D1293405

Books by Yehoshua Gilboa

Confess! Confess!

The Black Years of Soviet Jewry

THE BLACK YEARS OF SOVIET JEWRY

Translated from the Hebrew by

Yosef Shachter and Dov Ben-Abba

Boston, Toron

THE BLACK YEARS OF SOVIET JEWRY 1939-1953

Yehoshua A. Gilboa

Little, Brown and Company

WITHDRAWN

DELTA COLLEGE
Learning Resources Center

JUN 1972

COPYRIGHT © 1971 BY BRANDEIS UNIVERSITY

ALL RIGHTS RESERVED. NO PART OF THIS BOOK MAY BE REPRODUCED IN ANY FORM OR BY ANY ELECTRONIC OR MECHANICAL MEANS INCLUDING INFORMATION STORAGE AND RETRIEVAL SYSTEMS WITHOUT PERMISSION IN WRITING FROM THE PUBLISHER, EXCEPT BY A REVIEWER WHO MAY QUOTE BRIEF PASSAGES IN A REVIEW.

LIBRARY OF CONGRESS CATALOG CARD NO. 70–143716
TO5/71
FIRST EDITION

Published simultaneously in Canada
by Little, Brown & Company (Canada) Limited

PRINTED IN THE UNITED STATES OF AMERICA

This book is the result of a research project undertaken by the author while he was a senior research associate of the Institute of East European Jewish Studies of the Philip W. Lown School of Near Eastern and Judaic Studies of Brandeis University. The book was published with the cooperation and support of the Graduate Center for Contemporary Jewish Studies at Brandeis University.

AUTHOR'S NOTE

The Black Years of Soviet Jewry deals with the period from the beginning of World War II in 1939 to Stalin's death in 1953. Although the term "Black Years" is used in the text with reference to the period between 1948 and 1953, the book deals with a more extended period, 1939–1953. The author believes that the book's title adequately applies to the nature of the extended period in the life of Soviet Jewry.

The understanding of significant events in the life of the Soviet Jewish community between 1939 and 1953 requires the elucidation of previous developments in nearly every chapter. And as naturally the chronicle of Soviet Jewry is closely associated with the general developments in the USSR at the time, these are also discussed as required.

There are many difficulties inherent in the writing of contemporary history, most of them stemming from the conflict of immediate personal interest in the subject matter and the obligation to conduct dispassionate research and objective analysis. A state of tension exists between the sense of personal involvement and the need for scholarly detachment. The author wishes to make it clear that although the subject of this book is one that is very painful to him personally, he has endeavored to the best of his ability to present all the material objectively. Every researcher is also aware of the resolution that must be made between the tendency to include a plethora of notes and bibliographical citations and the need to be concise. The author chose a middle way between the two tendencies, attempting to include a list of sources and all pertinent documentation without imposing a burden on the reader.

This study concludes with the smashing of the doctors' libel case in April of 1953. From that point, conditions began to improve somewhat for Soviet Jewry with the advent of de-Stalinization. Unfortunately, however, evidence of anti-Jewish feeling continues in the years after 1953. The post-Stalin period is not discussed in this survey; nevertheless, the author wishes to point out that many of the motivating forces behind Soviet anti-Jewish policies in the past years can be explained in light of the treatment of the Jews between 1939 and 1953.

ACKNOWLEDGMENTS

I would like to express my gratitude to the individuals and institutions assisting in the preparation and publication of this book: the Institute of East European Jewish Studies at the Philip W. Lown Graduate Center for Contemporary Jewish Studies at Brandeis University, Waltham, Massachusetts (where I was invited to spend two years doing research for this book); and Professor Erich Goldhagen, director of the Graduate Center, who encouraged me in my endeavors; and the many libraries and archives whose collections I used, notably the Widener Library at Harvard University, Cambridge, Massachusetts; the United States Library of Congress; Brandeis University Library; the National Hebrew Library in Jerusalem; the Jewish Historical Society in Jerusalem; the YIVO Institute of Jewish Research in New York; the New York Public Library; Boston University Library; the Labor Archive in Tel Aviv; and the Diaspora Research Institute at the University of Tel Aviv.

For information, advice, and guidance regarding sources and critical comment I am grateful to many, notably Dr. Matityahu Mintz, Dr. Benjamin Pincus, Mr. Joshua Rothenberg, and Professor Khone Shmeruk. I would also like to express my appreciation to the translators who worked so assiduously and patiently: Dov Ben-Abba; and Yosef Shachter, who unfortunately died in the course of the project.

Finally, I wish to thank the publisher, Little, Brown and Company, and particularly my editor, Mr. Harry Sions, who gave the work its final polish.

I greatly appreciate the contribution of the individuals and institutions who helped make this book possible, but I would like to emphasize that I alone am responsible for its contents.

Y.A.G.

CONTENTS

THE BLACK YEARS OF SOVIET JEWRY

ONE

The War Years

Of all the countries that took part in World War II, the Soviet Union undoubtedly suffered the heaviest losses. Her toll of military and civilian life is estimated, according to Soviet sources, at 20 million.[1] In addition, the millions of infants that perished as a direct result of the privations of war and the German occupation severely stunted her natural increase potential.

The economic and material damage sustained by the Soviet Union was no less extensive: according to official Soviet figures, 1,710 towns and more than 70,000 villages were totally or partially destroyed and some 25 million inhabitants rendered homeless; 65,000 kilometers of railway tracks, 40,000 medical institutions, 84,000 schools and colleges and 43,000 libraries were destroyed or pillaged; livestock was vastly depleted — some 7 million horses, 17 million head of cattle, 20 million pigs, and 27 million sheep and goats were destroyed or looted by the German invaders. The total material damage, calculated at official current prices, is estimated at 679,000 million rubles.[2]

Dire distress and hardship pervaded the postwar scene. The victorious Soviet nation now numbered millions of orphans and widows, cripples and invalids, psychotics and persons otherwise disabled. Countless families were severely undernourished and underclad, and all this against a background of scorched fields, idle factories, and desolate towns and villages.

Starkly prominent in this scene of overall adversity is the particular tragedy of Soviet Jewry: of a total Jewish population estimated at 5¼ million,[3] some 2 million[4] perished in the war with Germany. For although the Jewish people as a whole had been singled out as the prime target of Nazi racism and aggression, it was on Russian ground that the German propaganda and exterminatory machinery found a particularly energizing and incendiary force. It was in the Soviet Union that the Nazis were able to point to a living example of their sworn enemy — the synthesis of Judaism and Bolshevism; and it was there that they could set about accomplishing their hope of eradicating the great twofold peril that threatened the human race and against which their Führer had warned in *Mein Kampf:* the Jew and his Marxist creed. It is noteworthy that the Berlin "Institute for Study of the Jewish Problem," set up shortly after Hitler's rise to power, devoted its first research to Judeo-Bolshevism and to the publication of a book, *Bolshevism and Jewry,* whose author strove to prove that Russia was ruled by "an international Jewish clique," and that the Soviet regime drew its inspiration from "the opium of Judeo-Marxism."[5] Numerous subsequent Nazi publications, in a similar vein, were at great pains to emphasize that Jews occupied key positions in all branches of the Soviet administration and services. To corroborate their claims of Soviet-Jewish complicity, the Nazis pointed out that many non-Jewish Communist leaders had Jewish wives, and even strove to prove that Lenin was of Jewish stock.[6] Alfred Rosenberg, the foremost Hitlerite theoretician, expressed this as a multiple equation: RUSSIA = BOLSHEVISM = JEWRY.[7] On June 23, 1941, immediately after the German invasion of Russia, Hitler himself hastened to reiterate his contention that his sole enemy was "Judeo-Bolshevism."[8]

Not only did the Nazis believe, by dint of long indoctrination and autosuggestion, that the Jews were the mainstay of the Soviet regime; they were also convinced that the Jews in occupied Soviet territory constituted a serious threat of revolt. This is borne out by the interpretation given by Marshal Erich von Mannstein, commander of the German 11th Corps in Transdniestria, to Himmler's orders to exterminate the Jewish population:

More than elsewhere in Europe they [the Jews] here occupy all key positions in the political and administrative leadership and in commerce and industry. They constitute the major element in [stirring up] possible disturbances and revolt. The Jewish Bolshevist regime must be liquidated once and for all. . . . The [German] soldier must understand that Jewry is to be severely punished, since it is the spiritual message-bearer of Bolshevism. . . . All likelihood of a revolt's being initiated by the Jews must be quelled.[9]

That the Jews were accorded "favored status" among the victims of Nazi oppression is dramatically expressed in a novel by the Russian Yiddish author Perets Markish, who has one of his characters say: "They [the Germans] want to make slaves of all the nations; of us [Jews] they want to make soap."[10] Vasily Grossman, another Russian Jewish writer, expresses a similar idea in a story where an old Jewish teacher explains to his Ukrainian friend that below the vast prison that the Fascists have made of Europe, they have reserved a cavernous dungeon especially for the Jews, "whose fate should make all other victims happy that they are not Jews."[11]

The "special status" accorded the Jews in this vast prison was particularly prominent in Nazi-occupied Soviet territory, albeit the fate suffered by the Russians, Ukrainians, and other national groupings was harsh. Already on June 1, 1941, several weeks before the German incursion, the Gestapo chief had issued specific orders to the commanders of the *Einsatzgruppen* detailed to operate in occupied Soviet territory to liquidate all the Jews there. One commander later testified that "the punitive detachments were given verbal orders, before going into action in the Russian theater of operations, to liquidate the Jews, as well as the Soviet political commissars."[12] These preliminary verbal orders were soon supplemented by a written order, issued on July 17, 1941, by the Gestapo's *Vierte Amt* to its units already operating in occupied Soviet territory, to track down primarily "all professional revolutionaries, all Comintern officials, all Red Army political commissars, all Soviet intelligentsia, and all Jews."[13] Hence, whereas a selective principle was applied in regard to all other national groupings, the repressive measures being aimed primarily at ideological and intellectual elements among the population, "all Jews" were sweepingly included in the category earmarked for liquidation or immediate suppression. That liquidation was the immediate object is conclusively borne out by the fact that very few Jewish ghettos, even of short duration, were set up in occupied Soviet territory. (Of these, only the Minsk ghetto was maintained till mid-September 1943, presumably as a reception center for Jews deported there for liquidation from other European countries.)[14]

Thus it was on Soviet soil that the Nazis proceeded to implement the "final solution" with the utmost urgency. This is corroborated by testimony at the Nuremberg Trial concerning the admission of SS commander Otto Ulendorf that his unit had murdered 90,000 men, women, and children, mostly Jews, in occupied Soviet territory. Ulendorf was reported to have stated that "if for years, tens of years, the doctrine is preached that the Slavs are an inferior race, and that the Jews are not even human, then this outcome was inevitable."[15]

Many Jews, admittedly, escaped death directly as a result of Soviet military operations. Hundreds of thousands were saved in the mass evacuations from occupied areas,[16] and not a few survived thanks to the help rendered, often at great peril, by some of their non-Jewish neighbors. Yet all this in no way mitigates the fact that some sections of the population in occupied areas actively collaborated with the Nazis in massacring the Jews. That this collaboration was not merely passive is extensively corroborated[17] despite the passivity implied by the Ukrainian Jewish poet Sava Golovanivsky in his poem *Abraham,* where he depicts a street scene in Kiev: an old Jew is led to his execution by Germans, while passersby turn away indifferently. (It was on account of this poem, incidentally, that Golovanivsky was later condemned for maligning the Soviet people.[18])

Anti-Semitic motives largely prompted significant sections of the population to extend a cordial welcome to the German invaders, who, they believed, had come to liberate them from the dual yoke of Bolshevism and "Jewish domination." If many were very quickly disabused of the faith they had placed in the "liberators" — who were not slow to show their true face — the Nazis' rabid anti-Jewish doctrine lost none of its attraction for them.

Obvious conclusions must be drawn from the undeniable fact that the Nazis were able to recruit collaborators in significant numbers in occupied Soviet areas, which was not the case in central and western Europe and in the Balkans. It is also significant that the incidence of Jewish survival was far higher in occupied European countries than in the Soviet Union (and also Poland), though it would appear at first sight that it should have been much easier to shelter Jews in the latter countries, where such possibilities were afforded by the profusion of villages clustered round the cities. Admittedly, this fact could be attributed in part to the higher "grading" which the Nazis accorded some conquered nations, chiefly in western Europe, and to the fact that the Jewish populations there were allowed to partake of some crumbs of this privileged status. But the chief difference lies in the attitudes of the populations themselves — a factor which the Germans took into account in the planning of their tactics.[19]

For Soviet Jewry, the attitude of their non-Jewish neighbors naturally came as a severe traumatic shock, over and above the agonies they suffered as a direct consequence of the war. If twenty-five years of Communist rule and education had failed to render Soviet society immune to the bestial anti-Semitism blared forth by Nazi propaganda, the Jews had every reason to be apprehensive, even without relation to the horrors of the occupation. Moreover, the official line of Soviet propaganda came as a further blow to the Jews: not only did the authorities gloss over the part played by sections of the population in aiding German extermination operations, they even deliberately suppressed or played down information concerning specifically anti-Jewish atrocities. At a time when the entire Soviet information machinery was geared to waging an all-out campaign to refute the lies and distortions of German propaganda and portray the invaders in the most hideous light, it largely refrained from backing up its campaign with what should have been the most illuminating corroboration: examples of anti-Jewish atrocities perpetrated by the Nazis (it should be noted that, as a rule, copious corroboration figures prominently in Soviet propaganda). Soviet announcements and publications during this period point to a deliberate attempt to conceal the Jewish tragedy behind general descriptions of German ferocity. Only rarely were massacres of Jews specifically mentioned, the dominant line adopted being not to single out such massacres from among the "criminal plans aimed at annihilating the Russian, Ukrainian, Belorussian, and other peoples of the Soviet Union."[20]

It was mainly in *Einikeit* and a few other publications with an exclusively Jewish readership, both inside and outside Russia, that the full, stark truth regarding the specific plight of the Jews was at all presented. Vasily Grossman, who in 1943 toured the newly liberated areas in the Ukraine as a correspondent of the daily *Krasnaya Zvezda* [Red Star], organ of the Soviet Defense Ministry, sent back reports of the widespread murder and pillage perpetrated by the German invaders. His most startling revelation, however, was: "A Ukraine without Jews . . . all have been slaughtered, in the hundreds and thousands. . . . The Germans have exterminated a whole nation in the Ukraine — a million children, women and old men, for the sole reason that they were Jews." But this bitter truth was never published in the general press, not even in Grossman's own paper, *Krasnaya Zvezda;* it appeared in the Yiddish-language *Einikeit,* and even there, Grossman's series of articles was soon discontinued.[21]

Though it might be unjust to assert that the USSR authorities were indifferent to the extermination of the Jews, yet from the political and moral points of view their attitude was no less reprehensible. Countenancing the prevalent anti-Semitic mood, they assumed that if prominence were to be given to the anti-Jewish aspect of the Nazi horrors, this might result in weakening the Soviet people's resistance to the invaders. In the frame of the total psychological warfare, Jewish suffering was considered an ineffectual means of stirring the population in the occupied areas to revolt. The German invader was therefore depicted as a monstrous beast whose fangs threatened the entire population indiscriminately, or were even sharper when non-Jews were the victims.

This being the case, the Jews had good reason to ask themselves: If the authorities feel obliged to take account of the prevailing anti-Semitic mood in combating Hitler, what assurance have we that even when conditions should change, they will not find it expedient to act similarly out of other internal considerations? The implications of this question must have been particularly ominous in view of the fact that the anti-Semitic mood, far from being confined to traitorous elements among the population, was rife even in circles whose loyalty to the Soviet homeland and readiness to fight the Germans was beyond question.

This phenomenon of Jew hatred alongside anti-Nazi resistance, incongruous as it was, also pervaded the partisan forces. It may be attributed to some extent to the lax discipline and lawlessness characteristic of most underground fighting organizations — though the fact remains that shortly after the German invasion, the *Partizanka* largely became part of the organized Soviet fighting forces and was subject to central control.

Many of the Jews who took to the "partisan forest" sought both refuge from the Germans and an outlet for their desire to fight and take revenge, only to meet with hostility, both concealed and overt, on the part of their comrades-in-arms. Anti-Jewish prejudice and slander were widespread among the forest partisans, whose frequently anti-Semitic attitude often deterred Jews from joining them though faced with extermination at home. "Why go looking for death in the forests when it is readily available in the ghetto?" was what Jews were prone to ask themselves. Not only rank-and-file partisans, but even high-ranking and heroic commanders of the underground were infected with the anti-Semitic virus; and even those that were not infected found it expedient to ignore or take no steps to curb its manifestations, since they feared that any active campaign against anti-Semitism would only serve to "back up the German propaganda directed against the partisans and deplete their ranks" and lend confirmation to the German claims that "the Red *Partizanka* is a creation of the Jews." Thus, the partisan leaders turned a blind eye to the anti-Jewish feeling that pervaded their forces, just as the Soviet government found it necessary, "for psychological and tactical reasons," to ignore the rising tide of anti-Semitism.

There is evidence that Jews were set upon and disarmed (chiefly by Ukrainian farmers and police), not only as they fled to the forests to join the partisans but also by the partisans themselves. Very often they were driven out of the forests, or interned in makeshift ghettos. Jewish property was not infrequently pillaged or "officially commandeered" on the orders of partisan group commanders. The partisan code was applied deliberately to Jews with utmost rigor and the most drastic penalties were imposed for minor contraventions — incredible as this might sound, some Jewish partisans were actually executed on trumped-up charges of spying for the enemy! In many instances, it is true, Russian partisans commendably manifested humanity and heroism in saving their Jewish comrades' lives. By and large, however, one may well appreciate the bitter feelings of the Jewish underground fighter, who, "while ready to lay down his life fighting the Germans, must also be ready for 'a settling of accounts' in the form of a bullet in the back from the gun of an anti-Semitic comrade"; and who, "even in the forest, was constantly subject tc the taunts, insults, reprimands and prejudice that turned his life into a living hell."[22]

Let us now turn from the partisan scene to the situation in the regular army. The magnitude of the Red Army's accomplishments on the battlefield in World War II will in no way be diminished by the assertion that its ranks were not proof against anti-Semitic trends. The Nazis concentrated the full force of their anti-Soviet propaganda, as has been mentioned, against what they termed "Judeo-Bolshevism." Moreover, with their famed German precision, they sought to impart factual substantiation to their propaganda during the fighting. On various fronts, where they faced Soviet units recruited from some specific district, the Germans would call out over loudspeakers the names of Jews who were presumably well known in those districts. "Are those Jews here among you?" they would ask the Red Army soldiers. "Or have they stayed at home to get rich by black-marketeering?" The German propagandists would often warn Russian soldiers against trusting their lives to Jewish officers, such as "Yankel" (Jacob) Kreiser (a famous Red Army general).[23] What is particularly deplorable, however, is that this malicious and primitive propaganda did not entirely miss the mark. The Nazi venom was allowed to seep through into an army where — unlike other armies — political inculcation formed an integral and formal part of its operational planning, structure and chain of command (every unit had its *politrook,* or political commissar, who ranked next to the commanding officer).

It might be useful, from this aspect, to point out that Soviet Jewry was still staggering under the profound shock caused by the Soviet-German pact, when it rallied to perform its full share in the "Great

Battle for the Homeland" — as the war with Germany was commonly called in the USSR.

This pact, signed in Moscow on August 23, 1939, by Soviet foreign minister Molotov and the foreign minister of the Third Reich, von Ribbentrop, is regarded as one of the most dramatic events in the whole course of international politics and diplomacy. The international developments that led to the conclusion of this pact are the subject of a complex of claims and counterclaims that have long engaged, and will continue to engage, the attention of historians and politicians. Its direct connection with the terrible bloodshed of World War II has made this pact one of the most bitterly controversial contemporary issues. What is illuminating, however, is that for many years following the signing of the pact it has been the subject of a spate of Soviet publications, largely in an apologetic vein. This would appear indicative of a spiritual and political need in some quarters to purge themselves of what might be a sense of guilt. Even Stalin himself, finding himself outflanked by the German invasion, saw fit to justify himself. In his first wartime broadcast to the Soviet people, on July 3, 1941, he stated:

> It might be asked: How could the Soviet government have agreed to sign a nonaggression pact with such vile and treacherous persons as Hitler and Ribbentrop? Was this not a mistake on the part of the Soviet government? Definitely not! A pact of nonaggression is a peace treaty between two countries. . . . I believe that no peace-loving country may refuse to sign a peace treaty with a neighboring country, even when the latter is headed by such villains and cannibals as Hitler and Ribbentrop. . . . Then what have we gained from concluding a pact of nonaggression with Germany? We have assured our country of peace for a year and a half, and have enabled it to prepare our forces to resist, in the event that Fascist Germany should dare attack our country despite the pact. This has definitely been to our advantage, and to the disadvantage of Fascist Germany.[24]

Not for long, however, did Stalin's appraisal remain sacrosanct in the Soviet Union. Many people subsequently began to entertain doubts even as to the initial expediency of Stalin's move. Was the temporary pact with Hitler — they wondered — worthwhile or necessary even as a pure "business deal"? Did it really give the Soviet Union a much-needed respite, or did the country pay dearly in the long run for its ruler's "shrewd" political maneuver? There is no doubt whatsoever, on the other hand, that towards the end of the Thirties a kind of grandiose political game was being played throughout Europe. In this game, which was practically devoid of any ethical considerations, each country staked everything solely on securing its own peace and gaining an advantage by diverting the Nazis' aggressive energy towards some other likely "enemy." Though the Molotov-Ribbentrop pact stands out conspicuously as the dramatic culmination of this game, casting a heavy stigma on the Soviet partner, some of its other offshoots — notably the Munich Agreement of October 1938 — hardly redound to the credit of the West. Churchill himself states in this connection: "The fact such an agreement [the Molotov-Ribbentrop pact] could be made marks the culminating failure of British and French foreign policy and diplomacy over several years."[25]

However, complex and controversial as this issue might be, there can be no disputing the fact that the Moscow-Berlin pact profoundly shocked world Jewry as a whole, and had a harrowing psychological and political effect on Soviet Jewry in particular. Whatever Stalin's motives might have been, and however prepared the Jews were to resign themselves to the mysteries of *Hochpolitik* and trust themselves to the genius of the Father of the People, surely they could not regard with equanimity an alliance which their country had formed with a regime whose professed object was the annihilation of the Jewish people! All the more so when the new political alignment was backed up with decorative effects and effusive courtesies: the Kremlin hall where the pact was signed was decorated with the swastika banner alongside the red flag, and Stalin personally toasted Hitler: he knew how much the German people loved its Führer, he said, and he therefore wished to drink his health.[26]

The impact of the Molotov-Ribbentrop pact was not limited to the emotional sphere, nor did it apply merely to the observance of the usual courtesies between friendly countries: the Nazi regime, and consequently Fascism as a whole (including that of Mussolini), were placed beyond the pale of criticism in the USSR. At first, admittedly, it was hinted in some Party circles, for internal consumption, that in regard to Nazism and Fascism some distinction would be maintained between the diplomatic and the ideological planes. It very soon transpired, however, that even the information drive against Hitler's racial and anti-Semitic doctrines had been silenced, and it was not long before all anti-Nazi and anti-Fascist publications disappeared from the bookstands.[27]

The ban on disparaging the German ally extended to belles-lettres, too. An illuminating example is Nikolai Shpanov's short novel *The First Blow,* which appeared in Moscow some time before September 1939. It gives an imaginary description of the first twenty-four hours of the Russo-German war that must inevitably break out and the bombing by the Soviet Air Force of industrial targets around Nuremberg. Though the book was circulated abroad, it was suppressed in the Soviet Union immediately after the Molotov-Ribbentrop pact was concluded.[28]

Ilya Ehrenburg in his *Memoirs,* published some twenty years later, reveals some illuminating details from personal experience regarding the ban imposed on making slighting references to Fascism. He had been trying for some time to publish his novel *The Fall of Paris.* Finally, at the beginning of 1941, he was informed that the first part of the novel had been approved "though there would have to be cuts." Ehrenburg writes, "Although it [the book] was only concerned with Paris in 1935–37, and there were no Germans in it, the word 'Fascism' had to be taken out. The text included a description of Paris demonstrations and I was asked to substitute for the slogan 'Down with Fascism!' 'Down with the reactionaries!' " He goes on to say that most of the articles he wrote for various periodicals at that time were turned down, since "in every line the editors discovered slanting references to the Fascists, whom wits called our 'deadly friends.' "[29]

So zealously did the Soviet authorities guard against any infringement of their friendship with Germany that a reign of terror was instituted to suppress all anti-German sentiments. One of its victims, for example, was the Soviet chargé d'affaires in Paris, Nikolai Ivanov, who returned or was recalled to Moscow in December 1940 and was arrested shortly afterwards.[30] Another case in point is that of a rabbi and Zionist leader who was imprisoned in Riga. Interrogated by an examining magistrate (especially brought over from Moscow) in

March 1941, he defended himself by adducing his share in the world struggle against Nazism, only to be told that "Hitler is our friend and ally, and we do not wish to hear anything said against him."[31]

Ribbentrop's visit to Moscow lasted no more than twenty-four hours. During this brief period, however, the signatories not only concluded the open treaty (with all the ceremonial courtesies) but also signed a secret protocol splitting up between them their respective European zones of influence (including Poland), as envisaged in the light of political and territorial readjustments. This fact alone clearly indicates that the pact was the result of lengthy prior negotiations. Furthermore, Moscow had anticipated the pact by calling off or toning down its anti-Nazi propaganda (just as Berlin had begun to play down its anti-Soviet propaganda). Thus, Ehrenburg states in his *Memoirs* that already in mid-April 1939 *Izvestia* stopped publishing the dispatches he sent from Paris as the paper's correspondent, though he continued to draw his usual salary. The reason for this "enforced leisure" was that "Paul Jocelyn [Ehrenburg's pen name] continued to denounce the Fascists, but the time of complicated diplomatic negotiations was drawing near."[32]

Nor were the incipient changes in the Kremlin's attitude to Germany confined to the sphere of propaganda only. On May 3, 1939, the Soviet commissar for foreign affairs, Maxim Litvinov (a Jew who had changed his name from Wallach), was replaced by Vyacheslav Molotov. Though this was attributable primarily to the imminent political realignment, Litvinov being considered the chief exponent of Soviet cooperation with the Western powers against Hitler, there is no doubt that his removal from office was intended as a preliminary "gift" to the Germans, or as Churchill put it: "The eminent Jew, the target of German antagonism, was flung aside for the time being like a broken tool, and, without being allowed a word of explanation, was bundled off the world stage to obscurity, a pittance, and police supervision. . . . The Jew Litvinov was gone, and Hitler's dominant prejudice placated."[33]

The few Jews who had been allowed to remain in key positions were also committed to upholding the new policy of Soviet-German friendship, despite its undeniable anti-Jewish implications. Thus, Jakob Suritz, the Soviet ambassador in Paris, whom Ehrenburg went to see when *Izvestia* stopped publishing his articles, could do little else but tell him to take this in his stride. "Take a rest," Suritz told him. "Write a novel. There are lots of interesting exhibitions on just now." When Ehrenburg returned to Moscow in mid-1940, he was received by Molotov's Jewish deputy, Solomon Lozovsky, whom he told about the situation in occupied France. "He listened to me absentmindedly," Ehrenburg recalls. ". . . I could not help saying: 'Doesn't this interest you at all?' Lozovsky smiled wryly: 'Personally I find it very interesting. But you know that we have a different policy.' "[34]

This "different policy" was expressed, among other things, in the Soviet claim that it was the British and the French who were the aggressors in Europe, whereas the Germans (after they had overrun Poland) only wished for peace; in the Soviet understanding for Germany's "defense measures"; in the felicitations Moscow extended to Berlin after each further conquest; and in the Soviet Foreign Office notifications to the Norwegian, Belgian, and Yugoslav legations in Moscow, in May 1941, that the Soviet Union no longer accorded them diplomatic status since their countries had forfeited their independence. Nor was the "different policy" limited merely to verbal declarations: the Soviet Union dispatched huge consignments of grain, petroleum, cotton, and other essential materials to Germany, significantly aiding the German war effort.[35] Hence, Molotov had good reason to be bitter when the Germans launched their assault on the USSR, for, according to him, during the whole time the Soviet-German pact had been in force, the German government had had no grounds to complain of any Soviet violation thereof.

It is relevant to mention the position taken by Communist Parties in other countries, under Moscow's direction and pressure, while the pact was in force. Those parties called for "neutralism" in Europe, preached isolationism in America, hampered the war effort, and resisted mobilization. Jewish Communist groups, too, were called upon to take this line. Shocked and perplexed at first by the news of the Ribbentrop–Molotov pact, some Jewish Communists had initially claimed that this was no more than a capitalist libel and provocation. On the other hand, Jewish Communist Party membership significantly dropped off. By and large, however, dialectics and orthodox acquiescence overcame doubts and misgivings, and Jewish Communists, too, were induced to see the problem "as a whole" rather than in the light of "narrow subjectivity." It should be noted that the Communist movement throughout the world had in any case long become spiritually atrophied, purged — as in the Soviet Union itself — of elements capable of independent thought and action. Unquestioning faith in the world revolutionary leadership, and all the more so in Stalin, had become an irrevocable tenet.

The Palestine Communist Party (PKP), too, was for some time subject to similar vacillation. Only a short time before the conclusion of the Moscow-Berlin pact and the outbreak of the war, the PKP had denounced not only Fascism, but also the neutralist policy of appeasement — a stand set forth in a pamphlet issued by the Party's Jewish Section on the occasion of "Anti-War Day" on August 1, 1939. Several days after the outbreak of war, the Jewish Section declared itself in support of the Jewish Agency's recruitment drive, but a few days after that, the PKP changed its tone and issued a manifesto condemning Jewish mobilization in Palestine. Some six months later, in March 1940, the Party condemned its Jewish Section, branding the latter's former position as "a criminal attitude, the direct result of Zionist nationalistic influences," and the war against Germany as "manifestly a capitalistic war." In the course of its vacillations the PKP retracted all slighting references to the "Hitlerite gang," which had meantime become Moscow's noble ally, and now leveled its abuse at Britain and her warmongering European and American accomplices. In a country that had given shelter to thousands of Jewish refugees from Germany, the Palestine Communists strove to hamper Jewish participation in the war against the Nazis; instead, they waged an all-out campaign against Zionist schemes "to sent thousands and tens of thousands of the Jewish working masses and youth to the imperialist slaughter." It was only after the German invasion of the USSR that the Palestine Communists also came to realize that "there is only one front, extending from Tobruk to Leningrad."[36]

Though the pattern of Soviet-German relations was by no means always idyllic and devoid of discordant notes, yet not even once did Moscow give the least intimation to her German ally — whether verbally or in writing — that her efforts to gain popular support for the pact were hampered by Germany's murderous campaign in general, and against the Jewish people in particular. Had they so wished, the Soviet authorities could have based such a contention on the mere fact that there were over five million Jews living on Soviet soil who might understandably show sensitivity on this point. Misunderstandings overshadowed the alliance on such issues as the ultimate fate of Finland, Bukovina, the Balkans, and the Dardanelles, but not over Germany's preparation of "a final solution." On the first anniversary of the signing of the pact, *Pravda* still acclaimed it in glowing terms. Shortly afterwards, on November 12, 1940, Molotov went to Berlin (this was the first visit of a top-level Soviet statesman to Nazi Germany) to negotiate certain disputes that had arisen. There was no subsequent intimation to the effect that Molotov, in his talks with Hitler and Ribbentrop, had taken the opportunity to express disapproval of the Nazi subjugation and butchery.

Before we proceed to describe the harrowing impact of the Ribbentrop-Molotov pact on Soviet Jewry, we must deal with a significant event that was connected with the pact and had a notable effect on subsequent developments. On September 17, 1939, the Red Army moved into Poland, and shortly afterwards, after minor disputes with the Germans were settled and certain modifications agreed upon, the USSR seized control of about half the territory of Poland — an area of more than 77,000 square miles with a population of 13,200,000. Of these, 1,109,000, or 8.5 percent, were Jews.[37] The annexed area had a similar Belorussian population (1,123,000) — a comparison that is called for in view of the Soviet explanation that the entry of Soviet forces into Poland had been motivated by "the need to extend assistance to our Ukrainian and Belorussian brothers, rendered helpless now that Poland has ceased to exist."[38] This contention, though smacking largely of political cant, nevertheless begs the question: If the Soviet Russians were permitted to stress the need to defend their brethren in the West against lawlessness, why were the Jews constrained to show indifference to the fate of millions of their brethren in German-occupied areas?

To the number of Jews living in the areas which in September 1939 became known as "Western Belorussia and Western Ukraine" must be added the thousands of refugees who had fled to the Soviet zone from the Nazi horrors in the German-occupied part of Poland. These refugees were, on the whole, grateful to the Soviet Union for giving them asylum, just as the majority of the local Jewish population, alive to the danger that Hitler might overrun the whole of Poland in a blitzkrieg assault, welcomed the Red Army's entry. This only served to deepen their shock when they found they must suppress the truth about the horrors of the German occupation; when they heard Molotov's statement, about two months after the war broke out, that "Hitlerism may be accepted or rejected like any other ideological system. It is merely a matter of political outlook. . . ."[39] When they learned from a leading article in the central government daily that Hitlerism was "a matter of taste"[40]; when they read of Hitler's congratulations to Stalin on his sixtieth birthday, and of Stalin's reply expressing his faith in the longevity and firmness of Soviet-German friendship, since this was "a friendship tempered in blood."[41]

For the writers among these Jewish refugees this came as a particularly staggering blow. Not only did they discover that all anti-Nazi publications, including those in Yiddish and dealing with the persecution of Jews, had disappeared in the USSR, but that they themselves were forbidden to publicize their own recent experiences.

Quite a large group of Jewish refugee writers had gathered several months after the outbreak of the war in Bialystok, a Polish city near the newly demarcated Soviet-German border. There is illuminating evidence of the mental and spiritual suffering that awaited them there. One of their number, Moshe Grossman, had been known as a so-called "proletarian writer" in Poland; though not a Communist, his professed views had stamped him as having leftist leanings. The first article he wrote on Russian soil, entitled "Happiness," was published in the local Yiddish-language *Bialystoker Shtern;* in it, he gave fervent expression to the happiness experienced by a Jew who has escaped from the horrors of the Nazi occupation to free soil. Meanwhile, streams of Jewish refugees kept arriving in Bialystok. One day, Grossman showed his editor a yellow patch which one of the refugees had brought with him, and was promptly requested to pen an article on the subject, but the article was suppressed. "The supreme authorities have banned it," the editor tried to excuse himself. "It's the present-

Moshe Broderzon expressed the general dejection thus: ". . . only a few kilometres away from the hell of Nazi butchery — and not a line, not a single word about the horrible fate of the Jews across the border, in that part of Poland flooded with Jewish blood."[43] Binem Heller, another Jewish poet who had aligned himself with Polish left-wing literary circles before the war, sent an anti-Nazi poem entitled "Warsaw 1939" to a Moscow publication early in 1940; the poem was rejected on various formal grounds.[44] "The only thing they allowed us, demanded of us in fact, was to write about the anti-Semitism of the former Polish rulers" — another refugee writer later recounted.[45]

When the refugee writers met Soviet Yiddish writers, they were obliged to communicate by means of veiled hints and looks; fearful of any slip of the tongue that might be construed as criticism of the Soviet-German pact, they refrained from making any overt reference to the great Jewish catastrophe.[46] This silence was officially enforced with increasing rigor. After Lithuania was declared a Soviet Republic in 1940, local Communist Party representatives advised a Hashomer Hatzair (Zionist left-wing youth organization) group in Vilna to "forget all about the Jews across the border in Nazi-occupied Poland."[47] It is ironical that this advice was given to a movement that produced young men who organized Jewish resistance in occupied Poland — men like Mordechai Anilewicz, leader of the Warsaw Ghetto rising, and other underground fighters. Only a few days before the German invasion of the USSR, Motl Grubian, who was in charge of the Yiddish Hour on the Minsk radio, was fired for using the term "Nazis" in a slighting tone.[48]

With all the tragedy implied in the examples quoted above, however, the period covered by the Soviet-German pact nevertheless had certain favorable aspects for Soviet Jewry. To understand this better, it might be useful to review the changing Jewish scene in the Soviet Union up to September 1939.

On the eve of the outbreak of World War II, Soviet Jewry was in the throes of a national and spiritual decline. This was still a far cry from the persecution and extermination meted out to them by Stalin in his latter years; but the belief that Russia would succeed Warsaw

The Moscow Yiddish daily *Emes* had stopped appearing in 1938, and both the number and circulation of other Yiddish publications had dwindled. Many Jewish cultural institutions had closed down. In 1932 there had been 160,000 pupils in Jewish schools.[50] In 1940, the enrollment was variously estimated at 85,000 to 90,000 (regarded by some as an exaggeration), or about 20 percent of the total number of Jewish schoolchildren.[51] The dream of an autonomous Jewish province in Birobidzhan had also evaporated. Intermarriage had become widespread. In a word: assimilation was rapidly gaining ground.

This development may be regarded as the outcome of a combination of factors, largely socio-economic. In the first place, there had been a large-scale migration of Jews from traditional Jewish townships and villages in Belorussia and the Ukraine to urban centers (beyond the "Pale of Jewish Settlement" under Tsarist rule), where they were soon integrated into the new construction and industrial projects. This change was aptly summed up by a Jewish demographic researcher as follows: "Tsarist Russia was the largest country of Jewish emigration in the world, but internal migration of Jews other than within the 'Pale of Settlement,' was forbidden. The revolution radically changed this: the borders were sealed against emigration, whereas the dispersal of Jews throughout the vast areas of the country was not only permitted, but even encouraged by the authorities. . . . This dispersal inevitably led to the decline of Jewish tradition and to assimilation."[52]

It must be borne in mind that the purges of the Thirties affected a significant number of Jewish writers and other prominent figures. Though the reign of terror made no deliberate national discrimination, it certainly was not conducive to the promotion of Jewish culture. The sudden disappearances came to be imprinted on the Jewish subconscious as a stigma of guilt, which heightened their dread. In consequence, potential Jewish creativity naturally declined.[53]

All this must be added to the fact that there was but little enthusiasm in the Jewish community to keep up what must be regarded, from many aspects, as merely a semblance of national identification. Jewish culture in the Soviet Union had not only undergone a process of secularization, but had been voided also of other essential national attributes. More than all other national cultures, it had been largely severed from its historical origins, both under external pressure and also by dint of internal developments induced by the Yevsektzia.[54] Ever since the revolution, Jewish religious observance had steadily declined to a low ebb. The last Pentateuch in Hebrew had been printed in 1918. A few devotional books were printed during the NEP years, and the last Hebrew prayerbook was published in 1928 (in 1956, a "Peace Prayer Book" was printed, photographed from the pages of old editions). Until the late Fifties, the last Jewish calendar had been issued in 1929, primitively printed with rubber stamps; thereafter, printers were obviously afraid to accept such "reactionary" printing jobs. The Bible was taboo. Hebrew was banned. The Hebrew theater company, Habimah, founded in Moscow in 1917, soon found itself in a precarious position; when the company left Russia in 1926 to tour Europe and America, its members saw no point in returning. The Yiddish language was de-Hebraized, and all remaining Hebrew traces were rendered indistinguishable by the introduction of phonetic spelling. Zionism was proscribed and its exponents persecuted. Even a sentimental attachment to the Land of Israel was regarded as a counterrevolutionary tendency. Spiritual or cultural ties with the Jewish heritage were looked upon as reactionary chauvinism. Heinrich Graetz's great *History of the Jews* had appeared in Tsarist Russia in Yiddish and Russian translations and was formerly to be found in the home of practically every educated Jew, but no new edition was published in the Soviet Union. Dubnow's universal history of the Jewish people had a similar fate: originally written in Russian, parts of it had appeared in various editions in Tsarist Russia; yet though completed after the revolution, the work was never published in the USSR.[55] Incidentally, it was Dubnow himself who referred to the cultural extinction of Soviet Jewry as a process of "de-historization." Added to this, Soviet Jews were kept in virtually hermetic isolation against any physical or spiritual contact with other Jewish communities and were completely cut off from their relatives abroad. The situation was aptly summed up in the phrase coined by Berl Katznelenson, the Palestine labor leader: "The soul is burnt out, while the body is kept alive."

The exponents of the new Soviet-Jewish culture, more than those of other national cultures, feared to deviate from the sacrosanct principle that culture must be "national in form and socialist in content." Hence, it was but a watered-down substitute that lacked sufficient nutritive elements to sustain it spiritually. Many parents must have asked themselves, for instance, what useful purpose could be served by Jewish schools which merely segregated their pupils linguistically from their surroundings, but did not teach them the Bible and Jewish history. Paradoxically, a Jewish child attending such a school might be inculcated with contempt for the spirit of Judaism, whereas at a general school he would at least be spared specific anti-Jewish indoctrination. This, indeed, was one of the reasons that deterred parents from sending their children to Jewish schools. In time, there was far less recourse to Jewish libraries, and Jewish theater audiences dwindled. This estrangement from things Jewish was no doubt also due to the attraction exercised by the rich Russian culture, while administrative measures, too, contributed to accelerating the process of assimilation.

For some time, nonetheless, the fact that Yiddish was still spoken and written and the existence of several Jewish cultural institutions, though starved of national content, served to keep the near extinguished torch of Jewish culture smoldering. The Yiddish language, steeped as it is in rich folklore and a host of historical and traditional associations with intrinsic national content, became a preserving force and assumed a distinctive role following the extirpation of Hebrew culture and the ban imposed on other national manifestations. "The Yiddish word," one Jewish writer states, "turned into a symbol, connoting all that was left of [Jewish] national existence."[56] The same thought was expressed, even more poignantly, by a Soviet Jewish writer who wrote under the pen name Der Nister: "We have been left with nothing. . . . We have no God and we have no Torah. All we have are the letters of the Yiddish alphabet."[57] K. Shmeruk, an authority on Soviet Jewish literature, rightly asserts that the following principle applied to that literature too: "So long as it was possible in the Soviet Union to preserve a system of education, culture and literature in the language of one or other national grouping, even the strongest ideological pressure was unable to abolish entirely their intrinsic national elements, even within the most stringent Soviet frameworks." Yet he, too, arrives at the conclusion that "it is not unlikely that already in 1939, Yiddish publishing had been doomed to gradual extinction; and though some Jewish writers and leaders might have resisted this process, they were powerless to stop it."[58]

It was against this cultural and spiritual background that Soviet Jewry was reinforced, in 1939 and 1940, with the addition of some two million Jews living in annexed territories in Poland, the Baltic States, Bessarabia, and northern Bukovina. The meeting with these Jews inevitably stirred up nostalgic memories. There is copious evidence (including the personal experiences of the author) that when Soviet Jews began talking freely with their new "co-citizens" many of them felt as though they had at long last returned to their cultural homeland. Eagerly they drank in every scrap of information about what was happening in the Jewish world and in the Land of Israel. At a time when Jewish culture in their own land was in its death throes, tragic circumstances had vouchsafed them a meeting with Jewish communities richly endowed with cultural values. Their own communal life all but extinct, they suddenly glimpsed a — to them — fabulous picture of intensive, dynamic Jewish life in the annexed provinces, where until quite recently the Jews had maintained extensive networks of Hebrew schools and teachers' training colleges, scientific research institutes, thousands of *yeshivot* (Talmudic colleges) and synagogues, flourishing publishing houses, rich libraries, active clubs with ramified activities, a variety of newspapers and periodicals of every shade of opinion, a great many theaters, charitable institutions, parties and societies of every political coloring, large-scale Zionist activities and the like.

After decades of separation, this meeting must have been significant for the "original" Soviet Jews. All at once they discovered that even under professed anti-Semitic regimes Jewish communities had been able to exercise their latent creative powers and maintain a large measure of national autonomy. Even Jewish Red Army soldiers, stationed in the annexed areas, were deeply moved by the distinctive Jewish pithiness and vivacity, devotion and adherence to tradition, which they encountered for the first time in their lives when they visited synagogues, or were invited to Jewish homes.[59] A Soviet Jewish demographer states that the addition of two million Jews was of value in "furthering the advance of socialist reconstruction among the Jewish masses in the Soviet Union, developing the Jewish autonomous region (Birobidzhan), and promoting the growth of Soviet Jewish culture."[60]

This quantitative and qualitative growth held out encouraging prospects, especially for the Yiddish writers, who had now acquired a far wider readership, as the number and circulation of Yiddish publications rose significantly in 1940.[61] It is, in fact, a paradoxical conclusion that "the outbreak of World War II in 1939 was what temporarily saved Yiddish literature in the USSR, putting off its total disappearance for nine more years."[62]

Yiddish writers began to write stirring poems acclaiming the liberation of the "Western areas" and the blessings this had brought their Jewish inhabitants. Thus, Leib Kvitko wrote a poem of thanksgiving entitled "From the Liberated to their Liberators." Perets Markish announced: "You Have Freedom." David Hofstein, in a poem on the liberation of Kishinev (former scene of bloody pogroms), wrote that the disgrace of its past was at last erased, "and we now mention your name with joy." Itsik Feffer assured the Jews of the Western areas that "no longer will you know disaster, you who live in Volozhin and Brody, in Grodno and Tarnopol." Already in 1939, there appeared a Yiddish anthology entitled *The Liberated Brothers.* Particularly illuminating is a poem by a young writer, Heinich Shvedik, in which he alludes obliquely to the difference between the Soviet liberators and the German conquerors, though he does not specifically mention the latter by name, thus circumventing the ban on criticizing the Nazi ally; addressing the "Ukrainians, Belorussians and Jews in the Western towns and Western villages," Shvedik lists the blessings that the advance of the Red Army has brought them: "They do not bring you horror and death," he writes, "but come to share with you their happiness and their bread."

A number of Soviet Yiddish writers came to the newly annexed areas, chiefly in organized Writers' Brigades. It is more than likely that they did not go there on their own initiative, but were charged with the task of instructing the new Jewish citizens of the Soviet Union, especially the local and refugee authors and intellectuals. Many of the latter had begun — willingly or perforce — to adjust themselves to the Soviet scheme of things. It may safely be assumed, however, that in their heart of hearts, the Soviet Jewish writers who toured the annexed territories did not always seek to discharge their imposed tasks of "instruction." Thus, Itsik Feffer, who attended a meeting of a group of Jewish refugee writers in Lvov (the capital of West Ukraine) and heard one of its members read out a superlatively patriotic poem in praise of the Soviet Union, was said to remark: "We can write like that about the Revolution far better than you can. . . . You go on writing as you did till now, as long as they let you."[63] At a reception held in Bialystok for visiting Soviet Jewish writers, when some of the refugee writers made a great show of demonstrating their leftist internationalist outlook, Motl Grubian, in reply, drank a fervent toast to "the life of the great Jewish nation."[64] Another Soviet Jewish poet, Zelik Akselrod from Minsk, was unable to hide his emotion when he saw Jewish stores in Bialystok closed on Saturday; and when Moshe Kusevitsky, the renowned Warsaw cantor, gave an operatic recital in that town, Akselrod earnestly pleaded with him to sing *Kol Nidre,* which he said he had not heard for over twenty years.[65]

Thus it would appear that the Soviet Jewish writers, notwithstanding their caution and trained ability to watch their step, occasionally gave vent to their inner feelings on meeting their fellow Jews in the annexed areas.

At the same time, however, while the Soviet Jews, including writers, were quenching their spiritual thirst at the founts of their "liberated" brethren, a rigorous campaign of full social and cultural Sovietization was initiated in the Western areas and enforced by dint of oppressive measures and heavy penalties. In regard to the Jews, this consisted at first in substituting Yiddish for Hebrew as the language of instruction at Jewish schools, in the liquidation of political parties and social and philanthropic organizations, and in other measures designed to mold Jewish culture to the Soviet pattern, rendering it "national in form and socialist in content."

Before long, the Jews were subjected to ruthless persecution, mass arrests, and deportations. Communal and political leaders were tried and sentenced for counterrevolutionary activities. Zionists were charged with being capitalist tools and serving as agents of foreign powers, especially Britain.[66] Jewish cultural activity in the Yiddish language was hemmed in with restrictions.

It was against this background that Akselrod met his death. As has been mentioned, Akselrod was unable to hide his feelings in Bialystok. For this and similar offenses he was reprimanded by the local political commissar for "manifesting Jewish nationalism." Subsequently he moved to Vilna, the "Lithuanian Jerusalem," and saw this flourishing Jewish center of learning depleted of its traditional essence. Learning that the sole remaining local Yiddish paper, *Vilner Emes,* was about to be closed down, he joined forces with another Soviet Jewish poet, Elia Kahan, in urging the local Jewish writers to protest against the closure and make representations to the authorities. Akselrod and Kahan were promptly arrested and imprisoned in Minsk. The following year, when the Germans were advancing on Minsk and the Russians were hastily evacuating the burning town, Akselrod was shot by his jailers in the prison yard or in an adjacent wood; he died on June 26, 1941, at the age of thirty-seven. Kahan, posing as a regular convict, was released with the other nonpolitical prisoners, joined the army, and was killed in action shortly afterwards.[67]

Indirect additional evidence on the events and prevailing atmosphere to which Akselrod fell a victim can be found in his poem "They Tell Me," which he wrote in 1940. There is no knowing whether those who interrogated and sentenced him read between its lines, but in the light of what is known of Akselrod's end and of the sentiments he shared with many Jews during the period of the Soviet-German alliance, this poem becomes as clear and meaningful as a document. In it, the poet begs his friends' forgiveness for his meager literary output, ascribing this to the fact that the year's events and experiences cannot be expressed openly: "Now I know the meaning of it all. . . . But I cannot say it plainly. Sometimes rain does not fall from heaven. Yet deep within me, I have surely preserved tomorrow's song for your sake."[68]

Other writers, too, preserved tomorrow's song in their hearts for the future. Those who gave expression to their grief at the fate of their fellow Jews across the border were forced, in abidance by the spirit of the Soviet-German pact, to add these writings to their other "drawer literature." Noteworthy among these writings is Perets Markish's Yiddish poem "To the Jewish Dancer" (1940), expressing pain and horror at the danger of extinction that menaces the Jewish people.

This danger is figuratively depicted as a violent storm raging across the River Bug (part of the frontier between the Soviet and German-occupied sections of Poland), from which masses of despondent survivors are fleeing. The poem, whose motif and opening line is the Hebrew verse from Lamentations, "I am the man that hath seen affliction," is charged with a host of Jewish historical and traditional associations and reminiscences: the refugees hang up their marks of exile, like the harps by the waters of Babylon, on the twisted candlesticks in the synagogues; a Jewish mother blesses the Sabbath candles, her hands clasped to her weeping eyes; the commandment "Thou shalt not kill" rises like dawn above the mountain summits. The Jewish dancer in the ghetto symbolizes the continuity of Jewish history, charged with the yearning of generations to attain spiritual heights, and their endless sufferings for their ideals and dreams. In the "eternal language of her weary feet" she tells only to the running brook how for two thousand years she has striven, fettered, to reach the mountain peak. Yet she has not yet fully paid the toll for "the wish to be free, the wish to think, to dream, to dare," for "a burning stake awaits you, condemned for loving the world." Others like the dancer "have had their eyes put out for gazing at the stars"; and again addressing the dancer: "Let not the yellow patch burden you . . . but walk erect, as did your father and your grandfather . . . as Akiva went with head held high towards the darkness . . . tempered like steel." And in the final accounting: "No sword but has been whetted on you, no sword but will be broken on you."

The Russian writer Boris Lavreniev said of this poem: "Personified in the dancer is the whole gamut of suffering and agony of the Jewish people, tortured and led to slaughter by German Fascism." Yet about six years had to pass after its author was executed before the poem was published.[69]

Hence it will be seen that in the period between August 1939 and June 1941, Soviet Jews underwent a deep inner conflict, torn between their natural human feelings towards their fellow Jews and their conditioned loyalty to the dictates of their government's foreign policy. That the Soviet authorities were aware of the Nazis' anti-Jewish atrocities is attested to by the spate of publications on the subject — intended chiefly for Jewish readers inside and outside the

USSR — that were issued immediately after the German invasion. Written in or translated into Yiddish, these publications bear such titles as *Under the Yoke of the Fascist Conquerors, German Fascism Subjugates the Nations, Blood Cries Out for Vengeance — Fascist Barbarity in Occupied Poland,* among others.[70] It is interesting to note that these publications describe the atrocities committed by the Nazis in the occupied territories, chiefly Poland, up to June 22, 1941 (the date of the German invasion). This means that the Soviet authorities had previously known what was happening, for it is inconceivable that these atrocities suddenly came to their knowledge as soon as the Soviet Union fell out with Germany. One example will suffice to prove beyond all doubt that the authorities had hitherto deliberately suppressed all such knowledge. In 1941, *Emes* published in Moscow a Yiddish translation of a booklet entitled *The Hitlerite Butchery in Poland,* written by the Russian author A. Golubiev. This booklet, as stated on the inside cover, went to press (which in the parlance of Soviet publishing means "was approved for publication") on August 11, 1941, that is, only one and a half months after the Germans launched their invasion. It must therefore have been written very soon after June 22. Yet the writer appears extremely well informed on the German barbarities in Poland, particularly against the Jews, during the whole period of their occupation since September 1939. Golubiev reports that "immediately after the entry of the German forces into Poland, there began a bloody massacre of innocent citizens — helpless old men, women, and children"; that "the deportation of the Jews is being carried out with especial ferocity. They are not only deported from western Poland, but are being exterminated." He describes the bloodshed and the pillage of the "hapless land" perpetrated by the Germans already in "the first days of their occupation" when "Jews were shot in masses."

The new situation that arose in 1941 brought Soviet Jews face to face with the stark realities of the German campaign of extermination. With all the physical horror this entailed, it must nevertheless have relieved the intense emotional stress and agony of conscience to which they had been subject hitherto; probably more than any other group of people at any time, Soviet Jews were torn between their divided loyalty during the period of the Soviet-German pact. Conversely, at no other time was the loyalty of Soviet Jews to their country firmer than during the war against Germany. "The Fascists are the great enemies of all peoples, the worst enemies of the Jewish people! Destroy the Fascists!" was the slogan printed under the name of the first issue of a Yiddish newspaper that began to appear in Moscow in 1942.[71] The ability to identify Hitler, the slaughterer of the Jewish people, with the deadly foe of the Soviet Union now eliminated any trace of split loyalty.

It is relevant at this point to dwell on Soviet Jewry's share in fighting the Germans. Different sources quote significantly disparate figures on the number of Jews in the Soviet armed forces, but it is statistically indisputable that proportionally they figured much more largely in the line of combat than the entire Soviet population. About half a million Jews saw active service in the Red Army. Many of them, according to a reliable mass of evidence, volunteered for front-line fighting, and a large number even resorted to subterfuge in order to circumvent the restrictions imposed on their mobilization. It must be borne in mind that only about half of the Soviet Union's five and a quarter million Jews (according to the 1941 estimate) were "native" Soviet citizens, that is, were not inhabitants of former German-occupied territories. Moreover, most of the Jews living in the areas annexed by the USSR in 1939 and 1940 were not enlisted in the Red Army proper, but served in auxiliary "labor corps," or in separate national military units organized inside the Soviet Union, some of which (e.g. the Lithuanian, Latvian, and Estonian contingents) operated within the frame of the Red Army, and others (the Polish and Czechoslovak units) operated independently.

Jewish enlistment in the Polish units is worth mentioning. These recruits included also Jews of "semi-Soviet" national status, i.e. those resident in West Belorussia and West Ukraine. Under an agreement concluded on August 14, 1941, between the Soviet government and the Polish exile government in London (following a previous basic agreement reestablishing Soviet-Polish relations), a Polish corps was formed in the USSR under General Wladislaw Anders. A large number of Jews served in this corps, despite the difficulties placed in the way of their enlistment. Thousands also served in the Polish Kosciuszko Division, formed in the Soviet Union in May 1943 (after the USSR broke off its relations with the Polish exile government).

Apart from the Jews who served in the regular forces, many fought in partisan units. Though their total number is difficult to assess, the fragmentary figures culled from numerous well-documented sources indicate that it was relatively high. Despite the aforementioned difficulties encountered by Jewish partisans, and the fact that their essentially urban background did not ease their adjustment to living conditions in the forests, many volunteered for the most daring and hazardous operations. In many localities it was the Jews who were foremost in organizing partisan resistance, and many distinguished themselves by heroic acts that became legendary.

It transpires, from Soviet official and semi-official sources, that the number of Jewish servicemen awarded the highest war decorations was proportionally much higher than that of any other national grouping. In all, 123,822 Jewish officers and other ranks were decorated for "bravery in action against the German invader." Over 100 Jews (Soviet sources variously quote figures ranging between 101 and 141) were awarded the highest order, Hero of the Soviet Union. There were between 100 and 104 Jewish generals in the Soviet army, and numerous other high-ranking Jewish commanders who saw distinguished action throughout the entire war against Germany. Jews were prominent on all fronts and in all fighting forces. They took part in the fiercest fighting in infantry, cavalry and armored units, served in artillery and tank brigades, on warships and submarines (the names of such distinguished submarine commanders as Simon Bogerad, Yitzhak Kobo, Israel Fisanavich and others became legendary); they excelled in airborne operations and as pilots (gallant exploits are related of fighter plane pilots Ilya Katunin and Yitzhak Irzhak); they served in reconnaissance and intelligence units, in front-line medical and engineering corps; skilled Jewish technicians and engineers were prominent in detachments dropped behind the enemy lines to carry out sabotage and establish underground lines of communications; to say nothing of the contribution of Jewish scientists to weapon development (for instance, Major-General Simon Lavochkin, who devised the fighter plane named after him).

It is of interest that the Lithuanian corps (the Sixteenth Division) was mentioned several times in the Orders of the Day issued by the Supreme Soviet Command, after having distinguished itself in breaking through the German lines. This would at first seem inconsistent with the fact that large sections of the Lithuanian population collaborated with the German enemy, especially when it came to persecuting and exterminating the Jews. The inconsistency is resolved, however, when we consider that some eighty percent of the corps' members, and ninety percent of its combat casualties, were Jews. Incidentally, this corps was pervaded by a distinctly popular Jewish atmosphere, with Yiddish community singing, traditional communal prayers, and even orders issued in Yiddish.

Jews also took a leading part in resistance activities. There is an accumulation of interesting evidence about Soviet Jews who organized and headed risings in various German concentration camps, and about Jewish Red Army prisoners of war who organized resistance in their prison camps.[72]

The participation of Soviet Yiddish writers in the war — in actual combat as distinct from their literary contribution to the war effort — is particularly significant in the light of subsequent postwar developments (which will be dealt with in detail later). According to an article published in January 1947, about three-quarters of the total number of Soviet Jewish writers fought on different fronts and in partisan units, and 38 of them "bravely gave their lives."[73] Subsequent figures, published in May 1965 on the twentieth anniversary of the defeat of Germany, list the names of 40 Jewish writers who fell in battle: 21 poets and 19 authors and literary critics.[74] Provisional figures published in 1958 put the number of Soviet writers who saw active fighting (including war correspondents and "political workers") at 980, and the number killed in action at 275.[75] Hence, the Jewish writers — many of them volunteers — shouldered a proportionately heavier burden than their non-Jewish colleagues.

A further observation is pertinent here. The dedication and heroism of the Soviet people in the war against Germany and the Red Army's crucial share in shattering the Wehrmacht is undisputed. Nevertheless, it is an established fact that treachery was not uncommon in the Soviet Union, encompassing millions of Soviet citizens especially shortly after the German invasion. Even Soviet sources abundantly admit the prevalence of this phenomenon, which assumed not only the passive form of welcoming the occupation forces, but extended also to active anti-Soviet military, terrorist, and espionage operations. Suffice it to mention, in this connection, that several autonomous Soviet republics were dissolved on account of the mass treachery of their inhabitants[76] (though this is by no means intended to condone the infliction of collective punishments). Even the Russian people, who undoubtedly formed the mainstay of Soviet resistance, were not free from the taint of large-scale treachery, as evidenced by the defection of General Vlasov and others. The collaborationist attitude of large sections of the Russian Orthodox Church, which the Soviet authorities accorded special privileges during the war, is also worthy of attention. Stalin himself had demonstrated a conciliatory gesture by inviting the Metropolis of Moscow to the Kremlin, and permitting the re-establishment of the Synod, thus elevating the Metropolis to the rank of Patriarch. But while the Church leaders in Moscow were exhorting their followers to wage unrelenting war against Hitler, whom they denounced as the anti-Christ, and threatening collaborators with excommunication, many members of the local clergy in the occupied zones were holding prayer services for the well-being of the Nazis, preaching impassioned sermons in their support, and making public appearances and having themselves photographed with German civil and military authorities. Some of these priests even served as spies and informers against the underground forces, especially its Jewish members, and actually took part in their liquidation.[77]

The Jews, on the other hand, constituted the most trustworthy and stable element among the population. They could hardly have been otherwise, admittedly, in view of the "New Order" that the Nazis wished to institute in Russia as in all the other countries they overran. Yet this does not alter the fact that there were no renegades and deserters among the Jews.

Though Soviet Jews as a whole distinguished themselves in the fighting and suffered conspicuous losses, they were nevertheless slanderously and sweepingly branded as shirkers and draft dodgers. This was but one more in the series of internal shocks administered to Soviet Jewry since 1939. Despite all facts and figures to the contrary (presented here in a fragmentary manner), the Jews were commonly said to have fled to the safety of the remote Central Asian republics, to which both non-Jewish and Jewish refugees had been evacuated. Malicious jokes, like "The Jews have conquered Tashkent," became increasingly current, with such witty additions as "and without a battle, too." "Abrasha" (the Russian diminutive for Abraham) was popularly represented as the wily Jew who managed to look after himself by having the right connections and elbowing others out of the way.

This vilification became so widespread that Ilya Ehrenburg saw fit to repudiate it. At a mass meeting convened by the Jewish Anti-Fascist Committee to intensify the Jewish war effort in the Soviet Union and throughout the world, Ehrenburg deplored the scurrilous anti-Jewish smear campaign, illustrating his point with the following story, which is worth reproducing in full:

> An elderly Jew came to see me, the father of a celebrated pilot whom the Army newspapers had written about. This pilot had been his only son. He had loved him dearly. And this is what the father told me: "I was speaking to a civilian manager [of a plant] and he asked me: 'Why are there no Jews at the front? Why are they nowhere to be seen in the war?' I didn't answer him. I found it hard to say anything. This was four days after I had been notified by the Army that my son had been killed."
>
> You have probably all heard about the Jews "not being seen at the front." There was a time when many of our soldiers were not aware they were Jews, until they started getting letters from their relatives in Uzbekistan and Kazakhstan asking them why people were openly saying that there were no Jews to be seen at the front, that they were not in the fighting. On reading such a letter on his way to the front or in a trench, a Jewish soldier becomes perturbed. He becomes anxious, not only for himself, but also for his relatives, who are being insulted without cause. . . .[78]

Ehrenburg's remarks carried great force of conviction and were published in a Yiddish paper, but were hardly able to curb the insidious anti-Jewish smear campaign, particularly as the authorities were not overly inclined to do anything about it. Even if they were not totally indifferent to such manifestations, considerations of expediency came first: surely at such a time — the authorities maintained — when we are engaged in such a mighty struggle, we cannot be sidetracked by such trivialities.

Some explanation can be found for the anti-Semitic feeling that had begun to pervade also the nonoccupied parts of the USSR. Many people arrived there by devious routes from German-occupied areas, where they had been infected by the Nazi anti-Jewish venom. The occupation lines were in a constant state of flux. The Germans set out to inculcate the fifty to sixty million Soviet citizens in the occupied areas with their Nazi, and especially their anti-Jewish, doctrines, and some of their propaganda publications somehow reached remote Russian villages far behind the lines. War shortages, too, were primitively laid at the door of the Jewish evacuees and refugees, whose sale of secondhand clothing and utensils in order to eke out a subsistence was magnified to the proportions of "profiteering." These and similar explanations could not, however, mitigate the depressive effect these anti-Semitic manifestations had on the Soviet Jews at a time when their country was fighting the Nazi enemy.

In 1943, the tide of war showed clear signs of changing as the Germans steadily retreated before the victorious Soviet army. Amidst the general air of hopefulness, it was only natural that Hitler's imminent defeat should hold out special hope for the Soviet Jews. They firmly believed that victory would effectively silence the Nazi anti-Semitic propaganda that had fed the population with warnings against the dangers of "Jewish domination" etc., and that, in consequence, the Soviet authorities would no longer hold it expedient to condone anti-Semitic manifestations and outbreaks inside the country.

These hopes were very soon shattered. As the German-occupied cities were liberated one after the other, the Jews who hastened to return to their former places of residence were met with a blast of anti-Semitism. While the morale of the population rose steadily higher as the Red Army victoriously pressed forward, the Jewish survivors who returned to the liberated areas found — not only the terrible bereavement of their people — but open hostility at their return.

This animosity towards the Jews was induced and fostered not only by social and psychological factors, but also by distinctly practical and material considerations. We shall enumerate several of them. First, in some localities, especially in liberated parts of the Ukraine, certain local elements were understandably afraid that the returning Jews might hold them to account for the murder of their families and either call for legal redress, or take the law into their own hands. Secondly, many of the local inhabitants were loath to restore the Jewish property which they had pillaged, or seized after the owners had been butchered, or which had been placed in their keeping. Thirdly, war damage had caused an acute housing shortage, and the returning Jews insisted on getting their homes back. Fourthly, the returning Jews were naturally entitled to be reinstated in their former posts and jobs, which meant that those who had occupied them during their absence would be ousted.

As for the official attitude — the Soviet authorities were not inclined to antagonize the local populations, especially since there was still fighting going on. Moreover, the newly liberated areas were infested by semi-lawless bands, whose support the authorities were eager to obtain in the initial process of reestablishing Soviet rule. The best way to achieve this would not be by reproaching the inhabitants for having committed crimes against the Jews.

Nikita Khrushchev, first secretary of the Ukrainian Communist Party and premier of the Ukrainian Republic, must have been aware that any public expression of symptahy for the Jews, as the prime victims of unparalleled Nazi ferocity, was hardly conducive to gaining popular support. Kiev, the Ukrainian capital, was liberated on November 6, 1943. On March 1, 1944, the Republic's Supreme Soviet convened for the first time since the German invasion. Addressing this session, Khrushchev dwelt at length on the horrors of the German occupation, and lauded the heroic and patriotic stand of the Soviet peoples in general, and of the Ukrainian people in particular. A perusal of the structure and content of this address will show that Khrushchev deliberately avoided mentioning the Jews. Yet he was obviously unable, on the other hand, to refrain from referring to the behavior and stand adopted by the Ukrainian nationalists, some of whom had fought against the Germans and others had actively collaborated with them, but neither element of which were favorably disposed towards the Soviet regime. His remarks on the subject imply a readiness to forget their sins in the recent past, so as to leave the door open for reconciliation.[79] At the same time he showed himself utterly callous with regard to the Jewish tragedy, such as that connected with the name of Babi Yar (in Kiev, scene of the butchery of tens of thousands of Jews). When Ehrenburg, in a letter to the Ukrainian premier, begged him to intervene with the city authorities who wanted to build a modern market on the site, Khrushchev replied: "I advise you not to interfere in matters that do not concern you. You had better keep to writing good novels."[80]

What Khrushchev said — or rather what he left unsaid — in his address and his letter must be regarded not only as a deliberate insult to the Jews, but also as an indication that the authorities would not meddle in the current attitude towards them. This no doubt encouraged some of the local population to brazenly "advise" returning Jewish survivors to go back to their hiding places.

There is abundant evidence of the surly welcome that awaited many Jews who came back to their homes in the liberated areas. Many accounts, of which the following is typical, are identical in many details:

> We came back to Kiev in July 1944 . . . and went straight to the courtyard [compound] where we had lived for fifteen years. I shall not forget that moment as long as I live. Our neighbors met us with furious looks, even . . . those we had been friendly with before the war and had helped to raise and bring up their children. When she saw us, one girl called Lydia called out: "I'll go and tell the Germans that the *Zhids* [derogative for Jews] are back." . . . Her mother, too, met us with a scowling face. I found a Russian called Kompantsiev occupying my apartment. He refused to vacate it, though we had lived there since 1930. But this was against the law. . . . In those days there was a great shortage of dwellings in Kiev, since much of the city had been destroyed. After a long struggle I got my apartment back practically by force. There were a lot of similar cases in Kiev. . . ."[81]

The hostile attitude that greeted the Jews often led to vituperative exchanges and blows. In some places Jews were afraid to venture out of doors after dark. Jews were occasionally set upon and beaten up. Severe anti-Semitic outbreaks were reported from Odessa,[82] among other places. The atmosphere in Kiev in mid-1944 was charged with the tension of an imminent pogrom. The ostensible reason was the rumor that a Jewish army officer, returning from the front, had tried to get his apartment back from a Ukrainian officer who occupied it, and, attacked by the latter, had killed him in the ensuing scuffle.[83]

The authorities not only proved reluctant to support Jewish claims for the restoration of their dwellings and property, but very soon began to obstruct the resettlement of the Jewish evacuees. From a letter sent from the Soviet Union in July 1944, it is learned that whereas at first the Jews were permitted to travel to the liberated areas, "now the Jews are no longer allowed to travel there because of the disturbances that have broken out in these places."[84] Those that did return met with increasing disappointments and frustration. An illustration in point is that of a Jewish lawyer who before the war had served as a prosecuting attorney in the Ukraine; on his return, he was appointed defense counsel for the pro-Nazi collaborators and others charged with crimes against the state, since, as a Jew — he was told — he would personally be far better off in this capacity.[85] A Jewish woman, a longtime Communist and underground fighter, was advised "as a friend" by Khrushchev to rewrite her curriculum vitae, as required by the Party's personnel department, and continue using the forged Aryan papers with which she had concealed her Jewish identity during the occupation, if she wished to keep her job in his secretariat.[86] It is reported that just before the end of the war, the Party Center in Moscow circulated a secret and carefully phrased directive to the local branches, urging them to take account of the anti-Semitic mood prevailing as a result of the German occupation, and refrain from employing Jews in key positions.[87]

We have dealt so far mainly with postwar physical manifestations of anti-Semitism, i.e. aimed at Jewish life, property, and employment. However, as borne out by a great deal of evidence, the official attitude towards Jewish cultural reconstruction was no less hostile. Vilna was liberated by the Red Army on July 13, 1944. The handful of Jewish survivors who returned to this formerly flourishing Jewish center found it a scene of utter devastation. Hoping to salvage something from the ruins, they tried to assemble some of the rare Jewish books, manuscripts, Torah scrolls, and other relics that had been zealously hidden away in the ghetto. Gradually, some five thousand Jews — not all of them former Vilna residents — settled in the city, and a group of writers set about restoring Jewish cultural life. They had great plans for setting up a publishing house, issuing a newspaper, forming a choir, and similar projects, and were confident of receiving government and Party help. However, they met with a solid wall of indifference and even antagonism, were sent rushing about from pillar to post, and found themselves obstructed at every step, not only by the authorities of the Lithuanian Republic, but also by Moscow officialdom — an attitude that could hardly have been attributed merely to red tape.[88] Their persistent, idealistic efforts thwarted by broken promises, cynical indifference, and even deliberate malice, they could not but infer that the government and Party officials wished in this way to "curry favor with the anti-Soviet majority of the Lithuanian population."[89]

This method of political bribery, far from being merely an isolated local manifestation, was applied also in regard to Soviet foreign policy, with distinctly anti-Jewish implications. This is aptly illustrated by the following.

Immediately following the German invasion, the entire Soviet literature and press were mobilized for a total anti-German campaign and were regarded as an integral part of Soviet war machinery. Prominent in this campaign throughout the war was Ilya Ehrenburg, whose daily articles and feuilletons became extremely popular. So great was their influence, that some Soviet leaders compared their impact to that of batteries of artillery or armored divisions, while the renegade "Vlasovchiks" claimed, on the other hand, that "the Jewish dog Ehrenburg is barking furiously." Hitler himself, aware of Ehrenburg's influence, referred to him in one of his later speeches as the "Commissar of Vengeance" (warning the German soldiers of what they might expect in case of a Russian victory, and thus exhorting them to fight to the death). Among the Russian people, too, Ehrenburg became similarly, though affectionately, known as the "Commissar of Hatred for the Conquerors" and was given other popular nicknames. Ehrenburg's literary activity during that period and his share in "developing the medium of Soviet anti-Fascist satire" was widely and glowingly acclaimed by critics, who stressed his contributions towards unmasking "the bestial face" of Hitlerism and the Nazi hordes. On several occasions Ehrenburg also expressed pride in the fact that the Soviet people, even in their darkest hours, never allowed their hatred of the

Nazi conquerors to be projected onto the German culture. "We shall punish the criminals who have drenched our soil in blood," he wrote, ". . . but none of us wished to burn down the house of Goethe in Weimar. . . . Our patriotism is pure, devoid of arrogance, devoid of zoological hatred."[90]

Ehrenburg's Jewish origin no doubt lent special fervor to his anti-Nazi sentiments. One of his articles, entitled "The Hangmen of the Jewish People Shall be Tried and Punished," opens with the words: "The hundreds of thousands that have been slain demand an answer."[91] The authorities viewed this fervor favorably for some time, but no sooner did the war show signs of coming to an end than Ehrenburg's anti-German temperament fell from grace. One article of his, *"Enough!,"*[92] which barely differed in tenor and contents from his countless previous articles, was severely censured in a manner suggesting official prompting. Georgi Aleksandrov, chief of the information department of the Party's Central Committee, countered with an article in *Pravda* entitled "Comrade Ehrenburg Over-Simplifies Matters," in which he claimed that Ehrenburg had carried his vengeful feelings towards the Germans too far, and reminded the "Commissar of Hatred" that "the Soviet people have never identified the German people with the criminal Fascist gang which rules Germany at present."[93]

It is reasonable to suppose that the official need to call Ehrenburg to account assumed special urgency, chiefly in view of his assertion in *"Enough!"* that the Germans feared Soviet occupation more than Anglo-American occupation — a claim that might well have spurred the Germans to offer more stubborn resistance to the Soviet forces. Years later, Ehrenburg himself termed Aleksandrov's attack on him as "the right move in the game of chess." In other words, he justified this as an expedient political move designed to break down the enemy's last-ditch resistance by promising impunity to Germans "of the rank-and-file who merely carried out the Hitlerite orders."[94] But it would appear that this was but a preliminary gambit in the larger chess game, in which East and West vied for the Germans' favor. It is significant, nevertheless, that the first person to be singled out for public condemnation for voicing exaggeratedly vengeful sentiments towards the Germans was Ehrenburg the Jew, though he was certainly not the only writer who had preached a "Doctrine of Hatred" (the name of an article published in 1942 by the Russian novelist Mikhail Sholokhov). This episode brings back certain associations from the years 1939–41, when Ehrenburg had been told: "Persons of a certain national origin are not pleased with our foreign policy. That is understandable. But they would do well to hide their feelings for the sake of their families."[95] It transpires that also in 1945, when the USSR was still at war with Germany, persons of Jewish origin were urged to "hide their feelings" for the same reason.

For the Jews, needless to say, the final defeat of Germany was a joyous event. Who, if not they, were entitled to exchange the traditional holiday greetings of *Mazel Tov* and *Gut Yontov?*[96] Yet it also goes without saying that the joy of "the slain people" — a phrase used by Yitzhak Katznelenson, poet of the Jewish holocaust — was uniquely overshadowed by boundless pain and grief. The celebration of victory was marred by an intense feeling of utter bereavement.

This ambivalence of feeling was frequently in evidence even before Germany's final surrender. The mood described by one Jewish partisan was no doubt shared by many: "At the beginning of July 1944, the Belorussian partisans marched in a victory parade through Minsk. The Jewish partisans also took part. Their eyes did not shine with the gleam of victory . . . theirs was a silent, proud, funeral march."[97]

The specific fate suffered by the Jews in the war was to leave its mark long after the war had ended. This was poignantly expressed by the Soviet Jewish poet Leib Kvitko: "My Ukrainian friends will still see their homes. . . . But I, who will I still find there? My Jewish brothers who lived there are no more. . . . Only pits and graves will I find there . . ."

The despondency of the Jews was heightened by the anti-Semitism manifested even at the time of the victory celebrations. That demobilized Jewish soldiers were frequently being asked where they had bought their medals hardly served to raise their spirits. The Nazi foe had been crushed, but not the "Accursed heritage"[98] of anti-Semitism. It may be added that whereas in the 1920's this "heritage" had been condemned and a campaign launched to curb its manifestations,[99] the authorities were not so inclined after the war.

Nevertheless the scales of this ambivalence sometimes tipped towards hopefulness. Russian Jews, like most other Jews during and immediately after the war, were imbued with an almost mystic faith that they would somehow be compensated for what they had suffered at the hands of the Nazis. Moreover, they were led to expect some kind of reward for their significant part in the fighting. These hopes were rationally grounded on certain wartime developments that seemed to promise the opening of a new chapter in the official attitude towards the Jews. These developments were connected, among other things, with the activities of the Soviet Jewish Anti-Fascist Committee, to which the following chapter is largely devoted.

TWO

"Our Jewish Brethren the World Over!"

The Jewish Anti-Fascist Committee of the Soviet Union (JAC) was founded in April 1942.[1] This might appear at first sight merely a technical and organizational measure. However, as will be seen, it set off developments that had a far-reaching political, cultural, and psychological impact on Soviet Jewry.

The establishment of the JAC was integrated into the overall plan for the total mobilization of resources for the war against Germany. It was founded alongside the All-Slav Committee, committees of Soviet women, of Soviet youth, and of Soviet scientists, each of which was allotted a specific sector in the political campaign and the psychological warfare against the Nazis. Its function was to appeal to world Jewish opinion, but this was by no means the ultimate aim. The Soviet authorities attached great significance to the influence of world Jewry in shaping general public opinion in the West, whose support in the struggle against Germany was considered vital. The aim was not only to obtain material aid, of great importance in itself, but to prompt Western Jewry to bring political pressure to bear. As the prime object of Nazi hatred, the Jews could be motivated to clamor for the opening of a second front in Europe and for America's entry into the war against Germany.

Over and above its ostensible aims outside the Soviet Union, the establishment of the JAC marked a sensational reversal of internal policy. For the first time since the Jewish Sections of the Communist Party were dissolved in 1930, Soviet Jewry was accorded some kind of organizational framework. The very formation of a specifically Jewish body and the recognition of its professed aims were tantamount to an official avowal of withdrawal from the established doctrine that Jewish unity did not extend beyond territorial boundaries; on the contrary, they implied that Jewish extraterritorialism was not inconsistent with the unity of the Jewish people. That the JAC's organ was named *Einikeit* [Unity][2] was in itself a refutation of the hitherto predominant theory.

The first signs of this revision of theory became evident some time before the Committee was officially recognized. A Jewish anti-Fascist rally held in Moscow on August 24, 1941, was described in the Soviet press as a "public gathering of representatives of the Jewish people."[3] This gathering might be regarded as having laid the ground for the establishment of the Jewish Anti-Fascist Committee.[4] This being the case, the question might well arise why official sanction of the Committee was withheld for more than seven months. There are grounds for assuming that during this period the Soviet authorities had reason to reconsider their initial attitude towards the formation of the JAC. It is possible that when the United States entered the war against Japan following the Japanese attack on Pearl Harbor, on December 7, 1941, Moscow felt confident that the United States would proceed to operate in the European theater, too, thus mitigating the urgent need to solicit the support of American Jewry by making a conciliatory gesture such as authorizing the founding of an all-Jewish committee. It is also possible that the plan for constituting a Jewish war committee would have been abandoned altogether, had the fortunes of war taken a radically different course at the time. But the Soviet victory was still far off, and political and strategic considerations proved of sufficient weight to relax the traditional attitude towards Jewry. No sooner was the Committee officially sanctioned, however, than the interpretation of its functions and objectives turned out to be far shallower than its protagonists had imagined. The case of Erlich and Alter is of special interest in this connection.

Henryk Erlich and Victor Alter, leaders of the Jewish Socialist Bund of Poland, had escaped in September 1939 from the German-occupied part of Poland to the area annexed by the Red Army. They were arrested shortly afterwards on charges of collaborating with the Polish secret police and planning to commit acts of sabotage in the Soviet Union, and were taken to Moscow for questioning. They were tried some time after the German invasion and sentenced to death, but the sentence was commuted into ten years' imprisonment. Following the intervention of the newly reopened Polish embassy in Moscow, they were both released from prison in mid-September 1941. Shortly after their release, Erlich and Alter were approached by Soviet government representatives with a proposal that they organize and head a *worldwide* Jewish committee to foster the fight against Fascism. From their talks with these officials, Erlich and Alter gathered that the Soviet government was interested in the establishment of a broadly based body that would comprise various Jewish groups from all over the world. In the initial plan they drew up and discussed with the Soviet authorities, the Committee was to be made up of Jewish representatives from the USSR, the United States, and Great Britain, as well as representatives of the Jewish population of the Nazi-dominated countries, such as Poland, Czechoslovakia, and Germany. The Committee's presidium was to consist of Erlich as chairman, Alter as secretary, and the renowned actor Solomon Mikhoels, director of the Moscow Jewish State Theater, as representative of Soviet Jewry.

On these lines, Erlich and Alter drafted a detailed plan outlining the structure and proposed activities of a Jewish Anti-Fascist Committee, which they were invited to discuss personally with Lavrenti P. Beria, people's commissar for the interior — chief of the NKVD. Beria advised them to apply to Stalin for authorization of the plan, since overseas activities were involved. They therefore addressed a memorandum to Stalin, expressing their fervent desire to mobilize Jewish help for the Soviet war effort, and requesting authorization to form the JAC, as outlined in a detailed plan which they appended to their memorandum.

It should be added that shortly after their release from prison, on September 24, 1941, Erlich and Alter notified the Polish ambassador in Moscow, Stanislaw Kot, that they had addressed an appeal to the Polish Jews in the USSR to enlist in the Polish forces that were then being organized on Soviet soil "in order to restore Poland's right to a life of freedom, and in order to liberate the world from brown [Nazi] servitude."

It would appear that the Soviet authorities at first set great store by Erlich and Alter. When all important institutions, as well as leading writers, diplomatic missions, and foreign news agencies were transferred to the interior from exposed Moscow on October 15, 1941, Erlich and Alter were evacuated, too, and lodged together with other VIP's at a hotel in Kuibyshev. But the request they had addressed to Stalin went unanswered. On December 4, 1941, Erlich and Alter were again arrested; shortly afterwards they were shot.

Whatever motives underlay the execution of these two men, the reason advanced by the Soviet authorities — that Erlich and Alter had collaborated with the Nazis and incited Red Army soldiers and the Soviet people to cease their fight against the Germans — sounds the least plausible. This may have been an act of vindictiveness on the part of Stalin, who not only harbored a deep-seated hatred of all Social Democrat and Bundist leaders, but was also probably aware of the two men's former attitude to him and his leadership, and especially their sharp criticism of the infamous Moscow trials. It is also possible that the Soviet secret police had intercepted letters that Erlich and Alter had tried to send abroad, suggesting that representations be made for the release of Polish labor leaders imprisoned in the USSR. Nor is it at all unlikely that the Soviet authorities, on second thoughts, became wary of letting Erlich and Alter be in direct contact with the Western world (particularly after the torture they had been subjected to during their imprisonment), since this might be more harmful than useful as propaganda. It has also been suggested that they paid the extreme penalty for daring to broach a proposal that a general amnesty be granted to prisoners throughout the USSR, as a gesture designed to rally the disaffected population to support the war effort. Though all this lies within the realm of conjecture, we may reasonably assume that, added to all their other sins, the enthusiasm with which they applied themselves to the task of initiating worldwide activities on behalf of the Committee did not meet with official favor. That they took the project too seriously must have contributed to the decision to put them out of the way.[5]

The execution of Erlich and Alter did not cause the JAC plan to be shelved, though it was radically modified both in structure and in terms of reference. Instead of a *World* Jewish Committee, as had been the original intention, the establishment of a *Soviet* Jewish Anti-Fascist Committee was announced in April 1942. Had the Committee been formed on the original lines — that is, comprising Jewish representatives from different parts of the world — it would have been necessary to accord it a certain freedom of thought and action, whereas as a Soviet body it could be, and was, placed under official direction and surveillance. The exercise of these latter functions, it appears, was delegated to Solomon Lozovsky, a longtime Bolshevik leader and deputy chief of the Soviet Information Bureau, who became a member of the Committee. Solomon Mikhoels, who was originally to have represented Soviet Jewry on the Committee, was appointed its chairman.

Not only was the representative basis of the JAC drastically narrowed, but its functions, too, were considerably whittled down. No mention was made of the proposal, raised by Erlich and Alter in the course of their negotiations, that the Committee also organize relief for Jews in German-occupied areas in Europe and materially support Jewish resistance activities. It was made clear that the JAC was to devote itself chiefly to influencing Jewish opinion outside the Soviet Union and enlisting Jewish financial support for the Soviet war effort. Its propaganda was designed to achieve two dovetailing objects: to intensify anti-German feeling, and to engender a pro-Soviet atmosphere among world Jewry. Thus, the JAC set out not only to publicize the German atrocities, but also to disseminate an idyllic picture of Jewish accomplishments in the Soviet Union against a background of national brotherhood and equality.

Coincident with its regular tasks of spreading Soviet propaganda abroad, however, the JAC brought about an extraordinary stirring of Jewish consciousness in its own ranks, reflecting the prevalent mood of Soviet Jewry as a whole. By dint of expressing feelings of national solidarity and Jewish pride, by employing traditional symbols taken from the Jewish heritage, and by similar means, the JAC leadership hoped to touch the right chords in appealing to Jewish communities outside the Soviet Union and enlisting their support for the Soviet war effort; but it soon became difficult to distinguish between mere campaigning devices and the manifestation of genuine feelings. The JAC workers were delighted with the harmonious relationship that had come about — or so they imagined — between the official line of propaganda and what they really thought and felt. In time, no doubt affected by the specific tragedy of the Jewish people, they were frequently so carried away by their faith and enthusiasm as to overlook the JAC's dominant objective, namely, that of spreading Soviet propaganda.

A "public gathering of representatives of the Jewish people" was held in Moscow in August 1941. At this gathering, Mikhoels addressed himself to "the Jews, my brothers," and other speakers spoke in a similar vein. Perets Markish, the Yiddish novelist and poet, said that "rivers and seas are no barrier"; and calling on his "Jewish brothers" to join in the struggle, he declared that "we are one people, and now we are become one army." For years Soviet Jewry had been denied the right to know what was going on among Jewish communities beyond their country's borders; now author David Bergelson publicly voiced deep pain that "we do not know how many Jews are alive today in Germany, Czechoslovakia, Poland, France, Belgium, Holland, Denmark, Rumania, Bulgaria, Yugoslavia, Greece, and in the Soviet areas which the Fascists have temporarily occupied." The unity of world Jewry was "endorsed" in a manifesto issued by the gathering, and addressed to "OUR JEWISH BRETHREN THE WORLD OVER!"

Nine months later, on May 24, 1942, Mikhoels broadcast an address on Moscow Radio to "the sons of the Jewish people in Great Britain, in the United States of America, in Palestine, in the South American republics, in South Africa, and in Australia," in which he declared: "I represent that part of the Jewish people that is living in the USSR," thereby stressing that Soviet Jewry was *part of a world entity.* In that same broadcast, a Jewish nurse who was serving in a military hospital appealed to "Jewish mothers and nurses in all countries in the world," and a Jewish physician and a scientist addressed their Jewish colleagues in other countries.

Though, as has been stated, the JAC was set up as an exclusively Soviet body, this limited status did not prevent it from adopting a resolution (at its plenary session of May 1942) calling on every son and daughter of the Jewish people, wherever they might be, to take an oath "not to rest . . . until Hitler and his gang of hangmen — the mortal enemies of all nations and the deadly foe of the Jewish people — have been wiped off the face of the earth." The text of the oath, which was to be taken on June 22, 1942 (the first anniversary of the German invasion of the Soviet Union), was published in an appeal which the JAC addressed to "the Jews of the United States, Britain, Canada, Cuba, Mexico, Palestine, Argentina, Brazil, Uruguay, Chile, South Africa, Australia, and other countries."

It was natural that the common German foe should be pointed up as being the dominant factor in the unity of the Jewish people, or, in the words of Mikhoels: "We are separated by vast oceans, but we are united by the ocean of the blood of our mothers and sisters, of our sons and brothers, which has been shed by the Fascists." But alongside this external and contemporary factor, the JAC spokesmen explicitly based the unity of the Jewish people also on its common history, tradition, cultural heritage, and wealth of associations. Thus, Mikhoels spoke of the German hatred for "the sons of the ancient people, the sons of a people that has been tortured and persecuted throughout the generations." JAC speakers and writers increasingly resorted to Biblical imagery, Talmudic references, and Jewish historical symbols. This applied not only to religious leaders, such as Moscow's Chief Rabbi Shlomo Shleifer (who quoted, "and He will render vengeance to His adversaries," or "the Glory of Israel shall not die"), but to eminently secular Jewish figures as well. David Bergelson, in an impassioned address, quoted from Psalms: "For the waters are come in even unto the soul" (that is, "our troubles have reached their climax") and "I shall not die but live"; Perets Markish referred to Job as the embodiment of the agonies of the Jewish people; Itsik Feffer recalled the symbolism of Ezekiel's vision of the valley of dry bones; scientist Lina Shtern stressed the continuity of the heroic tradition of the Maccabees and Bar-Cochba; Mikhoels exhorted his listeners to act according to "the words of our ancients: an eye for an eye, a tooth for a tooth." The Committee proposed naming the tank columns and aircraft squadrons donated to the Red Army by world Jewry after "heroes of the Jewish people and illustrious creators of

Jewish culture" (Bar-Cochba and Yehuda Halevi, among others), as well as in commemoration of contemporary Jewish war heroes.

Further examples of this trend are legion. We shall bring one more — an excerpt from an address given by Red Army General Jacob Kreiser, a member of the JAC, at a mass meeting held on August 31, 1942, at Ufa, capital of the Bashkir Autonomous Soviet Socialist Republic:

> The Jewish people, like the other people of the USSR, is steadfast in its resolution to fight the Hitlerite enemy to the death. My nation, which has given the world illustrious sages and brilliant thinkers, is also a nation that fights for its freedom. Jewish history tells of the glorious war waged by the Jews against the Romans, the ancestors of the present-day Italian Fascists. The name of Bar-Cochba has served as a shining example for many Jews. . . . I am proud of the thousands of Jews who are fighting heroically in the ranks of the Red Army and striking at the enemy [Kreiser mentioned here the names of several Jewish war heroes]. . . . A nation with sons like these will never be subjugated! Such a nation will never bow its head to the Hitlerite gangsters. . . . As a General of the Red Army and as a son of the Jewish people I solemnly swear not to lay down my arms until such time as the last Fascist has been exterminated from the earth.

At the JAC rallies and in its publications (unlike the general Soviet publications), emphasis was laid on the specific Jewish tragedy, on the fact that the Jews bore the brunt of the evil which the Fascists had brought upon mankind, and on active Jewish participation in the fighting. JAC speakers also specifically referred on various occasions to Jewish resistance outside the Soviet Union, thus: "The Jews of Poland, Yugoslavia, Czechoslovakia, Greece — all are following the example of their brethren in the Ukraine and Belorussia and are striking heavy blows at the Hitlerite butchers"; and, "The rising in the Warsaw Ghetto and in Bialystok, the resistance in the death camps of Treblinka and Auschwitz, the mass enlistment of Jews in partisan forces in France, Belgium, Yugoslavia, and Holland, as well as in the Ukraine and Belorussia, and the prominence of Jews in the United States forces — all these constitute glorious chapters of devotion and self-sacrifice in the history of the Jewish people."

In time, the JAC and its leadership began to voice also a "hymm for the future," as indicated in the manifesto which the Committee issued following its plenary session in 1943: "The day is not far off when Hitler and his gangs will be tried by the nations of the world. All the nations will present their reckonings, but the greatest reckoning of all will be that presented by the Jewish nation. Together with all other peace-loving nations, the Jewish nation will appear as a prosecutor at this trial." It is interesting to note that this statement speaks of the claims of "the Jewish nation," which the world had not yet accorded national status.

Overtones of a similar "hymn for the future" may be observed in an article published by David Bergelson at the end of March 1944, of which the following is an excerpt:

> Now that Hitlerism has been pushed back to the brink of defeat, it is of special importance that the Jews enlarge their already prominent participation in the war. This is important not only in order to bring victory nearer, but also for the purpose of determining clearly the contribution of the Jewish people towards achieving this victory. Hitler wished to exterminate us as a people, and the hundreds of thousands of our sons and daughters who have fought and are fighting with boundless devotion to defend the countries where they were born and are living — have fought and are fighting also for the honor of the Jewish people, in order to safeguard its future as a people.[6]

That these and similar sentiments were voiced indicates that the JAC had gradually come to exceed the narrow objectives it had originally been set. It should be pointed out, in this connection, that from the outset the Committee had divided itself into two opposing trends, which might be broadly termed maximalistic and minimalistic. The clashes that occurred between these two trends were a reflection not only of the independence of thought manifested by their respective adherents, but also of their faith, or lack of it, in the longevity of the "new Jewish policy" adopted by the Soviet authorities. At all events, deep-seated apprehensions and skepticism in regard to the benevolence of the authorities' motives caused the JAC leaders to exercise restraint, despite the official sanction and even encouragement of manifestations of "Jewishness." Already at the Committee's first session in June 1942, only two months after its inauguration,

Shakhno Epstein, the Committee's secretary, censured the tendency to burden the JAC with tasks that had nothing to do directly with the fight against Fascism.[7] But even Epstein's criticism — and his function of secretary no doubt lent his remarks the weight of authority — was unable to override this tendency. While some of the Committee's members regarded it merely as a temporary institution with limited functions mainly designed for overseas consumption, others held that it should grow into a living center for the entire Soviet Jewish population, directing its cultural and communal life both during the war and after it.

This exchange of views, as a rule, was largely restricted to private conversations, rather than aired publicly. Nevertheless it sometimes came out into the open, as in the debate at the Committee's second plenary session in February 1943. At this meeting it appeared that the maximalists gained the upper hand. Perets Markish, for example, claimed that "the Jewish Anti-Fascist Committee must in future expand its range of activities. . . . It must take an interest in the plight of the refugees and assist them to make a new life for themselves. . . . *Einikeit* must devote special attention to this question." Yitzhak Nusinov, a professor of literature, seconded this suggestion, maintaining that the Committee must not concern itself with propaganda only, but must also care for the Jewish evacuees. The poet David Hofstein, looking ahead, said that "the Red Army is liberating city after city, village after village. When we return there, what shall we find? Ruins and graves. We must prepare for extensive reconstruction. We must care for the living people who will have to engage in this work. Let us care for them in good time." Then he explicitly went on to say that "the Jewish Anti-Fascist Committee must become the center of Russian Jewry, and not merely an agency for raising funds in the United States." D. Shchupak, chairman of the "Naileben" *kolhoz,* urged the Committee to prepare actively for the reconstruction of Jewish collective farms of the Ukraine and the Crimea. Itsik Feffer reported that the Committee received numerous letters from evacuees, but "they come to us with problems which the Committee is unable to solve." He cautiously suggested that the Committee refer these questions to the appropriate institutions. Chairman Mikhoels's reply to these criticisms indicated his leanings, however mild, towards a broader interpretation of the Committee's functions. Though he reminded the meeting that the Committee had the clearly defined function of "mobilizing resources to combat Fascism," he nevertheless admitted that "there is a kernel of truth in the view that the Committee has not yet become, for the entire country, that living center of the Jewish population which it should be. People send letters and complaints to us from different parts of the country; the dispersed Jewish population is searching for an address [of a Jewish organization to which to appeal in their need]; we cannot be indifferent to such things."[8]

Some two months later, Mikhoels and Feffer went abroad on an official mission on behalf of the JAC to the Jewish communities in the United States, Mexico, Canada, and Britain. If the founding of a Jewish committee in the Soviet Union was in itself an astounding innovation, the fact that Soviet Jewish representatives were sent to make direct contact with their "Jewish brethren" overseas was all the more so. Some regarded this as an innovation not only from the Jewish point of view. One Russian literary critic, for example, wrote that Mikhoels and Feffer were the "first official representatives of Soviet art to go to the United States since [the visit there in the early Twenties of] Mayakovsky."[9]

This mission was decided on at the top government level. Stalin himself not only authorized it, but attached to it great political significance. Before they left, Mikhoels and Feffer were received by the Soviet president, Mikhail Kalinin. During the interview, Stalin "unexpectedly" came in to wish them a successful trip.[10]

Mikhoels and Feffer remained abroad for about seven months. Arriving in New York in mid-1943, they were given an official reception at the Soviet Consulate. They preceded their remarks with the traditional greeting, "*Shalom aleichem,* Jewish brothers!" and the general impression was that they were a "State delegation on behalf of Soviet Jewry."[11] According to Feffer's subsequent report, they toured forty-six cities and addressed Jewish audiences totaling some half a million. Though treated with reserve in some minor Jewish circles, this was barely noticed in the wave of general enthusiasm which met them wherever they went. Non-Jewish personages, too, readily joined the local reception committees. Addressing a mass rally in New York on July 8, 1943, Mikhoels used the form of address that had already become current in the Jewish appeals sent out from Moscow: "Brothers! Brothers of our people, brothers of those slaughtered by the Hitlerite butchers, of those burnt in the ghettoes . . . brothers of our fighting men who bring death to the Fascist hangmen on the Soviet battlefields . . ."

A pertinent bibliography lists as many as 260 articles and reports on the visit of Mikhoels and Feffer published in the Yiddish press in the United States, Mexico, and Canada; only thirty of these were unfavorable. Seven Jewish poets commemorated the event in verse.[12] An exhibition devoted to the visit of Mikhoels and Feffer in the three American countries was opened in New York on December 27, 1943. In his inaugural address, the Soviet consul general announced that "the two illustrious representatives of Soviet Jewry" had arrived safely in Moscow that same day.[13]

We do not propose to enlarge unduly on the political, propagandistic, or fund-raising objects of the visit. What is of interest is the profound effect of the visit on the Jewish communities in the West, as well as the fact that the visitors were no less profoundly stirred. Their public appearances and declarations were no doubt coordinated with the local Soviet representatives in conformity with the official line, but the heart follows a logic of its own. The representatives of the Jewish Anti-Fascist Committee were deeply moved by their meeting with Jewish masses who in some way or other maintained a Jewish national and communal life of their own. They could not but feel that their "Jewish brothers," who welcomed them with such warmth and sympathy, regarded them not only as representatives of the Soviet Union and its Jewish people who were in the throes of a bitter struggle, but also as harbingers of renewed contact between the Jewish communities of the East and West. Feffer remarked that though there was a certain "estrangement" between Soviet and American Jews, he was sure that "this is a matter of the past, and from now on the two important Jewish communities will be joined by bonds of unity."[14] He expressed the hope that "our coming here has created a possibility for living contact, and our books will frequently reach you, and your books will reach us." He then went on to speak about the "firm brotherly relations" that will persist after Hitlerism has been crushed.[15]

In the course of their tour, Mikhoels and Feffer came to be regarded as representatives of a lost tribe, as it were, which had now been restored at long last to the fold of world Jewry. This view was voiced explicitly by the Chief Rabbi of the British Commonwealth, Dr. J. H. Hertz, in connection with the visit of the Soviet Jewish representatives in Britain. Joining in an appeal for the Jewish Fund for Soviet Russia (affiliated to Mrs. Churchill's Red Cross Aid to Russia Fund), the Chief Rabbi stated: "Let us remember that, if we do our full duty, we not only help to smash Hitlerism, *but bring back Russian Jewry to the fold of Israel.*" (The italics appear in the original text.)

This and subsequent quotations are taken from a booklet issued in London by the Jewish Fund for Soviet Russia as a souvenir of the occasion of the visit of Mikhoels and Feffer to Britain, and, as stated in the preface, "as a mark of the friendship between the Jews of Great Britain and the Jews of the Soviet Union."[16] This booklet deserves special attention, since large parts of it point to new trends of thought among Russian Jewry, as well as to the belief entertained by significant sections of world Jewry that Moscow was prepared basically to revise its policy in regard to the Jews. Though published by a British organization, most of the material was supplied by the JAC. Here, too, we find Soviet Jewish writers using traditional imagery and phrases from Jewish sacred writings. We shall cite several examples.

In his message to the Jews of Britain and the United States, Mikhoels quoted from the prayer recited on the night of Yom Kippur: "May our supplication rise from eventide; may our cry come before you at the dawn. . . ." and he added: "Today we end the day with a curse against Fascism, and we arise with a curse against Fascism." His message ended with the words: "We are calling upon you to fulfil your national Jewish duty towards your people."

David Bergelson contributed an article on the personality and dramatic talent of actor Mikhoels, stressing his distinctive traditional Jewish traits and his profound knowledge of Jewish history: "King Lear is to Mikhoels one of the greatest figures in literature, ranking with Job and Ezekiel." Bergelson noted that when Mikhoels was feted on the occasion of a quarter century of dramatic achievements, "Jews assembled in the synagogues to extend their felicitations . . . because he had brought honor to the Jews."

The booklet contained a great deal of information about Jewish soldiers in the Red Army who had distinguished themselves in the fighting. Lieutenant-General Jacob Kreiser is referred to by his Jewish name of "Yankel-Osher" Kreiser. Mention is made of the fact that on the grave markers of Jewish war heroes their non-Jewish comrades had specifically inscribed the fact that they were "true sons of the Jewish people." In a letter from the mother of a famous submarine commander, Captain Israel Fisanavich, to her son (as quoted in the booklet), she urges him to "remember we Jews have a double account to settle with the Hitlerite murderers. You are fighting . . . not only to defeat the enemy of our country, but also to avenge hundreds of thousands of Jewish lives."

Since most of the material for the booklet was compiled in Moscow, it is not at all surprising that the accomplishments of celebrated Soviet Jewish scientists, inventors, writers, and artists should be acclaimed in glowing terms. What is surprising, however, is the warm reference made to an obscure "religious young poet," Israel Emyot, who "until the invasion of Poland wore Hassidic garb, which he exchanged for a Red Army uniform," and who wrote, among other things, of "the sacred Scrolls that were desecrated by the Nazis." Hebrew and the Hebrew theater had been banned in the USSR since the middle of the Twenties, yet the booklet tells of Natan Altman the painter and sculptor, who had "achieved initial fame with his stage-sets for the Habimah's production of Ansky's *The Dibbuk* in 1921." An article entitled "Cantor Kusevitzky of Warsaw Sings in Moscow" relates that after Kusevitsky had sung arias in several languages, "the great event of the evening was when the Cantor sang *Kol Nidre,* which deeply moved Jewish and non-Jewish members of the audience alike."

What is most surprising of all, however, is the religious sentiment that pervades this material. In an article entitled "The Old Type of Religious Jew Still Lives in Russia," the author quotes from a letter written by an old Jew in Sverdlovsk to his son, a Russian air force officer serving at the front: "During the High Holidays there was not enough room in our synagogue. . . . We prayed to God to send a speedy downfall upon this man of blood, Hitler, and his whole accursed gang." He also informs his son that "we have founded a *Chevra Tehillim,* and every day we say Psalms for the victory of the Red

Army and the well-being of our people." Another article tells of scrolls of the law that were saved, at great risk, from a burning synagogue in Stalingrad and transferred to Kuibyshev. "One of the Scrolls was so badly burnt that it had to be buried according to the Jewish rites. A large crowd of religious Jews followed the coffin . . . and one said *kaddish* at the graveside."

Though it was widely maintained that the contents, style, and coloring of these accounts were specially adapted for overseas consumption, nevertheless the unwonted "Jewish spirit" that now seemed to emanate from Russia was on the whole hopefully welcomed among world Jewry. Even those Jewish circles that had long been regarded by the Soviet authorities as "hostile elements" — religious and Zionist leaders, lovers of the Hebrew language, and Bundists — began to evince friendship and sympathy for the Soviet Union. This broad political attitude adopted by Jewry coincided with that voiced by Churchill in his broadcast on the day Germany invaded the USSR: "No-one has been a more consistent opponent of Communism than I have for the last twenty-five years. I will unsay no word that I have spoken about it. But all this fades away before the spectacle which is now unfolding . . . this is the concern of free men and free nations in every corner of the earth."[17]

So much the more was this the concern of Jews the world over, who were now ready to put aside all differences regarding the Communist attitude to religion and Zionism until after the defeat of Germany. Jewish pro-Soviet sympathies were no doubt also bolstered by the feeling, which grew stronger as the war continued, that it was particularly Russian Jewry — which many had already come to mourn as lost to the Jewish nation — which would keep alive the surviving embers of the rich, traditional spirit that had pervaded east European Jewry. The Jews naturally responded from humane considerations to the appeal to help the Soviet Union and particularly her Jews in their distress. But they also must have felt, consciously or subconsciously, that if they now opened their hearts to the Soviet Union, this might lay the foundation for a new pattern of relations between Jewry and the Soviet regime.

That Jewry set great store by the change that had seemingly occurred in Moscow's policy towards the Jews is indicated in particular by the impact this had on the Zionist movement as a whole and on the *yishuv* (Jewish population) in Palestine. Just before the arrival of Mikhoels and Feffer in Britain, a Zionist leader there had pointed out that the common struggle (against the Nazi foe) had again brought Russian Jewry, after twenty-five years of isolation, in contact with the entire Jewish world. He hoped that after the present war the Soviet Union would see its way to changing those aspects of its Jewish policy that were not favorably disposed towards the national Jewish movement (that is, towards Zionism), and maintained that there were no logical grounds for any conflict of interest between world Jewry and the Soviet Union, and that Russia should be among the foremost supporters of a Jewish national home in Palestine.[18] A similar idea had previously been broached in Jerusalem to the Zionist political leadership: "The joint war against the common enemy has for the first time afforded us an opportunity to make direct contact with Soviet representatives . . . and it is up to us to make use of this opportunity."[19]

This "direct contact," however, was extremely limited and cautious on the part of the Soviet representatives, who took great pains not to let it veer onto a political and ideological tack. Yet even so, the narrow channels of communication that were established between Zionist and Soviet bodies and representatives were considered to have broken the ice. At a meeting with the Soviet minister in Washington on July 17, 1941, American Zionist leaders stated that recent developments had prepared the ground for improved relations between Jewish organizations and the Soviet authorities. These "recent developments" also formed the political and psychological setting of a meeting, held in London some two weeks later, between Zionist leaders Zelig Brodetsky and Berl Locker, and the first secretary of the Soviet legation in Britain. And it was no doubt this prospect of "improved relations," and the legitimate hope to derive some political advantage from the newly arisen circumstances, that prompted David Ben-Gurion to meet Ivan Maisky, the Soviet minister to Great Britain, in September 1941, followed up by talks between Maisky and Moshe Shertok (later Sharett) and Berl Locker. At the beginning of October 1943, Maisky (accompanied by his wife) spent a day in Palestine, meeting Jewish Agency representatives Ben-Gurion and

Eliezer Kaplan and Histadrut executive representative Golda Meyerson (later Meir), who attached great political importance to his visit. He was taken round by Ben-Gurion to visit several kibbutzim and some Jewish quarters of Jerusalem, and obviously seemed favorably impressed. Golda Meyerson reported that Maisky's visit "was not merely a friendly call on the Jewish Agency, following his talks in London with Ben-Gurion, Shertok and Locker; he really wanted to find out whether something can be done in this country, so that when the time comes when a stand will have to be taken on the Jewish question and Palestine, he will have first-hand knowledge on the subject. We have the feeling that his visit has been of significant value." From indirect evidence it is learnt that Maisky submitted to his Moscow superiors a glowing — virtually "Zionist" — report on Jewish achievement in Palestine.[20]

In these and similar contacts the Zionist representatives pursued two dominant themes: one of immediate practical purport, and the other of long-range political perspective. In the first place, they raised such immediate questions as the release of Zionists from Soviet prisons, and the emigration to Palestine of Polish Jewish refugees. Secondly, they strove to mitigate the inimical Soviet attitude to Zionism by pointing not only to the present common interests shared by the Soviet Union and Jewry (the war against Nazism), but also to the absence of any conflict of interests between Zionist aspirations and the objectives of the Soviet regime. The Zionist leaders pinned their hopes, in particular, on the outcome of talks between Histadrut (Jewish Labor Federation) and Soviet representatives: if the latter were better informed about the Palestine labor movement and its cooperative enterprises, this might well serve to remove prejudices and make for some measure of rapprochement.

The outcome of these contacts, if judged in the light of practical and immediate achievements, could hardly be considered successful. This applied not only to the attempts to obtain emigration permits and secure the release of Zionists from Soviet prisons, but also to the endeavor to gain Soviet sympathy for the Zionist cause. Nevertheless, the Jewish leaders, encouraged by the mere fact that the Soviet representatives were prepared to meet them after a long period of stony aloofness, felt that some headway had been made. This feeling was apparent, for instance, in the report presented by Eliahu Epstein (later Elath), head of the Jewish Agency's Middle East division, on his meeting with the Soviet minister at Ankara, Sergei Vinogradov, in January 1942: "Throughout our talk I had the feeling that, although this was not advancing a solution to our problem, the very fact of having made direct contact with the Soviet minister was in itself an achievement that might still be of use to us."

This hope of a new chapter in the Soviet attitude was given fervent expression in Palestine Jewry's reply to the appeal made by the above-mentioned "public gathering of representatives of the Jewish people" in Moscow, on August 24, 1941. The reply was broadcast by eminent personalities on "The Voice of Jerusalem" Radio to Soviet Jewry on October 3, 1941. Some excerpts are worth quoting.

Menahem Ussishkin, chairman of the Jewish National Fund, who belonged to the Zionist right wing, left his sickbed to record his broadcast address (he died a few days later). "Dear brothers and sisters!" he said. "Twenty-two years have gone by since we parted. But our love for you and our spiritual ties have not abated. During all the years that my colleagues and I have labored to rebuild our historical homeland, we have not for a moment lost sight of the fact that we are building it for all sections of our people who are dispersed throughout the world, and also for you."

Chief Rabbi Isaac Herzog urged Russian Jewry at this hour to "draw courage, hope, and faith from our sacred Torah."

Poet Shaul Tschernikhovsky said: "We have never given up hope of being reunited with you. . . . We hope that the golden chain that links us together — temporarily severed — will be linked up again." He went on to express the hope that Hebrew literature would again flourish on Russian soil, the birthplace of some of the greatest Hebrew writers, and concluded with the solemn prayer: "Hear O Israel! All our scattered ones are One People!"

Yitzhak Ben-Zvi, chairman of the Vaad Leumi (representative National Council of Palestine Jewry) and later second president of Israel, stressed that "Russian Jewry was and has remained the cradle of the Jewish movement of national liberation," and that "we have never reconciled ourselves to being severed from this Jewry."

Labor leader Berl Katznelenson said: "For many years we have yearned to hear your voice. Now it has reached us . . . from those precious [Jewish] centers that have been razed to the ground. . . . And it sounds to our ears like a voice from the depths of Jewish history. . . . Now listen you to our voice, the voice of a young sprout from the stem of the ancient people — a sprout first planted in the soil of the Land of Israel by Russian Jews. . . . We shall continue to be one people despite all barriers."

Hannah Rovina, the leading Habimah actress, extended to Russian Jewry the greetings of the Habimah theater, which was "born in Moscow and made its home in the Land of Israel." All speakers expressed Palestine Jewry's admiration for the Soviet Union and its valiant Red Army, and stressed the joint struggle against the Nazi foe. They also pointed to the enternal bond that joined all sections of the Jewish people in normal times as well as in adversity.[21]

This expectation of a new chapter was further manifested in various ways. The Representative Assembly of Palestine Jewry, meeting in Jerusalem on March 9, 1942, published a statement in which it extended "heartfelt brotherly greetings to Russian Jewry" and warm greetings to "all the peoples of the USSR and their brave forces." The statement does not refrain from expressing concern for the fate of persons imprisoned, exiled, and persecuted in the Soviet Union "for their loyalty to Zion and their adherence to Israel's culture and religion" and refers to the Soviet regime's discrimination against "the national image of the Jewish community." Nevertheless, it reiterates the steadfast hope that "the barrier separating us from Soviet Jewry will now be removed, just as many barriers between nations that are confronting the common enemy have fallen."[22]

This hope is even more explicitly voiced in the platform published by Mapai (Israel Workers' Party, the largest political group in the country) prior to the 1942 Histadrut Conference: "There is now hope of establishing ties with the Soviet Union on the basis of its recognition of the Zionist undertaking and the creative activity of the workers' movement in our country. The community of interests shared by Soviet Russia and democratic countries is paving the way for setting up a solid front of workers throughout the world, in which the workers of Palestine will take their rightful place."

This last sentence deserves special attention. It was a clear indication that the hope of a change of Soviet attitude towards Jewry, the Zionist cause, and Jewish settlement in Palestine was based on the expectation of an overall change in Soviet policy, induced by the war and the USSR's alliance with the great Western democracies. To wide circles throughout the world, in fact, internal liberalization in the Soviet Union seemed a logical certainty, and this expectation could not but strengthen the hope for a revision of the Soviet Jewish policy, too.

This hopeful mood was also shared by Soviet Jewry. Mikhoels, for example, was confident that relations would develop freely between Soviet and world Jewry, a hope based on his faith that "Russian isolationism was coming to an end."[23]

The V League, established by the Palestine Jewish community in support of the USSR, largely contributed to furthering relations with the Soviet authorities. The League was founded as a nonparty organization with the object of enlisting aid for the Soviet war effort and promoting mutual understanding between the Soviet Union and the two (Jewish and Arab) communities in Palestine. Members of the Palestine Communist Party (PKP) were initially prominent among the League's active sponsors, but very soon the Histadrut and its affiliated Zionist workers' parties assumed leadership. The Communists subsequently withdrew from the League when it added to its articles of incorporation a resolution, adopted at its first national convention held in Jerusalem in August 1942, that "the League will strive to enlist Soviet support for the Zionist-Socialist undertaking in the Land of Israel."

The adoption of this article accorded great political significance to the League's convention, which was further enhanced by the participation of two Soviet representatives, Mikhailov and Pietrenko, who had come especially for the occasion from Ankara, where they occupied the respective posts of first secretary and press officer at the Soviet legation. Though informed by the PKP of its withdrawal from the League on account of the adoption of the "Zionist" article, and specifically requested not to attend the convention, Mikhailov and Pietrenko ignored this request. They heard the chairman, S. Kaplansky, say in his opening address:

Our comradeship-in-arms with the Red Army swells our hearts with pride. I feel you will not take it amiss if I say that this [comradeship] is all the more precious to us since it has renewed our ties — broken off for twenty years — with the Jews of Russia. The Jewish *yishuv* in Palestine has thousands of family and spiritual ties that connect it with the Soviet Union. . . . Under Russian skies was born the Jewish labor movement with all its ramifications. It was Russia that nurtured the Zionist movement. Russia gave us our modern Hebrew and Yiddish literature. Most Jews living in Palestine at present were born and raised in Russia. . . . In our readiness to help Russia, we do not present any claims or demands. . . . Yet, at the same time, we endeavor to make the Russian people aware of the real nature of Jewish settlement in Palestine. We, the Jews of Palestine, live in Zion, but we are Zionists not only in the geographical sense. The Jews of Palestine regard themselves as fulfilling an historic mission, as pioneers in the struggle for the national and social liberation of the Jewish nation on its ancient soil. . . . We trust that the claim we are presenting to the nations of the world for equality and freedom, and for a homeland that will be a refuge for our suffering people, will meet also with the sympathy and support of the Soviet Union.[24]

During their stay in Palestine the Soviet representatives did not, admittedly, identify themselves in any way with these Jewish national sentiments, confining their remarks to the common struggle against the Fascist enemy and stressing the fact that the Soviet Jews were deeply rooted in their home. But the very fact that they were prepared to listen to the voicing of such sentiments on various occasions created the impression that they, and those they represented, were giving these sentiments serious attention. This impression was reinforced by the message of greeting sent by the Soviet Jewish Anti-Fascist Committee to the League's convention. "It was on the soil of the Land of Israel," the message stated, "that Judah the Maccabee and Bar-Cochba once raised the banner of revolt against the forerunners of Hitler and Mussolini. It was on the soil of the Land of Israel that our illustrious poet, Yehuda Halevi, sang his swansong, his song of boundless love for the country and the eternity of his people. . . . We deeply appreciate the stirring words of the great poet, Shaul Tschernikhovsky, at the Israel Writers' Convention: 'The barrier has been demolished. Again we are united. We are one heart and one soul, one wish and one hope.' " The message concluded with an assurance that the ties of friendship would remain firm also after Fascism had been eradicated from the world.

The wording of this message could hardly be attributed to mere courtesy or tactical expedience. Immediately after the V League's convention, Martin Buber stated that for him, its greatest moment had been when the JAC's message had been read out, endorsing Tschernikhovsky's affirmation that "the barrier has been demolished."[25]

Some further particulars concerning the Soviet representatives' Palestine visit are pertinent. At the closing session of the V League convention, Mikhailov stated that the material help rendered by Palestine, though necessarily of limited extent, "will not be forgotten by the Soviet Union, which bears in mind the Russian saying [freely translated]: A friend in need is a friend indeed."[26] At a reception for the Soviet visitors, Zalman Rubashov (later Shazar, third president of Israel) said: "We know that among Soviet Jewry there are many who associate themselves in spirit with our work of rebuilding our country. Let them not be kept away from the actual process. Let them be given the possibility of taking part in this reconstruction!" At another reception held at Afikim (a Hashomer Hatzair kibbutz in the Jordan Valley, founded by settlers of Russian origin), Mikhailov and Pietrenko listened to the following remarks, among others, addressed to them by a kibbutz member:

> This kibbutz was founded by members who came from Soviet Russia eighteen years ago. It was our fervent desire, shared by thousands of young Jews in Russia, to return to our ancient homeland in order to reestablish our life on new foundations, the life of a free nation, living on the fruit of its toil, on a farm built up by socialist labor on a cooperative basis. Since then, emigration from Russia has been stopped. The Land of Israel has taken in Jews from other countries of the diaspora, and during these few years they have founded tens of settlements like ours, based on principles of equality and mutual aid. I hope that our ties with our Russian comrades will be resumed.

Though such appeals did not meet with any concrete response on the part of the Soviet visitors, they nevertheless frequently stated how struck they were by Jewish achievements in Palestine and promised to tell the Soviet people about all they had seen, despite the shortness of their stay. At Afikim, Mikhailov reminded his listeners that the sole object of their visit was to attend the V League convention, but added that "we are glad to have got to know something of this country, which is so important for Jewry."[27] It was obvious from this and similar statements that Mikhailov and Pietrenko were bent on making a clear distinction between the Jewish *yishuv* and the Zionist movement, though they must have realized that such a distinction must needs be artificial. Practically all the leaders of the *yishuv* were Zionist leaders too, the declarations and manifestoes issued by the representative Jewish bodies were identical in content with those issued by the Zionist bodies, as were the subjects discussed (emigration from the USSR and the fate of Jewish culture there) with the Soviet representatives. Nor could the ideology of the kibbutzim they visited be divorced from their intrinsic Zionist context.

According to one source, Mikhailov and Pietrenko summed up their Palestine visit in a comprehensive report to the appropriate Soviet authorities, expressing their enthusiastic admiration for the Jewish population of Palestine and its extensive resettlement project. This report appears to be somehow connected with a rather mysterious episode that has not been fully cleared up to this day, but which nevertheless has bearing on our subject. At the beginning of 1943, a man called Volkovich arrived in Palestine from the Soviet Union. He claimed that as a result of the favorable impression which the enthusiastic report submitted by Mikhailov and Pietrenko had made on the Soviet authorities, he had been sent by Solomon Lozovsky, head of the Soviet Information Bureau, to make a further study of Jewish settlement in Palestine and the prevalent mood in the *yishuv*. He could not, however, produce official credentials. Volkovich was a Jewish journalist of Polish origin who had come to the USSR as a refugee at the outbreak of the war. He explained that he had been chosen for this mission both on his own initiative, and also because of his firm connections with certain Soviet circles, who considered him trustworthy since he was a non-Zionist, among other reasons. He gave the impression that his visit had been semi-officially sanctioned, but that it deliberately did not bear the stamp of an official mission. Its object, he said, was to gather information and "send out feelers."

At the Jewish Agency and other representative bodies of the *yishuv,* Volkovich was treated with reserve and even some suspicion. Nevertheless, he met various Jewish leaders, to whom he pointed out the shift that had occurred in the Soviet position on the Jewish and Palestine questions. In the course of one such talk he stated: "I have observed in Russia a slow process of growing interest in the Palestine question. This is in evidence not only in Jewish circles, concentrated round the Jewish Anti-Fascist Committee, but also in Russian circles. This process, though extremely slow, is noticeable nevertheless, and has been boosted by the visit to Palestine of Mikhailov and Pietrenko." Volkovich urged Palestine Jewry to continue fostering good relations with the Soviet Union, of prime importance in view of Moscow's future role on the international scene after the war, but at the same time he stressed the need for caution and "delicacy." He promised that on his return to Russia he would work towards bringing about greater Soviet understanding for the Jewish and Palestine causes.

Volkovich did not go back to the Soviet Union, however. The breaking off of Soviet diplomatic relations with the Polish exile government in London and news of the arrest of many Polish refugees in the USSR obviously deterred him. Nevertheless, there is evidence that he drew up a sympathetic report, which he forwarded to Moscow, on the image and aspirations of the *yishuv.*[28]

As for the activities of the V League, these consistently continued to highlight Jewish national strivings. The League's main wartime activities consisted in organizing donations of ambulances and medical supplies from the *yishuv* to the Red Army. The first such consignment was presented at an impressive Soviet military ceremony held in Teheran on May 2, 1943. At this ceremony, the Palestine Jewish delegation extended the League's greetings, in Hebrew and Russian, to the Red Army and stressed the League's aim of "aiding the Soviet Union in its war against the Fascist enemy, and fostering understanding and friendship between the Soviet Union and the cause of national and social liberation of the Jewish people in the Land of Israel." Colonel Khoroshev, a commander of Soviet troops stationed in

Persia, warmly thanked "the Jewish workers of Palestine" for their gift of ambulances "sent to us from the far-away Jordan Valley, and from the ancient walls of Jerusalem."[29] One member of the Soviet legation in Teheran, in the course of a conversation with a member of the Palestine delegation, remarked that "twenty years ago they set up a closed box on which was inscribed: Zionism — Reaction" and that the box had not been opened since. He implied that for many years the Soviet Union had not properly appraised Jewish achievement in Palestine, but that "henceforth, a new era may begin in this respect."[30]

A second consignment of ambulances was sent to Teheran in December 1943, and a third (and last) in November 1944; and on each occasion the members of the Palestine delegation who made the presentations to the Soviet representatives took the opportunity of discussing questions relating to the Soviet attitude to Zionist aims and activities and the political future of Palestine. At the third presentation ceremony, a V League representative said: "The Jewish nation, which is striving for national and social liberation . . . has proved during the short period between the two World Wars its powerful will to survive, and the mighty creative ability of this ancient people. . . . We trust that the Soviet Union will give its genuine support so as to ensure that every nation, including the Jewish nation, is accorded the right to live a free, independent national life."[31] At an official reception given in honor of the Palestine delegation, the Soviet representative in Teheran stressed that "we are particularly moved by the assistance rendered by Jewish organizations in Palestine. . . . We know that these gifts consist not merely of metal, but of throbbing Jewish hearts."[32]

Information material in Russian was openly sent from Palestine directly to various organizations and individuals in the Soviet Union, chiefly by the Jewish Agency's Committee for USSR Affairs and the V League. Though these publications dealt mainly with the *yishuv's* share in the war against Germany, they also raised specific Zionist matters, such as immigration to Palestine offering the sole solution to the Jewish problem. These publications, it was learned, found their way to various Soviet libraries, including those of army units and hospitals. The Soviet authorities also permitted the dispatch of gift parcels to Jewish refugees in the Soviet Union; this was organized by the "Joint," the Jewish Agency, and other bodies (special stores to house these parcels in transit were set up in Teheran). A further gesture of goodwill on the part of the Soviet authorities was seen in the lively contact between Moscow's Rabbi Shleifer and Palestine's Chief Rabbi Herzog on *halachic* questions of religious law, and the fact that prayer books and devotional articles could now be sent to the Moscow Jewish community. There was some hope that the Soviet ban on the Hebrew language might be removed — a hope fostered by the fact that some of the material published by the JAC in Moscow was sent to Palestine with a Hebrew translation.

A further indication of a thaw in the adamant Soviet attitude to Jewish culture and the Hebrew language was seen in the case of the Soviet Hebrew poet, Elisha Rodin, whose son was killed in action early in 1942. Rodin had long been harrassed and persecuted for his tragic and unwavering love of Hebrew and his persistence in writing in this "reactionary" language. His guilt was rendered all the heavier by the fact that some of his poems occasionally found their way to Hebrew publications outside the Soviet Union, and that, in addition, he expressed in them his ardent love for the Land of Israel and for the Bible. Rodin dedicated to his son a collection of his poems, some of which he had written before his son's death. In 1942, Rodin applied to the Soviet military censorship, requesting permission to send these Hebrew poems to Palestine for publication. His application is here reproduced in full:

Esteemed Comrades in the Military Censorship,

The poems I enclose are dedicated to my son, Rodin Grigori Abramovich, who volunteered to fight on the battlefied and fell on the Kalinin front on March 14, 1942 [the name of his son's unit is here specified].

These poems are written in the language of the Bible, the language of my childhood, the language of my people, which I love as the instrument of my song, for it is only in this language that I am able to give fullest expression to my spiritual feelings and experiences.

I would request you to let them be scrutinized by a man who knows this language well enough, an upright man who is not prejudiced by personal feelings in regard to the Jewish national cause in Palestine.

I am confident that [after you have seen] an accurate and honest translation of my poems, [this] will enable you to send them without delay to Palestine, since my poems are devoted to our common cause: the defeat of Hitler.

For the sake of the memory of my brave son — who, when he learned a few days before he fell that I was writing about him, expressed his joy in his letter to me of March 5 — I beg you to treat these poems with respect and send them on to Palestine, where I propose to have them published.

It is my wish that my son's memory be perpetuated in the work of his father, who loved and respected him.

With greetings,
Elisha Rodin, Hebrew poet

Rodin's request was granted and his collection of poems *To My Son* was published in Palestine in 1943.[33] This gesture on the part of the Soviet authorities might very well have been motivated by considerations of propaganda, the publication of such Hebrew poems being an emotive means of enlisting support for the Soviet Union among Palestine Jewry. However, as such means were resorted to with increasing frequency, this inevitably raised the hope that Moscow was relaxing its inimical attitude towards Zionism.

The Zionist and *yishuv* representatives consistently maintained contact with Soviet officials throughout the war years. Mention may be made, for example, of a meeting between Yitzhak Ben-Zvi and the Soviet minister to Turkey, Vinogradov, which took place in Ankara in August 1943. At this meeting, Ben-Zvi raised the question of Palestine's postwar political status and the hope of obtaining Soviet support for Jewish claims (chiefly unrestricted immigration to Palestine, as offering the sole solution to the Jewish refugee problem). Vinogradov, though extremely cordial, pointed out that the object of the meeting was "not to conduct diplomatic negotiations." Nevertheless, he gave the impression that the Soviet government was not totally indifferent to the Jewish demands. The following year, Eliahu Epstein (Elath) met the Soviet chargé d'affaires in Cairo, D. Solod. The latter denied that Zionists were persecuted in the Soviet Union; yet despite his extremely cautious manner (characteristic of all Soviet diplomats), he gave Epstein the firm impression that the Soviets were keen "to get to know more about us than they knew in the past."

Encouraged by this ostensibly friendly atmosphere, some Zionist Organization leaders even contemplated trying to arrange for Chaim Weizmann to be received by Stalin. Churchill was asked to arrange for such an interview to take place at the time of the meeting of the Big Three at Yalta, in February 1945, but he did not consider this feasible.[34]

It is interesting to note that the V League kept up its contacts with Soviet representatives even after the war was over and the League's aid-to-Russia function had come to an end. In August 1945, three V League leaders — David Remez, Aharon Tsisling, and Shlomo Kaplansky — met the Soviet chargé d'affaires in London, Mr. Kukin, for a two-hour talk. Asked whether he thought the League should continue to function, Mr. Kukin "replied definitely in the affirmative," maintaining that "though the war is over, Fascism has not been wiped out, but has spread and penetrated to various parts of the world." Remez broached the question of sending a Palestine delegation to the Soviet Union, stressing the importance of establishing contact with the USSR on the whole, and with Soviet Jewry in particular. Kukin said he realized that Palestine Jewry was "eager to conduct propaganda among Soviet Jews," but thought it was still too early to talk about sending a delegation to the Soviet Union. He reiterated, however, that "Soviet circles have no doubt that the Jews of Palestine are a progressive element."[35]

These contacts did not always proceed smoothly, and Zionist circles were occasionally beset by grave doubts as to the sincerity of Moscow's placatory gestures. Even the apparent ties between the Jewish Anti-Fascist Committee and the Palestine *yishuv* showed signs of instability, and it began to appear as though the JAC itself was embarrassed by the overenthusiastic manner in which its activities had been hailed abroad. Following the Zionist overtones in the JAC's message to the V League convention, the League's leaders were not a little surprised at the tone adopted in a report on the convention published in *Einikeit,* which stressed that the League's sole object was to support the Soviet Union in its fight against Fascism, completely ignoring the League's professed object of "gaining Russia's support for the Zionist-Socialist cause in Palestine." There had also been disappointment over the fact that Palestine had been omitted from the itinerary of Mikhoels and Feffer, no doubt from political considerations. Y. Meriminsky, a Histadrut representative who met Mikhoels in the United States, was given to understand that the Soviet Jewish representatives ardently wished to see what was being achieved in Palestine, but this depended not only on their being invited there, but also on what the Soviet authorities decided.[36] Technically, Mikhoels and Feffer could easily have visited Palestine (Mikhoels actually passed through Lydda airport), but despite the numerous invitations extended to them, the visit did not come off.

These and similarly disappointing manifestations did not, however, weaken the general belief that Moscow's anti-Zionist policy had undergone a change. Firm evidence of this belief is to be found in Weizmann's appraisal of his three-hour meeting with Mikhoels and Feffer in the United States, which he termed as a great privilege and a most moving occasion, after having been severed from Russian Jewry for twenty-five years. Weizmann stated that this talk had given him a picture of the Jewish community in Russia, though Mikhoels and Feffer had been very noncommittal and had made no declarations. He said he believed they were interested in Zionism, or not opposed to it at all events.[37]

Apart from political considerations, Palestine Jewry also had personal, sentimental and nostalgic reasons for eagerly seeking the resumption of contact with the Soviet Union. The *yishuv* in the 1940's was still regarded as having been created largely by Russian Jewish endeavor, and the new winds that seemed to blow from Moscow satisfied a deep-seated personal and general craving. Every friendly gesture made by the Soviet Union had a tremendous impact in Palestine. Many entertained fond hopes of a great reconciliation between "our undertaking on the banks of the Jordan" and "the undertaking on the banks of the Volga" — as Yosef Sprinzak (who later became speaker of the Knesset) put it. Large sections of the *yishuv* sincerely believed that the defense of Stalingrad had saved Jerusalem.

Thus, the Jewish cataclysm was regarded as having provided the setting for some measure of reconciliation between Zionism and the Soviet Union. It was this atmosphere that produced such theses as that propounded for instance, by non-Zionist Chaim Zhitlovsky in 1943, that "the Jewish people now has two countries where a new, normal way of life is taking shape . . . Palestine and Birobidzhan."[38] And Mikhoels, during his visit to the United States, spoke not only of the "Jewish soap" which the Germans made from the bodies of their victims, but also of the future of the Jewish people: "Our people, the Jewish people, will appear together with other freedom-loving peoples as prosecutor and judge "

The overseas tour of Mikhoels and Feffer continued to boost expectations of a change in Soviet-Jewish relations, even after their return to the Soviet Union. Their reports and impressions indicated that they were gratified, on the whole, with their meeting with overseas Jewry. Mikhoels pointed to the fact that Zionists had joined the various reception committees. In a joint article about the American scene, Mikhoels and Feffer wrote that America was not a "one-storeyed structure" politically, but consisted of "friendly progressive tiers" as well as "hostile reactionary" ones. Yet they voiced no complaint of any unfriendly manifestations on the part of the Jewish organizations with which they came in contact.[39] Reporting on their visit to Mexico, they admittedly pointed to the existence there of several hostile elements (which they termed "venomous snakes") and Fascist newspapers, but stressed that "forty-six of Mexico's fifty-two Jewish organizations signed the invitation [to visit Mexico] that was sent to us in Washington, and participated actively in raising funds for the Red Army and for the relief of Soviet civilian victims of Fascism."[40] Stating that he was doing so at the request of American, Canadian, Mexican, and British Jews, Feffer conveyed on their behalf "warm regards to all the Jews in the Soviet Union."[41]

There was one definite conflict between the JAC representatives and those of the Joint Distribution Committee and of other Jewish welfare organizations in the USA that became public knowledge. It concerned relief activities among distressed Soviet citizens, especially refugees and displaced persons. It appears that some representatives of Jewish relief organizations suggested that Jewish contributions go towards relieving the distress of Soviet Jews; but subsequently they modified even this request, insisting that the consignments of food and clothing at least be distributed in localities where *also* Jews were living, so that the latter might get their fair share. There is no knowing what Mikhoels and Feffer really thought of these suggestions, which sounded fair and reasonable enough; nevertheless they rejected them, presumably in accordance with their instructions. When Feffer reported on this matter to the JAC plenary session in Moscow, in April 1944, he incorrectly asserted that the "Joint" and other relief organizations "wanted to help only the Jewish population of the Soviet Union" whereas the JAC representatives "did not deem it possible to single out in this respect Soviet Jews from the fraternity of peoples making tremendous sacrifices along with us in the war." However, this conflict appears to have been resolved, too, according to the information presented at that plenary session by Shakhno Epstein, the JAC secretary, who stated that "the most important event . . . is the successful outcome of the negotiations of Comrades Mikhoels and Feffer with the 'Joint,' the latter having begun to put into effect its decision to help, through the Red Cross, the evacuated population regardless of nationality."[42]

One facet of the development of relations between Soviet Jewry and Jewish communities in other parts of the world was manifested in the planning of a joint literary documentation project. It is interesting to note that the idea of assembling evidence on the extermination of Jews, on the one hand, and the Jewish share in the fighting, on the other, was mooted practically simultaneously at several Jewish centers and organizations throughout the world, including the JAC in the USSR, without there having been any prior contact or coordination between them. This notion was motivated, basically, by the same feelings and intentions that prompted individuals and groups in various places (including underground organizations) to keep a meticulous record of events and to preserve documents as testimony for future generations and corroborative material for the ultimate reckoning to be presented by the Jewish people.[43]

In time, an arrangement was made with the JAC whereby a *Black Book* was to be published simultaneously in the Soviet Union (in Russian and Yiddish), in the United States (in English), and in Palestine (in Hebrew). It was also decided to set up a *Black Book* Committee on which the following four organizations would be represented: the JAC of Moscow, the World Jewish Congress (New York Executive), the *Vaad Leumi* of Jerusalem, and the American Committee of Jewish Writers, Artists and Scientists. In August 1944, Ilya Ehrenburg sent a batch of material to the body that was preparing the publication of the *Black Book* in the United States, and it was firmly assumed that the same material would appear in the Russian edition. In his accompanying letter, Ehrenburg explained that this was not literature, but authentic stories from personal experience, letters, and diaries, and added: "Let all know that defenseless Jews died manfully, with words of contempt and revenge. . . . Let all know that Jews, when they could, killed their executioners. . . . Let this book burn like fire. Let it call for retribution."[44]

Significance attaches to the date when Ehrenburg sent his letter and the material, namely, August 1944. Large tracts of Soviet territory had already been liberated from the German occupation and the total defeat of the Nazis seemed imminent. Ehrenburg could reasonably have assumed that the war would be over by the time the *Black Book* appeared. Hence, his interest in its publication and the attention this was given by the JAC were probably prompted not solely by external propagandist and utilitarian considerations. They were motivated, no doubt, also by Jewish feelings rendered acute by the horrible slaughter perpetrated during the war, as well as by the desire to perpetuate Jewish acts of bravery as some proud redress for a bereaved nation. The publicizing of Jewish acts of bravery in the USSR was intended to serve also as a well-documented reply to the vilification of so-called Jewish shirkers.

That the desire of Soviet Jewish spokesmen to maintain contact with world Jewry was not prompted solely by Soviet wartime interests is borne out by the fact that the plan to publish the *Black Book* jointly persisted even after the Allied victory. At a meeting of the JAC presidium, the publication of a "book on Jewish heroes in the struggle against Fascism" was discussed, and Itsik Feffer reported that "the American Committee of Jewish Writers, Artists and Scientists has also made a similar proposal; the book is therefore being planned as a joint publication, in that it will describe the heroism of Jewish fighters on all World War II fronts, and, at the same time, it will prominently feature material on Jewish heroes who took part in the great struggle for the Soviet homeland."[45]

Contacts and exchange of views concerning the *Black Book* were still maintained in 1946 between the JAC and Jewish organizations outside the Soviet Union. When Ehrenburg visited the United States that year, he called on Albert Einstein at Princeton on May 14 (Einstein was then honorary president of the American Committee of Jewish Writers, Artists and Scientists). Ehrenburg later recalled, in his *Memoirs,* how deeply the few hours he had spent in Einstein's company had moved him. "I knew that Einstein was showing interest in the publication of the *Black Book* — the name given by tacit consent to the collection of human documents, diaries, letters and eyewitness accounts dealing with the slaughter of the Jewish population by the Germans in the occupied territory. I had brought along some published material and pictures. Einstein scrutinized them intently, then when he raised his eyes I saw sadness in them."[46] Ehrenburg adds that he, together with author Vasily Grossman, had started collecting "human documents concerning the total extinction of the Jews" towards the end of the war; "we called this preparatory collection the *Black Book.* It attested to the Facist crimes, but it also shed a great deal of light on manifestations of heroism and solidarity and love. The book was set up in type and ready to go to press. We were told it would appear at the end of 1948."[47]

The *Black Book* was never published in the Soviet Union: the typeset galleys were broken up in the Moscow printing press at the end of 1948.[48] The English edition, however, had already appeared in New York in 1946, published by the Jewish *Black Book* Committee.[49] The constitution of this committee — the four Jewish bodies in New York, Moscow, and Jerusalem — was shown on the cover, and Moscow's contribution was given prominence on the title page in the form of Itsik Feffer's slogan: "The globe is too small to contain both mankind and Fascism." Considerable sections of the book had manifestly been compiled and edited in Moscow, especially the chapters relating to the Soviet Union and Poland, and the Soviet Jewish partner's influence was perceptible throughout. At all events, there was nothing in the book that might be interpreted as an unfair or ungrateful reference to the Soviet Union, and certainly nothing of a provocative nature. No mention whatsoever was made of the Soviet-German pact, whereas the fact that after the outbreak of war, masses of refugees from east Europe had found shelter in the Soviet Union was highlighted, as well as the help rendered by non-Jewish Soviet citizens to persecuted Jews. The book twice mentioned the Katyn incident, for example, which had caused some tension in the anti-German bloc and had called forth anti-Moscow recriminations on the part of the Polish exile government in London; however, it quoted the Soviet version of the episode as being authoritative, namely, that it was the Germans who had massacred the ten thousand Polish officers in the Katyn forests.

The American Jewish partners in the publication of the *Black Book* scrupulously took into account the remarks and views of their Soviet counterparts, largely out of consideration for the latter's "delicate situation." It had been agreed, for example, that the preface to the *Black Book* would be written by Albert Einstein, but his preface presumably turned out to be too "Zionist" or "cosmopolitan" for Moscow's taste. In order not to stifle all prospects of publishing the book under joint aegis, Einstein's preface was suppressed and the English edition was published in New York without it. That Moscow took exception to the book's contents would indicate that shortly before the end of the war, the Soviet authorities seemed to have begun to retreat from what Soviet and world Jewry had come to see as a revision of the Soviet attitude towards the Jewish question. In other words, a "revision of the revision" may be said to have set in. Here are some excerpts from Einstein's unpublished preface, to which Moscow might well have objected:

> The purpose of this publication is manifest. It is to convince the reader that an international organization for safeguarding the sanctity of life can effectively fulfill its purpose only if it does not limit itself to protecting countries against military attack, but also extends its protection to national minorities within the individual countries. . . . The disasters of war are preceded by certain internal developments, and not merely by military and armaments preparations.
>
> Percentagewise the Jewish people have lost more than any other people affected by the disasters of recent years. If a truly just settlement is to be striven for, the Jewish people must be given special consideration in the organization of the peace. The fact that the Jews, in the formal political sense, cannot be regarded as a nation, insofar as they possess no country and no government, ought to be no impediment. Their status as a uniform political group is proved to be a fact by the behaviour of their enemies. . . .

> In parts of Europe Jewish life will probably be impossible for years to come. In decades of hard work and voluntary financial aid the Jews have restored the soil of Palestine to fertility. . . . Now . . . the demand must be put forward that Palestine, within the limits of its economic capacity, be thrown open to Jewish immigration. . . .[50]

Though Einstein's preface was suppressed, the Soviet edition of the *Black Book* was never brought out. This may be attributed to the fact that the Soviet authorities no longer favored any form of cooperation between Soviet and Western Jewry. Following the victory and the change in the international political climate, they were now inclined to look askance at the *Black Book*'s contents, too, which conformed with the Soviet wartime (but not postwar) line of propaganda; that is, the *Book* stressed Jewish interterritorial unity and national solidarity, rather than internal political, spiritual, and social antagonisms among the Jewish people.

Though the *Black Book* contained no ungenerous references to the Soviet Union, we shall nevertheless attempt to adduce some examples to which the Soviet authorities might have taken exception. To begin with, some sources of the material contained therein were obviously frowned upon: apart from material published in the USSR, the *Black Book* contained, for example, information and reports published by the Jewish Agency for Palestine (chiefly by its Jewish Rescue Committee), material issued by Zionist underground organizations and Zionist parties, excerpts from Jewish newspapers and bulletins from different parts of the world, news items and articles that had appeared in the American press, and like material. All this was likely to create the impression of ramified, intensive Jewish communal activity throughout the world, and of world public interest in the Jewish problem.

Secondly, the *Black Book* speaks glowingly of the part played by Jews from different countries and walks of life in the war against the Nazis. Thus we read of daring underground operations carried out in occupied Europe by commando raiders sent from Tel Aviv, and that these operations were financed from funds contributed by Jewish communities throughout the world; of Captain Guy de Rothschild who served as aide to General Koenig of the Free French forces; of the Chief Rabbi of Athens, Eliahu Barzilai, who fled to the mountains taking the community's archives with him. Had a Russian edition of the *Black Book* been published, Soviet Jewry would have been able to read, more than a year after the war had ended, that the leaders of the Warsaw Ghetto underground movement, alive to the gravity of the situation, had put aside all interparty differences, and that Josef Levartovsky, Communist-proletarian ghetto leader, had coined the slogan "We are all brothers and children of one family," which was adopted as a guiding principle not only in the Warsaw Ghetto, but by Jews in other ghettos and extermination camps as well.

In addition to the underlying theme of Jewish unity, Moscow must also have taken exception to the stress laid on the specific nature of Jewish retributive claims in the accounting with Germany. In a summarizing chapter entitled "Justice," its authors demand "in the name of the millions of Jews who were slaughtered" that their murderers be indicted also for "this specific crime." "Let no man say: What difference does it make what crime the Nazi is hanged for, so long as he is hanged? It is important that the Nazis, as well as their accomplices and followers and the world at large, should know what they are hanged for. No matter how many crimes they are charged with, the crime of murdering Jews must figure prominently among the charges." Remarks in this vein, acceptable or tolerated in Moscow up to 1945, had become inadmissible in 1946.

Joint publication of the *Black Book* was not the only project that was abandoned in accordance with the new (or rather, pre-1941) Soviet official line; it appears that the official veto extended also to other JAC projects, chiefly those concerned with fostering relations with Jewry overseas. One of these projects had been the organization of traveling exhibitions, for display both in the USSR and abroad, depicting "Jews in the Great War for the Soviet Homeland." The JAC had also planned to publish, jointly with the American Committee of Jewish Writers, Artists and Scientists, Yiddish yearbooks whose object was "to depict the life of the Jewish masses, chiefly in the USSR and the USA."[51] These projects remained a dead letter, however, and an indication of unfulfilled hopes and illusions. The Historical Committee that had been formed by the JAC met with a similar fate. Though the Historical Committee had contrived to collect and process a certain amount of documentary material, the bulk of this material was not allowed to be made public: it was seized or destroyed when the Jewish Anti-Fascist Committee was dissolved several several years later.

There are many indications that for the JAC members and other Jewish writers and public figures in the Soviet Union, 1946 and the subsequent years were a period of great perplexity. The official reversal to the pre-1941 attitude towards the Jews — in theory and in practice — did not emerge in a clearly defined manner and all at once. The permissive attitude towards manifestations of Jewish nationalism during the war had come to be regarded as the natural order of things, and the Jewish writers and leaders, psychologically unprepared for the reversal to the previous order, continued to act and express themselves accordingly by dint of inertia. Many of them doubtlessly found it hard to tear themselves away from the "Golden Age" when what had been demanded of them virtually coincided with their inmost feelings.

In actual fact, the JAC was beset by apprehension and insecurity ever since its inauguration. Thus it transpired several years later that, at the instance of the JAC, the Soviet Jewish historian Professor Y. Sosis had in 1943 compiled *A Short History of the Jews in Russia* in the Russian language, but this was never published in the Soviet Union. Part of this work was first published in Yiddish in Warsaw, in 1966,[52] and one may gather why the whole work had been suppressed in the USSR. This section, which deals with the end of the eighteenth and beginning of the nineteenth centuries, tells of Grigori Peretz, a Decembrist of Jewish origin, who "spoke a great deal of the need to form an organization to liberate the Jews scattered throughout Russia and even Europe and settle them in the Crimea, or somewhere else in the East, as a distinct nation."

However, notwithstanding its misgivings and doubts, the knowledge of its limitations and that it was under surveillance, as well as internal difference of opinion and temperament, the Soviet Jewish Anti-Fascist Committee clearly came to be regarded as a central Jewish national body. It gained this reputation among Soviet Jews chiefly because the latter, with their down-to-earth instinct, reasoned that the Committee's very existence and activities accorded with the official line of thought. The gravitational force of this body increased as the extent of the Jewish catastrophe became known: the Jewish nation's bereavement enhanced the JAC's status and heightened the hopes that were placed in it.

The JAC's prestige was also enhanced by the eminence of its membership and of the other personages who associated themselves with it. Modern Jewish history provides several illuminating examples of the manner in which persons hitherto far removed from Jewish life and problems suddenly became deeply affected by manifestations of a Jewish national reawakening. The charm that men like Herzl and Nordau, for example, exercised on their followers was no doubt greatly magnified by the fact that they had come from "the outside" to dedicate themselves to the Jewish cause, after they had previously distinguished themselves in the non-Jewish world. A rather similar phenomenon became manifest in the Soviet Union in the latter half of 1941. We find among the members and supporters of the JAC not only prominent Yiddish writers and members of the Jewish theater, but also well-known Jewish Russian writers, top-ranking officers, recipients of state awards, distinguished physicians and scientists and eminent artists. The appeal addressed by the "public gathering of representatives of the Jewish people," on August 24, 1941, to "our Jewish brothers the world over" was signed by persons who had not only never associated themselves with things Jewish, but whose Jewish or semi-Jewish origin had hitherto been a secret. The JAC's image was greatly enhanced by such names as Professor P. Kapitza,[53] film director Sergei Eisenstein, violinist David Oistrakh, pianist Emil Gilels, authors Ilya Ehrenburg, Vasily Grossman, and Samuel Maharshak, and scientists Lina Shtern and Ilya Trainin. Nor was it merely their names that added to the Committee's prestige; the fact that they participated in the activities of the newly established Jewish body, appeared at public Jewish functions and signed appeals addressed "by Jews to Jews" — all this bolstered up hopes of a change in the Soviet policy towards the Jews.

Some Jewish circles may possibly have pinned unduly great hopes on the JAC. In this regard, however, we may reliably accept the appraisal of Vilna Jewish writer Shmerl Kaczerginsky, who closely observed the JAC's activities and was intimately acquainted with its leaders. Though not overly impressed, Kaczerginsky was nevertheless prompted to state: "Whatever opinion one might form of the Committee's work and its leadership, it must be pointed out that within the frame of the rights they were accorded they did everything possible, and sometimes even overshot the mark."[54] The fate of most of the Committee's members — which will be dealt with in a later chapter — would also indicate that they did everything possible (and even more than that) within the Committee's terms of reference. Unfortunately for them, however, these terms of reference were by no means constant, and the Committee was not always able to adapt itself quickly enough to the changing official mood. Thus, for example, after the defeat of Germany the JAC addressed a manifesto "to Jews the world over" in which it stated that "during the war years there has been increased mutual understanding between Jews in different countries, and a basis has been established for firmer unity between us in the struggle for the life, propserity, and culture of our people." There is reason to assume that the emphasis laid on Jewish unity was already not to the taste of the Soviet authorities, although the same manifesto also stressed the need to intensify the struggle against "reactionary manifestations in Jewish circles" and against "those who openly or secretly hold brief for Fascism."[55]

It is relevant to point out here that in the course of time, particularly in the postwar years, the JAC came to engage in activities which it certainly had not been assigned beforehand: to relieve Jewish distress and to intervene on behalf of Jewish victims of unfair treatment and discrimination in regard to employment, housing, and rehabilitation. These functions, prompted no doubt by the Jewish wartime disaster, were largely undertaken by the JAC chairman himself, Solomon Mikhoels, whose help was sought by large numbers of distressed Jews, who considered him an influential person with a wide range of connections. Mikhoels's office at the Jewish State Theater building in Moscow was constantly besieged by applicants for help — Ehrenburg recalls that "after the victory, thousands of people applied to Mikhoels, whom they regarded as a wise rabbi, defender of the oppressed."[56]

The watchful eye that kept the JAC under surveillance no doubt noted the manner in which Mikhoels was exceeding his functions and added this to the list of his "deviations." That the JAC had committed the crime of engaging in philanthropic activities was brought up by Soviet spokesmen as long afterwards as over three years after Stalin's death, when the rigidity of his regime had ostensibly been relaxed. A Canadian (Communist) Progressive Labor Party delegation was told in Moscow, in the course of a talk on Jewish affairs, that the Jewish Anti-Fascist Committee "became a kind of welfare society towards the end, devoting itself to obtaining jobs and apartments for Jews," and that this activity caused "resentment in certain circles; there were people who wondered why the Committee was intervening and trying to obtain special concessions for Jewish citizens, when all other citizens addressed their problems directly to their local governmental institutions."[57]

Many JAC members and Jewish authors and intellectuals paid dearly for their sin of entertaining "nationalist views," or rather, for the illusions they had harbored as to the permissive attitude towards holding such views. It is characteristic that already before the great purge was initiated, entailing the mass arrest and execution of prominent Jewish figures and the total suppression of Jewish cultural activity, the first victim to be selected was Mikhoels. His death was but the first link in the chain of brutal blows deliberately aimed at Soviet Jewry.

Mikhoels was murdered in Minsk, capital of the Belorussian Republic, on the night of January 13, 1948. A news item, which carried the authority of an official announcement, stated that he had "lost his life in tragic circumstances," without specifying what these circumstances were. Official encouragement was given to the propagation of rumors that he had been killed in a road accident or had been the victim of a violent robbery, but these were refuted by various other versions. Mikhoels's death thus became a mystery that was not cleared up until several years later, but which aroused grave misgivings at the time.

Mikhoels had come to Minsk on behalf of the Stalin Prize Committee, as a member of its Theater Section. He had been charged with recommending prize-winning plays. On the evening of January 13, a strange telephone message had called him away from his hotel: according to one version, he had been invited to a private home for a drink, while another claimed he had been called to some office for an urgent meeting. At all events, he had left in the company of theater critic Golubov-Potapov, also a Jew, who had come with him to Minsk on the same mission. Early the following morning, the snow-covered bodies of both men were found near the Minsk railway station. Why they had gone there remained a mystery. Some claimed that the person who had called Mikhoels away by phone was the secretary of the Minsk District Communist Party; others believed it was the Belorussian Party secretary, Ponomarenko, who had had a hand in carrying out the Moscow-laid plan to liquidate Mikhoels.

An anonymous telephone call received at the Jewish Theater in Moscow threatened: "We have finished off your first Jew, and now comes the turn of all the rest of you"; in the mounting tension, this was regarded as being more ominous than a coarse joke.

The magnificent funeral Mikholes was given in Moscow could harldy dispel the all-pervasive air of perplexity. Tens of thousands filed past the coffin, which lay in state at the Jewish State Theater building, with the police keeping an especially watchful eye. It became known that Professor Zbarsky, the expert mortician who had embalmed Lenin's body, had been charged with restoring Mikhoels's lacerated face.[58] The funeral turned into a mass demonstration of the general esteem in which the deceased had been held, the eulogies and obituaries expressed the grief and dismay felt in wide circles, and eminent figures in the field of art and literature kept vigil at the catafalque. At the same time, however, it was rumored that Mikhoels's apartment had been ransacked by the secret police. Shortly afterwards the news got about that a Jewish criminal investigator called Lev Sheinin had "disappeared"; rumor had it that he had attempted to initiate and conduct an inquiry into the circumstances of Mikhoels's death.

Jewish grief at Mikhoels's passing soon became tempered with grave apprehension, for the anti-Jewish implications of this tragic, mysterious occurrence were inescapable. Whereas Ehrenburg mourned Mikhoels as "a comrade to those that fell in the war," Perets Markish openly invoked the Jewish aspect in his perfervid poem "To S. Mikhoels — An Eternal Lamp at the Coffinside." In the most moving terms, Markish adds the victim of the Minsk murder to the six million Jews who perished in the holocaust: "Your disaster has riven the heart of the whole nation. The six million arise in their graves to honor you, as you have honored their memory when you fell among the ruins of Minsk." The poem is charged with traditional Jewish symbolism ("Like the two blessed candles, your hands shine forth from the coffin"), and lyrically compares Mikhoels with Rabbi Levi Yitzhak of Berdichev, the illustrious defense advocate of the Jewish people. This analogy was no doubt inspired by the deceased's philanthropic work in his latter years.

Subsequent events and the climate they engendered did nothing to allay the fears of Soviet Jews. The mysterious murder continued to evoke various speculations and conjectures. One explanation, apparently deliberately leaked out by Moscow to Jewish Communist and leftist circles abroad to supersede previously circulated versions (which had become totally discredited by now), is significant in the light of subsequent happenings: it claimed that Mikhoels had been silenced by American intelligence agents after the Soviet security services had uncovered an extensive spy ring, operated in the USSR by the American Joint Distribution Committee and headed by Mikhoels on behalf of U. S. intelligence. This explanation was designed to stress Mikhoels's traitorous role as the agent of a foreign power. It will be shown, in subsequent chapters, that what had been initially launched as a rumored conjecture shortly after Mikhoels's death was played up four of five years later as an important element in the fabric of lies on which the doctors' plot allegations were based. This clearly points to a tie-in between Mikhoels's murder and the plans that were already then being laid for the fantastic charges brought against the Jewish physicians. As for Mikhoels's alleged espionage activities, he was said — according to the abovementioned explanation — to have headed the spy ring ever since his visit to the United States in 1943 on behalf of the JAC. The implications are obvious: Mikhoels's alleged treachery coincided with his meeting with Jewish communities in the West, at a time when there had been high hopes of a change in the Soviet attitude towards Jewry, and when Mikhoels himself had been profoundly stirred by his contacts with his Jewish brethren overseas.

Mikhoels's murder was a planned, deliberate move. To be assured of this, it was not necessary to wait fifteen years until a Soviet Lithuanian paper should report that Mikhoels had been killed by Beria's agents; already towards the end of 1948 it had become increasingly clear that the alleged accident in Minsk had been an official act. "When Zuskin was arrested," Ehrenburg wrote, "everybody started wondering how Mikhoels had lost his life."[59] Binyamin Zuskin, who had ranked second to Mikhoels at the Jewish State Theater in Moscow, had been appointed its director on Mikhoels's death. His arrest at the end of 1948 was a link in the chain of mass arrests and liquidations.

Nevertheless, a number of questions concerning Mikhoels's death inevitably arise. If there were political motives behind it, how does this sort with his impressive funeral, with the glowing eulogies that were delivered, with the laudatory obituaries published in the Soviet press and in a special anthology dedicated to his memory?[60] Furthermore, why did the Soviet authorities have to resort to clandestine methods?

Several explanations may be advanced: in the first half of 1948 the authorities, still somewhat hesitant as to the line they were adopting, chose to launch their anti-Jewish campaign in an indirect manner so as to be able to observe the initial reactions; the security services were not operating in full coordination with other governmental agencies —after Stalin's death it transpired that Beria's secret police constituted a self-contained empire within the Soviet administration; the circumstances of the murder were in keeping with the sadistic instincts of the secret police — Ehrenburg, for instance, assumes that Beria resorted to malicious concealment not because he took public opinion into account, but because he considered such methods a kind of amusement.[61]

Some seventeen years after Mikhoels's murder, Ehrenburg noted in his *Memoirs:* "Now I realize that the commencement of certain events . . . [the anti-Jewish campaign] is connected with Mikhoels's tragic death."[62] This conclusion holds good only insofar as the chronological order of these "events" is concerned, whereas their roots are to be found in Mikhoels's activities in his latter years, in the significant processes undergone by Soviet Jewry and personified in Mikhoels's personality, stature, and activities.

Mikhoels's murder was obviously intended to do away with a public figure who had personified, since 1941, the trend towards organized Jewish communal life in the Soviet Union. Mikhoels was singled out as the first victim of the purge not only because of his official post of chairman of the Jewish Anti-Fascist Committee, but also because he had manifested dangerous "public-minded" leanings. Apart from his eminence as an actor, he had enjoyed growing prestige as spokesman of his people. Exaggerated rumors had circulated among Soviet Jews regarding the great measure of influence he wielded and his connections with leading Soviet personalities. He was believed to have had constant access to the Kremlin, and even to have enjoyed Stalin's friendship (the latter was said to have called him affectionately "Solomon the Wise"). The functions he had been assigned (including his overseas mission) and the esteem in which he had been held by leading members of Soviet society (his Yiddish stage performances attracted many non-Jewish admirers) had all served to enhance his influential image in Jewish minds. Gradually he had begun to figure, not merely as the chairman of a Jewish body, but as the leader of Soviet Jewry.

Mikhoels imparted to his appearance on the public scene some of his artistic talents: internal pathos, poetic imagination, and identification with the role he assumed. A study of his activities and public appearances and of the memoirs written about him would indicate that he gradually came to regard himself as a Jewish leader or spokesman. Though far removed from any feelings of chauvinistic nationalism or Jewish isolationist trends, he was profoundly affected by the Jewish wartime tragedy, which he felt called upon to voice. At the same time, he was prompted to oversimplify his interpretation of the official gestures towards Jewish sentiments and aspirations. Though known to be a clever man, it is doubtful whether he had an astute, realistic poliltical sense. During the war years he was largely guided by emotions and wishful thinking. The momentous events he lived through and the functions delegated to him must have had a profound spiritual effect on him. On April 7, 1942, he had recorded in his diary: "There are people who bear within them a revolution, the birth of a new era. The fate of such people is not fortuitous. Spinoza was not merely a glass grinder; he ground lenses through which a new world might be seen."[63]

Mention has already been made of Mikhoels's role as "defender of the oppressed." It is relevant, in the light of developments that followed his death, to mention a widely held conjecture regarding his attempt to broach the subject of anti-Semitic manifestiations to Stalin personally. Though the veracity of this report cannot be vouched for, it nevertheless appears to be quite plausible. At a reception given by Stalin in mid-1944, to which representatives of public wartime bodies, including the JAC, were also invited, Mikhoels was said to have taken the opportunity of appealing to the Soviet ruler, in the presence of other prominent Jewish figures, to stamp out anti-Semitic manifestations. Mikhoels might well have been emboldened to broach this to Stalin, prompted by several motives: the full extent of the annihilation of the Jews at the hands of the Nazis had already become apparent by that time, and he could count on the "unpleasant flavor" attaching to anti-Semitism inside the USSR; victory was very near, and Stalin could now be expected to devote himself more to internal questions; Mikhoels considered this a favorable occasion to raise the Jewish question in view of his successful overseas mission, in which Stalin himself had shown some interest. Stalin's reply, according to this report, was disappointing: he said that anti-Semitism was a kind of "time flow" that could not be arrested all at once.[64] What this implied was that not only the lower and local echelons of officialdom, but also the highest authorites were prone to condone anti-Semitism for reasons of expediency.

Was the fact that Mikhoels had dared to broach specifically Jewish questions to the ruling powers put down as a black mark against him? We believe that it was not any particular incident that sealed his fate, but the fact that he had been the ideal personification of the Jewish collective "crime," compared to which any specific charges paled in significance. His murder was designed to clear the way for an extensive anti-Jewish purge.

Soviet Jewry was indeed overwhelmed by the feeling that Mikhoels had died for his people. This feeling was eloquently expressed by author Der Nister in a memorial article: "They say that in Moscow the mirrors have been covered in many Jewish houses, as after the death of a relative."[65]

THREE

The National Awakening in Soviet Jewish Literature

We have stated in a previous chapter: "On the eve of the outbreak of World War II, Soviet Jewry was in the throes of a national and spiritual decline." This process of actual assimilation, or of passive renunciation of Jewish problems and way of life, was due to a combination of factors.[1]

During the war, a contrary process became evident, namely, a return to the Jewish heritage and a resurge of national sentiment. This reawakening was intensified by the Nazis' vilification and persecution of Jewry. Jewish solidarity was an instinctive reaction to the Hitlerite schemes and acts, whereby every person of Jewish descent was doomed to extinction. Hyman Levy, a leading British Communist, and a rationalist by predisposition and by dint of his scientific occupation, noted this "imponderable" phenomenon many years after the war, summing up his impressions of a visit to the USSR in the following terms: ". . . as an unconscious force that intensified Jewish nationalism, Hitler towers head and shoulders above all others."[2] It would appear that this unconscious force countervailed all current events that might reasonably have been expected to intensify the process of "denationalization" among Soviet Jewry. True, the German occupation of the Ukraine and White Russia, where the large majority of Russian Jews had been concentrated before the war,[3] had destroyed, together with the Jewish communities themselves, also "most of the Jewish administrative, cultural, and communal institutions still in existence [in the Soviet Union]."[4] Yet despite these material factors and the increasing dispersal of Jews throughout the Soviet Union, which hardly served to bolster Jewish life during — and after — the war, the feeling of Jewish solidarity was reinforced rather than weakened. This sense of national awakening pervaded even those young people who had never received the bare rudiments of a Jewish education and knew practically nothing of the history and culture of their people. Thus we find many Jewish Red Army soldiers, among them youngsters and even Komsomol members, seeking a chance to visit a synagogue, especially during the Red Army's westward advance.

An illuminating appraisal of the resurge of Jewish national identity was given by a leading Russian writer, Alexei Surkov, in the course of a conversation with the Israeli poet Avraham Shlonsky during the latter's visit to the USSR:

> There were times when we thought that the process of Jewish assimilation was being intensified by dint of the historical logic of Soviet conditions, and that the Jewish problem was being resolved of itself. Then came the war and its horrors, then the aftermath, and all of a sudden Jews began to seek one another out and to cling to one another.[5]

We propose to illustrate this national awakening with examples culled from Soviet literature. We shall dwell, to begin with, on a series of works in the Russian language written by authors of Jewish origin who were, as a rule, far removed from Judaism, having become assimilated to the dominant Soviet culture. We shall not appraise these works for their literary value, our aim being merely to pinpoint the Jewish motifs inherent in them, as being indicative of the prevalent mood among Soviet Jewry.

We have already mentioned Ilya Ehrenburg's journalistic writing during the war, when his name had become a kind of popular symbol of burning hatred for the enemy. Even those who regard Ehrenburg as a person quick to adapt himself to climatic changes may reasonably assume that during those war years, for all that his writing adhered to the official line, it also largely mirrored what he himself thought and felt, especially in regard to Jews and Jewry. He professed it was an honor to belong to a people persecuted by the Nazi monster, which sought to suppress the cultural values inherent in the genius and works of such Jews as Heine, Bergson, Tuvim, Einstein, Chagall, and others. Thus he declared:

> They [the Nazis] have used us as targets like beasts. In order not to miss the mark they have branded us [with the yellow star]. Let this be a mark of honor! . . . We are those whom Hitler hates the most, and this adorns us.

Nor does the pathos of another of his declarations strike a less sincere note:

> I grew up in a Russian city. My mother tongue is Russian. Like all Russians, I am defending my homeland. But the Nazis have made me remember something else, too. My mother was called Hanna. I am a Jew. I say it with pride.[6]

In his abundant descriptions of the martyrdom and heroism of the Soviet people, Ehrenburg never fails to work in a great many instances of Jewish suffering and bravery, and, what is more, interlace them with Jewish historical references and traditional symbols. Recalling the Jewish mourning customs of rending the garments and strewing ashes on the head, he exclaims: "Wherefrom shall I take the language of the prophet [Jeremiah], that I may describe the great destruction, the sorrow and the fury?" When he toured former German-occupied areas immediately after their liberation, he surveyed not only the total physical destruction; in the Ukrainian townships he also imagined he heard the footsteps of Baal Shem Tov and the ringing notes of Bialik's verses, and saw Sholem Aleichem's smile. . . .

Ehrenburg's novel *The Storm* is of special interest. It was published after the war, when Soviet policy had already taken an anti-West turn. Soviet Jews were being increasingly accused of harboring nationalistic tendencies, and "hints" were being dropped to writers, enjoining them not to highlight the specific Jewish wartime tragedy. It is inconceivable that a writer as experienced in political shifts as Ehrenburg should not have been aware of the pendulum's swing. Large sections of *The Storm* indeed give the impression that the writer adapted his appraisal of wartime happenings to the Soviet postwar line of policy. Thus he points up East-West differences, whereas only a couple of years back he had pointed to the factors common to them both — hence the acclaim accorded to *The Storm.* In short, Ehrenburg surely knew which way the wind was blowing. Nevertheless, several Jewish characters figure prominently in the broad plot of the novel, alongside Russians, Frenchmen, Englishmen, and Americans; and what is more significant, they are generally shown in a positive light. The author even points to instances of non-Jewish indifference to, and in some cases even active participation in, the Nazi persecution of their Jewish countrymen.

It is most relevant to our discussion to dwell on the two main characters in *The Storm:* the brothers Osip Alper of Kiev, and Leo Alper of Paris, who represent two widely separated branches of the same family.

The author spares no effort in endowing the Kiev brother with fine, and rather standardized, attributes. He is shown as a perfect Soviet prototype — a man of conviction imbued with a keen sense of duty, an engineer who is dedicated to his work of construction in peacetime, and a brave fighter in wartime. He is not ruled by emotions, but is invariably firm and cool-headed, making strict demands both on himself and of others. As for his origin, this is beyond the pale of his thoughts or concern. His marriage to a non-Jewess, Raya, is to be regarded as an extremely common occurrence. His mother, Hanna Alper, who lives with them, still clings to some of the old Jewish ways, but this in no way impinges on her son's world.

Osip is the only survivor of his family, all of whom perished in Kiev. He is deeply shocked by the massacre at Babi Yar, which he visits on his return to the liberated city; but even here, he does not unbend so far as to manifest any specifically Jewish sentiment — a "subjectivism" that would have been out of keeping with his solidly rationalistic way of thinking. As against this, the author focuses a particularly strong light on objective facts. Osip's mother, Hanna, and his little daughter, Alya, have perished together with the tens of thousands of other Jewish victims at Babi Yar (his wife, Raya, fell at the front).

Then the Jewish fate obtrudes from the far edge of the plot: Leo Alper, the brother in Paris, is sent to Auschwitz.

Hence there is a continuous Jewish thread that joins Kiev with Paris, Babi Yar with Auschwitz. The Alper family had long ago split up, one branch casting in its lot with the Communist regime, and the other establishing itself under the capitalist system. It must be pointed out that Ehrenburg not only protrays Leo Alper, the prosperous manufacturer and businessman, as a warm, sympathetic person; through him he gives forceful expression, amidst the raging storm of war, to Jewish anguish and Jewish pride (an old French scholar, fulminating against both the Germans and their collaborators, regards the yellow star which Leo Alper is forced to wear as a mark of distinction).

It should be noted that Ehrenburg's association with Judaism had been practically nonexistent. In describing his parents' home, he states that contrary to the popular saying, "An apple doesn't fall far from the tree," his father had already strayed far from the tree, since he "belonged to the first generation of Jews who had broken out of the ghetto."[7] As for Ilya Ehrenburg himself, he was so far removed from his origins as to have completely disassociated himself from them. It is against this background that the descriptions contained in *The Storm* acquire added force, for, consciously or not, Ehrenburg gives eloquent expression to the Jewish common fate, regardless of the territorial boundaries that may separate various sections of the Jewish people.

From Ehrenburg, who was born in 1891, let us pass on to a poetess, Margarita Aliger, born in 1915, who was brought up under the Soviet regime. Though she wholeheartedly indentifies herself with the tragic heroism of Russia as a whole, she is also prompted to express her especial identification with the suffering of her fellow-Jews. Her poem *Your Victory* contains a "Jewish chapter" in the form of a dialogue between a Jewish woman, a refugee, and her daughter. The latter is fervidly attached to her Russian homeland, to its language and culture, its broad fields and endless spaces, its poets and fighters. In the same fervent breath she speaks about the Russian *muzhik* (peasant) and Lenin. Her Jewish descent had left no trace in her consciousness, until the Nazi horrors have come to remind her of it, and she herself now wonders how she could have been so unaware of it all the time. In answer to her mother's reproachful "We are Jews. How did you dare forget?", the daughter tries to justify herself: how could she have imagined, in those free, happy times, that there would come a day when she would only be able to glimpse the blue sky by stealth? How could she have conceived of such horrors as Treblinka and the gas chambers and gallows? "We were a freeborn generation in a young, free homeland; unwittingly we forgot our people, but the Fascists remembered only too well." She has heard the cry of human blood in many languages, joining together into "the roar of a storm-tossed ocean," which has not, however, drowned the cry of Jewish blood: "Now I hear the dread moaning of my people." And hearing this moan, the poetess becomes aware of her persecuted people, a nation of great-spirited, gifted men, of workers and fighters, descendants of the heroic Maccabees.[8]

We propose to add a few comments on Vasily Grossman's novel *The Aged Teacher,* mentioned in Chapter One, which treats chiefly of Jewish suffering under the German occupation in a small Ukrainian town. The author voices the specific Jewish tragedy in a parenthetical remark, as it were, to the effect that despite their sufferings the Jews could not believe that so terrible a fate awaited them: *"The murder of a whole nation* [italics added] seemed too horrible in their eyes." On reading this novel, one cannot but sense the warmth and probity with which the author endows his Jewish characters, both intellectuals and simple folk. Nor is it merely by chance that he portrays several typical Jewish artisans, honest working men, and calls them by such authentic Jewish names as Baruch, Leib, Mendel, and the like. In illustration, we shall point to one passage which expresses most dramatically this sense of identification with the Jewish people at its most terrible hour: a Jewish boy, who looks like and could pass as a Christian, rejects a neighbor woman's offer to pose as her boy in order to escape the slaughter that threatens the Jews of the town. "I want to look like a Jew," the boy says. "Wherever they take my father, there will I go too."[9]

Pavel Antokolsky born in 1896 in St. Petersburg and grandson of the famous sculptor Marc Antokolsky was a Russian poet who, judging by the body of his work, had not the least attachment to Jewish culture and tradition. It is of interest that his wartime poetry should contain distinctly Jewish overtones. Thus he ends one of his poems with the *Shema Israel!* of Jewish martyrs throughout the ages, and establishes a connection between Jewish suffering at the hands of the Nazi and the nation's two-thousand-year-old anguish. For him, Babi Yar is not an isolated episode, but a link in this continuous chain of martyrdom.

The Ukrainian Jewish writer Leonid Pervomaisky similarly turns to the Jewish past. In his dramatic poem *Olexa Dovbush,* the rebel hero leads his people to the ancient Land of Israel; and in his poem *Under Alien Skies,* the Romanian township of Sinaya evokes nostalgic associations with Mount Sinai.[10]

Jewish devotional articles become a symbol of morality, the antithesis of Nazi evil, in Tatyana Velednitskaya's story *The Sun Sets from the East,* where the *tallit*-wrapped rabbi, beaten and tortured by the Gestapo, collapses onto the mutilated scrolls of the law.

In one of Yaakov Khelmsky's poems, dedicated to the liberation of Riga, every house in the ghetto is become a "Wailing Wall."

Samuel Maharshak, whose wartime poems were said to "lash at the enemy," in a memorial poem dedicated to Sholem Aleichem (1946), laments: "The last vestige of Kasrilievka's soul has been erased; the war has erased all, has erased the *bet-hamidrash.* What has it not wiped out?"

The Russian writers enumerated above differed greatly in age, mode of expression, attributes, and talent, but their wartime writing (and that of other writers) showed common indications of a change induced by their Jewish origin, or as one critic put it: "They began to feel anew, at this grave hour, the ties of blood and the spiritual bonds that bound them to Judaism."[11]

It is relevant to take note of a similar surge of feeling that manifestly overwhelmed writers and philosophers of Jewish origin in other countries, too. French philosopher Henri Bergson had increasingly been attracted to Roman Catholicism in his later years, but refused any concessions on the part of the Nazis when they occupied France; the ailing octogenarian was reported to have queued up for many hours to register as a Jew. There was a return to Judaism on the part of several Polish writers of Jewish origin. Adolf Rudnitsky made Jewish martyrdom his central theme, since he was unable, as he put it, "to break away from the era of the crematoria." Stanislav Vygodsky identified himself as "the biographer of silence and violence, of streets dead and desolate, of charred shoes and clothes, mine and yours . . . ." Christian-born Antoni Slonimsky — his father was a baptized Jew — elegizes the small Jewish townships that have vanished from the Polish scene, and mourns "my kinsfolk, the boy-poets."

A striking illustration of this phenomenon among Polish writers of Jewish origin is poet Julian Tuwim's impassioned and rather unexpected article, *We the Jews of Poland* — penned in New York in April 1944. This is a confession and a lament, where the poet reaffirms his love for the Polish language, for the River Vistula, for the Polish birch trees and willows, in short, his boundless attachment to his Polish homeland. But he also points to a powerful factor that has reminded him — and those like him — of his Jewishness: this is not so much the blood that flows *through* the veins, as the blood that ebbed *from* the veins — the blood *of Jews,* rather than the Jewish blood. The blood of the Jewish millions, in the poet's eyes, is a "new Jordan River" in which he wishes to immerse himself in ritual baptism so as to join the Jewish brotherhood of sacred martyrdom, and he entreats his Jewish brethren to accept him into the "greatly honored fellowship of those whose innocent blood was shed."[12]

The "blood that ebbed from the veins" inspired a great many Russian Jewish writers to seek "an emotional return" to Judaism. But if this was merely a fragmentary manifestation in Russian wartime writing, it became a dominant feature of the Yiddish literature that was produced in the Soviet Union. Practically all the Yiddish writers expressed a yearning for the Jewish past and heritage, employed distinctly Jewish symbols, showed emotional attachment for Jews wherever they might be, and manifested love for all things Jewish. This is aptly illustrated in the words of one character in a story by Y. Rabin, who mourns his father who has been hanged by the Germans in a Belorussian township. This has left him in "such a state of mind that every grain of Jewishness is become lovable, agonizingly dear to him; he reveres the mere fingernail of a Jew, the splendor of a Jewish feast day, the weeping at a Jewish funeral, the winsomeness of Jewish children."

In Russian Yiddish literature, the phenomenon we refer to as a "national awakening" evolved till it assumed the form of a sharp swerve away from the former trend. In order to become cognizant of the implications of this, we must survey retrospectively the course of this literature during the 1920's and 1930's.

The course of Yiddish literature during those years was hardly different from that of Soviet literature as a whole. The Yiddish writers, like their Russian colleagues, were constrained to abide by the formula that charged literature with the function of being a recruiting force for the fulfillment of present tasks, of being an auxiliary instrument of the Party in waging its external and internal political campaigns, of helping to carry out the five-year plans of reconstruction, industrialization, collectivization, and the like. Like the literatures of all the Soviet peoples, Yiddish literature, too, assumed a dominant rhetorical propagandist note; it abounded in paeans of praise for the heroic Soviet people, for the Red Army and each and every one of its corps, for the Red Flag, for the Stalinist Constitution, for the October Celebrations and the First of May, for the Party and the Komsomol, for the Pioneers and the Octobrists, for Russia's great cities and Moscow in particular, for the gigantic construction works in progress, for the *kolhozes* and Stakhanovites, for the heads of state in general, and for Lenin and Stalin in particular. The favorite themes were the civil war, the repulsion of outside intervention, the shattering of internal resistance, the upsurge of Soviet industrial and agricultural output, the joys of creative labor and the joy of living as a whole. Under the pressures of "socialist realism" writers turned into mere functionaries, subject to the ideological surveillance of the Party. This severely limited the scope of their art, forced them into a uniform standard mold, and even laid down the ingredients of their plots and themes. Like all the national literatures in the Soviet Union, Yiddish literature, too, became imbued with the official optimism, hence the syrupy plots in fiction and the primitive versification in poetry.

All Soviet writers found it hazardous to break away from the conformist line; nor could they resort to silence, which would only have rendered them suspect and liable to be charged not only with passivity, but even with manifesting deliberate inimical tendencies. Against this general setting, some Jewish writers exceeded their colleagues of other national groups in their strident patriotism and their militant tones. The wish to excel in this manner stemmed from special psychological motives. There were some who were possessed of the fears and perplexities of "latecomers," having climbed onto the bandwagon of the revolution after it had traversed quite a distance without them, and were now classified among the waverers or "fellow travelers." On reading their impassioned declamations one has the feeling that some writers were trying to escape the haunting shadows of their past: their petit bourgeois origin, their traditional Jewish upbringing, the "decadent," liberalist tendencies manifested in their prerevolution writings. Some were certainly unable to rid themselves of the lifelong fears that haunted them because of the praises they had once lavished on Trotsky. Others tried to erase from their biographies such stigmata as having once written in Hebrew, or belonged to some Zionist group, or having been Bundists or Folkisten (Jewish political party in Poland, founded in 1916, which advocated Jewish national and cultural autonomy). Some were haunted by the fact of their having been "émigrés": such well-known authors as David Bergelson, Leib Kvitko, and Der Nister had left Russia (the Ukraine) shortly after the revolution and lived for several years in Berlin, even entertaining hopes of setting up a Jewish literary center there. David Hofstein had gone to Palestine and had thought of settling there, and even Perets Markish had been there on a visit in the early 1920's. Poet Moshe Kulbak and researcher Max Erik had come to Russia from Poland in 1928 and 1929 respectively, and several other Jewish writers were not of Russian origin, but had come to the Soviet Union from various countries in Europe and America, and even from Palestine. This may possibly account, in part, for the markedly aggressive attitude adopted by Soviet Yiddish writers towards Jewish writers abroad — a phenomenon described, with sad irony, as being "the sole national right accorded to Jewish literature in the Soviet Union: the right to revile Jewish literature abroad."[13]

Though, as we have stated, the course of Yiddish literature in the USSR did not differ greatly from that of the literatures of other national groupings, it did nevertheless treat of themes that were, in part, specifically Jewish, and especially of the change that Jewish life was undergoing: the process of productivization; the Jewish population shift from town to country; the changeover from small town crafts to industrial trades; the Jewish settlements set up in the Crimea, the Ukraine and Belorussia, and particularly in Birobidzhan. Yiddish writing might occasionally depict the tribulations and suffering which Jews underwent in the course of this transformation, but on the whole the general tenor was that of abundant enthusiasm and happiness. It should be borne in mind that a strain of sadness was not looked upon favorably in Soviet literature during most of Stalin's rule; hence the Yiddish literature submerged itself, in its own way, in the many-tongued chorus of optimism. Sometimes this was done, for example, by way of giving a Soviet twist to Sholem Aleichem; thus in Faivel Sito's story, Motel son of Pessi the blacksmith does not say, as did Sholem Aleichem's Motel son of Pessi the cantor: "I feel good, I'm an orphan." Instead, he declares: "The revolution means that there aren't any orphans."

What distinguishes Soviet Jewish literature, however, is the fact that apart from the general functions with which it was charged, it was also assigned the specific "national" task of deepening the scission between Russian Jews and their national historical sources, and of severing any spiritual and emotional ties they might still have with other Jewish communities. In all fairness it must be stated that it was not without an inner struggle that the Jewish writers, at least part of them, undertook this task. The first indications of the pressure that was brought to bear on Yiddish writers and protagonists of Jewish culture to "disavow their heritage" became manifest already at the beginning of Stalin's regime and the abolition of the New Economic Policy, mounting in intensity in the wake of the developments of the 1930's. In 1927, the Association of Jewish Revolutionary Writers in the Ukraine declared that "all vestiges of nationalistic afterpains that are still in evidence among Jewish writers, and which lead only to isolationism and helplessness, must be eradicated." The aims of the class struggle called for a literature that was realistic and militant, rather than a romanticism that hovered in the past. In keeping with these proletarian principles, sharp criticism was leveled at various "nationalistic and petit bourgeois" manifestations. If Jewish themes appeared to be dealt with excessively, if too many Jewish characters were portrayed in a novel, or if some of the phrasing suggested a nostalgia for the Jewish township — these were regarded as "deviations." In the course of the campaign waged against what was termed "nationalistic apologia," even the presentation of Jewish characters in a favorable light was condemned as "isolationism." Excessive portrayal of the Jewish *kolhoz* member, for example, was branded as a narrow, "Pale of Settlement" approach, which smacked of *Yiddishkeit* and distracted attention from the main issue — that of the general process of collectivization and the class struggle in the villages, a process in which the Jewish community was also called upon to take part.

One may easily imagine the alarm that seized Soviet Jewish writers when campaigns were launched against Ukrainian, Georgian, and other nationalistic manifestations. Hence, many of these writers endeavored to clear themselves, a priori, of any such suspicion, and much of the contempt for the Jewish past that was voiced in the Soviet Jewish literature of that period may be regarded as a preventive measure taken by the writers to allay or absolve themselves of any possible charge of Jewish nationalism that might be or had already been laid against them.

Not all these indications of repudiation of the past and dissociation from Judaism were necessarily forced upon the Soviet Jewish writers. Some were essentially genuine, especially in the early part of the Soviet regime, when external pressures had not yet become overpowering. In the Jewish writing of those years one may discern a genuine passion for destroying and withdrawing from the old traditions, tragic and mistaken as this passion was — a passion emanating from the ebullition of the revolution, and enflamed by the sight of the old world being torn down and a new one built up. It was particularly the younger Jewish writers who were seized by this passion to break away from the past of "Jewish shopkeepers and the dusty marketplace," in the belief that the new order would amend the social structure of the Jewish community.

It must be added that shortly after the revolution there were many *Russian* writers who, in an emotional state of rebellious intoxication, were fit to tear down art galleries, burn Raphael's paintings and throw Pushkin overboard. Yet it was just when the Russian writers were sobering up from their destructive frenzy that Soviet *Jewish* literature was being increasingly exhorted to break away from the Jewish heritage. To state that a Jewish writer had succeeded in throwing off the burden of the past was a common meed of praise.

We shall cite several instances of this process of "emancipation" from the burden of the past and from Jewishness as a whole in Soviet Yiddish literature, and subsequently some further examples of the reverse process, that is, of the national awakening during and after the war.

In 1925, literary critic N. Oislender asked: why spin out "the thread of the development of all-Jewish literature" now that the revolution had shattered "the old all-Jewish communal existence"? Moshe Litvakov insisted that "the folkloristic beauty" of Jewish culture be separated from and safeguarded against "the reactionary laminations" that had accumulated on it over the years. A. Veviurka claimed that "Mendele, Peretz, and Sholem Aleichem left no heirs in the bourgeois Jewish literature," which he described as "pornography and filth." Critic Yasha Bronstein reminded Jewish writers that "it is our duty to eradicate the *Kerenshchina* from our literature, as we have done from our politics." Izi Kharik, a tragic poet of socialist protest and of anguished belief in the greatness of the new day that had dawned on the worthlessness of the past, saw the Jewish marketplace abandoned and rusting: "We, the poverty stricken of those sleepy alleys, shall trample and forget you like rotting straw." Critic I. Druker, in discussing the "young prose," pointed out that Elie Shechtman for example, "has rearmed himself and is drawing nearer to proletarian literature: in his novel *Ploughed Furrows,* he has rid himself of his former 'objectivism,' of his petit bourgeois 'humanism'; instead of mourning and bewailing the decline of the rich, propertied *Aaron-Moishes,* he now justifies their annihilation and extinction."

Naturally, this breaking away from the past and rejection of the idea of world Jewish unity called for a demonstrative repudiation on the part of Jewish writers of any attachment for the Land of Israel. They assiduously performed this duty, especially in stories set in Birobidzhan. S. Godiner, for instance, in his story, *The Sun Rises in the East,* writes about a certain Israel Yehudin who is packing his belongings before leaving his little town for Birobidzhan, and who leaves behind his grandfather's sacred books, kept in the family for generations ("This is a life that has long become putrefied"); not content with that, however, the author takes issue with a little bag of soil from the Holy Land, from which three generations of mothers have made amulets and hung about their children's necks: "Israel Yehudin jerked his head, as though stung in the chest, in the spot where the amulet used to hang in his childhood. . . . Angrily he kicked the little bag of dust away."

Many were the Jewish writers who showed outstanding diligence when it came to jeering at Jewish religious values and customs, some even resorting to blatant coarseness. These antireligious outbursts were indicative of a mixture of sadism and masochism, of insolence and servility of spirit. Many were plainly overjoyed at the sight of synagogues being converted into workers' clubs. The idealization of mixed marriages became prominent in a great many literary works, yet somehow in a manner that lacked assurance and conviction. Religious faith was often represented as being contrary to hygiene. In an "agro-play" depicting life in a Jewish *kolhoz,* Y. Dobrushin presents an insipid dialogue between Avrom-Yossi, a former *melammed,* religious teacher of small children, and Naftali, a former porter, who is here representative of progress and the new era: speaking of the communal bathhouse that is going up, Naftali remarks that, "Now we'll be able to get rid of lice and God!" Paltry versifiers pounced on the fortuitous Yiddish rhyme *Got* and *Bankrot* ("God" and "Bankrupt"). Izi Kharik's socialist protest was tempered with antireligious fury: in his poetic vision, he somehow manages to associate the Sabbath and the houses of the rich with . . . brothels, and he charges God with being custodian of "the shopkeepers' keys." The demand to eradicate all Hebraisms from the Yiddish language was explained, inter alia, by the need to purge the language from all religious connotation. Similar reasons were advanced for the selective approach to certain former Jewish writers. Thus, the Peretz who voiced the rage of the underprivileged was acclaimed, while the Peretz who idealized *hassidism* was execrated. Former writers of the Haskala (Jewish Enlightenment) school were elevated to prominence, especially those who had fought against "religious backwardness." The Sabbath and Jewish festivals were laughed to scorn in scores of literary works — a favorite butt were the New Year and Day of Atonement. *The Holy Brigade,* a short play by Y. Gordon and Y. Zeldin, ridicules the *minyan,* the minimum congregation of ten, which some *shammes* (beadle) is trying to get together for communal prayer in the *kolhoz* during the High Holidays; whereas the Jewish farmers are too busy with their "socialist contest" of labor to have anything but contempt for the "brigade of holy idlers." Vilification of religious symbols and devotional articles was not infrequently interwoven into the pattern of praises for the homeland, its leaders and defenders, and its vast enterprises, so as to point up the contrast between progress and backwardness and stress that religious faith and ritual are inimical to everything the great Soviet people holds dear. Hence, Passover is contrasted with the October Celebrations; the *shochet,* or ritual slaughterer, and the *gabbai,* or synagogue warden, with the Stakhanovites; the crumpled curtain of the Holy Ark with the Red Flag; the Holy Scriptures with the works of Marx; the Sabbath candles with the electrification projects.

Special prominence was accorded in Soviet Jewish literature to the "pork" motif. It should be pointed out that despite the secularization that marked world Yiddish literature up to the beginning of World War II, even in its most violent anticlerical manifestations, the pig — abhorred by Jews throughout the ages — was rarely introduced as an element indicative of a reversal in the Jewish way of life and thought. Hence, this is essentially a Soviet Jewish "contribution," partly explained by the fact that Soviet Jews began for the first time to engage in pig breeding. Yet one cannot help feeling that the pampering and affection lavished on the pig in Soviet Jewish literature of that period was intended as a deliberate demonstration of so-called Jewish emancipation.

It must be reiterated that in depicting what it claimed to be Jewish life, Yiddish literature was actually reflecting the official line, or the line adopted by Jewish bodies and circles considered to be empowered by the Party authorities to decide in Jewish affairs. Hence, much of this literature cannot be taken as a true mirror of Jewish life and thought, or even as an expression of the authors' real thoughts and feelings. After Stalin's death it was frequently stated in the Soviet Union that Soviet literature as a whole had been guilty of distorting reality during his lifetime — and this no doubt applied to Yiddish literature, too, as well as to a great part of its descriptions of Jewish life. Nor must we lose sight of the general atmosphere that pervaded Yiddish literature, or all Jewish cultural activity for that matter — an atmosphere of fear and surveillance, of self-condemnation and terror. That this atmosphere existed is borne out by the very fact that some of those same writers, examples from whose works we have here quoted, were liquidated during the 1920's and 1930's, despite the ultrapatriotism they had manifested and their ostentatious repudiation of the Jewish heritage and unity.

A further observation is called for: even during the 1920's and 1930's — which abound in illustrations of the repudiation of the Jewish past and its traditional values — Soviet Jewish literature at the same time showed indications of a reverse trend of Jewish nostalgia, whether overt or implied. We may cite the case of Moshe Kulbak in illustration: during his stay in the USSR he wrote a novel called *The Zalmans,* which depicts the decline of Jewish life in a typical courtyard, tenanted by craftsmen and simple folk who cannot readily adjust themselves to the new way of life, to the huge factory and the conveyor belt system. Tonka, representative of the new generation in the Zalman courtyard, diagnostically opines that, "The courtyard must be demolished before it caves in of itself." Yet it may be that Moshe Kulbak and other Jewish writers are conveying what they really feel, not through Tonka, but through the ludicrous figure of Uncle Yudeh, who says: "It was a vital necessity, a need as great as life itself, to depose the Tsar. This Tsar was just a worthless good-for-nothing and not a ruler. . . . But, you see, this thing that they've done, to do away with the last tiny shred of *Yiddishkeit* — it's not right . . . no, it's not right at all . . . it simply isn't nice . . ."

Such expressions of nostalgia for *Yiddishkeit* and of "national pain," which had already become quite rare in Soviet Yiddish literature during the 1920's and virtually nonexistent in the 1930's, surged up again in a mighty wave in the wartime writing. Nor was the yearning for a shred of *Yiddishkeit* confined merely to odd types, psychological leftovers of a bygone, outgrown past; it became a legitimate feeling expressed even by the staunchest supporters of the Soviet regime, by industrious workers and brave fighters, including members of the younger generation.

Cautious as we are in delineating hard-and-fast periods in Yiddish literature in the Soviet Union, there is an inescapable contrast between the writing turned out prior to the German invasion of the USSR, and that produced after June 21, 1941. Naturally the indications and depth of the national awakening were not identical in all the Yiddish authors, just as their renunciation of the Jewish heritage in the 1920's and 1930's differed greatly in degree. Yet the shift in the tenor of Soviet Jewish literature in mid-1941 was clearcut, and its readers might well have been surprised by the new tone adopted. Alongside the usual themes of Soviet patriotism, the brotherhood of nations, the heroism of the people, praise of their leaders, and the like — specifically Jewish motifs were given prominence. These motifs may be summed up in the following general terms:

1. The annihilation of the Jewish people during the war.
2. A sentimental attachment, sometimes expressed in primitive or melodramatic terms, for everything associated with Jews and Jewishness.
3. A manifest yearning for traditional symbols and devotional associations — the Sabbath and festivals, the ritual candles, the Passover *seder,* the synagogue and the scrolls of the law, verses from the Scriptures and prayer book, Jewish burial rites, and the like.
4. The highlighting of Jewish national integrity, on both the historical and geographical planes.
5. Meditations on the peculiar fate of the Jewish people, its history, wanderings, dispersion, and the mystery of its survival.
6. Demonstrative recourse to Jewish history for manifestations of greatness, heroism, and humanitarian values.
7. Assertion of present Jewish greatness and heroism.
8. Closely interconnected with the two previous items: manifest pride in the accomplishments of distinguished Jews (prominent among these, understandably, are Soviet Jewish generals, prize-winners, scientists, inventors, etc.).
9. A new approach in depicting Jewish characters, no longer classi-

fied a priori according to social class or ideological outlook. Wealthy persons and even members of the clergy were not condemned from the outset on account of their social origins or their present occupations and status, but were depicted in a warm light by virtue of their endearing human, and specifically Jewish, qualities.

10. Lastly, in direct contrast to the motif of destruction — firm faith that the Jewish people would arise and flourish once more.

The ten motifs enumerated above may be summed up as representing a Judeophile trend, strange as this term must sound when applied to literature produced by Jews in the Jewish language. Parenthetically it may be observed that this change in the content and human scene of Soviet Jewish literature also served to widen its general scope, enabling it, in some degree, to shed its former oversimplification by which persons and events were appraised in terms of stark black and white. The national renaissance, moreover, afforded Jewish literature some hope of raising its artistic standards.

There is no doubt that the official permissive attitude was significantly conducive to bringing about this shift in tenor. The Soviet authorities, in their efforts to mobilize for the war effort all possible forces and public emotions, both inside and outside the Soviet Union, were ready to sanction and even encourage the expression of national sentiment. Within the frame of the total strategy of "Everything for Victory," the national factor was recognized as being a powerfully rousing incentive; hence, Soviet literature as a whole — charged with political and educational tasks in peacetime, too — was called upon to rouse national sentiments and channel them in the service of the war effort.

The Soviet leaders saw fit, admittedly, to stimulate Russian patriotism, in particular, a trend that became apparent already in the 1930's. If Stalin was shrewd enough to pander to feelings of Russian national pride in order to consolidate his regime and further socialist construction in time of peace, he would naturally use this national pride as a powerful lever when the nation was at war with the invaders. The exigencies of war dispelling all remaining "proletarian" misgivings on this score, the heroism manifested by the Soviet people during the war fed largely on traditional Russian national pride. It may be assumed, moreover, that some Russian writers responded more readily to the nationalist call during the war than they had formerly complied with the dictates of the Party. It is noteworthy that a number of Russian writers who for years had been virtually banned, again began to appear in print during the war.

With Russian nationalism and heroism in powerful focus, the multinational character of the Soviet Union was in no way overlooked, however, and non-Russian literatures, too, were permitted to voice warm national sentiments. In the circumstances, the Jewish writers also began to draw the obvious inference: if the authorities were encouraging the glorification of past Russian heroes and even bolstering the national pride of other Soviet peoples, why should not this apply, say, to David and Samson, to the Maccabees and Hanna and her seven sons, to Bar-Cochba and Rabbi Akiva? If Russian Orthodox priests were depicted in several Russian novels as brave underground fighters, why not a rabbi-partisan in a Jewish story? Solomon Mikhoels, during his New York visit in 1943, recounted at a meeting with YKUF leaders that a Russian artillery officer was in the habit of interlacing his orders with literary terms, thus: "Fire, for the sake of Anna Karenina, for the sake of our revolutionary Russian literature!" And Mikhoels added: "That is exactly what our own Rabbi Akiva used to do, when he rallied the Jewish fighters to do battle in the name of the Torah."[14]

It must be stressed that this drawing of analogies was merely an ancillary factor that contributed to the national awakening in Soviet Yiddish literature, whereas the awakening itself stemmed from sources of deep inner experience. We shall endeavor to prove, in this and following chapters, that the Jewish writers erred in regarding the official sanction of nationalist manifestations not merely as a temporary tactical measure, but as a basic reversal of policy that had come to stay. Their realistic perception, though sharpened by years of experience must no doubt have been dulled by the profundity of Jewish suffering. At all events, the feelings that the Jewish writers had stifled throughout many years, or had deliberately striven to eradicate from their consciousness, began to flood their writing in the latter half of 1941. Thus, as Isaac Yanasovich, a Polish Jewish writer who came to the USSR as a refugee, put it: the Soviet Jewish authors seemed to tear the masks off their faces, revealing their true selves in the genuine enthusiasm with which they responded to the call to adopt a Jewish national attitude during the war.[15] Though still careful, during that period of relative liberalization, not to give their pens too free rein, nevertheless their writing abounds, as a rule, in Jewish sentiment.

The change undergone by Soviet Jewish literature during this period also becomes apparent in the light of the absence of some of its former elements: between June 22, 1941, and the end of 1945, "not a single antireligious work appeared in Yiddish."[16] A scrutiny of all Yiddish works published during that period shows about two-thirds of them to be of intrinsic Jewish content, which calls for the obvious conclusion that "although during the war years — 1941 to 1945 — there appeared only some 21 percent of the number of books published in 1940, this small volume is inherently far greater from the Jewish aspect than the former spate of writing."[17]

This preoccupation with matters of Jewish interest persisted in Soviet Yiddish literature after the war as well, or at all events, the writers strove to sustain it. The Jewish tragedy, which had nurtured the change towards nationalism in this literature, rather than ending with the cessation of the fighting, was only then unfolding in its true magnitude. And indeed, "there was no great change in the composition of Soviet Yiddish publications between 1946 and 1948, as compared to the war years, despite the ideological pressures that were increasingly brought to bear during those years. . . . After the war, too, at least 80 percent of all the Yiddish books published in the Soviet Union respond in some way to spiritual needs of Soviet Jews following the war and the holocaust."[18]

The national awakening in Soviet Jewish literature is also confirmed by the manner in which it was appraised in the Soviet Union itself. "The war has enhanced the national feeling in our literature," is asserted in one article that appeared in 1947.[19] Another article, which appeared in the same periodical, states that "the growth of national awareness and national pride in the Soviet Jew during the thirty years of the Revolution is now an unassailable fact!"[20] Though the article refers to all "the thirty years of the Revolution," the author may be assumed to have drawn his inspiration from the wartime developments.

We shall now present a series of illustrations of the prominence given to Jewish motifs in various wartime and postwar literary works.

To begin with, the notion of exacting retribution from the Germans, in evidence in all Soviet wartime literature, was stressed from the specific Jewish aspect in Yiddish writing. Thus, Yiddish poet Lipeh Reznik — in his poem "To Demand and Repay" — again leafs through "the old, forgotten pages," where he finds "the glory of my people, its suffering, and its wrath"; he recalls the slaughter of Worms, of Magenza, and "our believing forefathers" who were martyred. In another poem, "The Hour Has Come," he associates his hatred for the enemy with "the brilliant spark of hereditary splendor."

Soviet Jewish soldiers went into battle "with the sacred Russian rifle in their hands and Jewish songs on the lips," in Mottel Grobian's war poem. This poet, who wrote of "mountains of skeletons," did not refrain from hinting at his countrymen's callousness to the fate of the Jews.

In a story by Hershel Polianker, Red Army Sergeant Avrom Ginsburg carves his name and that of his home town on the stones of conquered Berlin, as did many other soldiers, but he does so in Yiddish.

Even though the enemy be "a Goliath," Moshe Khashchevatsky asserts in one of his poems, a "new David" will arise to defeat him. Other poems of his, too, were based on Biblical and historical motifs; noteworthy among them is the poem "Hanna and Her Seven Sons," recalling the martyrdom of the Jewish mother and her seven children who staunchly refused to abandon their faith and people, whose blood has been shed these two thousand years and more — "My heart goes out to my people and my faith," the poet affirms.

For Avraham Velednitsky, *Mount Ararat* is become "well loved and near," for "my people know it, and the Bible tells of it."

"Mother Rachel" is the title of a poem in which Aaron Kushnirov depicts the slaughter at Babi Yar. It was said of this poet that when he reached liberated Vilna with the Soviet Army (in which he held the rank of captain), he asked local surviving Jewish writers to get him a Bible, preferably with a Yiddish translation.[21]

Poet Ezra Fininberg, who had at one time exhorted the little townships to cleanse themselves by getting rid of their rabbis and priests, now sees Isaiah and Jeremiah treading their mournful paths. He compares the defeat of Germany with the fall of Babylon, taking as his motif a verse from Jeremiah, "They have crushed all her hosts," and ends his poem with the words: "Babylon writhes in agony, and the nations of the world rejoice. . . . Thus it is eternally written in the Book that will never wane."

In his story, "Heirs of the Angel of Death," Shmuel Gordon portrays an aged Jew in a little township in the Crimea who does not leave his home after the German invasion. Confidently the old man ties in Russia's fate with that of the Jews, or as he puts it: no king has ever been able to conquer Russia, just as no Haman has ever succeeded in destroying the Jewish people. On the eve of the Day of Atonement he lights the candles, puts on his *kittel* (white ritual garment) and *tallit,* and is at prayer when the Germans come and torture him to death, staining his white *kittel* (also used as a shroud) with his blood. That same night a partisan band, led by the old Jew's grandson, blows up an officers' club where the Germans are carousing. In another story, Gordon describes the evacuation of Jews from their township supervised by "Elie Yehudin" (the title of the story); Elie notices a group of Jews in holiday attire carrying with great care cases containing scrolls of the law, which they will not abandon to the "cursed Hamans."

Poet Avraham Gontar, mourning the devastation of his home town, recalls not only its former happy life, but also the Sabbath candles that shone from every window.

On the liberation of Minsk, Uri Finkel wrote: "Minsk! Will your streets no longer ring with Yiddish sounds? Will your houses nevermore echo with beloved Jewish songs?" By the grave of poet M. Z. Manne in the town of Radozskowice, where the Nazis had butchered thousands of Jews in the cemetery, the words of Manne's poem about the "Eternal People" still cry out in Uri Finkel's ears.

A rabbi-partisan, in a story by Hirsh Orland, stressing the historical fact that the Jews were the first to be martyred in the war, observes that "the more precious the pelt of an animal is, the more fiercely it is hunted down."

In his poem "The Jews," young Lithuanian poet Hirsh Osherovich depicts a whole Jewish community burned to death in their synagogue, and, together with them, devotional articles that had soaked up the prayers of ages, holy writings and sacred poems.

In a story by Shireh Gorshman, a Jewish child born in the ghetto is named *"Haim Meir"* (Life, Light) as a symbol of hope, and the mother explains the meaning of the Hebrew words. Another story by Gorshman, "Bathsheva the Shochet's Wife," is worthy of note for its plot and the atmosphere it conveys. Shabtai, the aged *shochet* (ritual slaughterer), is reciting from the Book of Lamentations when the Germans irrupt into his small Lithuanian town. He collapses under their blows and kicks, but rises to his feet clasping his skullcap to his head lest it be uncovered. The Germans take him away, then return his body to his house, where they drunkenly carouse. The author depicts their sadistic sport in detail: they set a roast pig on the table and adorn its head with the dead *shochet*'s skullcap, festoon the room with his *kittel,* and drink out of his Passover goblets. In the end, Bathsheva, the *shochet*'s wife, cuts the throats of two Germans with her husband's slaughtering-knife.

Noah Luria, in his story "By the Open Grave," describes a German *Aktzia* (liquidation operation) in a Ukrainian town in the autumn of 1941; we hear Jews reciting psalms, the confessional, and other prayers. To allay suspicion, the German commander has ordered all the Jews to take with them food for three days and a valise with essential belongings; but Mates, the night watchman, takes with him only a crust of bread and a prayerbook . . .

Y. Rabin's story "The Road Back" depicts the return of two Jews to their home town after the war; they are among the fifteen survivors of the town's fifty thousand Jewish inhabitants, and they find their homes converted into a graveyard. As one of the solitary survivors walks through the desolate streets, he feels that many generations are watching him — "the sole heir to hundreds of years' existence."

There is a distinctive Jewish symbolism to be found also in Aaron Vergelis's poem dedicated to Yosef Bumagin (a Birobidzhan Jew who fell when the city of Breslau was taken, and was posthumously awarded the order of Hero of the Soviet Union). The poet wishes Bumagin's glorious deeds to be included in the treasury of Jewish legend: "May Yosef be a modern Song of Songs of his ancient people in Birobidzhan . . ."

Moshe Pinchevsky, an author who went through many different phases, at one time exceeded many of his fellow writers with his clamorous ultrapatriotic sentiments and his vilification of "enemies" of every description. He did his patriotic duty by Trotsky (whom he referred to as "Judas Iscariot"), by Zinoviev ("the harlot") and others. In Jewish matters, Pinchevsky resorted to blatant coarseness and obscenity in reviling Jewish symbols and values, the Hebrew language, Zionism, and the like. Against this setting, therefore, particular significance attaches to his play *I Live,* written during the war. The play was first performed in Czernowitz, and the Jewish State Theater in Kiev reopened with it on August 30, 1945. An official Soviet Jewish periodical noted the success of this play in the city "where the Fascists slaughtered hundreds of thousands of Jews. . . . The inscription 'The Jewish Nation Lives' on the curtain aroused stormy applause."[22] The main characters in the play are Rabbi Bezalel ("Zaleh") Shafir and his daughter. The bearded, skullcap-wearing father stirs the Jews in the ghetto to revolt, and the daughter kills the local Gestapo commandant.

Shortly afterwards, presumably on the instructions of the political literary censors, Pinchevsky (obviously not the sort of man to stand up for his principles) was forced to change the play, substituting a Russian professor of history for the rabbi, thus acquiescing in the claim that "a rabbi and his daughter can surely not be allowed to be the exponents of Soviet ideology." But even this change did not prove adequate, as may be learned from the criticism leveled at the play in September 1946. It should be remembered that it was in August and September 1946 that the Zhdanovist campaign was launched to purge Soviet cultural life of any ideological deviations and political frailty. Pinchevsky was then accused of having allowed the professor to mouth "all the phraseology of Rabbi Zaleh Shafir," thereby compromising the reputation of a Soviet scholar. The further criticism leveled at the play and the enumeration of its shortcomings may give some indication of the atmosphere it initially set out to depict. The author is condemned for retaining the play's "narrow nationalistic" content, even after he substituted the professor for the rabbi; for retaining its outworn Jewish romanticism (for example, the blessing on lighting the Sabbath candles); and for presenting the ghetto as being dissociated from the overall Soviet underground fighting.[23]

The above illustrations have not embraced the works of eight of the most prominent Soviet Jewish writers, each of whom we propose to review separately. The fate of these writers is of special interest. Four of them — David Bergelson, Itsik Feffer, Perets Markish and Leib Kvitko — were executed in August 1952; two — David Hofstein and Der Nister — died in prison; and the other two — Shmuel Halkin and Itsik Kipnis — after languishing in prisons and labor camps from the end of the 1940's, were released several years after Stalin's death. We do not propose to dwell on the literary quality of their writings, but on those aspects of it that might illustrate — chiefly by way of analogy — the national awakening that Soviet Jewish literature underwent at the time.

We shall begin with David Bergelson, a celebrated prose writer, whose works were regarded by some as ranking among the great classics, alongside those of Mendele Mocher Seforim, Yitzhak Leib Peretz, and Sholem Aleichem. For the purpose of our discussion we may pass over his prerevolution writing, though it was chiefly then that he produced some of his finest work; we merely wish to point out that by the time of the October Revolution Bergelson had already distinguished himself in the realm of Yiddish literature and was widely acclaimed for his refined taste, his distinctive style and his subtle pyschological insight into the environment that served as his subject matter.

Like many other Russian intellectuals in the early days of the Soviet regime, Bergelson (born in 1884 in a small Ukrainian town) was assailed by inner conflict. In 1921 he left Kiev, where he had lived since 1908, and settled in Berlin, but found no inner peace there, either. After undergoing a series of spiritual crises, and prompted by considerations concerning the future of Jewish literature and the course of his own writing (as well as by his friends' urging), he returned to the Soviet Union in the early 1930's. The time he was away from Russia may be regarded as an intermediate phase in his writing, which reflected his self-probing, but which might be assumed already then to have gained him admission into the world of Soviet literature.

It was during this intermediate phase that Bergelson published his novel *Measure of Justice* (1925), a romanticized glorification of the iron fist of the revolution. The principal character, portrayed in a sympathetic light, is Filipov, *Nachalnik* of the "Special Section" (political police) in an outlying Russian town. Filipov, far from being cruel by nature, is rather a modest, amiable man, in failing health after he had spent most of his life working down in the coal mines. When he orders a man to be shot, "it is not he, but History, that gives the order." His philosophy is this: "There's a revolution on. We're not playing games with dolls. Just don't tangle with the revolution." If a "red bullet" cuts someone down, it is by dint of Filipov's sense of fairness, which demands "in the name of the Great Justice of the revolution . . . that all the petty wormlike justices be crushed and burnt in ruthless flames."

Just before Bergelson returned to the Soviet Union, the first part of his two-volume novel *By the Dnieper* was published (1932). The main character is young Penek, a boy raised in the luxury of the spacious "white house" of his father the merchant, yet who is irresistibly drawn to the servants, the scullions, and stableboys. Penek is boon companion to the inhabitants of the "twisty back lanes" who "go to sleep early so as to live a few hours less." He loves them and they love him, for he spiritually and emotionally shares not only their want and poverty, but also their hatred for his father's house. The plot is heavily charged with social emotionalism, and one cannot escape the feeling that the author has made a ten-year-old boy spout revolutionary phrases like an adult. The whole novel, in fact, abounds in the "retroflexive" proletarian wisdom of the new Bergelson, who now seems eager to dismiss his own past. Penek, the young rebel, is portrayed as an accomplished ideologist, sometimes as a Bolshevist or Yevsektsist orator, well versed in the laws of historical evolution, who speaks in a self-assured Marxist vein. Parenthetically, this is where Bergelson fails in the artistic literary sense: he discards the somber truth of an end-nineteenth-century Jewish townlet and the innocent protest of a child, in favor of brochure-like phrases and schematic formulas.

We shall not enlarge on the degree of artistic and human refinement inherent in endowing Penek and the slum dwellers with sadistic qualities, as in the great moment of satisfaction in their dreary lives when the boy's father, wealthy Reb Michoel Levin, is in his death agonies and is soon buried. What is far more important for the purpose of our discussion is the means which Bergelson resorts to in order to interlace the joy of the town's underprivileged and the rebel son with their abuse of Jewish tradition. Just as the author associates the hateful, grasping figure of the father with piety and Jewish scholarship, he similarly causes Penek to reflect at his father's funeral that "it is the rich, pious Jews who have buried in the grave the 613 precepts of the wealthy." Though the first part of *By the Dnieper* was written outside the Soviet Union, it is nevertheless pervaded by an agnostic, *bezbozhnik* (Godless) spirit. The old pauper, Maites, who breaks his back working at the grindstones, with the sweat streaming onto his *arba kanfot,* reflects that "This must be the way God likes it." Through the medium of Yeshie Freides, who works as a cashier in Reb Michoel Levin's business, Bergelson propounds a kind of Marxist-Leninist thesis that religion is the opium of the masses: Yeshie has a lot of sacred books at home, which cannot provide a festival meal, of course, but which "can make you forget for a few hours that there are rich men and poor men, just as a bit of vodka can make a drunkard forget all his troubles."

The author sends many a barbed shaft at the Jewish High Holidays and their ostensible religious significance. Penek observes that the two days of New Year ("Days of Awe") fill the town with a sense of dread, though he is well aware, having already turned twelve, how groundless are the fears aroused by the blowing of a horn called a *shofar* and by prayers charged with dire threats of death by starvation and by the sword. This, he reasons, is merely a subterfuge employed by the religious in order to bring poor folk to the synagogue and have them mingle with the profiteering merchants and usurers who are in league with God. Bergelson spares no device in making Penek revile God, the synagogue, and prayers, sometimes in the most obscene terms. At times the author reaches a pitch of masochism in the self-abasement he exhibits, as when he compares the drawing aside of the curtain of the Holy Ark to the lifting of a Jewish woman's skirts! On the eve of the Day of Atonement, Penek's loneliness is somewhat relieved by the company of a gentile peasant, who was swindled by a mean little Jew . . .

Bergelson wrote the second part of *By the Dnieper* (entitled *The Youthful Years*) after his return to the Soviet Union. The scene is laid at the beginning of the twentieth century, when the revolutionary awakening had begun to manifest itself in underground societies, strikes, demonstrations, and like activities, in which some sections of the Jewish population were swept up as well. Thus, young Penek not only aligns himself on the proletarian side, but his sympathies fully lie with the Iskra, Lenin's supporters, who embody the ardent revolutionary spirit and revolutionary ability. The plot, however, is subject to the historiographic influences of the Stalinist period and already augurs Stalin's subsequent greatness when it tells of the mighty impact of the "strikes and demonstrations staged in Batum and other Caucasian towns."

In the province of specific Jewish problems in particular, Bergelson charges Penek with the task of discrediting the Bundist movement, as well as Zionism and Jewish tradition as a whole. Penek is also led to the conviction that he must sever his connections with the Hebrew language — a need that seems to arise from Bergelson's wish to atone for his own sin of having started his literary career by writing in Hebrew. By the most artificial process of character development, Penek is represented early in the second part of *By the Dnieper* as a "Hebrew scribbler." Though vaguely in favor of the Iskra, he nevertheless for some reason continues to fill the pages of his diary in Hebrew until his revolutionary awareness makes him realize that his Hebrew scribbling is utterly divorced from matters "that are of present moment to living people." After the Kishinev pogroms Penek is not only firmly convinced that the bourgeois order is responsible for the bloodshed; he also discovers a "manifesto" signed by rabbis (the tools of Jewish bourgeoisie) calling upon Jews to fulfill a "sacred duty" by handing over to the authorities all provocateurs and those who rebel against "our exalted Government."

Bergelson rendered faithful Jewish service to the Stalinist cause in his series of *Birobidzhan Stories* (1934). Not content with glorifying the great Jewish settlement project being carried out by the Soviet government, he depicts persons and events in such a manner as to stress his contempt for any vestige of Jewish tradition. Much of the praise he lavishes on his favorably depicted characters consists in the fact of their repudiation of "nationalistic nonsense" and "moldering beliefs," whereas his villains are guilty of adherence to religious customs. Bergelson obviously strove in this way to preclude any suggestion of an association between the Birobidzhan project and the concept of a Jewish national renaissance in the traditional historic sense. It was only natural that amidst this new, healthy Jewish environment the romanticization of the pig should not be absent. And indeed, the author describes with exceptional pathos the heartrending tears of a Jewish girl when the sow under her care (in a bright, gleaming pigsty) bears a litter of nine dead piglets.

In considering the illustrations we have cited, account must be taken not only of the atmosphere prevailing in the USSR in the 1930's, but also of Bergelson's particular frame of mind engendered by his rich non-Soviet past. This will become somewhat more apparent when we consider his preface to an *amended* edition of his stories on the subject of the civil war (*Step by Step,* 1938). He had first written these stories, he states, "when the new world outlook had just begun to stir me," but over the years, having come to see things more clearly, he had begun to feel the need to rewrite the stories and remove the shortcomings "which were revealed to the author in the new light of our age."

Let us now turn to Bergelson's writing after the German invasion, beginning with his play *Ch'vel Leben* (I Will Live — see Psalm 118: 17). The main character is Avrom-Ber, an old Jew who is proud of being a Soviet citizen, but is also filled with national Jewish pride. He lost his eldest son in World War I, then his second son, commander of a Red Army brigade, in the present war. When his son's body is brought to his house, the old man does not break down. Instead, he says to the commissar who has come to offer condolences: "We, simple Jews, have seen many dead. But the more of us that die, the stronger is our will to live." Avrom-Ber is surprised that a certain Professor Kornblit, of German origin, declares himself a Jew only after the German invasion. "Are you a Jew? It took you long enough to admit it!" When the professor, in despair under the Nazi occupation, contemplates suicide, Avrom-Ber is not so much concerned with the personal aspect of such a way out as with the public aspect. "And who does the professor intend to abandon, if not all the other Jews, the Jewish people, who despite all the persecution and inquisitions and expulsions never took their own lives? He is abandoning his people, who in the face of all their hardships and decrees never ceased declaring to the world: 'I shall not die, but live!' " Avrom-Ber staunchly reaffirms "I shall not die, but live!" just before he is put to death.[24]

This change of tone is mild compared to that voiced by Bergelson in another play of his, *Prince Reuveni.* Set in the sixteenth century, the plot revolves around the Jewish messianic movements, the Inquisition and the life of the Marranos, but its projection on current events is easily discernible. A distinct parallel, in fact, is drawn between the two periods, with obvious references to the Zionist struggle to open the gates of the Land of Israel to the Jewish refugees and the demand for an independent Jewish homeland. *Prince Reuveni* is a clear indication of Bergelson's recourse to the past in order to attain greater freedom of expression in present affairs.

David Reuveni is an envoy of an imaginary Jewish kingdom that is fighting against the Turks from the rear. Reuveni seeks the help of Christian powers — money, ships, and men — for this conflict, and he musters three hundred thousand armed men. He negotiates with financiers and diplomats, and draws up alliances based on common interests. Granted an audience by the Pope, he states: "The Jews have always appealed to popes on grounds of compassion, but now, for the first time since Bar-Cochba, there stands before you a Jew who makes claims backed by Jewish strength." and he further affirms: "Beware of those whose only choice lies between the auto-da-fé and victory." It is a time when new lands are being discovered, yet only one nation, Reuveni complains, has not been accorded a tract of land. "Possibly only we ourselves are to blame, in that we did not take from time what it was able to grant us." In Reuveni, Bergelson personifies the resurgence of Jewish yearning for a homeland. Yet alongside the admiration of physical force expressed in the play, it also praises the spiritual fortitude of the Jewish people: "The world is a balance, with force on one scale and grace on the other. Force is [represented by] Amalek, Edom, Rome, the Inquisition. Grace — the Jewish people. By the Jews, nations are judged. By the Jews, the world is judged." But one cannot rely on grace alone, Reuveni maintains: "A tract of land* is due to a nation not only after its death, but also during its lifetime." A motif representing the tenor of the play may be found in the words of one of the characters, suggestive of a paraphrase of Descartes' famous phrase, "You, my people, fight, therefore you, my people, exist."

Reuveni is the antithesis of Penek in *By the Dnieper.* Whereas the latter derides the Day of Atonement, a Yom Kippur prayer is offered up amidst a solemn atmosphere in *Prince Reuveni.* The same author who flung stones at the moldering national tradition hoists "the banner of Judah" at the masthead of Reuveni's man-of-war. Through the medium of his characters Bergelson even seems to be condemning his own course in the none too distant past, as in the words of Reb Shabtai: "More than one of them passed themselves off there as Christians. Very many of them changed their dinars there; some out of fear, some in order to gain happiness. . . . They traded and bartered, and gradually they sold their fathers, and themselves."[25]

After the bold Jewish nationalism expressed in *Prince Reuveni,* Bergelson's subsequent postwar writing appears to be rather an anticlimax, for all that it forms a striking contrast with his *By the Dnieper* or *Birobidzhan Stories.* In *New Stories,* a collection published in 1947, the first story, "In the Mountains," treats of the observance of tradition among Caucasian Jews. It tells of twenty-four-year-old Gadashvili, a soldier who comes home on leave after having been wounded on the front and escaping capture by the Germans. The young man's father, we are told, "is still a little religious, like many mountain Jews"; he does not shave his beard, yet the son feels good when he

* Literally, "four ells," which has the dual connotation of "living space" and "a grave."

clings to his father's unshaven cheeks. Closing his eyes for a moment, the young soldier recalls a childhood memory, when his father observed one of the fasts that "took him far back to the ancient days of the Jews."

The scene of the "The Sculptor" is laid in a townlet famous for its Jewish printing craft. One of the first to return to his home town after the war, the sculptor is overwhelmed by a flood of memories at the sight of every object in his home. He clutches a wooden board on which his mother used to salt the meat (to make it *kasher*). As he sits on the front steps, the wind carries a swirl of scraps of paper, among them charred *mezuzot* and half-burnt promissory notes, which for some reason unknown to him had been made out in Hebrew . . .

The central character in "The Witness" is a sixty-year-old Jew, one of the handful of survivors of the Nazi occupation, who gives an eyewitness account of his experiences to a Jewish woman employee of the town council. His account is but a pale rendering of the horrors of the holocaust, and the author finds it necessary to emphasize the common lot and feelings of the Jews and non-Jews. Yet when the woman who is taking down the deposition asks him whether she has translated it correctly from Yiddish into Russian, the Jew observes: "What can I say? Our troubles, surely, were in Yiddish . . ."

In the story "She of All People," a Jewish woman, Doctor Niuta, wishes to reestablish contact with her family, having been prompted by revolutionary zeal to sever it at the beginning of the century — "she of all people, whom her father had once mourned by sitting *shiva* [seven days of mourning] and rending his garments."

Dr. Soifer, a character in the story "Memorial Candles," is an accomplished eye surgeon who successfully performs an operation that saves the eyesight of Trofimov, former *kolhoz* chairman, who was wounded in the war. The doctor regards this operation as symbolic of lighting a candle in memory of his mother. On the way to the hospital, he glimpses his white surgeon's coat peeping out from under his shabby furs, and remembers the *kittel* worn by Jews on their way to the *Kol Nidre* service on Yom Kippur eve. When the operation proves successful and Trofimov opens his eyes with a cry of "I can see!" the surgeon murmurs from the memorial prayer: "May her soul be bound up in the bond of eternal life . . . mother . . . mother . . ." Dr. Soifer, a survivor from a Nazi extermination camp, tries to draw a comparison between his patient and himself. "Here are two people," he muses. "One has lost what he sees with, and certainly arouses sympathy — a blind man! But the other has lost what to see." He originates from Vilna, where "all the life's tradition he imbibed since his childhood has been wiped out. Some people may be orphaned of their father and mother, but he has been orphaned of a whole city, of a third of his nation." The author voices this analogy even more poignantly when he says: "Sometimes nations lose their sons, and this is certainly a loss. But here is Dr. Soifer with his loss — he is one of those who have lost a people."

We shall conclude with Bergelson's review of *Freilechs,* a series of sketches depicting a Jewish wedding, performed by the Moscow Jewish State Theater shortly after the war. Here, too, our primary concern is not with his appraisal of the artistic quality of the performance, but with his attitude to its theme. We find that the writer, who had formerly extolled the virtues of intermarriage, now manifests a sharp reversal of attitude on this point. In his review of *Freilechs* he lays particular emphasis on the significance of Jewish marriages in general, and at this time in particular, and stresses that among the Jews the concept of family has always been closely bound up with the national concept. He states that, "Among the Jews, a people that had long been unable to entrench itself behind territorial frontiers, the other bond — that of the family — was therefore strengthened all the more. Hence the grave importance the Jews attach to family life and their particularly serious air at their children's weddings. When a Jew marries off his son or daughter, he does not merely make a match with another Jewish family; he re-allies himself with the Jewish nation as a whole." The author then goes on to describe the custom of the Seven Benedictions which "apply not only to the newly married couple, but to all Jews wherever they might be." Moreover, the rejoicing is not confined to the houses of the celebrants, but sweeps the entire Jewish neighborhoods. "Enemies invariably make up before the wedding, for their personal differences would appear paltry at a time when a whole nation, whose sons had often been led to the slaughter, was reaffirming the establishment of further generations." It is particularly these aspects, prominently brought out in *Freilechs,* that are ungrudgingly praised by Bergelson.[26]

Itsik Feffer, born in 1900, published his first collection of poems in 1922. Hence, the whole of his prolific literary output was produced under the Soviet regime. His pre-World War II writing shows hardly any indications of an inner conflict in regard to the Jewish cultural heritage; he endeavored, in fact, to prove himself an authoritative exponent of the official line in Soviet Yiddish literature. In the manner of Mayakovsky in his later years (who expressed the wish that the pen be as a bayonet, and that Stalin speak of verse before the Central Committee as he speaks of coal and petroleum), Feffer declares in his Yiddish verses (freely rendered): "What we need are poetry-making brigades, a political poetry that will sweep away the lyrical gibberish; for we build up our poetry as one now puts up a building, as the Party builds up its theses." Feffer casts off all restraint in his ardent enthusiasm for the new order: "Let us glorify our age — in height and depth, in breadth and distance." The mere names of his books of poems are indicative: *May Life Live, The Lucky Hour, Arrows Far and Wide.* He declares his love for "barefoot poems" and for "simple words," and indeed, he reviles and abuses and threatens in the plainest language, as when he warns the propertied class that "the Moscow spirit will accompany you to the next world." Nor does he spare his Soviet Jewish fellow writers, of whom he is the most aggressive, militant, and scornful, sometimes in a clumsy and even obscene manner. He reminds his colleagues that one cannot shirk one's duty of proceeding in the march of time by keeping silent: "At present, silence smacks of treachery." His poetry is charged with exaltation of the greatness of actual events, of mighty socialist reconstruction, of "electrified days," days when "the electric wires are singing." Who cares about "squeaky outpourings about the moon and the night," about "lyrical sighing"? Feffer's only lapse into lyricism is a "metallic lyricism," his paeans of praise for the Dnieper Project or the coal-mining program. He is most vociferous in the chorus of abuse hurled at the "traitors, spies, and assassins" who were hounded out of cover during the 1930's: "Dogs who trade in conscience — we shoot you down like mad dogs. . . . Cursed are the names of Tukhachevsky and Yakir, the names of the Trotskyite scum. . . . Death to the assassins, even today, even today!" Feffer's loyalty to the Soviet regime is boundless: "I have forgotten where is the house I live in, where is the courtyard and the fence. I remember only this: the duties I must perform to the end of my days."

Feffer proves his performance of his duties also by dint of his blatant repudiation of the Jewish past. Not content with the hymns he sings to "my Russia," to the "wondrous heart" of Stalin, and even to the "blond Komsomol girls," he loudly boasts of the fact that he has shaken off "the dust of ages" and calls upon other Yiddish writers to discard themes that exude "the bad odor of the [Jewish] townlet of Talne." In his poem "In the Museum" he declares that he will not allow his clear path to be sullied by dust, and jeeringly enumerates the Sabbath candlesticks, the ancient curtain of the Holy Ark, and Mendele Mocher Seforim's *tallit* among the dust-covered objects. True to the *bezbozhnik* concept that identifies the war against religion with the class struggle, he calls for an all-out attack on "poverty and nakedness, the *bet midrash* and God" all in the same breath; or he boasts that "I have never put on *tefillim* [phylacteries] and have never traded in the marketplace." He is amused by the thought that he is named after the saintly Reb Itzikel; and as for his Jewish origin, "What matters it," he asks, "that they have circumcised my flesh?"

The tenor of Feffer's prewar writing is aptly summed up by another Jewish writer thus: "In Jewish poetry, never has a man of his talent stripped himself so bare, giving his last poetic shirt to his country, as has Feffer."[27] It is in contrast with his blatant spurning of Jewish traditional and sacred values that Feffer's wartime poetry is all the more significant for its utter change of tone. The same poet who formerly hurled his venomous shafts at the Jewish past now "seeks refuge" with Rabbi Levi Yitzhak of Berdichev* or "in the shade of our ancient grandfather-oak." Even such an outspoken, confirmed heretic as Feffer is overwhelmed by "penitent feelings." Whoever is familiar with his propagandist poems, which voice full-throated contempt of Jewish tradition, cannot but be astounded by the new notes

* Eighteenth-century Hassidic leader whose central doctrine was "love for Israel," legendary defense advocate of his people and intercessor for divine justice.

emerging from his pen (sounds which formerly resembled the beating of drums). For all that he is still rather careful not to manifest exaggerated Jewish sentiments, the intensity of which he sometimes tones down within "permissible" limits, or which might possibly have alarmed even himself, his wartime poetry is nevertheless characterized by such poems as "I am a Jew," "Shades of the Warsaw Ghetto," and others in a similar emotive vein.

Each of the fourteen stanzas of "I am a Jew" ends with this declaration. Here, the poet weaves the thread of generations, inspired by belief in the eternity of Israel as symbolized in the locks of Samson and Isaiah's prophetic vision, as affirmed in Solomon's wisdom and the bravery of the Maccabees, in the tones of Yehuda Halevi's songs and the philosophic reflections of Spinoza, in the meditations of Heine and Mendele, in the sunset of painter Levitan, in the throbbing of a Jewish heart in Buenos Aires, in the sounds of a Jewish song in New York, and even in the moaning of the waves in Haifa harbor. Admittedly, Feffer adds to all these also his adulation of Marx, Stalin, Sverdlov, and Kaganovich (Stalin's friends), but this appears to be no more than mere lip service, for behind all these verbal gyrations one may easily discern whither the new Feffer might be bound if he were really to give his feelings free rein; thus, "More than gold, I have cherished the stubborn fortitude of my ancestors; neither Pharaoh nor Haman, neither Titus nor the auto-da-fés of Madrid have crushed the eternity of Israel — nor will Hitler and the edicts of Berlin."

In "Shades of the Warsaw Ghetto," the poet puts a question that would have been inconceivable in his earlier poetry: "Lord of Creation! Is it here that Jews wove the golden thread of generations?" He associates the heroism of the ghetto fighters with the eve of Passover, the Feast of Freedom, to which he gives the Hebrew calendar date of "the night of the fourteenth of Nissan." He depicts the *seder* in detail and with pronounced feeling: the festive table, the goblets, the plates inscribed *kasher le-Pessach,* the leather-bound prayer books. He emphasizes the special contemporary significance of the passage "We were once slaves . . ." and affirms that the Nazi gallows await all Jews without distinction — rabbi and bathhouse attendant, rich man and pauper. Tenderly he now recalls the "*tefillim* bag" concealing arms with which thirteen-year-olds dealt death to their enemies;

the confessional prayer which the martyrs never completed; a page from an old *haggada,* swirled by the wind — which moans "Pour down thy wrath . . ." — together with resistance fighters' letters; a desecrated fragment of a scroll of the law.

The new Feffer now reveres the memory of his grandfather and great-grandfather, from whom he has inherited his "proud conscience."

Perets Markish, born in 1895, was prone by nature to be fired by revolutionary slogans, without analyzing their purport. A man of stormy temperament, who instinctively loathed all that was static and conventional, he was enchanted by the very idea of launching an assault against the fortress of conservatism — a predisposition manifested also in the titles he gave his collections of poems, titles like *Stam* [Just Like That] or *Hefker* [Carefree]. He loved ferment for its own sake, constant innovation, the tension of the unknown. An impulsive poet, he eagerly grasps at every new message: "I seize on all that comes my way. . . . I lie abandoned on the ways, the paths of dawn"; "Unknowing if I am at home or in foreign parts — I run! . . . I belong to no one, I am carefree, without beginning, without end." He compares himself to a bursting cloud, to a heavy downpour that rains down on his own head. He strives to reach no shore, content to plunge along with the current. It is not the objective that is important, but the march of present time, or as he puts it: "My name is Now."

Yet with all his abandonment, his intoxication with all that is new, his love of the untrammeled, Markish nevertheless appears at times to be chastened by ambivalence, unable to discard his deep roots in Jewish life and tradition: his early education in the *cheder,* his experiences as a choirboy in the Berdichev synagogue. Prominent among his earlier work is the poem "*Die Kupeh*" (The Heap — a popular appellation given to the Ukraine pogroms of the late 1920's, i.e. the "heaps of slain"). Here he voices a bitter cry of protest and mourning: "For you, the slain of the Ukraine that fill the land, the slaughtered that lie in a heap in Horodishch on the Dnieper's banks — I say *Kaddish!*"[28]

Though fired with enthusiasm by revolutionary slogans, Markish might nevertheless be said to have uprooted himself from the soil of his native tradition not merely for the sake of giving vent to his rebellious spirit, but also out of deep faith that the revolution bore a message of a new world that would arise, and a message of redemption for the Jewish people. He was far from insensible to the sufferings, both physical and spiritual, that the new order was inflicting on the Jews, yet he believed that these were the temporary pains that inevitably accompany a serious surgical operation, or the throes of the birth of a new Jewry. Thus we see Markish consciously resigning himself to the lancet of revolution as it cuts into the living flesh of his people: "It may be that the stone feels pain when it is ground and honed and shaped. It may be that at every blow . . . there moans the primal helpless agony. Yet we, we alone, are ordained to allay that pain." It would appear, however, that the old traditions exercise an attraction that exceeds the bounds of reason, for the poet feels he must brace himself "to mar and sully the shriveled, parchment-yellow breasts of antiquity, that my lips may no more crave to touch them."

Settling in the USSR in 1928, Markish continued to be assailed by ambivalent emotions, as evidenced by the elegiac, even resigned, note that had crept into his pathos-charged poetry: "If you still have a shred of heart, silence it! If you would be silent, cry out unto death!" In time he was beset by mounting misgiving, for not only were his human and national expectations of the Soviet system gradually shattered in the face of the grim reality, but he also underwent a crisis as a creative writer. His work was widely acclaimed, admittedly, yet he found himself forced to moderate and even relinquish his tempestuous spirit. The Stalinist regime had no use for revolutionary visionaries, however stormy their temperament, and certainly not for men who struck out in search of new paths. He found himself constrained to repudiate his own ardor and bow his head to the yoke of orderliness and discipline. At first he might have found some outlet in romanticizing the new birth engendered by the revolution, but he was very soon reduced to patching up the lacerations in his soul by dint of shrewd rationalization: "Ah, my wise generation, my many-faceted age! How sweet is the burden — the burden of understanding you!" Having accepted this sweet burden, Markish did not have too far to go in order to sing paltry songs in praise of the regime and its ways, of Stalin, and so on. His ardor became mechanical, his joy declamatory, his conviction gave way to artificial confessions and breast-beating for his former erroneous course. Illustrative of this is his preface to the second volume of his *Collected Works* (1936), which reads like an abject confession:

> Most of the poems in this volume belong to different periods when my artistic and ideological patterns were being molded. They bear the mark of failures common to the whole of my generation of poets. They are, first and foremost, the failures of a cultural heritage from which we parted with difficulty, being called upon by the dictates of history to discard this national cultural burden in favor of the new socialist culture of the proletarian revolution. . . . Apart from this, we were lured away from our course by the relics of decadence, which inevitably engendered [in us] a neutral individualism. This was only one step removed from nationalistic narrow-sightedness.

There are many indications that Markish's spirit did not break all at once. That he was subjected to a prolonged downfall is attested to by the numerous harsh attacks aimed at him by reviewers who considered themselves custodians of the offical line. Already in the early 1930's, for example, when Markish had not a few "revolutionary works" to his credit, his critics reminded him that "in most of them there emerge nationalistic sentiments." The poems in which he depicted Eretz Israel landscapes or made Biblical allusions were branded as "appurtenances from the Zionist lexicon." He was charged with idealizing a life that was outmoded, reactionary, pious, patriarchal, whereas "Markish might have been expected finally to discard his former nationalistic idols." He was censured for his "benign" attitude towards his petit bourgeois characters from the small Jewish township; for the manner in which he depicts a group of Jews who happen to get together at an inn and "snatch" a communal prayer, or his description of a *seder* conducted in a regal manner; for the fact that, on the other hand, "we do not find a single line that would indicate the author's negative attitude to this patriarchalism."[29] He was severely condemned for manifesting compassion and pain at "the decline of the Jewish shopkeeper race" — a tenderness symptomatic of rotten liberalism, indicating that the author has not yet sufficiently assimilated the revolutionary ideology.[30]

These and similar criticisms had no small effect. In the latter part of the 1930's Markish's work suffered a perceptible decline in artistic quality. His writing became insipid, his plots watery. He gave in to the demands made of him in general, and in regard to Jewish themes in particular. Before long, in fact, he depicts as a "Shylock and venerable profiteer" a Caucasian Jew, enclosed in his ghetto, who is unable to break away from the traditions of his ancestors. In contrast, he writes glowingly of the neighboring Jewish *kolhoz* members in propagandist, un-Markish-like terms: "Only our Socialist Revolution, which has engraved 'Re-education' on its banner, could have succeeded in making useful men of this rabble of a thousand years." Of the chairmen of one such *kolhoz* he writes, that at the age of forty-two "the Revolution severed his 'glorious' lineage of penny-pinching petty shopkeepers with their hallowed *arshin* [lineal measure common in old Russia], which his forefathers seemed to have received together with the Torah on Mount Sinai and handed down from one generation to the other"; whereas now this former shopkeeper is become a working man, a farmer, possessed of a "new physique," who is happy with the produce of his fields and orchards, and who "takes particular pride in the fact that his pomegranates are sent to the Kremlin in Moscow." It is particularly distressing to see Markish resort to primitive abuse of religious symbols and values, which is not devoid of the hackneyed glorification of the pig.

The examples cited in the previous paragraph were taken from a collection of Markish's stories that appeared in 1939. We have already remarked, in the first chapter, on the profound shock experienced by the author at the beginning of World War II, culminating in the German invasion of the Soviet Union. This deepening sense of shock, coupled with the apparent change in the official line, swung the tenor of his writing onto a diametrically opposed tack. His Soviet patriotism, to be sure, becomes still more pronounced as he sings of blood-drenched Leningrad, of Kiev groaning under the conqueror's yoke, of war-ravaged Odessa and Sevastopol, of Mother-River Volga; but he also suprisingly exhorts, in the poem "To the Jewish Fighter": "Do not part from your rifle, Jewish soldier, just as your forefathers have never parted from the *Sefer Torah.*" He reminds the Jewish fighter of the Ten Commandments handed down on Mount Sinai, which have endowed the world with moral values, and which Jews still stand by, though their throats be butchered and their mouths incinerated.

Movingly, he tells of a whole Jewish community that is being herded to its death; of the old woman from Pervomaisk, with the gleam of Sabbath candlesticks peeping out of her bundle, who keeps asking, "Isn't it Friday, Sabbath eve, today?"; of the Hungarian Jew who keeps fingering his bundle every moment — he has been a wandering refugee for three years, but has always managed to keep his *tallit,* in which he wishes to be buried. On the brink of the death pit, he and other victims cover their heads with their *tallitot,* like *cohanim* blessing the congregation. In another poem, a Jewish wood engraver, wearing a *kittel* and *tallit,* kills two Germans on the eve of the Day of Atonement, just before the *Kol Nidre* prayer.

In the person of Dr. Kagan, and other characters, the poet presents not only the concept of Jewish unity that transcends territorial boundaries, but also the specific fate of the Jewish people down the ages (a fate, incidentally, against which Zionism has rebelled). During the fifty-six years of his life, Kagan has been a trespasser, as it were, "the land all around him — an illicit homeland. . . . Nowhere has he been at home, nowhere has he confidently set his foot." Kagan-Markish ponders the enigma of his people: "How grew such a tree, whose every branch is of a different land, whose every bough speaks another tongue and drinks a different sap?" He seems to throw off all restraint in expressing his inmost feelings, in depicting the Jew as a man doomed to flit stealthily from one land to the other, an unwelcome guest at the table of strangers, who pays with his heart in return for a night's lodging, and is led to the death pit when he gazes at the stars.

The change that occurred in Markish's writing is prominently reflected in his four-volume epic *War,* containing over twenty thousand lines of poetry, which was published some three years after the war ended. Significant parts of this work are actually variations on the themes of poems he had written previously. The genre and form of *War* are extremely difficult to classify. In part it is a sweeping epic that tells of what happened to Jews in different parts of the country, describes different frontline battles, camps and ghettos, Nazi atrocities and partisan revolts, depicts the defense of Moscow and Stalingrad, the Red Army's victory march through Berlin, and other episodes. The popular style at times makes way for a style that is charged with pathos, quietly elegiac or rhetorical. The poetry abounds in rational analyses, emotional moods, philosophical questioning, descriptions of the horrors of war, scenes of destruction and heroism, unanswerable questions, exchange of views between the different characters and their unspoken reflections on such matters as the homeland, the revolution, the course of their lives.

The principal characters in *War* are a young Jew, Gur-Aryeh,* and Alexei Sadovsky, a young Russian officer who is an agronomist in civilian life. Their meetings and conversations are the principal media through which Markish conveys his thoughts and experiences. Despite the two men's friendship and mutual understanding, their respective fates and outlooks differ significantly. Gur-Aryeh, who somehow manages to escape from the butchery at Babi Yar, wonders: "Is there a road that leads away from the grave?" He meets Sadovsky, and when the latter asks him who he is, he replies: "I belong to a race that possibly is now extinct." Immediately after the war they both visit Babi Yar at Gur-Aryeh's suggestion to his "Comrade Commander": "I want to take you where the earth heaved for seven days over the grave of those buried alive . . . it still heaves, the earth, and will never be still." Gur-Aryeh explains to his companion, or possibly to himself, why the Jews had let themselves be led unresistingly to the slaughter: long before that, he asserts, they had already died of humiliation and anguish. The Nazis had drained their souls, turned them into kneaded clay, so that many of them looked forward to the salvation of death, while others, who did try to escape, were mowed down by heavy fire. Gur-Aryeh also mentions the fact that "the local toadies [collaborators] led the way to the death pits."

Sadovsky and Gur-Aryeh, who become close friends, are utterly different in character and temperament. The former's reactions are natural and straightforward. The latter is filled with self-questioning, must probe into the reason of his existence, his citizenship, the war he is fighting. Sadovsky is firmly rooted in his native soil: one hundred and fifty years ago one of his ancestors fell defending Moscow; one

* Hebrew: lion's whelp. The name, a metonym for Judah (The Lion of Judah), is significant.

hundred years ago an ancestor of his fought at Sevastopol; his family fought at Port Arthur in Manchuria fifty years ago; and now he himself is fighting in his country's war. Gur-Aryeh, no less a brave fighter, muses on the meaning of things. He wonders, for example, about the fate of his people — "a tenant among the nations." When he comes upon a ruined synagogue, he compares the fate of the Jews with that of the stork in the fable, which extracted the bone lodged in the wolf's throat only to be devoured for its pains; this is so, he concludes, not only because the wolf is wolfish by nature, but also because the stork has no talons.

The epic abounds in religious symbolism and Biblical metaphor. At Babi Yar a Sabbath candlestick, handed down from one generation to the other and pervaded by age-old anguish, lies discarded on the ground. Gur-Aryeh conjures up a distant memory of stories the old folk used to tell of the dead leaving their graves at night to recite the New Moon Blessing. He recalls Ezekiel's vision of the dry bones that come to life. There are references to Daniel in the lions' den, the parting of the Red Sea, Elijah's miracles, the starlit dew of the Song of Songs, Gideon by the Stream of Harod. Jews walk to their mass graves carrying bundles filled with "four thousand years of prophecy, of tears, of sad striving, of revelation and of joy, of *galut,* of compassion." In the devastated synagogue, the "Gates of God" of the Holy Ark lie open, and there is the odor of charred sacred scrolls and fragments of holy writings. "There is not a living soul in this ruin," Gur-Aryeh reflects, "yet what a fullness presses down from the walls." From all sides there echo in his ears the sounds of prayers offered up by the congregation before they were slaughtered.

Markish's *War* is not devoid of praise for the Soviet regime, for Stalin and the Russian people, nor is it sparing in its condemnation of the West for arming Hitler — and it is difficult to determine how much of this is sincere and how much is lip service. At all events, it may be assumed that while he was producing this work Markish was not free of the feeling that somebody was watching over his shoulder. According to one account, hundreds of lines which Markish had read out to a fellow writer and close friend were not included in the published version of *War:* "Each day the political line veered in a different direction, and his fear of this unclear situation forced Markish to strike out what he was not sure of, and substitute what the authorities might consider favorable."[31] Be this as it may, *War,* may well be regarded as a great Jewish literary work conceived under the stress of the Jewish national catastrophe.[32]

We shall conclude by quoting two poignant reminiscences that reaffirm Markish's change of heart induced by the Jewish wartime catastrophe. Bernard Mark recalls that at a memorial gathering held by Polish Jews in Moscow after the war, in memory of the millions of Polish Jewish martyrs, Markish "buried his face in his delicate fingers . . . the proud figure sagged, and from the eyes there burst a flood of tears. He wept over the nameless grave. Then he addressed the Jews who were returning to their burned-out homes in order to rebuild a Jewish life and continue to bear the Jewish message that Hitler and his accomplices had doomed to extinction."[33] When Itsik Feffer stated at this gathering that it demonstrated "the friendship of the Jewish peoples," Markish remonstrated that "there are no two Jewish peoples. The Jewish nation is one. Just as a heart cannot be cut up and divided, similarly one cannot split up the Jewish people into Polish Jews and Russian Jews. Everywhere, we are and shall remain one entity."[34]

Leib Kvitko was born on December 31, 1893, and was already deeply imbued with Jewish life and culture by the time he embarked on his literary career. The new Soviet order understandably filled him with misgivings and induced a great deal of soul-searching. He left Kiev for Berlin, where in 1923 he published a book of poems entitled *1919.* Most of these poems voice the shattering of the poet's world following the Ukrainian pogroms. In his preface to this volume, Kvitko points out what "my Ukraine" had meant to him: "a limb of Great Russia," where he had heard and seen the gigantic march of the revolution and its hosts, who with song on their lips and ardent faith in their hearts had "gone forward to liberate not only our enslaved land, but an entire world." Yet it was during those momentous, fateful days that the poet had been forced to stand face to face with "Petlura's people," to see the slaughter perpetrated by rioting bands. These scenes, especially the harrowing sight of butchered Jewish children and of "orphans with heads proudly erect," continued to haunt Kvitko for many years. He returned to the Soviet Union and settled in Kharkov, presumably prompted by the fact that the Soviet regime was out to suppress those "rioting bands."

As a poet, Kvitko is not vociferous by nature. His early poems show self-restraint, for all that they abound in thought and feeling. Yet in time his work becomes increasingly pervaded by a militant note, subordinating his "Incidental Desires" — the title of one of his poems. He still attempts to rebel against the Party bureaucracy that has set itself up as a watchdog of the "integrity" of Soviet Yiddish literature, but this attempt is harshly condemned as scurrilous anti-Soviet slander. Finally, Kvitko subsides into the hackneyed groove: writing of the 1930's shows him to have joined the general chorus of abuse hurled at the spies and traitors and assassins — "Trample on them, the vermin!" he fulminates. "Good housewives begrudge the honest bread that falls into their verminous mouths!"

Kvitko established his reputation, particularly as a writer of children's stories. His works were translated into many languages, excerpts were included in Russian and other text books, and the sale of his books was considered "astronomical" for a Yiddish writer. Persons who knew him claim that he came to support the Soviet system wholeheartedly, rather than under constraint.[35] Hence, Jewish motifs grew rarer in his writing, which at all events was devoid of anything that might smack of "nationalism."

It may well be that just because Kvitko — both as a Jew and a Soviet citizen — was so firmly convinced of the justice of the system, that his spiritual anguish was all the deeper when he came up against wartime manifestations of anti-Semitism on the part of the authorities and the machinery of the Party, of which he was a member.[36]

Kvitko's resurgence of Jewish feeling during and after the war, however, stems chiefly from his horror at the Nazi slaughter. As in the work of other Jewish writers, we now find him pointedly employing Jewish traditional symbols and metaphors. His Jewish fighter pilot swoops down from the sky to destroy Haman; the pilot comes from Berdichev, and the author is at great pains to stress this town's distinction as a Hassidic and Jewish cultural stronghold. His Jewish submarine captain, Yitzhak Kobo, performs his duty (*avodah** — which also has the connotation of "divine service") with religious fervor. In enumerating the qualities of another Jewish submarine captain, Yisrael Fisanavich, the author does not fail to mention that he attended a Jewish school. Ettele, the cobbler's daughter, has been torn away from her dolls at the age of eight to bear on her shoulders "the ancient burden of her people." Hunted by the ferocious (Nazi) beasts, she seeks in her dreams some resting place, like the dove that was sent forth from Noah's ark; the girl's beauty is described in terms of the Song of Songs, yet the look in her eyes seems to say "All is Vanity." When the wife of Hirsch the blacksmith gives birth to twins, the poet rejoices that "the Jews now have two more sons to reinforce their numbers."

David Hofstein, born in 1889, began to figure prominently in Soviet Yiddish literature immediately after the October Revolution. His poetry, which is lyrical, picturesque and rich in imagery, is also charged with philosophical elements. His pre-World War I writing, chiefly in Hebrew and Russian, shows him to have been richly imbued with Jewish and universal culture at the time of the revolution. From the inception of the new regime, however, his work shows a conflict, as he puts it, between "love for what is breaking through and emerging, and sorrow at what has declined." His enthusiasm for the new reality is genuine and profound: "to walk along a broad, new, untrodden path"; yet he is unable to discard his nostalgia for the evanescing past. He declares with pathos, "We walk at the head of your columns, forward-marching humanity"; yet his poetry is charged at the same time with elegiac overtones. The revolution had fired his zeal and captivated his spirit, but had failed to subordinate all his moods and conflicts to its "whims." This conflict breached his spiritual world already in the early 1920's, and he put his name to a memorandum drawn up by a group of Soviet intellectuals protesting against the suppression of Hebrew in the Soviet Union — a deviation that was condemned by the Yevesektzia. This engendered an atmosphere of

* Hebrew-Yiddish term applied to an impressive section of the Day of Atonement prayers recounting the Temple sacrificial service and the ritual officiation of the high priest on that day.

ostracism, presumably one of the reasons that induced him to leave Russia for Palestine, where he lived for several years and published a few Hebrew poems. Subsequently he returned to Russia. The reasons for this are not fully clear: he might have found it difficult to adjust himself in Palestine from the material or spiritual points of view; he might have been overwhelmed by nostalgia for his childhood scenes and native tongue; or he might have been conscious-stricken for having left his children in the USSR. At all events, after his return his literary ability again became manifest and was acclaimed, though his "Hebrew and Palestine deviations" continued to haunt him like a persistent shadow, which he strove hard to get rid of. In a poem he published in 1926, shortly after his return to the Soviet Union, we find what seems like a tragic premonition of his own end: "The ruler of the great land, he is almighty and all-powerful . . . the choice of sacrificial victims lies in his hand. . . . Let us, then, close our ranks, silently and gravely bow our heads, and raise our hands and bravely swear allegiance to the ruler of the great land, to hearken and obey."

Henceforth, the poet forces himself to discard his reflective nature and assume "an everyday lightheartedness, to drive away all cries of woe." More concretely, in the specific Jewish sphere, he maintains: "What if a small child once learnt a verse from the Book of Job? . . . This is no time to bewail the past." He refers to Moscow as the "Third Rome." His poetry reechoes with the whistle of trains, the vibration of railway lines, the humming of electric wires. Nonetheless, his writing is constantly under critical scrutiny. Thus in 1934, for instance, he is charged with having written several poems that adopt outworn attitudes; with the fact that most of his associations, as an "associative poet," are taken from the ancient Jewish culture, and that they have occasionally served "nationalistic ends."[37] In time, Hofstein's creative art gradually becomes impoverished. His fine sensitivity gives way to vulgarity, to such officially prompted hackneyed phrasing as: "A new humanity, creative and eager, its vanguard is the worker, and in the vanguard's front line — the Communist Party, and the Party is led, as the whole world knows, by that man called Stalin."

Even during the wartime period Hofstein does not relax his wary attitude, born of habit and constant apprehensiveness. Nevertheless, he cannot but be stirred by the rivers of Jewish blood, and he invokes vengeance, devoid of "Jewish sympathy." Moreover, he has recourse to associations "taken from the ancient Jewish culture," as when he exhorts: "Forget not the lamentation of Mother Rachel at Ramah." According to one account, he wrote "for himself" (that is, not for publication) a series of wartime poems on the Jewish catastrophe, voicing his horror at the acts perpetrated against Jews by Soviet (and especially Ukrainian) nationals.[38] His anguish is intensified by sharp pangs of conscience at the false note that he allowed to intrude into his own prewar poetry, and he tries to find some mitigating justification for himself and other Yiddish writers: "Do not bear down hard on us. No one knows what we went through. It is altogether a miracle that we somehow preserved our human image."[39]

It appears that the birth of Israel caught Hofstein off his guard, or unable to distinguish between what was a passing phase in Soviet policy (of supporting Israel) and what was the permanent official line. No sooner was the establishment of the state declared than he cabled the vice-president of the Ukrainian Academy of Sciences, suggesting that a chair of Hebrew be set up at its Department of Jewish Culture — so firm was his conviction that this turning point in Jewish history had opened a new chapter also in the history of Soviet Jewry.[40]

Hofstein's frame of mind in those days is most convincingly borne out in one of his poems, whose apparent obscurities are easily unraveled. We quote several excerpts:

> Yes, I am proud of belonging to a nation that grows not weary, that builds and believes. In order to achieve immortality, one does not necessarily have first to die! . . . And again there separates, crumbles, and is dispersed what was once united. Yet my people still believes that though it has been ordained to be everywhere — does that mean nowhere? Every place has its somewhere! Be it in the center of the world! . . . That somewhere that all the world remembers; but more than all the world, my people remembers, whether in castle or in hovel, wherever it may be. . . . And I am proud to belong to such a people.

Der Nister* was the pseudonym of Pinhas Kahananovitz, born in 1884, an unusual figure in Soviet Yiddish literature. Embarking on

* "The Hidden One." This has distinct esoteric associations with Jewish mysticism.

his literary course at the beginning of the century, his work soon showed maturity and depth of perception, and was imbued with mysticism. Hence, presumably, his pen name, which in time became largely indicative also of his behavior. As his literary ability achieved prominence, however, he proved his possession of another capacity under the Soviet regime — the capacity for remaining silent: for years he did not publish a single line. Amidst the prevailing atmosphere where Jewish writers vied with one another in praising the system and denigrating things Jewish, it must have required great spiritual strength on the part of a writer to abstain from joining in the general chorus. Meanwhile, the critics proceeded to heap censure on the works he had previously published, charging him with "speaking through closed lips, in veiled hints and secret allusions" — a way of writing, they claimed, that enabled him to cover up both his "backward and forward steps" and conceal all his "petit bourgeois zigzagging and wavering irresolution in regard to the revolution."[41]

This is not meant to suggest that Der Nister was unmoved by the great progress achieved in the Soviet Union. In his novel *Capital Cities* (1934) he depicts, with manifestly warm admiration, the vast socialist reconstruction projects accomplished in Kharkov, Leningrad, and Moscow. Yet at the same time he shows that a Soviet Jewish citizen may praise his country without necessarily befouling the wellsprings of his Jewish origins.

In 1939, Der Nister began to publish his historical novel of Jewish life, *House of Mashber,* the first volume of which appeared in Moscow in 1939, and the second in New York in 1948, printed from a manuscript which the author had sent there.[42] This work was never completed, however. Critics are convinced that the town of N., described in minute detail in *House of Mashber,* is none other than Berdichev. Be this as it may, the novel is eminently a Jewish saga, weaving a broad historical pattern of Jewish life, social and interpersonal relations, the struggle for existence, and the quest for spiritual deliverance, and portraying a wide array of characters set in the previous century. The author asserts that he has kindled, "here in the heart of the marketplace, a memorial candle that burns silently in memory of the soul of the marketplace." This does not necessarily imply that he would like to bring that Jewish market back to life, but there is no doubt of his yearning for that which is gone by, never to return. Confronted by what must have appeared to him to be a Jewish spiritual vacuum, Der Nister warmly evokes the generations-old accumulation of Jewish life and culture, and the way in which he does so leaves no doubt whatsoever as to where his own sympathies lie.

In his wartime and postwar writing, Der Nister reveals even more of his true self. In a series of stories depicting Jewish life in occupied Poland, he presents in a warm light Jews of various social strata, endowing them with noble human and Jewish attributes, which seem to sparkle with a holy radiance amidst the sea of evil and defilement. A pious Jewish widow clutches her silver Sabbath candlesticks as she walks to her death together with the rest of the congregation. In her dire anguish she has almost forgotten that it is Friday, Sabbath eve, but on the brink of the death pit she raises her eyes and enjoins her sisters in calamity to repeat after her the benediction: "Blessed art thou, O Lord our God, King of the Universe, who has sanctified us by thy commandments, and commanded us to kindle the Sabbath light."

In another story we meet Rabbi Aaron Moneses, who lives in a spiritual world and scrupulously observes every religious precept, and his grandson Itsikel — a confirmed Communist who rebels against both God and the prevailing order of things. They represent two worlds that are diametrically opposed, yet under the stress of adversity there is harmony between them. In the end, they are both hanged at the same time by the Nazis, the rabbi clasping a *Sefer Torah* to his breast, and his grandson clutching a portrait of Lenin. The Nazi hangman tries to induce the rabbi to spit at the portrait, and Itsikel to spit at the sacred scroll, but both refuse. The author erects a joint monument, in traditional Hebrew wording, in their memory.

Another story, "Regrowth" (whose title speaks for itself), is of special interest. It tells of a Jewish widow and widower — "two half families" — who occupy adjoining flats in a Moscow tenement house. The widower's son has been killed at the front. The widow's daughter, a nurse, was killed when the hospital she worked at was bombed. The bereaved father and mother are drawn closer to one another, though not only because of their common fate, but also "against the background of a more transcendental community of interest . . . the fate of the community as a whole, from which they felt they had too long dissociated themselves." This dissociation from, and subsequent reunion with, their people, in fact form the central theme of the story, several excerpts from which are worth quoting. The author writes of Dr. Zemelman (the widower): "Estranged as he had been from his community for many years, without the least contact, nevertheless when the great cloud of destruction loomed over this community, he began to feel himself very closely associated with it and its destruction. This must have occurred not only to people of the type of Dr. Zemelman, but also to many others who had formerly stood aloof. . . . He felt some ancient hidden sense of his origin surge up inside him, like the instinct of sheep which in time of danger huddle together for protection." Dr. Zemelman, who had long been so completely cut off from his community as to forget his origin, wonders that it should now occur to him to identify himself with "a fountainhead he had never had recurse to, and which now began to fill him with a sense of guilt." His dead son appears in his dreams to reproach him for his repudiation of this fountainhead, and other ghosts, too, admonish him for breaking loose from the "Jewish harness." He dreams of the death pit, on whose brink stand an old couple dressed in Oriental garments. Intuitively, he feels he recognizes them as the ancestors of the people to which the new martyrs belong — "Say, an Abraham and Sarah." A host of childhood memories surge up in his mind: his grandfather and grandmother poring over the ancient books "on the day they mourned the Destruction [of Jerusalem]." Finally, Dr. Zemelman, alone in his flat in the evening, "would turn to the Book of Books that had long been hidden away in a corner of his bookcase," searching for some reassociation with his origins, with his people throughout the distant generations, as far back as the early Patriarchs. Later in the story Dr. Zemelman adopts a son, and the widow likewise adopts a daughter — both refugees who have survived the holocaust. The foster-parents urge the youngsters to speak Yiddish again, a language they have almost forgotten. When the young people fall in love, their foster-parents regard this as being more than an ordinary attachment between boy and girl; it is a union between members of the same nation, destined to perpetuate its existence, necessitated by nature and by fate. Dr. Zemelman and Mrs. Zaits (the widow) contemplate marriage, too, both out of human and practical considerations, and also in answer to some "hidden command" that enjoins regrowth, despite the adversity "that has affected all, and particularly ourselves."[43]

"Flora," another of Der Nister's highly illuminating stories, is in a vein similar to that of "Regrowth." Flora is a Jewish girl whose father, a highly respected member of the community in a large Polish town, committed suicide when arrested by the Germans. The girl makes her way to the Soviet Union, where she joins the partisans. The story takes us back to the time when Flora has just completed her studies at school. Her father takes out from his jewel chest an "antique, finely wrought gold ring, inlaid with a precious stone shaped like a Star of David," which has been a familiy heirloom for generations. He says to her: "Maybe this [ring] is rather too romantic, but never mind. Take it and wear it in good health and with honor, as did your grandparents further back than I can remember." On this occasion the father also announces that he is betrothing his daughter "to her past." Flora recalls in her diary (much of the story is written in diary form) her "Hebrew teacher [she uses the Hebrew *moreh* in the original], who was specially brought over from Palestine to teach at our school." She describes him with sentimental, romantic innocence, noting the fact that he never parted from his Bible; each time he entered the classroom, he would hold out the Bible (which he invariably kept in his pocket) and say: "You see, children, more than our people have preserved this Book; this Book has preserved our people."

The author relates that he first made Flora's acquaintance on May 9, 1945, at a victory celebration held by a Jewish public institution that had been established during the war. Her beauty and deportment, her clothes and the way she danced charmed everybody present, who found it hard to believe that this girl had been a partisan fighter. Flora sat at the table (together with the Jewish commander of her underground unit) facing leading members of the Moscow Jewish community, headed by Rabbi Shirer (whose only son had been killed in combat). Flora was among those who addressed the gathering, and, the author notes, "when she saw herself surrounded by her own kinsmen, from whom she had been cut off for some time, she began to speak in her native Yiddish — a language she had grown out of the habit of using with the partisans in the forest. All those present felt proud both of her, and also of the fact that the nation's fountain-head had not run dry." After recounting several episodes about the partisans' operations and life in the ghetto, Flora held up her glittering gold ring and addressed the women thus: "My sisters, this is a heir-loom I received from my father, who perished. In giving it to me he betrothed me to our past, and this past now enjoins us to establish a generation worthy of continuing the thread of the eternity of our existence as a nation." Her audience was profoundly stirred, and when Rabbi Shirer rose to speak, he was so moved that he could only quote the Scriptural blessing (Genesis, 24:60): ". . . Our sister, be thou the mother of thousands of ten thousands!", to the loud applause of the gathering.[44]

In 1944, Der Nister published in Moscow an article entitled "Hate" (for the Nazi butchers), wherein he reports a conversation he had with sixteen-year-old Shloimke Olitsky, a Jewish partisan from Poland, sole surviving member of his family. The boy, as depicted by the author, has been through experiences that have given him the outlook of an old man. He bears on his young shoulders the yoke of suffering that "no Jeremiah, no testimony to the manifold destructions of our long-suffering people is able to lament." Yet the author exhorts Shloimke, and himself as well, to find consolation in the inevitable downfall of the enemy and in the better days that are sure to follow — in a flight of fancy that is nevertheless firmly based on reality he pronounces: "And it shall be on that day — one yearns to use the noble language of the Prophets — that the kingdom of wickedness shall perish . . . and then you, Shloimke, the wounded child of our nation, shall discard your Methuselah's years and be young again. . . . Then shall we see you among those who rebuild the ruins on our Mount [Zion], where jackals have prowled not long since. We shall see you fetching bricks and mortar to rebuild the nation, which we shall be proud of, as all men are proud of all reconstructed buildings. And we, the gray-haired old ones, shall help in this building work as well as we can, and lend a hand. And when our strength should fail us, we shall stand and watch, and our lips shall murmur a blessing:

And it shall come about on that day, a day of redemption, and peace on earth, and understanding among nations."

It may be gathered from their dialogue that Shloimke has revealed to the author his intention to emigrate to Palestine, and this has prompted Der Nister to convey his inmost feelings — both overtly and by allusion — on the subject of the Jewish renaissance in the ancient homeland.[45]

A further indication of Der Nister's cast of soul is to be found in his account of his journey to Birobidzhan in 1947, on a train conveying Jewish settlers to the autonomous province. He considers the time ripe for a large-scale resettlement project in Birobidzhan — both from the objective standpoint, since the state is now able, after the victory, to give the matter the necessary attention, and also from the subjective aspect, "since the Jewish masses have recently received such a dire historical warning and such ominous danger signals that it has become of vital urgency to consider 'the question of consolidation.' " His descriptions of the passengers show his deep attachment for popular Jewish traits and way of life. He is profoundly struck, in particular, by the typically Jewish features of the children: in the innocent face of one child he discerns traces of an ancient, two-thousand-year-old prototype; the eyes of another child suggest a sun-scorched desert somewhere in the Middle East, or central Asia, or even further away. These children inspire faith that "the last line of our life's account has not yet been summed up, that our fountainsprings have not run dry." He also describes a wedding held in one of the wagons of the immigrant train. The marriage is perforce solemnized by a *shochet* — the only clergyman available among the passengers — and nobody can produce a wedding ring, everything having been looted by the Germans. But, as one Jewish passenger puts it, the wedding ceremony is conducted "in poverty but with joy . . . we weep and dance at the marriage of a son and daughter of our people which has almost perished, the son and daughter of a nation with such a power of survival that it has always emerged alive from all its hells and catastrophes." The same Jew, when he drinks to the author's health, pronounces: "May the House of Israel be built up [this is reproduced in the Hebrew original], may a home be rebuilt for our people, and for our children and children's children."[46]

Shmuel Halkin was born in 1897, like Der Nister. He is one of the few Jewish authors in the Soviet Union who was not swept up in the general wave of decrying Jewish national tradition and of self-abasement. The blaring of trumpets and beating of drums that characterized the writing of his fellow authors were unable to drown the soft lyricism of his poetry of the 1920's and 1930's. Many of his poems of those years, in fact, were like solitary islands of pure feeling in a tumultuous sea of vociferation. This does not mean that he stood aloof from the mainstream of events in the Soviet Union, or refrained from lauding the regime and its leaders, nor can it be stated that this was mere lip service. Yet it was not in this that Shmuel Halkin revealed his true self. Throughout the vacillations of the Soviet order and the different phases of his own writing Halkin remained essentially a sensitive, subtly expressive poet. What is particularly noteworthy is the fact that he never spurned Judaism and its traditions. For many years he remained inspired by the spirit of *Habad hassidism* that had pervaded his father's house — a spirit that continued to permeate his poetry — and he did not hasten, like many of his contemporaries, to throw his *tallit* and *tefillim* overboard.

A few illustrations will suffice in order to prove that Halkin never allowed his revolutionary convictions to override and stifle his Jewish feelings. In his poem, "Grandfather's Goblet," a Jewish workman opens up his heart: "The First of May — that's my holiday, of course. But there's something that troubles me: the festive table, the white cloth that covers the swelling *halot* [Sabbath loaves], and the hymns — all that hurts. What crime is it? Where's the disloyalty? Why shouldn't my Marat [his son] know that he once had a grandfather who was named Reb Motele? That there was such a Jew who lived in this world and harmed nobody? What crime is it? Where's the disloyalty?" In another poem, "To the Newborn Infant," Halkin reveals a soul torn between yearning for universal deliverance and apprehension for his nation's survival: "Blessings on the newborn infant: may he imbibe with his mother's milk the thirst to bring light to humanity, but that this light shine also on his people. And when a new star is revealed unto the world, let not the darkness thicken around his people."

It was only natural that Halkin thereby rendered himself a clear target for harsh literary and political censure. And indeed, his poetry was criticized for its pervasive "nationalism and petit bourgeois pessimism," for being permeated by the "burdensome heritage" of an outworn world order, and similar lapses. But though he could hardly ignore such charges completely, he did not readily allow his poetry to lapse into the hackneyed groove. It is not surprising, therefore, that towards the end of the 1930's he seized upon the opportunity presented by the change in the dominant Soviet historiosophic concept in order to give expression again to his national Jewish feelings. These are particularly prominent in his dramatic poem "Bar-Cochba" (1939), which is not devoid, however, of the said historiosophic concept. In this poem, Halkin brings out in sharp relief the contrast between Bar-Cochba and Rabbi Akiva, the commander and the spiritual leader of the revolt against Rome, on the one hand, and the influential wealthy class that stood aloof from the rising or actively opposed it, on the other. What is astounding about this poem is the fact that a Soviet Jewish author should have recourse to Jewish figures from the distant past, and his very boldness in personifying the notions of national integrity and social justice through the medium of sages and freedom fighters of ancient times. One cannot but be stirred by the ardor of the Jewish patriotism expressed, for instance, in the words of Rabbi Akiva: "Whoever loses the way to his nation, whoever shuts his eyes to the splendor of his nation — his memory shall sink into everlasting oblivion."

In view of the foregoing, one cannot point to any specific change in Halkin's writing induced by the Jewish catastrophe. For him, Jewish traditional and sacred symbols were not analogous to a loss restored, as was the case with other Soviet Jewish writers. His mourning for the Jewish holocaust, too, is less "sensational," more restrained and quietly lyrical than that of his fellow writers, though its inner forcefulness is in no way less pronounced. Of a townlet that has been wiped off the face of the earth, the poet writes, only the stab of a bayonet has remained, a stab that is all his own. His poem "Deep Pits, Reddened Clay" evokes an anguished memory of "a house that once belonged to me," and conveys a restrained hope that times and fortunes will change, and that next to the deep, full pits, next to the

frolic. His play *For Life and Unto Death* depicts a ghetto rising in a Polish town. The original title, *Ghettograd,* was obviously an allusion to the defense of Stalingrad. Noteworthy among the elements of the plot is the emphasis laid on the manner in which various Jewish groups — Communists, Zionists, Hassidim, and so forth — all rallied round the common cause of the underground struggle against the Nazi conquerors.[47]

Itsik Kipnis, born in 1896, conveys the mood induced by the Jewish catastrophe in his article "Babi Yar," published on the occasion of September 29, 1944, the third anniversary of the terrible butchery of the Jews in his native town of Kiev. "Let us revisit that place on foot," he enjoins, "as our brethren went there." He alludes to the specific Jewish wound, against the background of the indifference — or what is worse, the share — of various local elements in causing this wound. "Go to Babi Yar on foot," he repeats, "and not by tram," for the latter is pervaded by an everyday atmosphere that is too stifling to bear, and "an alien look may unwittingly coarsely abrade my wound. Yes, coarsely, for the agony is great, and the wound has not yet healed." Writing of the sad, quiet return to the deserted hearth and home, he asserts: "There are certain wrongs suffered at the hands of people on the inside that should not be bruited about, that should be settled quietly as matters that must remain amongst ourselves." He describes in retrospect the people carrying their bundles as they walked to the valley of slaughter. They left their mothers' candlesticks behind, for they were too heavy to carry, but they took with them "their ancient, little yellow goblets, handed down to them as heirlooms." On the anniversary of the slaughter, a group of mourning survivors gathers near the huge mass grave. But amidst the lamentation a consoling note is heard: "A people, half and three-quarters of which has been annihilated, is like a globule of mercury. Wrench half of it away, and the other half will become rounded and be whole again. . . . Let us therefore rise from the ground, let us straighten up. . . . Jews, dear brothers, let us rise from the ground, shake off the dust, and glow in the splendid light that

in his story "Bluntly, Without Reckonings." This is about a kind-hearted Ukrainian woman who, at great personal risk, saves a Jewish boy and girl at the time of the German occupation and lavishes so much tenderness and motherly love on them, that they become part of the family and are totally assimilated to their environment, losing all trace of their Jewishness. The author, while lauding the kindness of this noble-hearted woman, also voices regret at the fact that these children will never return to their Jewish origins. He gives his pen free rein on this score: "In recent years I have become most jealous; I am zealous to preserve what has survived and remained whole. When I see a pretty young Jewish girl-student, a well-built, brave soldier, an academician, or just an ordinary Jew — I yearn to hear them speak Yiddish to me." He expresses a further wish that "All Jews who now walk victoriously in the streets of Berlin should wear on their chests, next to their medals and decorations, also a little Star of David. He [Hitler] wanted all to see the Jew tortured, abused, and spat upon. Now I wish all to see that I am a Jew, and that my Jewish pride and honor is not one whit less than that of all other freedom-loving citizens."

This story was first published in *Einikeit* in Moscow, but not before certain "nationalistic" and "chauvinistic" passages (like the reference to the Star of David) had been expunged by the editors. Kipnis, however, added to his crimes by sending his uncensored story to a Jewish newspaper in Poland, which reproduced it in full.[49]

Kipnis was subjected to a hail of criticism and condemnation on the part of his Jewish fellow writers, the intensity of this attack showing every indication of an organized "campaign." Nor is there any doubt of the alarm that overwhelmed Jewish literary circles, which went to great pains to dissociate themselves from Kipnis and what he had written. His critics asserted that "only a nationalist could have drawn a parallel between Soviet orders and medals, which are insignia of honor, glory, and heroism, and . . . a Star of David"; that "Jewish combatants will certainly reject the decoration offered by Kipnis";[50] that Kipnis had "ignored the fact that the Star of David has long been the badge of political belligerent Zionism, a movement we hate for its essentially bourgeois and anti-Soviet objectives";[51] that though Kipnis had been warned more than once, "he has regrettably refused to learn a lesson. Not only has he permitted himself to ignore criticism, but he has persisted in committing more grievous errors."[52] In a transparent bid to cleanse Soviet Jewish literature of the stain of Kipnis, one critic remarks that the said story had not been presented (in full) to the Soviet reader, "who would certainly have rejected it in an appropriate manner," and expressed confidence that "Polish Jews, too, will be duly wary" (of the chauvinistic ideas contained in the unexpurgated version).[53] It may be added that Kipnis's critics seized this oportunity to impeach him with his past nationalistic sins, such as that of his "Months and Days";[54] in this story, published in 1926, Kipnis describes the 1919 pogroms in his native town of Sloveshnye, when his Ukrainian townsmen butchered scores of Jews, including the family of his first wife.

The stifling of Jewish culture in the Soviet Union and the physical liquidation of many of its exponents and moving spirits will be the subject of a separate chapter. We shall merely point out at this stage that it was not long before Itsik Kipnis's accusers were thrown into prison together with him. All their desperate attempts to show implicit adherence to the old-new line, to purge themselves of un-Soviet impurities, had not availed them, and certainly not their prewar righteousness, their boundless praise for the regime and its leaders, and their abuse of the Jewish heritage. There came the day when the "measure of justice" — to use Bergelson's phrasing — was fully, ruthlessly, and inexorably meted out to Jewish culture in the Soviet Union, and "Filipov's sense of fairness" demanded that Soviet Yiddish writers "do not tangle with the revolution."

FOUR

The Rootless Cosmopolitans

The anti-Jewish campaign waged in the Soviet Union in the late 1940's and early 1950's, despite its specific character and form, was closely bound up with the general development of Soviet foreign relations and internal events after the war.

Hardly any time elapsed between Germany's defeat by the Allies and the upsurge of the cold war, interbloc suspicion and tension having come into evidence when World War II was in its final stages. Indeed, towards the end of the 1940's and at the beginning of the 1950's the view had become widespread in both camps that an armed conflict between them was a real possibility, at least, in the none too distant future. Some even felt that the world was on the brink of a blowup. As for the Soviet leadership, they were not finally and irrevocably committed to the prospect of the inevitability of a new war; ideas of coexistence had been voiced in Moscow even during Stalin's latter years, and these could hardly be regarded as merely propagandist slogans designed to mislead the West. Yet at the same time it was clear that Soviet domestic policy was actually adapting itself to the prospect of a conflict with the West as a very concrete possibility. In other words: though this conflict was not yet regarded as inevitable, it was nevertheless adapted and subjected to a brink-of-war outlook.

What is chiefly relevant to our subject as regards this outlook is not the military preparations, but rather the moral, spiritual, and political preparation of the Soviet people for the possibility of an interbloc conflict. The psychological warfare launched against the West assumed total proportions, leaving no room for any fine distinctions in appraising the enemy. The West must be shown up as the embodiment of all that was evil, rotten, and diabolical. The masses must be given the blackest picture of the West, and not one that might be arrived at by dint of selective criticism. Its image must be totally villainous, presenting an absolute contrast to the glorified self-image of the Soviet Union. Moreover, maligning of the West was applied retrospectively: the West had always been inferior to Russia in culture and scientific attainment.

The campaign against cosmopolitanism was one of the principal manifestations of the anti-West campaign, whose purpose was to instill loathing and hostility for the West — feelings that would bolster a militant spirit when the expected conflict came about. One of the criticisms leveled against the cosmopolitans was that they were not sufficiently imbued with, or did not show, a spirit of battle against Russia's former allies. With the Stalinization of east and central European countries, where Western influence was more in evidence, they too were incorporated into the ramified campaign of de-Westernization. It would appear that the mood in the whole of the Communist bloc was very soon adapted to Stalin's wartime premise that "one cannot defeat the enemy unless one has learned to hate him with one's full spiritual forces."

It was not long after the war that a popular old term, that had disappeared from the Soviet lexicon during the anti-German alliance, made its reappearance, namely "capitalist encirclement." Together with it there came back into use its permanent companion: the need for "vigilance" against the capitalist enemy. This vigilance was not only military or relating to security (against spies and saboteurs), but also *ideological;* it was directed against any vestiges of Western capitalist culture and art, regarded as instruments for disarming the Communist state and making Soviet citizens relax their alertness. The "kowtowing to the West" as reflected in the form and content of works of literature and art, or merely in praising the European and

American achievements, was regarded as heinous defeatism in time of "war."

Even for a totalitarian regime which controlled all propaganda and information media it was no easy task to vilify the West such a short time after the Soviet-West military alliance. There were many indications that to the Soviet masses — and to the artistic and intellectual circles among them — the wartime friendship with the West appeared to be not only an emergency expedient, but also an ideal for normal times. Both instinctively and rationally Soviet citizens were inclined to believe that the continuation of Soviet-West friendship would bring *them* a relaxation of the rigid regime. Though the Allied delay in opening a second front aroused some suspicion and resentment also among the Soviet people as a whole, the war had nevertheless made them genuinely sympathetic and grateful towards the West. It was this popular feeling, presumably, that prompted the authorities to intensify their anti-West campaign.

Zhdanovism was a kind of declaration of a state of war in the Soviet Union. It was not mere chance that the man from whose name the term was coined, Andrei Zhdanov, was both one of the leading Party spokesmen on the internal "cultural front," and also the principal Soviet speaker at the inaugural meeting of the Cominform (founded in September 1947).[1] And in this state of war, as in real war, one must need refrain from any praise of the enemy. In 1942, when Ilya Ehrenburg had sought to stress the greatness of the Russians, he found that this greatness resulted, among other things, from the fact that they had not set up a barrier between themselves and the rest of Europe, but had rather learned a great deal from Europe, just as they had exerted an influence over the continent. Ehrenburg did not fail to mention that Peter the Great had attended school in Holland, or remark on the influence of Voltaire and Hegel over Russian philosophers, Pushkin's love for foreign poets, the debt that the Decembrists owed the French Revolution, and even the benefits the Russian proletariat had derived from the experience gained by European workers' movements.[2] In the latter half of the Forties, however, such voices had to be silenced, in accordance with the rule prescribing that a new political climate entails new cultural tones. These tones were sounded by, among many others, P. Vyshinsky:

> Servility and fawning on foreign countries is the most loathsome and harmful antipatriotic vestige. This vestige has not evanesced from the consciousness of certain Soviet people and is still present in the minds of a backward section of the Soviet intelligentsia. . . . Certain authors have a stubborn slavish habit, in their research on the history of Russian literature, sciences, and arts, of regarding Russian philosophers, artists, and writers as adherents of west European patterns.[3]

The campaign to render the West odious was given the supreme authoritative stamp of approval in a series of resolutions adopted by the Central Committee of the Soviet Communist Party on matters relating to literary, theatrical, musical, and other cultural creation. The campaign took as its gospel the speeches of Zhdanov at conferences of authors, philosophers, and artists, and there was no doubt that he was backed by Stalin.[4] It is hardly to be imagined that Stalin, Zhdanov, Vyshinsky, and others really believed that Russian supremacy was undisputed in all fields, from literature to biology and from music to technical invention. But the factual truth was unimportant here when set against the mobilizatory consideration: in recruiting all spiritual resources against the enemy, the latter's drawbacks and worthlessness must be magnified and stressed. This total mobilization for the anti-West campaign was in time blown up to both horrifying and absurd proportions, proving that there is but a short step from the sublime to the ridiculous. Authors had to be careful not to extol the beauties of foreign landscapes. It was stated that the Russian Mozhaisky had preceded by tens of years the Wright brothers in designing the first aircraft; that modern aircraft production was based on Zhukovsky's discoveries in the field of aeromechanics; that Lubachevsky's geometrical system had laid the mathematical foundations for Einstein's theory; that Russians were the first to have evolved the painless birth method; that the Russian Lunin was one of the first to discover vitamins; that insulin was discovered by Sobolev; that penicillin was discovered by Monacein and Polotenov, and not by Fleming; that jaundice was actually "Botkin's Disease" (named after the Russian doctor who was claimed to have first diagnosed it); that Lebedev had discovered synthetic rubber; that Yablochkov had preceded Edison; that Lodygin had invented the electric light bulb; that Russians had been familiar with the art of printing before Gutenberg; that Afanasi Nikitin, a merchant from the Russian town of Tver (the Soviet Kalinin) had sailed around the world before Vasco da Gama; that Ivan Polzunov had invented the steam engine twenty years before James Watt. . . .

This eagerness to prove that the Russians were first in everything extended to the tractor and combine, to the telephone and telegraph, to the electric motor and dynamite. To set forth all these Russian claims would take up a great many pages. It will not detract from the true greatness of the Russian people, however, when we state that not a few of these claims were contradictory to facts in a manner beyond all proportion. In time, the conductors of the anti-West campaign were so ungenerous as to deny the Americans even the credit of having invented baseball: in 1952, an illustrated magazine for young readers explained that baseball was an American distortion (chiefly by the addition of brutal elements) of a rural game called Lapti, which Russian villagers had played centuries before the Americans.[5] It was even deemed necessary, for ideological purposes, no doubt, to discredit the authenticity of French Camembert cheese. Ehrenburg, who refers to this instance, says in a general manner: "It is enough to glance at the Great Soviet Encyclopedia — or to be more precise, at the volumes that appeared up to 1954 — in order to see the distortions brought about by the campaign against fawning [on the West]."[6] The Encyclopedia, however, was but one authoritative voice in the varied chorus of propaganda. The history of the development of whole branches of science and the biographies of scientists were written or rewritten, with the explicit object of proving the primacy of Russian science.[7] Alongside the favorable descriptions, aimed at proving Russian potential capacity, authors took pains to prove that certain advantages held by the West stemmed from scientific fraud and plagiarism. Lavoisier's discoveries in chemistry were claimed to have been made by the Russian Lomonosov, and Marconi was accused of stealing the idea of wireless telegraphy from Alexander Popov. It was no longer enough to praise the beauty of the Russian language, or repeat Ivan Turgenev's remark that such a language must have been endowed to a truly great people; it was even asserted that Russian excelled French and English and would supplant them as the universal language of socialism. Nor were these ideas divorced from practice. With xenophobic zeal the Russian language was purged of many foreign terms; parents were criticized for having given their children foreign names that were not in keeping with the Russian spirit; steps were taken to make hotels give up their foreign names. Hundreds of works, including scores of university textbooks, were banned because they contained indications of "fawning" on Western culture.

Stalinism-Zhdanovism did not content itself with waging a campaign against what was commonly termed "blind emulation" of foreign culture. It aimed at maintaining a kind of total spiritual autarchy which would supplement the physical isolation of the Soviet people. Herein lay one of the paradoxes of postwar Stalinism, in that it set out to intensify the isolation of the Soviet citizens from the outside world just at a time when their country had actually become a world power. On the one hand, the Soviet Union had never been so concerned with and directly involved in what was happening in the world arena as she was after Germany's defeat. For the first time her physical presence extended over a large area beyond her borders. It was just at the time when it appeared as though the doctrine of "Socialism in One Country" was dying out in the face of the new international political reality, that Stalinism looked askance at any manifestation of affinity or contact with the outside world. It seemed that Stalin continued to believe in the possibility of exerting Soviet influence over the world, while keeping the Soviet Union immune to outside influences. To maintain the Soviet Union, now a world power, in this state of isolation was tantamount to squaring the circle. It could be effected somehow by dint of heightened terror, which indeed became manifest immediately after the war.

This intensified Soviet isolationism entailed due consideration of the trends that were developing on the world scene. The period immediately following the war was naturally favorable for the burgeoning of ideas of a "united world" in the sense of mutual ties between nations and countries. Alongside the clear manifestations of national pride that inevitably followed the defeat of Hitlerite Germany, there was also a widespread "internationalistic" mood among various circles throughout the world, with leanings towards wider regional, continental, and intercontinental association. These trends did not appear to Moscow to be consistent with her practical political interests. She appraised them, in the present circumstances, as reinforcing the dominant position held by the United States. Soviet writers, thinkers, and scientists saw fit to unmask what, according to them, lay behind the explanations proffered in the West that in the world of the present day there was no escape from some renunciation of national sovereignty. They set out to debunk what lay behind the call for a "World State"; what lay behind the concepts of regionalism, continentalism, and universalism, which, they claimed, merely camouflaged the expansionist aims of the West, and particularly of America. This was stated by Zhdanov at the inaugural conference of the Cominform, thus:

> One of the aims of the ideological "campaign" concerned with the plan to subjugate Europe consists in an attack on the principle of national integrity, in the call on nations to renounce their sovereign rights, and in the exchange of these rights for notions of an "All-World Government." The sole object of this campaign is to cover up the vigorous expansion of American imperialism, which ruthlessly impairs the sovereign rights of the nations. Its object is to represent the United States as performing the function of fighting for [the preservation of] the laws of mankind as a whole, and to depict those who oppose the American penetration as siding with "egoistic" nationalism that has become outdated.[8]

In a similar vein, Soviet propaganda presented cosmopolitanism as being a disguise for racism, chauvinism, and imperialism. An Austrian socialist newspaper had defined a cosmopolitan as "a citizen of the world, whose thoughts and feelings are directed towards all the nations of the world; in other words, a man who aspires to internationalism." In the light of this definition, the paper asked, what was the crime in cosmopolitanism, and what was wrong in being called a cosmopolitan?[9] To which Moscow replied:

> Present-day cosmopolitanism reflects the trends towards world hegemony that is inherent in imperialism . . . [towards] domination of the world by a group of the strongest capitalist countries, or by one country. The present upholder of this trend is Anglo-American imperialism. Present-day cosmopolitanism, therefore, is the other side

of the ideology of racial supremacy, fostered by the Anglo-Saxon imperialists.[10]

In similar phrasing, hundreds of Soviet publications tore the mask off the face of cosmopolitanism, thus: "With high-sounding phrases about mankind's community of interests, world culture, the reciprocal influence and fecundation of cultures — cosmopolitanism is a cover either for the chauvinism of world powers towards other nations, or for a man's nihilistic attitude towards his own nation, and treachery against its national interests."[11] As against this, the principle of national sovereignty performs a "great progressive function" in the imperialistic era, for in present-day conditions it is a "weapon of war in the hands of the workers against the aggressive policy of the American imperialists, who aim to rule the world."[12] It is of interest to note the Soviet reaction to the idea expressed by Albert Einstein after the war advocating the establishment of an authoritative supranational organization, with the individual nations renouncing certain sovereign rights, failing which, "there can never be complete agreement on international control and the administration of atomic energy or on general disarmament."[13] Four well-known Soviet scientists, in an open letter, drew attention to "Dr. Einstein's mistaken notions." They claimed that the ideas of "world government" or of a "superstate," which Western pacifists and liberals had also taken up, were no more than "a reflection of the fact that the capitalist monopolies, which dominate the major industrial countries, find their own national boundaries too narrow."[14] The firm connection between the internal campaign against cosmopolitanism and factors relating to the international scene was also apparent in the attacks on notions of "abstract world science" which should transcend national boundaries. The contention of a celebrated Soviet scientist that "science must be international" was condemned as a "subversive claim."[15] The scientist was very soon obliged to admit his mistake publicly, by recognizing the fact that "every mistake of a cosmopolitan nature is not only theoretical, but political as well, for it directly impairs the cause of educating our people in the spirit of Soviet patriotism."[16] Even from a distinctly propagandist address that Ehrenburg gave abroad, at the Second Congress for Peace in November 1950, and which was published in the Soviet press, the censor blue-penciled a passage which stated that "the development of humanity's culture is impossible amidst isolation and artificial barriers."[17]

The need to vilify the West was intensified following the "polarization," when the United States was "confirmed" as being the chief enemy of the Soviet Union. The Soviet people still greatly admired America because of the large-scale help in war materials and staples she had rendered during the war — help which millions of Soviet citizens (chiefly army personnel) knew about and had directly benefited from. It should be pointed out that during the war the Soviet authorities themselves had taken pains, for reasons of expediency, to enhance the image of the Western allies. When the Soviet-German war was in its early stages, and particular when the Soviet forces seemed on the verge of collapse, stressing the might of the Western allies served to raise the morale of the Soviet people. Soviet publications, in fact, lauded Britain for her brave stand, alone, against the overwhelming German forces, and pointed to the United States' vast resources and industrial potential as being a guarantee of victory. What is more, they even praised the prevailing *systems* of the Western partners to the anti-German alliance. Stalin himself rejected the attacks of Nazi propaganda which termed the Anglo-American system a "plutocratic regime," and called them a Hitlerite attempt to cover up their own "reactionary black-hundred essence," pointing out that "in England and in the United States there are elementary democratic liberties." True, this form of praise for the Western democracies was not long-lived, but the popularity of the West, chiefly of the United States, was still widespread among the Soviet masses, whose thoughts are not prompted twenty-four hours a day by political considerations and ideological directives. Many people in the Soviet Union toyed with the idea that the Soviet-West meeting on the River Elbe was not merely a transitory wartime episode, but that it also heralded future rapprochement. It is worth noting that a certain admiration for the United States was unwittingly fostered by Soviet objectives and slogans right from the beginning of the Communist regime. As much as the authorities strove to arouse hatred for the American capitalist-exploitation system, America's plenty and industrial capacity became an object of admiration and envy in the Soviet society, which had been educated to stand in awe of material and technological achievements. In fact, Lenin himself had laid down that socialism meant "Soviet rule plus electrification," while Stalin had set the Soviet people the supreme, explicit objective of "catching up with America" (and later of outstripping her).

It was this favorable popular mood towards America, however, that led to a stiffening of the anti-American campaign. It is characteristic that in the various waves of the purges and public trials, the principal external foes, which the "enemies of the people" were accused of serving, were changed. This reflected to some degree the connection between the internal terror and Soviet external relations, or — to be more precise — it was an answer to the question: where, externally, is the "vigilance" to be chiefly directed? The early purge trials, for example, laid bare the schemes allegedly laid by the accused in the service of Britain, France, and Poland, to which were added Germany and Japan during the Thirties; whereas after the war, it was primarily the United States that was claimed to be behind the persons accused in the various trials held in the East European countries, and the main source of inspiration for all sorts of deviationist sinners in the Soviet Union.[18] In doing so, Soviet propaganda did not content itself with showing up the imperialist role that the United States was currently performing, but depicted her as enemy number one of the revolution since its inception and as the most active factor in the military intervention against the young Soviet republic, and even took pains to stress the brutality of American intervention against the Soviet population of the far north and east. There is no point discussing the accuracy of these descriptions, since the drawing of a historical or scientific conclusion was considered to be essentially a function of actual political-strategic considerations. The object of this description of American behavior of forty years ago was to prove that the Americans were *still like that.* Soviet citizens could get to know the real nature of the Americans, for instance, from a play whose action takes place in a small town in the state of Missouri (where President Truman comes from). The main character, a haberdasher, looks rather like Hitler, and a gang of local politicians decide that his place is in the White House . . .[19]

Various circles — from professional Party propagandists to institutions of the Academy of Sciences — joined in depicting the United States in an atrocious light and in humiliating Soviet citizens who "kowtowed" to her and to the West in general. To foreign observers, the proportions and indiscrimination of the anti-West campaign might well have appeared like a fit of madness. To certain Soviet intellectual circles this, too, must have appeared like an anomalous outbreak. At a London press conference, in 1950, Ehrenburg tried to avoid speaking about the persecution of the cosmopolitans; yet when pressed by a barrage of questions, he admitted that he did not agree with all that was written on the subject in his country, and that it is harder to do away with stupidity than to do away with capitalism.[20] It appears, however, that recourse to pathological explanations would be too facile, evading the essence of the development under discussion. It might be said, at least, that there was method in this madness.

At first, the campaign against cosmopolitanism and "kowtowing to the West" did not show any anti-Jewish trends. In September 1946, in the first of a series of speeches delivered by Zhdanov before the conferences of authors, philosophers, and scientists, as mentioned above, he sharply attacked, to begin with, satirist Mikhail Zoshchenko and poetess Anna Akhmatova, the publication of whose "works" (the inverted commas are Zhdanov's) was among the gravest mistakes committed by the Leningrad journals *Zvezda* and *Leningrad.* Zhdanov used the blackest colors in depicting the "rotten and degenerate image" of Zoshchenko and in humiliating Akhmatova, whose poetry was that of a "demented lady rushing about between her boudoir and the prayer-room." Neither Zoshchenko nor Akhmatova are Jews. The campaign against anti-Party trends on the "philosophical front" was authoritatively endorsed by Zhdanov, in June 1947, in his remarks on *The History of Philosophy in Western Europe,* a textbook written by Georgi Aleksandrov, a non-Jew. Aleksandrov, it transpired, had failed to fulfill one of the most important requirements in regard to the writing of a good textbook on the history of philosophy, namely, "to equip our intelligentsia, our cadres, and our youth with a new, powerful ideological weapon." Herein, in fact, lay the sin of the entire "philosophical front," which "is not conscious, in its philosophical activity, either of the spirit of battle or of the Bolshevist rhythm." Sergei Prokofiev, Dmitri Shostakovich, Aram Khatchaturian, and V. Muradeli, who were attacked for their deviations from the "ideological course" of Soviet music, are not Jews, either.[21] On the whole, the names of well-known Russians, Ukrainians, and others are to be found among the victims of the anticosmopolitan purges. In the struggle against "national nihilism," derogatory mention was made also of prerevolution Russian intellectuals who, it was claimed, had degraded the Russian national pride and fawned on everything that was foreign. What was more, there were Jews among the philosophers, writers, and scientists who participated in the anticosmopolitan campaign, and even Yiddish writers took a hand in it. Characteristic of this is the article "Sholem Aleichem on America" written by Y. Dobrushin shortly before Yiddish literature was liquidated in the Soviet Union, wherein he sets out to show how much the great popular writer's work was charged with sarcasm and mockery for America.[22]

However, the more extensive and intensified the campaign against cosmopolitanism became, the more pronounced was its anti-Jewish spearhead. (It may be observed, parenthetically, that the Soviet authorities and writers did not originate the notion of cosmopolitanism being a contemptible Jewish attribute; they were preceded by German anti-Semitic philosophers of the nineteenth century, notably historian Heinrich von Treitschke, who is considered one of the leading theoreticians of modern anti-Semitism.) Several factors contributed to the "Judaization" of the anticosmopolitan campaign. One of these might be termed operational. It was readily realized that imparting to the campaign an anti-Jewish coloring increased its prospects of being assimilated by the public. Whereas lengthy general explanations of the pernicious nature of cosmopolitanism must sound like abstract phrases, the addition of a great many distinctly Jewish names of cosmopolitans lent these explanations concrete and easily assimilated substance. Such personification was likely to render the abstract ideological offense more readily understood. Instead of unwieldy terms, or alongside them, there was presented a list of foreign-sounding names that could stir the imaginaition. All the more so, the evil and diabolical was effectively symbolized in cartoons, in which cosmopolitans of various kinds were given the Jewish hook nose. A cartoon in

Krokodil, the Soviet humorous magazine, showed a traveler with distinctly Jewish features and flamboyant clothes; the labels on his bag present the names of such cosmopolitans as André Gide, Somerset Maugham, D. W. Griffith, Walter Lippmann, André Malraux and Jean Paul Sartre.[23] This identification of despicable cosmopolitans with foreign Jews is even more pronounced in a cartoon showing hook-nosed people throwing saxophones and ink blots at the portraits of the Russian composers Glinka, Tchaikovsky, and Borodin.[24] Such plastic representations no doubt wrought their effect on popular instincts and turned the campaign against cosmopolitanism into negotiable currency.

It is quite possible that the anti-Jewish barb of the campaign was designed, in part, to gain the sympathies of circles hostile to the regime, or to still disaffection among the population that had no part in the ideological front." At all events, the addition of an anti-Semitic flavor was likely to make the anticosmopolitan dish more appetizing for the lower echelons of the Party and state personnel, who, more than the top levels, were susceptible to the popular anti-Semitic mood.

In waging the anticosmopolitan campaign, the Soviet press and public speakers reiterated abusive terms and definitions that could leave no doubt as to their intention to identify the antipatriotic elements chiefly with an alien body, in fact with the collective Jewish image. Suffice it to point to the stock phrases and epithets that appeared in both popular and theoretical publications, affording further proof that the entire campaign was not only centrally directed, but was routed from above into anti-Jewish channels. In the face of such stereotyped, illustrative epithets as "homeless," "rootless," "passportless wanderers," "strangers to the people and its national culture," "tribeless vagabonds" — it could hardly be claimed that the Jews were just being too sensitive.

Not only were the newspaper columns filled with "typical names" of cosmopolitans, distinctly pointing to their Jewish origin — from names ending in "man" to "Tsymbal"; beginning in mid-February 1949, when the campaign rose to a fevered pitch, the Soviet press would add in brackets the original Jewish names of persons charged with cosmopolitanism, alongside the names they were known by, if the latter had a misleading Russian or Ukrainian sound. Thus, persons who used pseudonyms in various fields of activity were identified: Yefim Markovich Stebun was shown to be Chaim Mordkovich Katznelson (added after his name in brackets); Alexander Isbakh (Isak Bakhrakh); Zhadanov (Lifshits); Martich (Finkelstein); Yakovlev (Holtsman); Melnikov (Melman); Yasny (Finkelstein); Kholodov (Meirovich); Viktorov (Zlochevsky); Sanov (Smulson); Volin (Katz); Gan (Kagan); Burlachenko (Berdichevsky); Svetlov (Sheidlin).

It will be recalled that it was a common practice of Nazi propagandists to point to the Jewish origin of Soviet personages by revealing their former names — a practice that had also been adopted by anti-Semitic White Russians in their endeavors to discredit the Bolshevist regime. Thus, Bronstein would be added to Trotsky, Sobelson to Radek, Rosenfeld to Kamenev, Valakh to Litvinov, and so forth. That a similar method was applied in regard to the cosmopolitans indicated an intention to malign something (in this case the West) by resorting to anti-Semitic devices. Moreover, the addition of bracketed names hinted at the cunning, the infiltration, and the subterfuge of the "foreigners."[25] Altogether, the fact that so many Jewish names appeared — in or out of brackets — among the publicly pilloried cosmopolitans could not but be interpreted as the Kremlin's indirect yet official sanction of an anti-Jewish line, to be applied by the various institutions and personnel. True, non-Jewish authors were denounced too, but taking into account the proportion of Jews among the population, or even among the intellectual circles, the Jews figured disproportionately largely among those branded as cosmopolitans. According to a cautious estimate made in 1949, intellectuals with Jewish names constituted some 60 percent of those condemned in Soviet publications for fawning on the West and showing other deviationist cosmopolitan tendencies.[26] In view of this demonstratively prominent place accorded to Jews among the deviationists (some estimates accord them even more significant status), hardly any importance attaches to the fact that some Jewish names were to be found also among those who attacked and denounced cosmopolitanism. The latter fact may no doubt be attributed to such factors as proneness to adaptation, attempts at self-exoneration, inertial habits of compliance, and even some measure of genuine conviction. That Jews participated, or were called upon to participate in a campaign that became anti-Jewish in nature calls to mind a remark made by a former mayor of Vienna and notorious anti-Semite, Dr. Leuger (Hitler admitted having been inspired by him), who had Jewish friends: "*Wer Jude ist bestimme ich*" ("I decide who is a Jew"). The Soviet authorities even reserved the right to decide when so-and-so "began" to be a Jew — when Yefim Markovich Stebun, for instance, turned into Chaim Mordkovich Katznelson.

We shall quote one of the victims of the anticosmopolitan campaign — film director Mikhail Romm. At a meeting of writers and artists with Khrushchev, he recalled that during Stalin's latter years "the expression 'cosmopolite without a fatherland' was invented to replace that other expression 'dirty Jew.' " He also recounted the following:

> On the cover of the [satirical] magazine *Krokodil* a cartoon appeared during those years presenting a "cosmopolite without a fatherland" of clearly Jewish type, holding a book in his hands on which one could read in big characters the word "GID." Not "André Gide" but simply "Gid."[27]

A cheap trick, no doubt, but an effective one for all that.

As we have previously explained, the popular sympathy for the United States placed difficulties in the way of the Soviet propaganda campaign against that country; the introduction of an anti-Jewish note, it appears, was designed to make the obloquious descriptions of America more readily assimilable by the masses. The Jew, citizen of the world, was shown up not merely as a wanderer without a homeland, but as a servant of American venality and imperialism. This identification of America with the Jews was not done in such a blatant, unbridled manner as by the Nazis, who went so far as to attribute to Roosevelt the Jewish name of Rosenfeld; nevertheless, Soviet cartoons did not stop at endowing Wall Street types with distinctly Jewish features. It is noteworthy that when Jewish cultural institutions were already being systematically liquidated, they were charged, among other things, with "Americanism." Thus, N. Gusarov, secretary of the Belorussian Communist Party, claimed in February 1949 that there was only one theater left in the republic — the

Jewish theater — which until recently had staged antipatriotic plays. This antipatriotism, according to him, was manifest in two aspects of the repertoire: an idealization of the partiarchal way of life of the Jewish petit bourgeoisie, and praise for the American bourgeois way of life.[28] In other words, Jewish nationalism was here associated with fawning on America.

It is relevant to point out that in Soviet belletristic writing after Stalin's death, which abounds in somber descriptions of the reign of terror conducted during his lifetime, there are also references to the persecution of Jewish cosmopolitans, or of Russians who sought to defend them. In *Battle on the Way,* a novel by Galina Nikolayeva,[29] we meet Professor Geizman, an old scholar, whose eyes radiate sheer purity. Geizman is a frequent visitor at the house of Boris Karamish, commander of the partisan unit in which old Geizman had served and from which he refused to be sent back behind the lines. After the war, Geizman is charged with ideological deviation, as allegedly reflected in his scientific works on the cosmos and the star systems; in fact he is accused of "idealism, cosmopolitanism, and other such isms." This is only a short step away from being indicted for subversion and espionage. The old man is arrested. Karamish, who believes in the total innocence of his friend and former fellow partisan, tries to ascertain the old man's fate and do something for him. In the end Karamish is arrested, too. In "Stillness," a story by Yuri Bondarev,[30] the painter Mokomulov and the critic Leikman are mentioned. At a meeting of artists, Leikman is reviled as a cosmopolitan. Mokomulov, an upright man, tries to defend Leikman, whom he knows to be a refined man and a loyal Communist, but his defense is drowned by the hooting of his audience, and he himself is charged with cosmopolitanism. Anna Valtseva, in her story "Apartment No. 13,"[31] depicts a vicious, repugnant character, former colonel Sergei Kovalev. He addresses a Jewish neighbor, who calls at his flat, by his name and his patronymic, as is customary in Russia; but instead of calling him Yacob Arkadevich, which is the Jew's real name, he insists on calling him Yacob Abramovich, though his mistake is pointed out to him. In the ensuing exchange on this subject between some of the characters in the story, we read that "if you scratch an anti-Semite you will always find something of the scoundrel in him; not that every scoundrel is an anti-Semite, but every anti-Semite is a scoundrel." Recalling the case of one ruffian who molested a Jewish woman in the subway, one character asserts that types like Kovalev are "brave when they have to deal with defenseless old women and children, as a rule," and that "up to the war we did not have such goings-on; it was during the war that the Fascist venom seeped through . . . racialism, self-reproach expressed through degrading others . . . a means as old as the world."

We have dealt, so far, with the opportunistic or "operational" considerations that channeled the campaign against cosmopolitanism in an anti-Jewish direction. Another reason for giving this campaign a Jewish direction lay in the fact that there was no difficulty in shifting this "crime" onto the Jewish intelligentsia, in view of certain hereditary qualities and characteristics which they manifested (this is by way of a generalization, of course).

In dealing with this aspect of our discussion, we shall begin by referring to the views of a man who was intimately familiar with the political and psychological processes current in the Communist Party and in the Soviet Union. In connection with the Slansky Trial, held in Prague in 1952, Milovan Djilas claimed that its anti-Semitic manifestations were symptomatic of all the countries dominated by Stalinism, including the Soviet Union itself — an indication of the struggle against the last vestiges of "the spirit that still links East European nations with the rest of the world, irrespective of whether this is the spirit of socialism, or of 'Jewish cosmopolitanism.' " This spirit, Djilas explained, is alive in the Jews, hence the fury that is vented on them; by dint of historical developments Jewish people — as a result of being scattered all over the globe, among other reasons — have become pervaded by the spirit of internationalism; the Jews are "helpless to suppress this spirit, hence they are doomed to be persecuted wherever a regime isolates itself."[32]

And indeed, with all the inherent historical irony this implies, it was just these internationalist universal elements of Judaism that aroused suspicion and hostility on the part of those same rulers who proclaimed that their country was a stronghold of internationalism. Writers and artists, the historic fate of whose nation had rendered them, more than others, open to the influences of the wide world, began to be branded as an alien and even hostile element by a regime zealous to preserve its monolithic character and keep its subjects in a kind of spiritual quarantine. In the late Forties and early Fifties, when the Soviet Union became increasingly sensitive to any potential centrifugal element, political fuel was added to the smoldering suspicion in which the Jews were held.

It must be stressed that the "Jewish" internationalism or universalism were prone to evoke suspicion even though devoid of organizational features or political expression. Their spiritual substance was quite enough. Illuminating in this connection is an observation made by Ehrenburg, who fled from his Jewish image nearly all his life, in New York in 1946: "What unites us all [the Jews] is our thirst. Jews thirst for the truth, for honesty and freedom — and this eternal thirst unites all the Jews."[33] A totalitarian regime, by its very nature, hardly tends to favor such spiritual unrest. A uniformist regime cannot tolerate the eternal wandering of the Jew — not merely the physical wandering, but the constant spiritual quest. A Soviet Russian poet of Jewish origin, whose work shows no trace of what might be defined as a "Jewish theme," once referred in the course of a casual conversation to "the right of the eternal Jew, who bridges between cultures, who suffers for his sensitivity, and is able to sense the most delicate tremor of future progress."[34] No doubt the poet was not referring to physical wandering but to moral soul-searching and intercultural communication. The latter kind of "wandering," however, seemed to suffice in stirring the uniformist regime to adopt a vigilant attitude towards it.

Reviewing former years and generations, we find that Jews — even though they later repudiated their Jewish origin or were indifferent to it from the outset — endowed the revolutionary movement in many parts of the world with some of their own qualities: inner disquiet and a search for new, transcendental values. Great as was their share in radical-national organizations in various countries, they endowed them with a kind of spiritual extraterritoriality. Aaron Liebermann (1845–1880), considered a pioneer Jewish socialist, though imbued with strong nationalist feelings and deeply attached to Hebrew literature, once claimed that as a Jewish socialist he was a cosmopolitan or a "cosmo-socialist (to coin a term)."[35] These cosmopolitan or cosmo-socialist tendencies were well known to the leaders and theoreticians of the revolutionary movements, including those of the October Revolution, and as a rule they welcomed these qualities. Lenin remarked favorably on the fact that "the percentage of Jews in the democratic and proletarian movements is everywhere greater than their proportion among the population at large," and he was aware that this fact was not only a result of economic conditions or persecution, but was to some extent also connected with the "great, universal, progressive attributes" to be found in Jewish culture, in "its internationalism, its readiness to respond to the avant-garde movement of the age."[36]

However, the more firmly Stalinism became entrenched, the less the Soviet Union felt the need to have recourse to the spiritual attributes which the Jews had imparted to the revolutionary movement. Stalinism based itself on regimentation, rather than on spiritual sweep of vision. It called for implicit obedience rather than for the devotion that comes of conviction. It preferred constraint to the zeal of idealism. It certainly did not approve of a visionary-admonitory uprising against injustice. It may be added, in this connection, that a successful revolution does not, as a rule, look favorably upon those who are revolutionaries by nature; enriched by its own experience, it fears rebellious, restless types and tends to keep an eye on potential heretics.

The beginning of Stalin's rule already marked the end of the Communist internationalism, which had attracted a great many Jews. This internationalism was supplanted by arbitrary dialectical exercises, according to which "an internationalist is a man who, without reserve, without hesitation, unconditionally, is prepared to defend the Soviet Union, since the Soviet Union is the base of the world revolutionary movement."[37] Concomitantly, there was fostered in the Soviet Union the belief in the central position occupied by the Russian nation among the Soviet family of nations. Some twenty-five years after the revolution, the Russian émigré philosopher Berdaiev admitted that the view which he and others had held in 1917 that Communism had engulfed Russia had proved false; on the contrary, he had become convinced that "Russia had swallowed up Communism." In time it became apparent that the authorities regarded the Russian people not only as "first among equals" among the Soviet peoples, but were according it a dominant role. Indeed, many observed the interesting fact that Stalin, of Georgian origin, was more of a Russian chauvinist than the average Russian. This was due, no doubt, not to a sentimental, romantic, and mystical love of Mother Russia on the part of Stalin, but to sober, practical considerations. We have observed how Russian patriotism was blown up to ludicrous proportions in the postwar anti-West campaign, almost to the point of creating a Russian superman legend. The deliberate fostering of the Russian mythos, indeed, had already become clearly apparent by the mid-Thirties, as evidenced by the "posthumous metamorphoses" of historian Mikhail Pokrovsky. In the Twenties, he had dominated Soviet historiography, which had stressed the imperialist, reactionary, and backward image of Tsarist Russia (thereby glorifying Soviet Russia all the more, by way of contrast). At Pokrovsky's funeral, in 1932, his coffin was borne, among others, by Stalin, Molotov, and Kalinin, and the urn containing his ashes was laid in the wall of the pantheon (reserved for the nation's illustrious dead) behind Lenin's mausoleum in Moscow. Two years later, however, he was declared a Trotskyist and enemy of the people, and his works were banned. The whole school that had associated itself with him was pronounced "anti-Marxist" when the Stalinist regime came to the conclusion that certain historical episodes and celebrated figures from the Tsarist days might effectively serve its interests and ends. And indeed, kings, princes, generals, and war heroes of Old Russia began to be a source of inspiration for writers and artists. Though this process did not entail the renunciation of "proletarian internationalism," nevertheless the latter was patently overshadowed by such grandiose figures as those of Ivan the Terrible and Peter the Great — who no doubt had greater appeal for Stalin, the new Russian emperor. In keeping with this revision of Russian historiography (once the Pokrovsky school was stamped out), not only was minimal weight attached to the social inherence of the historical Russian heroes, but even the revolutionary definition that Tsarist Russia had been "a prison of the peoples" was discarded. This was replaced at first by propounding the theory that Russia's domination of other nations was a kind of lesser evil. This was but a short step away from the notion that Russia had always served as a guide for Europe and a pattern for other nations, and had always come to the assistance of suppressed peoples. The crux of this notion was that Russia's past imperialist expansion and conquests had been, from an objective standpoint, a favorable and progressive phenomenon rather than Tsarist "piracy," as they had frequently been termed before.

Naturally, these assumptions on which the Russian neopatriotism was founded were apt to alienate persons whose love and devotion for the Soviet Union had largely been nurtured by the fact that it had dissociated itself from Old Russia. It was also natural that these assumptions, in addition to impairing the sincere internationalist convictions of not a few Soviet citizens, proved to be particularly hard to assimilate for Soviet Jews. They certainly "found it hard to work up convincing enthusiasm for a historical past marked by Pales [of residence] and pogroms, for national heroes like Ivan the Terrible and Khmelnitsky."[38]

Reference has already been made in a previous chapter to the increased wartime recourse to Russian nationalism. After the war was over, however, this orientation proved to have become even more pronounced. The line adopted during the Thirties and emphasized during the "Great War for the Homeland" became reinforced after victory was achieved. A leading article of an authoritative Party organ, in the issue that bears the date of the day following Germany's capitulation, stated that:

> The Russian nation has genius and is extremely talented! It has given to mankind the greatest writers, poets, scientists, and musicians . . . the most brilliant military leaders — Marshals Zhukov, Konev, Rokosovsky, and others — all sons of the Russian nation and all imbued with the distinctive characteristics of the Russian nation.[39]

Two weeks later, on May 24, 1945, this view was voiced most authoritatively and solemnly by Stalin himself at a magnificent reception which he held for Red Army commanders at the Kremlin. Stalin pledged a toast to the Soviet people and, in particular, in his own words:

> . . . to the Russian people, since it is the most outstanding of the nations which make up the Soviet Union. In this war, it has gained universal admiration among all the peoples of our country as the

guiding force of the Soviet Union. I raise my glass [in a toast] to the Russian people not only because it is the guiding force of the Soviet Union, but because it is a people endowed with a clear brain, a stable character, and endurance.[40]

This reference to "endurance" suggests that Stalin not only admired this quality in the Russian people as its contribution to victory; he also took this endurance into account as an indication of its ability to face up to future trials. This might have been some kind of advance compensation accorded to the people, by way of bolstering up the national pride, in return for the years of tribulation and tension that lay ahead, in addition to the want and hardship that was already felt at the time of the exultation over the great victory. The wording of the toast might also have been a kind of carefully considered prologue to the anti-West campaign. At all events, it became increasingly apparent that this policy of stirring up Russian nationalism was far from being a passing phase; on the contrary, it was being geared to the highest pitch. And once the flames of Russian nationalism, for purposes of political expedience, had been fanned to fanatical xenophobia, it was only natural that the Jews should be made to feel ill at ease: against this newly created emotional setting they figured conspicuously as an "alien element." Within a short time, in fact, the Jews became painfully aware that this xenophobia, though aimed primarily at the outside world, also created a hostile atmosphere with pervaded the general attitude towards them inside the country.

Alongside the disappearance, or distortion beyond all recognition, of the internationalistic principle in the Stalinist regime, Communism itself — in the Soviet Union as well as on a worldwide scale — was rapidly changing into a kind of doctrinaire Church, with its sacrosanct writings and ritual, which inexorably attributed infallibility to its "pope" in the Kremlin. The protagonists of a unitarian trend such as this could hardly feel favorably disposed towards elements who might view such a development with skepticism or irony, and who therefore came to be regarded by the regime as dangerous islands of independent thought in a sea of unanimous agreement. Men of an inquiring disposition, who are prone to look at both sides of every question, are liable to hinder the imposition of absolute authority. They are regarded at the outset as a disintegrative element in a society that has set out to trammel conduct and thought in the shackles of collectivism. The Stalinist concept could hardly favor individuals who think too much, or as the Russian-Jewish writer Isaac Babel phrased it, who "wear spectacles on their noses and autumn in their hearts." Such men do not readily fit into the acquiescent chorus that dances to the official tune and sings the praises of the happy new era.

The last years of Stalin's life saw mounting hostility towards such types and elements in the Soviet Union, alongside a growing tendency to see in the Jewish community, or in the Jewish nature, fertile ground for the growth of the "rank weeds" of nonconformism. Several years after Stalin's death, Khrushchev himself aptly illustrated what must have been not only his own emotional attitude towards Jews, but also that common to quite a large section of the Soviet leadership that had been nurtured on the Stalinist doctrine. (It should be noted that Khrushchev, an impulsive speaker, was perhaps the first Soviet leader who revealed some of the inner feelings that he doubtlessly shared with others.) Among the shortcomings Khrushchev attributed to the Jews, he pointed to their proneness to scrutinize every occurrence and manifestation: "They take an interest in everything, always probe deeply [into every problem], argue about everything, and end up by holding divergent views."[41] This reflects some apprehensiveness of the inquiring, probing "Jewish mind." Nor could the Jewish love of debating controversial issues have been to the taste of the regime. At a time when the bureaucracy was striving to attain complete control not only of the nation's production and administration, but also of its thought processes, it could hardly have condoned any manifestation of pluralistic tendencies, that is to say, of "divergent views." Whether or not Khrushchev was anti-Semitic is not relevant to our present discussion. What is far more illuminating is his instinctive resentment of the fact that the Jews "take an interest in everything."

This skepticism and analytical disposition — attributed to the Jewish intelligentsia — must have proved increasingly irksome and suspicious to the authorities as they exerted mounting pressure to homogenize the Russian society. The regime, which demanded an all-out national effort to achieve such aims as industrial and military growth by dint of totally imposed discipline, could hardly be tolerant of individuals who were not prepared to swallow ready-made ideas.

All unitarianism — which is closely akin to autocracy — is not only instinctively haunted by Julius Caesar's fear of Cassius, who "thinks too much" ("such men are dangerous"), but also develops a singular propensity for detecting treacherous conspiracy in every manifestation of thought. "Give me six lines written by the most honest man," said Richelieu, "and I shall find in them something on which to hang him." And indeed, once the seeds of the "Jewish agitator" image had been sown in the minds of the authorities, this sufficed to make them regard the Jews as a threat to the regime. Political prophylaxis called for keeping the Jewish intelligentsia under surveillance. Restless by nature, and regarded as a likely breeding ground for the germs of skepticism and susceptible to the attractions of the wide world, this intelligentsia was liable to impair the uniformity of thought and breach the wall of isolationism. When the Stalin-Zhdanov regime, against the backdrop of international developments, performed a psychological "dress rehearsal" inside the Soviet Union in preparation for the impending showdown with the West, characteristics commonly regarded as distinctively Jewish were blown up to the proportions of sabotage and treason. Seen through the magnifying glass of Bolshevist terror, possession of these characteristics verged on criminal guilt.

It may perhaps be asked: did the Jews really possess all the characteristics that were imputed to them, and which the Soviet regime found so unpalatable? It would appear, from the foregoing, that these characteristics were quite common among the Jewish intelligentsia; nor were they such as to put their possessors or their national heritage to shame, to our mind. We may add, parenthetically, that the very fact that these so-called "Jewish characteristics," as outlined above, came to be so hated and suspect in the Soviet Union pointed to a degeneration of the regime and a dissolution of those selfsame values for which so many had fought dedicatedly in the revolution. There is no doubt that the Soviet leaders exaggerated the exposure of those characteristics particularly among the Jews, and grossly overrated their potentiality, to say nothing of the absence of any grounds for considering them a real threat. Herein, perhaps, lies some explanation for the apparently strange fact that the campaign against cosmopolitanism did not spare even those Jews who had long conformed to the demands of the regime and had served it faithfully to the best of their ability. The suspicion-ridden totalitarian regime was not prepared to believe that the Jewish intelligentsia, with its distinctive spiritual makeup and heritage, was capable of slavish obedience. This may be borne out by a further example adduced from Ehrenburg. Although he invariably toed the current line, he nevertheless affirms in his memoirs that all his life he himself had doubted the absolute value of accepted truths, and that blind faith had always been alien to his spirit. The sharp Stalinist nose would no doubt have smelled a distinctive Jewish flavor in these words, though their writer had veered far away from his Jewish origin.

This suspicion inevitably brings up associations from Jewish history. At the time of the Spanish Inquisition, the enmity and suspicion of the Church extended not only to the observant Jews who practiced their religion openly, or even to the Marranos who did so in secret, but also or even primarily to converts who had embraced Christianity of their own accord.[42] Thus, the Jews were being coerced into undergoing baptism, to begin with, and, having done so, the converts found themselves under relentless suspicion, as though the state and Church authorities were firmly convinced that they could never be true Christians. Similarly in the mid-twentieth century, Stalinism would not accept the assimilation of the Jewish intelligentsia as proof of their implicit loyalty, as though doubting whether "the Ethiopian could change his skin." When Stalin singled out for liquidation, in the purges of the Twenties and Thirties, many suspected opponents of Jewish origin who had long repudiated all Judaism, he may very well have been prompted by the inner thought: they are *Jews* by nature and in temperament, despite their repudiation of their Jewish origin. And indeed, if the liquidation of such men as Trotsky, Kamenev, and Radek had been put off until the time of the anticosmopolitan campaign, it is almost certain that their long-discarded Jewish names would have been raked up and added, in brackets, to their current names.

In addition to considering these Jewish human and spiritual attributes harmful, the Soviet policy makers, when the cold war became exacerbated, could not but seize upon the patent fact that the preponderant majority of the Jewish people was concentrated and well-established in the West, and that many Soviet Jews had relatives there. With their sound logic, and in the face of reality, the Soviet authorities realized that in the wake of the wartime tragedy family ties and yearning must have become strengthened among the Jews all over the world, and there was no reason why the natural desire to find relatives somewhere in the world should not overwhelm Soviet Jews as well. That Soviet Jews had relatives in the West also made them more prone to being regarded as a destructive element, inasmuch as they might be tempted to compare their living conditions with those of their relatives abroad, especially persons in the same or similar professional categories.[43] A further germane fact: there were five million Jews — prominent among them Jews of Russian origin or their children — living in the territory of Soviet Russia's chief potential enemy, namely, the United States. Thus, world Jewish unity emerged from beyond the confines of its spiritual-religious-historical nature and — as seen through the magnifying glass of Bolshevik vigilance — assumed the form of a potential danger transcending all boundaries. Against this danger it became necessary to apply the system of "prophylactic justice," or the legal concept of imposing criminal responsibility in accordance with the "analogy" principle (which makes it possible to relate a "socially dangerous act," even though not provided for in the law, to similar crimes provided for in specific enactments).[44] The need to take preventive measures against the Jews was further induced by the consideration that they were the only one of the larger Soviet peoples that did not have a territory of their own. Birobidzhan's official status as a Jewish autonomous region — there were several tens of thousands of Jews living there at the end of the Forties — was hardly enough to detract from the extraterritorial image of the Soviet Jewish minority. Since territorial-ethnic concentration makes for easier political surveillance in the "professional" sense, it may be assumed that the fact that the Jews were scattered throughout the Soviet Union made the authorities all the more suspicious of them. The Israel factor, too, blended harmoniously with all those other considerations: not only were not the Soviet Jews settled in their own territory; they were the only minority of any significant size that might have allegiance to "their" country outside the Soviet Union. The wave of enthusiasm that engulfed Soviet Jewry when the state of Israel was born — and on the arrival of its mission in Moscow in 1948 — was enough to bear out the contention of those members of the Soviet leadership who claimed that the Jews were a fifth column. According to the above-mentioned principle of "analogy," there was no great distance between discovering various "nationalistic" manifestations in the works of Soviet Jewish writers and regarding the Jews collectively as a security risk. By and large, as had frequently happened in the course of history, the Soviet authorities, too, grossly magnified the "community spirit" with which the Jews were imbued. Against the background of the "state of war," this magnification had an ancient ring about it: ". . . and it come to pass, that, when any war should chance, they also join our enemies and fight against us . . ." (Exodus, 1: 10). The stage now appeared to be set for the anti-Jewish terror and liquidation, for "throughout history, the barbarous notion of 'objective' or potential danger has been at the origin of every massacre of innocents."[45]

We shall now adduce details, based on Soviet publications, in illustration of the special status accorded the Jews among the various categories of cosmopolitans. These details no doubt served to enhance the awareness of Soviet readers and listeners of Jewish "infiltration" into all spheres of literary, scientific, artistic, and other cultural activity.

We shall begin our survey with reference to the theater. Here we must first point to the apparently surprising fact that the campaign against cosmopolitanism was leveled with particular rigor against dramatic art and criticism. "Why did the campaign commence with a secondary subject, that of dramatic criticism?" asked Ehrenburg. "I don't know," he replied to his own question, but proffered the assumption that "Maybe an outraged playwright once complained to Stalin, and maybe it was mere chance."[46] This is hard to accept. What appears more plausible is the assumption that the Soviet leadership was aware that the sugary literature of "socialist realism" was losing its hold, whereas the cinema and theater were assuming increasing importance as media for guiding the masses. "The theater and dramaturgy are an important and sensitive section of the ideological struggle," asserted an *Izvestia* leading article.[47] This "ideological struggle" was essentially an anti-West struggle, for which Soviet drama had to be urgently mobilized. Just as anti-West and anti-American plays had to be staged with all possible haste, similarly theatrical circles had to be quickly purged of all elements whose hostility towards foreign culture was not assured, and especially of critics who might attach more weight to the artistic aspect of the plays than to their ideological and militant content. The fact that there was a relatively large number of persons of Jewish origin among these critics might very well have added zeal to the purge and gained it wide support.

A "personal" article published in *Pravda* towards the end of 1948 by Anatoli Sofronov, who began to achieve prominence as the trusted spokesman of the authorities in the realm of literature, clearly indicated which way the wind was blowing. Here, the author not only coined the epithet "cosmopolitans without a homeland" with application to the leading theater critics, but even mentioned such names as Y. Yuzovsky, A. Gurvich, Y. Warshavsky, and L. Malyugin.[48] The latter were subsequently a target for repeated attacks.

The attacks launched against the theater critics assumed an increasingly militant note. The alien nature of these cosmopolitans was stressed. The barrier separating them from the people was underlined. They were maligned in the most colorful terms. It was pointed out, among other things, that they did not even master the Russian language or use it properly.[49] The frequency and intensity of these attacks bear out what Ehrenburg relates, quoting Soviet author Alexander Fadeyev, that "the campaign against a group of antipatriotic critics was launched on Stalin's instructions."[50] The source that inspired the campaign and the importance attaching to it was attested to by a four-column *Pravda* leader entitled "About One Antipatriotic Group of Theater Critics." In addition to the serious charge of antipatriotism contained in the title, the use of the word "group" was in itself of ominous significance. And indeed, the critics, who were alleged to have infiltrated into the Soviet press, were referred to as a "literary underground" that had set out to denigrate all that was good in Soviet drama. They were described as adherents of bourgeois aestheticism who degraded Soviet art and literature and impeded their development. "These critics have lost all [sense of] responsibility towards the people. They are the bearers of homeless cosmopolitanism, which is opposed to the Soviet person and which arouses his profound disgust.

. . . The feeling of Soviet national pride is alien to them." This antipatriotic group, the article went on to assert, had decided to set itself the aim of "obstructing and maligning all the patriotic works of Soviet playwrights, all the plays that have a blood relationship with the life of the people and the homeland." Critics Y. Yuzovsky and A. Gurvich, in particular, were charged with deliberately maligning Soviet characters in a series of recent plays. Gurvich had stated that in the complacent humor and naive optimism and faith which pervaded Nikolai Pogodin's plays the observer found a reflection of his own self; he was charged with slandering the Soviet Russian character: "It is just because self-complacency is foreign to us that we cannot but reject this attempt to malign the Soviet national character." The Soviet reader, accustomed to reading meaning into allusions, could hardly fail to perceive the specific implication of the question: "What notion can A. Gurvich possibly have of the national character of the Soviet Russian," if he writes as he wrote about Pogodin's plays?[51]

The Party cell of the Soviet Writers' Association convened about two weeks after this leading article appeared in *Pravda.* Anatoli Sofranov attacked the "ring" of antipatriotic theater critics, among them Y. Altman, L. Subotsky, A. Leites, A. Erlich, D. Danin, A. Holtsman, K. Kholodov, A. Kron, and F. Levin. The bureau of the cell was charged with looking into the question of the Party membership of Altman, Levin, Subotsky and Danin. The report on that meeting referred to A. Kron as the *former* chairman of the Dramaturgy Committee of the Writers' Association;[52] hence it may be assumed that he had recently been ousted from office.

Shortly afterwards, Moscow playwrights and critics met to discuss the deviations of the "antipatriotic group" and hear an address by Konstantin Simonov, deputy secretary general of the Writers' Association. According to him, cosmopolitanism inhered in "the desire to demolish the national roots and national pride, since persons whose roots have been severed are more easily prone to degenerate and sell out to the enslavement of American imperialism." He dwelt at length on the "bourgeois cosmopolites devoid of natural feelings of Soviet national pride and indifferent to the life and heroic struggle of the Soviet people." It did not require a great stretch of imagination to understand whom "devoid of natural feelings" alluded to, particularly as the speaker referred specifically to A. Gurvich, whose writing he branded as a "maltreatment of the Russian nation, of the Russian individual, and of Russian national traditions." (It may be added, parenthetically, that after the Twentieth Congress in 1956, the same Konstantin Simonov asserted that the measures taken against the theater critics at the end of the Forties were, in fact, a punishment meted out to those who had dared to point to the true shortcomings of Soviet drama.)[53] Playwright Boris Romashov claimed that "all those Tsymbals, Yankovskys, and Dreidens [Jewish names] grew excited over every trivial thing of European origin and looked down with snobbish contempt on our Soviet drama."[54] It should be noted that the use of Jewish names in the plural — Tsymbals and Yankovskys, or Gurviches and Yuzkovskys, and so on — was common during the anticosmopolitan campaign.

From time to time one member of the antipatriotic group was singled out as the target for a concentrated and intensive attack. Thus, for example, a special article was devoted to Altman, who was branded "the nationalist bourgeois Altman." The author stated that "Altman hates everything Soviet. His bourgeois nationalism and loathing for everything Russian has inevitably led him to fawn on the West."[55] Another article, by N. Gribachev, was devoted chiefly to poetry critics, and specifically to an attack on D. Danin, branded as an "arch-cosmopolite," thus: "Only a passportless wanderer like him could have written as he did."[56]

Among those charged with denigrating Russian creation and thought was Boris Eichenbaum. His crime lay, for instance, in regarding Schopenhauer as an important source of philosophic inspiration for Leo Tolstoy, and in pointing to West European influences in *Anna Karenina.* In this way he had shown himself "devoid of any pride in our literature . . . lacking in self-respect in regard to things Russian, our own."[57] Eichenbaum's attackers strove to shatter his reputation as a scholar, which appeared to be extremely firm. The man who occupied the chair of Russian Literature in the faculty of philology at the Leningrad University was said to have "surrounded himself with a circle of students, who deliberately exaggerated his authority at Leningrad." His "Trotskyist" views on literature, which he had voiced in 1924, were brought up against him. No less illuminating was the devastating attack directed at certain autobiographical notes which Eichenbaum had published in 1929. In them, he was alleged to have revealed the hereditary roots wherein inhered his contempt for Russian culture and his kowtowing to things European. The tone adopted in this attack shows that the barbs of mockery and enmity were not directed at Eichenbaum alone, thus:

> Eichenbaum lauds his ancestors. Mosei [Moses] Golber, according to the author (Eichenbaum), was a genius pure and simple, "a man of extraordinary talent." He "studied the Talmud and the Bible," attained "an outstanding degree of perfection" and became "a Luminary of Israel." One of his forbears was "abundantly endowed" by nature with "extraordinary qualities." Similarly all his ancestors. One of them published a poem in the Yiddish language, on which the author lavishes particular praise.[58]

Charges of attempting to "Europeanize" classical Russian literature were laid against Yitzhak Nusinov, a critic and researcher of Yiddish literature, who had at one time been a professor of European literature at the Moscow University. In the early stages of the anticosmopolitan campaign, a work by Nusinov entitled *Pushkin and World Literature,* published as far back as 1941, was wrathfully brought up against him. Actually, the views of Nusinov and his fellow sinners were rooted chiefly in the comparative school of Alexander Veselovsky, a nineteenth-century Russian literary researcher. But the attacks leveled at Nusinov left no doubt as to the fact that they were inspired by concrete considerations of the late Forties, rather than by a quest for scientific-literary truth. In his book, Nusinov had pointed to the European spirit that pervaded Pushkin's works. Such a view was interpreted as an insult to the Russian genius, as a distortion of Pushkin's image and as politically and educationally harmful. Alexander Fadeyev, for example, denounced the "denationalization" of Pushkin by Nusinov, who had turned the Russian poet into "something universal, pan-European, all-embracing"; he claimed that "Nusinov preaches eternal universalistic ideas that allegedly have an abstract existence."[59] It is relevant to call attention, in this connection, to the relatively large share assumed by researchers of Jewish origin in the field of comparative literature — due, no doubt, to the large number of Jews who mastered various European languages. Nor is it surprising that the men who engaged in this field were, as a rule, singled out for attack during the anti-West campaign. But the onslaught directed at Nusinov was of special intensity, hardly warranted by the small work he had published in 1941. Could this have been due to the fact that this "comparativist" was one of the leading exponents of Soviet Yiddish literature? It would be difficult to affirm this definitely. It should however be noted that in the subsequent Moscow trial of Jewish writers and public figures, in 1952, Nusinov figured among the victims.

A further literary episode of interest occurred in 1949, when the anticosmopolitan campaign was at its height. The Leningrad periodical *Zvezda* had published an installment of a story entitled "Podpolkovnik [Lieutenant-Colonel] of the Medical Corps" by Yuri German, a Russian writer of Jewish origin, with the notation that the concluding installment would follow. The central character in the story is a Doctor Levin, the Lieutenant-Colonel.[60] The story was harshly criticized and the concluding installment was not published. The essence of the criticism leveled at the story may be found in the confession of the author himself, in his letter to the *Zvezda* editorial office:

> My story . . . has been subjected to fundamental and just criticism on the part of the readers. They have shown that the main character, Doctor Levin, lives shut away in his own limited world, completely preoccupied with his suffering, and that such a man does not deserve to be regarded as a favorable character. The defective hero's soul-searching and the complexity of his interpersonal relations — all these have formed an untrue picture of life at the hospital and in the garrison force. In recognition of these mistakes, I do not think it possible to publish the continuation of my story in *Zvezda,* since it must be thoroughly revised from the first chapter to the last.[61]

The *Zvezda* editors, in announcing that the publication of "Podpolkovnik of the Medical Corps" would be discontinued, added a note admitting their mistake in publishing the first chapters of the story. The main character, they stated, "is divorced from life, defective, individualistic, and sensitive to a sick degree."[62]

Jews occupied a leading role in Soviet cinematographic art, but figured even more prominently among those attacked for cosmopolitan heresies. A central butt of attack was L. Trauberg, a Leningrad film director, who was branded "the head cosmopolite" in the realm of the cinema. Among the charges leveled at him was that Soviet cinematographic art had been greatly influenced by American, French, and German directors and actors — a crime that fitted in with Trauberg's praise of the foreign bourgeois cinema. From the point of view of our discussion it is interesting to note the remarks made by the Soviet minister of cinematography about Trauberg: "The cosmopolitanism and antipatriotism of Trauberg are not surprising, since he has long harbored antinational views that are alien to the great cultural tradition of Russia." The day after these remarks were published, the deputy minister of cinematography explained that cosmopolitanism upheld the banner of reactionary American imperialism, "which strives to disarm nations culturally, deprive them of the will to struggle, and subjugate the peoples of the world to the Wall Street masters." Immediately following this explanation the deputy minister added: "It was this very thing, actually, that Gurvich, Trauberg, and Bleiman called for, in maligning Soviet art, in sneering at the national forms of our culture." Bleiman's view that D. W. Griffith was the father of the world cinema called down especial wrath. Others charged with "subversive activities" in the realm of the cinema included Yutkevich, Volkenstein, Sutyrin, and Kovarsky.[63]

In the realm of music, charges of "formalism" and similar deviations were laid against a number of music critics, prominently Belza, Zhitomirsky, Weinkop, and Shlaifstein.

The same applied to the plastic arts. Among those denounced for degrading the national spirit we find the names of such cosmopolitan art critics as Efros, Romm, Arkin, Pasternak, and Baskin.

Jews were the first cosmopolitans to be unmasked in the field of architecture, too. Here, a wrathful attack was concentrated on the pupils of Moises Gintsburg. E. Levinson was branded as the head of a school entirely infected with cosmopolitanism. Among those charged with fawning on American architecture there figured Khiger and Gabrichevsky.

Cosmopolitan subversion was also manifested in sport, or to be more precise, in sports newswriting. Those denounced in this regard included L. Shneider, G. Yasny (Finkelstein), A. Svetov (Sheidlin), V. Viktorov (Zlochevsky), and G. Gurevich. Their sins were as follows: one writer had once asserted that Soviet sportsmen were petty-minded glory seekers; another had once revealed that some employees of the Indo-European Cable Company had originally brought football to Russia; a third had reported that a Soviet wrestler, just before an international match, had been inspired by Jack London, and not by his love for his homeland.[64]

Practically in all the sciences Jews were featured prominently as kowtowing to the West in an abject manner, and hence as maligning Soviet and Russian science. It was S. Altshuler, author of popular essays on science, who was charged with attributing the discovery of penicillin to Sir Alexander Fleming, and of diminishing the role of Russian physicists in his article on atoms and isotopes. It is noteworthy that the denunciation of Altshuler pointed out that he had used the Russian pseudonyms of S. Zveriev and S. Vladimirov. This cosmopolitan triumvirate — Altshuler - Zveriev - Vladimirov — was one and the same person, who had actively "maligned and distorted the image of Soviet science."[65]

As for the cosmopolitan deviations in historical research, the floodlights of denunciation were turned onto such "rootless ones" or "national nihilists" as Mintz, Gorodetsky, Feigina, Kafengauz, Khankin, and Razgun. The author of *Elements of General Psychology,* S. Rubinstein, was charged, among other things, with dealing with the history of psychology in too "objectivist" a manner and with "academic detachment." In the field of political economy and the history of economics we find such fawners on the West as I. Blyumin, D. Rosenberg, L. Roitburd, I. Trachtenberg, V. Lan, M. Bukashitsky, Professor Urlanis, I. Baransky, Professor Boyarsky, Bernstein-Kogan, and Boris Stein. The latter (he was a member of the Soviet delegation to the United Nations in 1947, when the Palestine question was under deliberation) was said to hold cosmopolitan views closely allied to those of the economist John Normano, whose real name was Levin (given in brackets). Hence, a Soviet source took pains to stress the Jewish origin of a foreign "cosmopolitan nihilist" whose theories had tainted a local cosmopolitan — nor was this the only instance of this kind. Incidentally, it was the Nazis who in 1933 first revealed Normano's identity as Levin, when he escaped from Germany to America, but Normano himself later denied this.[66]

In the field of jurisprudence, those denounced included B. Osherovich; in his work *On the History of Russian Legal Thought* he had exaggerated his appraisal of "the degree of the influence of West European philosophical and legal concepts in molding Russian social thinking," and had not duly recognized the originality and independence of Russian social thinking in the fields of philosophy and law. Among other jurists denounced were Trainin, Gringaus, Eisenstadt, Rabinovich, Karp, and Gertsenson (the latter had opposed the application of the "analogy" principle).

Turning to philosophy, we find such names as Z. Kamensky, V. Hofenshafer, Y. Cherniak, M. Slektor, and M. Rosental among those charged with denigrating Russian thought.[67]

In regard to Rosental, we feel we should point to an important detail concerned with the campaign against cosmopolitanism. Rosental was described as constituting the link between cosmopolitans in the realm of philosophy and those in the field of literary criticism; just as in another instance, Bleiman was charged with serving as a link between the antipatriotic group in the field of the cinema and the cosmopolitan theater critics.[68]

The press also pointed to the ties maintained by cosmopolitans in different cities and districts. At first, readers were told, some of the leading cosmopolitans in the field of dramatic criticism denied that they formed a "group," but "on being pressed to the wall, they were forced to confess, albeit reluctantly and holding back certain facts, to the existence of a group, to plotting, and to deliberate, coordinated activity." This admission was made by Y. Yuzovsky, a leading author and teacher of dramatic art (he was alleged, on one occasion, to have had no interest in getting to know the Russian language, the Russian people and its culture). Yuzovsky disclosed that the group aimed "to cause harm to Russian drama by dint of flank attacks."[69] In other words: those who directed the anticosmopolitan campaign endeavored to prove that the views held by the various nihilists and antipatriots were not merely indirectly harmful thoughts, but actually constituted a real conspiracy. Cosmopolitans were also charged with covering up for one another and praising one another in the course of their subversive activity. Thus, for example, it was said of one critic that "the antipatriotic nature of the homeless cosmopolitan Levin is most clearly shown in his sympathies" for Pasternak, Melnikov (Melman), Yuzovsky, and Gurvich; whereas, on the other hand, he had run down such patriotic works as the *Pedagogic Poem* by A. Makarenko, *Thus the Steel was Tempered* by N. Ostrovsky, and *Far from Moscow* by V. Azhayev.[70] This was intended to allude to the prevalence of Jewish communal solidarity that was opposed to the general spirit of the country — an age-old anti-Semitic device.

In not a few cases, the rootless cosmopolitans were branded as elements hostile not only to the Soviet homeland as a whole, but also as persons who despised the national cultures of specific Soviet peoples. This practice was particularly in evidence in the Ukraine, where it was natural to stir up latent or overt anti-Jewish feelings. The charge was laid against Stebun (Katznelson) that throughout all his literary activity he had maligned the Ukrainian classical literature. Burlachenko (Berdichevsky) was accused of denigrating the Ukrainian theater and of finding no more then mere "vestiges of nationalism" in the Ukrainian culture. Such critics as Y. Gordon and A. Shamrai were denounced for discovering the influences of Heine and of English poets in the work of the Ukrainian national poetess Lesa Ukrainka. Theater critics like G. Gelfandbein, L. Yukhvid, and L. Zhadanov (Lifshits) were alleged to have instituted a reign of terror against local Ukrainian theaters. A list of people with distinctly Jewish-sounding names (in or out of brackets) — persons alien to Ukrainian dramatic art — were charged with having ensconced themselves among the staff of the Ukrainian Theater Association, from which position they were able to besmirch Ukrainian drama and theater. Other nihilistic besmirchers include A. Gozenpud, Y. Gan (Kagan), Adelheim, C. Tokar, E. Martich (Finkelstein), and Sanov (Smulson).[71]

In the phrasing of these attacks on the "rootless ones" in the Ukraine we find concessions to Ukrainian nationalism at the expense of the Jews. This was obviously an attempt to accord some degree of emotional compensation to those who resented the political and cultural Russification that was aimed at Ukrainian nationalism. Here there emerges the apparently surprising fact that whereas cosmopolitans of Jewish origin were denounced for disparaging the national

Ukrainian culture which was foreign to them, at the same time criticism was leveled at indications of nationalistic deviation or recidivism in Ukrainian literature and art (similar phenomena were manifest also in regard to local national cultures elsewhere). Thus, one eye kept nationalistic manifestations under surveillance, while the other winked at them seductively.

We shall list further names of "passportless wanderers" who were alleged to have maligned or set out to demolish Ukrainian culture and its institutions — men who had "infiltrated" into various fields of activity: M. Stein, Y. Pustynsky, A. Grin, Eselson, Halperin, Hilikh, M. Grinshpon, and Leonid Pervomaisky. One had maligned Ukrainian music, another had sneered at the Ukrainian theater; one had fawned on the bourgeois gangster films, and the other had lauded the degeneracy of Europe . . .

What the abovenamed had done in the Ukraine, such nihilists as Y. Gertsevich, M. Model, L. Berg, Meyerovich, and others had wrought to the Belorussian people and its culture. They, chiefly, were alleged to have asserted that the Belorussian people was not capable of original artistic creation, or possessed no folklore of its own.[72]

In various places and in various fields of endeavor a venomous atmosphere was deliberately engendered around the cosmopolitans. Not only was their literary or philosophical worthlessness exposed, but they were also stigmatized as being possessed of base personal and social characteristics. Thus, for example, Stebun (Katznelson) and Sanov (Smulson) were pilloried as liars and swindlers.[73] The nihilists and rootless wanderers were often denounced as saboteurs and subversives and compared to spies. Of the "traitorous cosmopolitans" who muddied the "pure waters" of Soviet culture (among them such men as Yuzovsky, Gurvich, Borshchagovsky, Altman, Warshavsky, Malyugin, and Kholodov) it was written that "they have infiltrated to us . . . like enemy saboteurs and spies. To open fire on them — this is our patriotic duty!"[74] *Pravda* wrote: "Cosmopolitans without a homeland, who know nothing of creative work, of truth and honor, have infiltrated into our editorial offices, our scientific institutions and universities. They are persons devoid of any sense of duty towards the people, the state, or the Party. It is our pressing task, therefore, to smoke them out of their lairs, for these people, who lack a nation and a country, impede the development of Soviet literature."[75] Such remarks could not but be regarded as a manifest, practically official, call to oust the parasitic nihilists from the institutions referred to in the article. And indeed, there is every reason to believe that this call met with an enthusiastic response. It may also be assumed that, in addition to such promptings and allusions, there were explicit instructions to carry out the purge. At a meeting of the Party cell of the Gorky Institute of World Literature it was decided to expel B. Yakovlev (Holtsman) from the Party, and to investigate the "conciliatory attitude" towards him of several authors — among them E. Bialik. Shortly afterwards, G. Brovman, head of the Department of Soviet Literature, and consultants Feodor Levin and Pavel Antokolsky were dismissed from their posts at the Gorky Institute.[76]

Several further particulars concerning Antokolsky are relevant. At the beginning of 1947 he had published an article which might be said to have contained an admission that Soviet citizens — chiefly young people — returning from European countries where they had served in the army or in other capacities, had become prone to an idealization of Western culture. Antokolsky had in fact deplored this idealization, which, he claimed, stemmed from an admiration of such achievements of personal convenience as good roads, bathrooms, bicycles, cameras, cigarette lighters, and the like. It was not in such things, Antokolsky maintained, that true culture inhered, such as was prevalent particularly in the Soviet Union.[77] Such views are hardly an indication of fawning on the West, nevertheless the anticosmopolitan campaign did not pass over Antokolsky. Though he was far from Jewish culture and affairs, he was charged with cosmopolitanism tainted with Jewish nationalism, as attested to by a series of his poems, allegedly "inspired by Zionist feeling and bourgeois nationalism."[78]

Similar charges, though more concrete and aggressive, were leveled at Alexander Isbakh (readers were informed, as has been previously mentioned, that his real name was Isak Bakhrakh). In a story included in his autobiographical collection *Years of Life,* published in 1948, he had sinned in describing Jewish ritual practices in detail — he had depicted his own bar mitzvah ceremony, the synagogue service, and the calling up to the reading of the Torah, which his critics termed "a glorification of the Jewish religion." Moreover, Isbakh had pointed out that he had been influenced by Zionism in his early youth, and had even quoted some lines of *Hatikva,* the Zionist anthem, in the original Hebrew (transliterated) and in translation. This was denounced as "overt Zionist propaganda." Equally heinous was the fact that Isbakh was allegedly inspired by literary critic Levin.[79]

And indeed — as was frequently explained to Soviet readers and listeners — cosmopolitanism assumed various guises, such as pan-Americanism, Catholicism, or Zionism. Yet whatever its guise might be, it "objectively served the interests of imperialist reaction."[80] Such sweeping definitions naturally afforded extensive possibilities for persecution and purge operations. In the light of these definitions it was not difficult, for example, to attribute "cosmopolitan deviations" to a number of Orientalists charged with adopting too conciliatory an attitude towards Zionism. A special conference, in fact, was convened in order to combat "manifestations of bourgeois cosmopolitanism in scientific Orientalist works." One of the leading speakers at this conference was V. Lutsky, who devoted part of his address to "the functions of the Oriental research front in the struggle against Zionism — the reactionary ideology of Jewish bourgeois nationalism." To engage in this struggle was hardly a new task, but it had assumed particular urgency in view of the fact that "Zionism is one of the operative weapons of American and British imperialistic policy in the Near East." Lutsky went on to say that "the immediate task of Soviet Orientalists engaged in [research of] the Near East is to unmask and demolish the cosmopolitan ideology of 'a united Jewish nation' — an ideology that was shatteringly condemned both by Lenin and by Stalin."[81]

Once cosmopolitanism — in literature, science, and politics — was associated with Jewish sentiments, with the reprehensible mythos of world Jewish unity, with Zionist concepts and the like, this augured the adoption of the most stringent measures against Jewish culture in the Soviet Union. These measures were chiefly directed against Yiddish literature which, it will be recalled, abundantly manifested Jewish national feelings following the war.

We shall endeavor to reconstruct the total liquidation of Soviet Jewish culture in the following chapter. At this point, we shall content ourselves with adducing one particular, pointing to the incorporation of the campaign against Jewish culture within the frame of the general campaign against cosmopolitanism. In February 1949, there was published a denunciation of "cosmopolitan objectivist views" prominently reflected in the attitude to Jewish literature adopted by the authors of a plan for a glossary for the Great Soviet Encyclopedia (second edition). These "Cosmopolitans without a Homeland" (the title of the article in question) were charged with allotting a similar place in the glossary to contemporary Jewish literature to that allotted to the Uzbek, Kazakh, and Georgian literatures all together. The authors, it was ironically remarked, had "added the highly interesting observation that the glossary embraced the *entire* Jewish literature." This, it appeared, was a nationalist deviation that fitted in with the cosmopolitan infraction, thus:

> They [the compilers of the glossary] take "the entire Jewish literature" regardless of countries and political systems, and extract the cosmopolitan, nationalist-bourgeois idea — helpful to the enemies of our homeland — concerning the alleged existence of an all-world Jewish literature. In [compiling] their list, these Soviet writers place themselves on the same level as confirmed present-day businessmen in America, Palestine, and other countries. The harboring of such a concept can be termed nothing other than slavish fawning on inimical, nationalist-bourgeois concepts.[82]

Thus we may see that the anti-Jewish campaign had recourse to a kind of point and counterpoint. On the one hand Jews were widely branded as cosmopolitans, and on the other, many Jews (often the same ones) were accused of harboring excessive communal and nationalistic feelings — an apparent inconsistency deriving from the fact that Judaism combines universal elements with a desire for national integrity. In the words of Yaacov Talmon: the distinctiveness of Judaism inheres in "the constant tension between that indomitable desire to preserve our identity, despite those forces which strive to efface or even eradicate it, and between that deep adherence to universal content and values, of which the Jewish nation is one of the fathers."[83]

In Stalin's latter years, it appears, this dichotomy contributed its share towards regarding the Jewish community in the Soviet Union as a collective persona non grata. The Jews came to be considered a differentiative element, both because of their inherent desire for a national existence and also because of their innate susceptibility to all-human values. History abounds in instances of Jews being hated as foreigners. Rationalization of this hatred was based — either alternately or at one and the same time — both on the Jewish adherence to specific traditions and way of life, and also on their taking root and becoming assimilated to their environment. It is well known, similarly, that in some countries clerical circles despised both the bearded *kapota*-clad Jew, symbol of communal isolation, and also the modern type of Jew, whom they regarded as being infected with the germs of atheism. From the aspect of the atmosphere that was engendered, the postwar attitude to the Jews in the Soviet Union was not very different. Against the background of the prevailing political, social, and cultural trends, the Jews were regarded by the authorities as an anomalous element both for the excessive "universalism" and the excessive "Jewishness" they manifested.

Thus they paid the penalty both for their "cosmopolitanism" and for their "nationalism."

FIVE

A Culture Uprooted — A People Effaced

The campaign against cosmopolitanism had only indirectly pursued an anti-Jewish trend; within a short time the Soviet authorities took direct, deliberately planned, and definitive measures to liquidate the entire Jewish culture in the country.

Einikeit, the official organ of the Jewish Anti-Fascist Committee, had appeared thrice weekly since February 24, 1945; its last issue came out, or was circulated, at all events, on November 20, 1948. This also marked the dissolution of the Jewish Anti-Fascist Committee. A few weeks later, the *Emes* Moscow publishing house was closed down. The bimonthly *Heimland,* founded in 1947, had appeared regularly since the beginning of 1948; its last — the seventh — issue came off the press in September 1948 but its circulation was suppressed. The Kiev *Der Shtern,* which had begun to appear in 1947, met with a similar fate: its seventh issue, at the end of 1948, had also been printed but was suppressed, though the sixth issue, dated November 1, 1948, had featured an advertisement soliciting subscriptions for the year 1949. In stating the need to close down *Der Shtern,* this periodical was alleged to have been "severed from the Soviet people, from the wide Jewish toiling masses. It fostered nationalistic tendencies and a small-town psychology, and went so far as to presume to draw a comparison between the Soviet Jew and the Jew abroad."[1]

Soviet Jewry was thus deprived of any vehicle of written expression, apart from *Birobidzhaner Shtern.* That this paper — the sole organ that survived the eradication of Jewish culture throughout the country — was allowed to continue to appear may be attributed to the authorities' desire to retain some sort of alibi in case of need, or possibly there may have been a number of Jews in Birobidzhan who knew no language other than Yiddish and the authorities wished to retain some medium of communication with them. At all events, the continued appearance of *Birobidzhaner Shtern* — of narrow local content — hardly changes the picture. According to various reports, after 1948 the paper was printed in about one thousand copies — a number that exceeded its actual circulation — as a rule thrice weekly. It usually ran to no more than two pages and its contents, though printed in Jewish typescript, were not even remotely connected with Jewish affairs. It is an intersting fact that even the most competent bibliographers have been unable to ascertain exact particulars concerning the appearance of this paper after 1948. Not only was it not sent abroad, but even in the Soviet Union it was virtually impossible to get a copy outside the Birobidzhan province.[2]

By the end of 1948 it had already become apparent that the campaign to liquidate Jewish culture was assuming total proportions, and, what was more, was pursuing a distinctly vandal course. When the *Emes* Publishing house and the abovementioned periodicals were closed down, not only were manuscripts confiscated, but Jewish linotype machines were dismantled and Jewish type destroyed as well. When the reprinting of the Jewish prayer book was permitted several years after Stalin's death, this was perforce done from old photographic plates.[3]

Later, in the mid-Fifties, Soviet spokesmen pointed to the difficulties besetting the reappearance of Jewish literature in the Soviet Union, due, they claimed, to the absence of a "polygraphic basis." Strange as this contention must sound against the background of the technological potential of a country that launched the first satellite — the Sputnik — into space in 1957, it nonetheless reflects the cruel aftermath of the liquidation of Jewish culture. When the Yiddish magazine *Sovetish Heimland* began to appear in August 1961, containing the first Yiddish writing to be published in the Soviet Union (apart from *Birobidzhaner Shtern*) since the end of 1948, plates etched from drawings were for some time used for the headlines, presumably for lack of suitable size type.

The authorities did not merely suppress the further publication of Jewish literary creation; they imposed the ban retroactively. Bookshops were purged of all Jewish writing. Jewish libraries were closed down and Jewish books disappeared from other public libraries, or withdrawn to a classified *Spetsodel* (Special Section), to which the general public were denied access.[4] It was not so much the contents of these books that decided their fate, as the very fact that they were in the Yiddish language and were formally associated with overall Jewish expression. The entire Jewish literature — and not merely "dangerous" writing — was included in the Soviet "Index," in the same way as Hebrew literature had been banned twenty years before. Yiddish was denied even the right to continue praising Stalin, and the most patriotic works in this language were suppressed or banned. Jewish gramophone records met a similar fate. By that time there were practically no Jewish schools in the Soviet Union: those that had been destroyed in the war were not reconstructed. The two last Jewish educational institutions, the schools in Vilna and Kovno, were closed down in the summer of 1949.[5] By the end of the Forties, the liquidation operations had extended to the last remaining Jewish workers' clubs, together with their amateur art and drama groups and choirs. All Jewish professional theaters, which had resumed their regular activities in Moscow, Kiev, Minsk, Odessa, Kharkov, Czernovitz, and Birobidzhan towards the end of the war or after it, were liquidated in 1949. The Jewish State Theater in Moscow survived a little longer — it was last billed in a newspaper notice in November 1949 — but its last year was overshadowed by an inexorable death sentence. This theater had, in fact, been pervaded by an atmosphere of dread since the murder of Solomon Mikhoels in January 1948. Following his death in Minsk, several members of the Theater's personnel disappeared. It may reasonably be assumed that the authorities prolonged the death throes of the Moscow Jewish Theater so that it might serve as a trap to identify those who still clung to the culture that was doomed to extinction. Before its end, in fact, the theater was sparsely attended.

Several facts concerning the last years of the Moscow Jewish State Theater are relevant. It is a cruel irony, indeed, that after the theater staged its first postwar production, *Freilechs,* director Solomon Mikhoels, actor Binyamin Zuskin and stage artist Alexander Tishler were given the 1945 Stalin Award — a distinction that elated the members of the theater and the exponents of Jewish culture as a whole. Mikhoels then stated that this honor had not been conferred on individuals; it was a celebration, a victory for the entire Soviet Jewish people. Zuskin, who pointed out that the staging of *Freilechs* gave expression to the concept that "The Jewish People Lives!" stressed with pride: "Where, when, and in what country is it possibile that the exponents of Jewish culture should be awarded such a high mark of appreciation on the part of the government!"[6] The conferment of the award was variously celebrated, and the national implications of *Freilechs* were repeatedly stressed. It was pointed out, for instance, that when Zuskin, in a voice charged with both sad and joyful overtones, uttered the words, "Let there be a people — and let there be celebrations among Jews!" the hall shook with the thunderous storm of applause.[7]

This elation was short-lived. Not only had Mikhoels's murder engendered a general air of despondency, but the manifestly inimical administrative attitude adopted by the authorities towards the Moscow Jewish Theater also boded no good. This theater (like other Jewish theaters in the country) was in straitened financial circumstances. According to a general government directive, Soviet theaters had to provide their own budgets, apart from the theaters of national minorities which were subsidized. The subsidy was withdrawn from the Moscow Jewish Theater, however. Various reports indicate that the Jewish public showed a readiness to help the theater remain financially self-sufficient. The issue of subscription tickets met with an enthusiastic response, but this "Jewish fund-raising" aroused the vigilance of the authorities, who regarded this as an attempt at national organization. (Subsequently, many of the subscribers were arrested.)

In January 1949, the Department of Jewish Culture at the Ukrainian Academy of Sciences in Kiev was closed down. This department — a diminished resuscitation of the Cultural Institute that had been liquidated in 1936–37 and many of its staff executed in the purge —

had resumed its activities after the war, and Soviet Jewish cultural circles had regarded it as a promising scientific center. It was again headed by Eliahu Spivak, a celebrated scholar and one of the noblest figures on the Soviet Jewish public scene, who dedicated himself to his task. The same fate, however, was meted out to Spivak and to the institution he headed: he was arrested on the day the police authorities arrived to close down the department.[8]

The atmosphere of dread grew so heavy that many Jews performed an auto-da-fé on their books in the Yiddish language or on Jewish subjects; they even destroyed Judaica translated into Russian from other languages, such as works by Leon Feuchtwanger dealing with themes from Jewish history. There is shocking evidence of this self-inquisition, which consisted of throwing books into garbage bins or burning them in stoves — which often called for a great measure of resourcefulness to cover up the traces.[9]

The liquidation operations claimed both institutions and individuals as victims.[10] The leading Jewish writers in Moscow were arrested at the end of 1948 and beginning of 1949. Itsik Feffer, who had accompanied Solomon Mikhoels on his overseas visit in 1943 and was one of the leading spokesmen of the Jewish Anti-Fascist Committee, was one of the first to be arrested, together with his wife and sister-in-law. Within a short time they were followed by Perets Markish, David Bergelson, Leib Kvitko, Shmuel Halkin, David Hofstein, Yitzhak Nusinov, Yehezkel Dobrushin, and Der Nister. Each no doubt fearfully awaited his inexorable turn. Der Nister, for instance, was said to have exclaimed "At last!" to the policemen who came to arrest him. This waiting must have been too much for Aaron Kushnirov, whose death in mid-1949 thwarted his certain arrest; his widow was deported together with the wives of the other imprisoned writers. Binyamin Zuskin, director of the Moscow Jewish State Theater and its leading actor, was also arrested at about that time.

So far we have enumerated only the most representative figures among the victims, but this listing is enough to show that the Soviet authorities had urgently set out to "decapitate" Soviet Jewry, for it is difficult to imagine that Jewish culture could survive once it was deprived of its most creative forces practically at one sweep. The liquidation now extended its range to other Jewish centers. We have mentioned the liquidation of the Department of Jewish Culture in Kiev. Together with Spivak there were arrested, one by one, a large number of Jewish writers and practically all the members of the department's staff. They included: Itzik Kipnis, Avraham Velednitsky, Abraham Kahan, Motl Talalayevsky, Riva Balyasnaya, Hershel Polianker, Chaim Loitsker, Moshe Maydansky, R. Lerner, Moshe Beregovsky, Z. Skoditsky, Benjamin Gutyansky, Elie Shechtman, Nathan Zabare, Shlomo Cherniavsky, and David Volkenstein.

Those arrested in Minsk included: Isaac Platner, Hershel Kamenetsky. In Vilna, Kovno, and Riga: Mark Razumny, M. Shatz-Anin, Hirsh Osherovich, Mikhail Yo, and A. Movshovich.

In the purge of the Bessarabian (Moldavian) or "Romanian" branch of Soviet Jewish literature, the victims included its central representative, author-actor-director Yaakov Sternberg, and also Moshe Altman, Motl Sakzier, Yankel Yakir, Hertz Rivkin, Meir Kharatz, and Yehiel Shreibman.

The liquidation perpetrated in Birobidzhan deserves to be dwelt on at length in view of the official status accorded the "Jewish Autonomous Province." Developments in the region during several years preceding 1948 should, however, first be reviewed.[11]

At the end of the war there were some 25,000 Jews living in Birobidzhan, among a total population of about 100,000. The resumption of Jewish migration there after the war brought about some sort of national Jewish awakening in the province. Though the Jews were a minority, they were nevertheless easily recognized there as an ethnic group, and Jewish communal activity could be promoted and backed by formal territorial rights.

The literary periodical *Birobidzhan* was launched in 1946, already before Jewish periodicals in Moscow and Kiev began to make their postwar reappearance. In the same year, the Birobidzhan Jewish State Theater, named after Lazar Kaganovich, resumed and enlarged its scope of activity, recruiting new talent; in the 1947–48 season it staged a series of new plays and laid ambitious plans for the future. A regional Jewish publishing house was founded in Birobidzhan in 1946. It brought out two collections of poems, in 1947 and 1948, and announced an enlarged publishing program for 1949.

In *Einikeit*'s last year, 1948, it abundantly featured news items, stories, and articles about Birobidzhan, about the arrival there and integration of new settlers, and about achievements and future projects. The paper adopted a generally optimistic tone, frequently stressing that "Birobidzhan Awaits New Builders" — the title of one of the articles.[12] M. Levitin, chairman of the Provincial Executive of the Jewish Autonomous Province, published an article in *Einikeit* towards the end of July 1948, which contained several "summings-up and prospects" of renewed migration to the region, and was generally charged with a note of gratification and assurance.[13] It should be noted that although the material published on Birobidzhan aimed to bring out the general prospects of the region and stress that Soviet patriotism was the principal factor that motivated settlement there, a manifestly Jewish note was also introduced, albeit indirectly. The articles and feature stories told of the *Jews* who migrated there and the Jews who welcomed them, of Jews building factories and founding farms, of Jews who were establishing their lives anew — not to speak of the reports, sparse though they were, of specifically Jewish communal and cultural activity. Such publication was no doubt a direct answer to the yearning of a great many Jews during that period to live among their own people.

It was not long before the hopes fostered by Birobidzhan were cruelly shattered. The Kaganovich Theater, the Jewish publishing house and the *Birobidzhan* magazine (of which only three numbers are known to have appeared) were closed down, as were the surviving Jewish schools. Nor were they replaced by other institutions, and all the various schemes were abolished.

Birobidzhan had been proud of its Sholem Aleichem Library, which in 1947–48 had run to 130,000 volumes, including some 30,000 Jewish works. The library had contained a rich collection of Judaica in various languages, including a considerable number of works in Hebrew. Practically the entire collection of Jewish works, or those dealing with Jewish subjects, was destroyed in the liquidation operations. One censor was said to have used these books as kindling to heat his flat in winter. From firsthand reports of overseas visitors to Birobidzhan after Stalin's death, it is learned that a mere few hundred Yiddish books remained on the library shelves, in the "foreign language book" section. Most of these were translations from other languages, especially the translated works of Marx, Engels, Lenin, and Stalin (of the latter, presumably up to the Twentieth Congress). Some Jewish books might have remained in the library's vaults.[14] A similar situation was revealed to a *New York Times* correspondent who visited the province in June 1954 and inquired at a local bookshop. The only Yiddish books he found there were a few dusty volumes of Sholem Aleichem, Stalin's *Problems of Leninism,* and *Short History of the Communist Party.*[15]

Another important Birobidzhan institution was the regional geographical museum, which had been officially opened in June 1945. One of its four sections was assigned to Jewish culture; this section collected material relating to the Jewish contribution to civilization, rare Jewish books, exhibits depicting Jewish traditional life (before the revolution), and also material on the Jewish share in the war against Germany. It was headed by author Ber Slutsky, who, though nearly seventy years of age, threw himself wholeheartedly into his task. Already before the official opening of the museum, the man who was appointed its director had appealed to all "Jewish writers, artists, actors, and cultural leaders in the Soviet Union," asking them to help him in collecting books, manuscripts, objects of historical interest, and the like. He stated then that the aim of the museum was "to assemble everything of value to the history of the Jewish people, to collect and reconstitute any relics of the cultural treasures of the Jewish people that have survived the terrible destruction wrought by the Fascist vandals." It appears that the entire museum was closed down in 1949. To an American journalist who visited it in 1954 it seemed quite new, as if opened less than a year before; but, he writes, "there wasn't a word in the museum about Jewish culture or the Jewish language or the Jewish contribution to the oblast [region]. The only indication that Jews had had any part in Birobidzhan was three old copies of the Yiddish paper [*Birobidzhaner Shtern*] which I saw in one obscure cabinet."[16]

The anti-Jewish purge in Birobidzhan claimed a great many writers, artists, and communal leaders as its victims. About forty of them were sentenced to long terms of imprisonment. Some of them received death sentences which were later commuted to long terms of imprisonment.[17] Those arrested included: Mikhail Levitin, who had only recently published his authoritative "summings-up and prospects" of Jewish migration to the region (he died in prison); Alexander Bakhmutsky, secretary of the regional Party Committee; Moshe Zilberstein, former chairman of the Regional Executive Committee; and the locally resident Jewish writers: Israel Emyot, Ber Slutsky (he died in prison), Buzi Miller, Hershel Rabinkov, Liuba Vasserman and Chaim Maltinsky.

They were charged, primarily, with nationalist activity, of which various "proofs" were adduced. The Jewish theater, for example, was alleged to have devoted itself entirely to a repertoire of Jewish reactionary and petit bourgeois content. The Birobidzhan museum was alleged to have engaged not only in the local geographic and ethnic field, but to have set out to highlight Jewish history. Israel Emyot had arrived in the Soviet Union from occupied Poland during the war together with other refugee writers: in 1944 he had moved from Moscow to Birobidzhan, at the instance of the Jewish Anti-Fascist Committee, to promote cultural activity in the region. On his arrest, however, he was charged, like his fellow victims, with artificially fostering Jewish culture in a region with a predominantly non-Jewish population. Jewish writers and communal leaders were accused of attempting to expand the local Yiddish newspaper, and even of planning to establish a Yiddish-language university. They were denounced for stressing the Jewish aspect of life and endeavor in the region, for organizing the rousing welcoming receptions that were held for the new arrivals. According to the authorities' reactions, this alleged nationalism was not merely a sentimental or spiritual manifestation, but was associated in devious ways with espionage and sabotage conspiracies. It was characteristic that the Jewish "plot" exposed in Birobidzhan — as in other places in the Soviet Union — should be alleged to be in the service of America. Just as in the Thirties the purged Birobidzhan leaders had been accused of serving Japanese intelligence and imperialism, they were similarly now accused chiefly of being Washington's agents and of plotting to deliver the region into American hands. Had not Birobidzhan Jews continued to receive food and clothing parcels from America long after the cessation of lend-lease? Birobidzhan, it was charged, had been turned into a hotbed of espionage, in accordance with the plans that JAC emissaries Mikhoels and Feffer had been handed during their visit to the USA in 1943.

The liquidation operations in the region were directed primarily at leading Jewish citizens and institutions, in a Birobidzhanian version of the "decapitation" of Soviet Jewry. All distinctive Jewish signs were virtually effaced. Migration to the region was halted. Yiddish stopped being a language in administrative use. The Yiddish inscription was removed from the postmarks. A street sign bearing the name of Henekh Kazakevich, first eiditor of *Birobidzhaner Shtern,* was changed. Some signs in both languages were still allowed to remain on a few streets and offices and also on the local railway station, but they, like the Yiddish paper, seemed like a flickering memorial to the Jewishness of the "Jewish Autonomous Province." In the 1950 general elections to the Supreme Soviet, only one of the five elected Birobidzhan deputies to the Soviet of Nationalities was a Jew. The previously quoted *New York Times* correspondent who visited the province in 1954 found that "it was plain that Birobidjan had lost its significance as a Jewish center a long time ago."[18]

At the end of 1948, the Jewish population of Birobidzhan, including the new settlers, was estimated at about 30,000. According to the census taken in 1959, the Jews in the region numbered no more than 14,269 — or less than 8.8 percent of the total population of 162,856. It is possible that in 1959 there were Jews living in Birobidzhan who chose not to identify themselves as such, or the 1948 estimate might have been exaggerated. There is no doubt however — as is affirmed by an Israeli who visited the region in the Fifties, after Stalin's death — that after 1948 "thousands of Jews left the region, not in an organized manner, of course, but as individuals. They simply dropped off and got away." It is practically certain, moreover, that most of the Jews who moved from Birobidzhan during the purges did not return to their former homes in the Ukraine and Belorussia, but remained in the outlying northeastern areas. There, they were able to discard the label of "Jewish autonomy" — an anonymity that no doubt rendered their lives somewhat easier. In Khabarovsk, for example, the Israeli visitor found that the Jews who had arrived from Birobidzhan felt better than they had in their own "national province."[19] The American correspondent records the interesting fact that in the "transfers" of Jewish population that took place during the purges of 1948–49, they were sent to such places as Yakutia (in eastern Siberia, where there is a large Tartar population), and not to the Jewish province. On the other hand, he found in Birobidzhan a sizable Tartar minority, survivors of those who had been deported from Crimea at the end of the war.[20]

It is interesting to note the surveillance under which the American correspondent was kept during his Birobidzhan visit. Though he had lived in the Soviet Union during Stalin's last years, he affirms that "Never, in my stay in Russia, had I experienced such surveillance." He could hardly take a single step without being tailed by a troop of detectives, who behaved roughly and with barely any attempt at concealment. Very soon he discovered that his hotel manager was the local secret police chief.[21] Though, as has been mentioned, the visit took place in June 1954, the stringent measures taken by the authorities no doubt reflected the heavy atmosphere engendered in Birobidzhan and its surroundings in previous years.

In the light of what happened in Birobidzhan and the grim reality of the "Autonomous Jewish Province," there inevitably arises the question: why did not the authorities rescind the region's formal status? The fact that this status has been retained until the final preparation of this work for print (1970) adds cogency to the question. Any answers that are offered must needs be largely hypothetical. It is possible that the noncommittal status of Birobidzhan has been kept in reserve against the need to make a change in the official line adopted in regard to the Jews. It may possibly be intended to serve the ends of external propaganda. Or it may be used by the Soviet authorities as proof of their attempt to accord Jews full national rights. That is to say: the Jews, and not the regime, are to blame for not having made use of the chance they were given. Or it may possibly be motivated by "reluctance to admit ideological failure."[22] Another possible reason why the Jewish Autonomous Province was not abolished may lie in the fact that its existence, like that of other autonomous provinces, is laid down in the Constitution (paragraph 22). And it may be that all these reasons together (with others) account for the retention of Birobidzhan's formal status quo. Nevertheless, it is beyond all doubt that in the late Forties and early Fifties the "Autonomous Jewish Province" had become a mere fiction.

Let us go back to the liquidation of Jewish culture and its exponents on a countrywide scale. With a certainty backed by reliable evidence we are able to list many additional names of victims from different places. They include: Z. Vendrof (David Vendrovsky), Elie Falkovich, Moshe Broderzon, Moshe Taif, Noah Luria, Moshe Byelenky, Shlomo Rabinovich, Mikhoel Apelbaum, Zinovi Shulman, Saul Lyubimov, Shmuel Gordon, Leib Avram, Shmuel Agursky, Avraham Gontar, Yosef Rabin, I. Lyumkis, Naftali Hertz Kon, M. Mizhritsky, and A. Frumkin.

From a scrutiny of the names of the writers and artists who were arrested it transpires that some of them were in their seventies, and others in their thirties. Not a few of them had fought in the war, had been wounded and decorated. Chaim Maltinsky, born in 1910, for example, is known to have fought in combat units from the beginning of the Soviet-German war, and to have returned from the conquest of Berlin with a great many decorations and an amputated leg. This did not save him from the purge, however, and he was sentenced to ten years in a "rigid discipline" camp. Some of the victims were writers who had taken part in public affairs and had from time to time become involved in literary controversies; others had kept away from the public scene, devoting themselves entirely to their work. Some had been outstanding authors, while others had been failures. Some had incessantly sung the praises of the regime; others had shown restraint in professing patriotic sentiments. We may add that some of them were men of integrity, while others had occasionally been suspected of denouncing their colleagues. The mills of Stalinist justice, however, ground them all with indiscriminate violence.

The trepidation caused by the liquidation operations caused Jewish writers and artists to shut themselves up in their homes. After the arrest of several leading Moscow writers, police officials stayed in their apartments to keep track of all who came there. Such was the atmosphere of terror, that one Jewish writer, who had been hidden by a non-Jewish woman during the Nazi occupation, was again saved from arrest by the same woman: she hid him in her pigsty, where he remained until Stalin's death.[23]

The wives and families of the prisoners, including parents and brothers and sisters, were subjected to humiliation and want; many of them were exiled to remote regions. Those writers who were not immediately arrested, as well as the few who survived the ravaging terror, were left without means of support, having become outcasts, expelled from the Writers' Association, and from the Party, if they had been members. The prevailing atmosphere was hardly conducive to their finding literary work outside the Yiddish field. Writers, artists, and actors sought jobs as bathhouse janitors or cloakroom attendants in barbershops, and some took to stitching handkerchiefs for a living. A number of them had to be supported by their children, or, contrariwise, by their aged parents.

Later in this chapter we shall dwell on a large group of Jewish authors, artists, and other leading personages who were put to death. Others, as has been stated, died in prisons and labor camps. Dozens who were released in the mid-Fifties were shattered in body and spirit.

How many were arrested in the wave of anti-Jewish purges perpetrated between 1948 and 1953, and how many perished? Any attempt at arithmetical reconstruction can hardly lead to a complete, accurate figure. There are, however, several key systems that may be — and have been — used in attempting to arrive at an estimated figure.

A list compiled on the strength of data culled from Soviet Yiddish publications (dailies, periodicals, and single issues) from 1936 to 1940 included the names of some eight hundred Jewish authors, journalists, literary critics, researchers, translators, editors, etc.[24] In mid-1956, a Communist source in the United States set the number of surviving Jewish writers at seventy-one.[25] The first issue of *Sovetish Heimland,* which began to appear in Moscow in August 1961, listed 112 Soviet writers who would contribute to the new Yiddish magazine. Later, the names of more contributors to it were mentioned, among them several dozen names that first became known in the Sixties, and had not appeared on the list for 1936–1940. What, then, had happened to those eight hundred? Many of them no doubt died a natural death, and scores had perished in the purges of the Thirties. About forty writers had fallen in the war, and several had been murdered by the Nazis. It may also be assumed that some had quietly given up writing in Yiddish and had turned to Russian or Ukrainian,[26] and some no doubt chose — chiefly for safety's sake — the anonymity of nonliterary occupations. At all events, whatever had remained of the Yiddish literary manpower at the end of the war suffered a crushing blow between 1948 and 1953. A similar fate befell those men engaged in other branches of Jewish culture. The number of those arrested ran into the hundreds. According to a Communist source, of the 140 Yiddish authors who were living in the Soviet Union in 1964, "eighty had not been arrested by Beria."[27] This is in effect an admission that sixty of those living authors had been among those arrested, in addition to those who had been executed, those who had died in prison or after their release, and those who had not resumed their Yiddish literary activity. The number thus arrived at still does not include men who were engaged in other cultural branches. It must again be pointed out that the eighty authors who "had not been arrested by Beria" included a number who had not yet been active in the field of Yiddish literature at the end of the Forties.

What, actually, were the crimes of the writers and other exponents of Jewish culture who were arrested, interrogated, and sentenced? It will have been seen in Chapter Three that their crime lay in the spiritual and emotional trends they had manifested during the Forties — as revealed, explicitly or implicitly, in their recent writing, in the expression of their inner convictions, or in their incorrect appraisal of what was permissible and what was not. Their fate was sealed because they had become an undesirable, and hence, according to the rule of prophylactic justice, a dangerous element.

The various writers and artists were primarily charged with nationalistic and chauvinistic tendencies, with Jewish egocentricity and with adopting a universal Jewish ideology — crimes compatible with those of insufficiently or incorrectly representing the Soviet brotherhood of nations, and of indifference to the theme of postwar reconstruction. For several years, Jewish periodicals had published criticisms of harmful trends in Soviet Jewish literature and had condemned a great many writers — especially following the resolutions of the Communist Party's Central Committee and Zhdanov's speeches on literary and artistic matters. Such criticism could well have been interpreted as a warning sounded by the authorities.

This criticism has been referred to in our discussion of the national awakening in Soviet Jewish literature, in Chapter Three. We shall adduce some further examples in illustration of the point we are presently discussing. *Einikeit* had stated, in September 1946, that the said resolutions of the Central Committee had "a direct application to Soviet Jewish literature and to the Jewish theater"; alongside useful works, there had been published also works "that were lacking in ideas and were apolitical, and even nationalistic poems and stories"; the repertoire of the Jewish theaters was "not in keeping with the educational aims that are mandatory for Soviet art."[28] On other occasions, *Einikeit* had censured "distorted concepts regarding the cultural heritage," pointing out that such concepts were prominently defined by poet David Hofstein, who spoke about "the mold from which penicillin is made; mold that can serve as a cure also in cultural life."[29] An article in another journal, which spoke of "an uncritical and apologetic approach to questions of the national heritage," had decried the distortion of sharply outlined social contours and the exaggeration of national feelings in Soviet Jewish writing.[30] A Kiev Jewish periodical had urged Soviet Jewish literature — in the year that turned out to be its last — to "efface the vestiges of capitalistic convictions, to uproot all signs of bourgeois nationalism," and had upbraided a number of writers for their various nationalistic manifestations.[31] Nearly all of these writers are known to have been arrested, as was the author of the condemnatory article himself.

In time, the ideological infractions became more concrete and thus a basis for criminal accusations. *Einikeit*'s application to the authorities for a larger allocation of newsprint, or its tentative attempt to obtain permission to appear as a daily, "laid bare" the schemes of the Jewish cultural leaders to imbue the readers with their nationalistic trends. Similar motives were attributed to Der Nister, who, during a month's stay in Birobidzhan in 1947, had sought to enlarge the scope of cultural activity in the region. For speculating on what really lay behind the "accident" that had claimed the life of Mikhoels in Minsk in 1947, writers and artists were called to account for their "vilification." The widespread mourning at Mikhoels's death and the mass attendance at his funeral were interpreted by the authorities as an organized demonstration rather than a spontaneous reaction, and the complaints of anti-Semitism were construed as subversive activity. Expressions of sympathy for Israel added to the incriminatory material; the author heard it affirmed that a number of Jewish writers were requested to put their names to an anti-Israel manifesto shortly after the state was established. They tried to get out of doing so, or did not respond with sufficient eagerness.

Some were interrogated and harassed for attempting to contact and help the prisoners' families. Some were accused of hiding Hebrew books, or books in Yiddish which had suddenly become illicit. Among the charges laid against one writer, married to a non-Jewish woman — apart from those of manifesting chauvinism in his work — he was accused of resorting to cruelty to prevent his son from having his Russian nationality, like that of his mother, entered in his passport; a child of a mixed marriage may, on maturity, choose between the nationalities of the parents.

Many of those arrested were confronted with the names of American friends, chiefly Jewish writers — some of whom, incidentally, were known for their warm sympathies for the Soviet Union — with whom they had corresponded, or from whom they had even received gifts. Personal contacts with several American Jewish writers who had visited the Soviet Union after the war (similar to the contacts made by Mikhoels and Feffer during the visit to the United States in 1943) were used as proof of extensively planned anti-Soviet subversive activities.[32]

The final act in the cruel campaign aimed at totally uprooting Jewish culture took place in July and August 1952: this was the trial and execution of twenty-four men and the sentencing of one woman to life imprisonment. Most of the victims were celebrated Soviet Jewish writers. Scraps of information combine to form a picture of the tortures they were subjected to during their interrogation and trial. For nearly four years they were held in the notorious Lubianka Prison in Moscow, where they were brutalized and confessions were wrung out of them. They were indicted on a most grievous charge: an attempt to sever Crimea from the Soviet Union (this will be enlarged on in the next chapter). This fantastic allegation, together with the special treatment meted out to the accused, lead to the assumption that their case was intended to serve as the culminating act of the liquidation of Jewish culture, and the opening act of a series of further anti-Jewish operations: their planned extent and resourcefulness emerged clearly in the Doctors' Plot six months later.

The trial of the twenty-five accused lasted from July 11 to July 18. According to various accounts, special courage was shown during the trial by Perets Markish, who defended himself in a dramatic and forceful speech and claimed that his accusers were the real criminals, and by seventy-four-year-old Solomon Lozovsky who, though subjected to merciless tortures, still showed the spiritual strength, obstinacy, and dignity that had marked his stormy revolutionary youth. Actor Binyamin Zuskin broke down as soon as he tried to say something in his defense.

Up to the time this work has gone to press, all attempts to compile a complete list of the twenty-five accused have failed. It is practically certain, however, that they include David Bergelson, Perets Markish, Solomon Lozovsky, Eliahu Spivak, Leib Kvitko, Binyamin Zuskin, Shmuel Persov, Yitzhak Nusinov, Itsik Feffer, and Lina Shtern. The latter, a member of the USSR Academy of Sciences, had made important contributions in the field of biochemistry. She had apparently been a member of the Moscow Jewish Anti-Fascist Committee, which presumably wished to enhance its reputation with names of celebrated Jewish scientists. This woman, fondly nicknamed "an Einstein in skirts," though far from aspiring to be a public figure, was deeply sensitive to suffering on the one hand and falsehood on the other. To a "responsible comrade" who had once explained to her that the German-Soviet pact of 1939 was "a marriage of convenience," she had replied that "even such a marriage can produce offspring."[33] The war had drawn her nearer to the Jewish tragedy and Jewish life.

Lina Shtern was the only one of the accused to be sentenced to life imprisonment.[34] All the other twenty-four were executed, presumably in the cellars of the Lubianka Prison, on August 12, 1952.[35] A perusal of the Soviet press on that day, and on those before and after, gives no indication of the slaughter that was planned and perpetrated. "Public opinion" followed its even course. The newspaper columns told of output achievements, of the campaign for peace, of democratic developments in the Communist Party, of gigantic enterprises, of the happiness of life in the Soviet Union and of similar rosy matters. For many months after the executions the wives of the victims still knew nothing about their fate; the security authorities still accepted money remittances from the families, then stopped doing so on the grounds that the prisoners lacked nothing. Nothing at all became known of what was done with the bodies.[36]

Various rumors and allusions have accumulated over the years as to the persons who lent a hand in building up the fabric of accusations against their colleagues. It has proved impossible to determine what measure of truth there is in these rumors. It must be stated, however, that the interpersonal relations in the Soviet Jewish literary and art circles were influenced in no small degree by rivalry for official favor — fertile soil for the germs of corruption and degeneration. It must also be borne in mind that Stalinism not only encouraged jousting in external verbal manifestations of patriotism and loyalty; it turned the denunciation of alleged "enemies" into a kind of sacred, honorable national duty. This "ideological" attitude naturally made way for kowtowing, careerism, pressures, mutual suspicion, and a struggle to survive, with each man out to save his own skin. Many were swept into this slough of degeneracy, some up to the knees and others up to their necks. In addition, we know something of the means, both psychological and physical, to which the authorities resorted during the Stalinist reign of terror in order to extract depositions and confessions. It must be stressed, however, that it was not merely this or that word of denunciation that swayed the authorities in their decisions concerning Jewish culture and its exponents. Moreover, the purges and arrests claimed as victims also those who were rumored not to have been quite guiltless, and who were among those executed in August 1952.[37]

Against the background of the pogrom launched against Jewish culture, it is not surprising that persistent rumors and hints should become widespread concerning the "unclean hands" of those writers who escaped the terror. More concretely, suspicion was cast on the Yiddish writer Aaron Vergelis, and the Russian writer of Jewish origin, Ilya Ehrenburg. The suspicion in which the former was held was presumably reinforced by the following fact: when the first attempts were made to revive Yiddish literature somewhat in the Soviet Union, Vergelis became its leading exponent and a kind of an official spokesman on Jewish affairs. The suspicion cast on Ehrenburg derived from his reputation as a man quick to adapt himself — even in Stalin's latter years he was sent on representative missions abroad. Moreover, there were two incontrovertible facts: though Ehrenburg had been on the Jewish Anti-Fascist Committee, practically all of whose members were imprisoned or liquidated, he himself had come through unscathed; the second fact inheres in his article of September 21, 1948, in *Pravda* ("About a Certain Letter"), which was construed as a radical change in Soviet policy both towards Israel and also towards the indications of the Jewish national awakening in the Soviet Union, particularly as the liquidation of Jewish culture set in shortly after the publication of this article.

More concrete evidence may eventually turn up. At all events, that Vergelis and Ehrenburg actively contributed to the liquidation operations cannot be conclusively established on the strength of the rumors, hints, suspicions, and indirect allusions at our disposal at the time of this writing. One Communist source saw fit to point out that Vergelis did not escape the repressive measures, either, in that he was expelled from the Communist Party and the Writers' Association.[38] As for Ehrenburg, he himself sought on various occasions to repudiate what he termed a "smear campaign" against him; whatever credence one attaches to him, one cannot but admit the logic of his contention that the charges against him were founded chiefly on the fact that he had survived: "He remained alive? That means he is a traitor."[39] Undoubtedly, the above-mentioned *Pravda* article of Ehrenburg was officially inspired. Yet this is hardly sufficient proof that the author was privy to the authorities' schemes to liquidate Jewish culture and its exponents. A prominent Soviet writer, "who is presumably not among Ehrenburg's personal friends," said something quite reasonable concerning the charges laid against the latter: "To think that he had a share in the liquidation of the Jewish writers — that is stupid! Utter nonsense! You may dislike Ehrenburg, you may oppose him, but it is stupid to think that Stalin at that time took the opinion of any Soviet writer into account."[40]

There is no doubt, however, that Ehrenburg and many other Soviet writers knew of the terror launched against Jewish public life and activity immediately after it commenced, and evinced no reaction. A few non-Jewish writers, it is true, at least showed the courage of trying to help the prisoners' families,[41] but on the whole a conspiracy of silence prevailed in regard to what was happening to Jewish culture and its leaders. This silence, which raises complex moral questions of our time, is beyond the scope of our present discussion. We shall merely point out that some Soviet writers, when asked about the mystery enshrouding Jewish culture in the Soviet Union, deliberately lied when they answered that they knew of nothing untoward that had occurred, or assured their listeners that all was well.

For about six years — between 1949 and the summit conference held in Geneva in July 1955 — frequent attempts were made (chiefly by Jewish institutions and personages, but also by non-Jews) to obtain authoritative Soviet information concerning the rumors and assumptions of the liquidation of Jewish culture in the Soviet Union. In the main, the inquiries addressed to Moscow and to Soviet representatives at the United Nations (in the form of questions, memoranda, appeals, and protests) were not even answered. The few replies that were proffered took either the form of firm denials, accompanied by angry claims of anti-Soviet vilification, or of conciliatory statements. Leading members of the American Committee of Jewish Writers, Artists, and Scientists — founded during the war with the chief aim of promoting friendship for the USSR — were received by the Soviet ambassador in Washington. When they asked him about the fate of the Jewish writers, "he pretended that the very fact that we put such questions was an insult to his country. How could we imagine such a thing, that innocent people should be imprisoned in the Soviet Union?" They were also received by Andrei Gromyko, who was in New York to attend a United Nations General Assembly session, but he gave evasive replies to their questions concerning the fate of Jewish writers and institutions in the USSR. Letters addressed to the Jewish Anti-Fascist Committee in Moscow, to Soviet institutions for the promotion of cultural relations and to the Soviet Writers' Association did nothing to clear up the mystery, nor did the personal queries addressed by American authors and journalists to Soviet colleagues — to quote one writer, "their replies clouded rather than cleared up the matter."[42] Ehrenburg was glib about it, and his shrugging and denials hardly inspired credence. Concern for the fate of Soviet Yiddish writers and literature was conveyed to Alexander Fadeyev, who had come to America in the spring of 1949. He calmed these fears by asserting that "everything is all right," and that the writers whose names had been mentioned to him were "alive, working, and creating"; on his return to Moscow, Fadeyev promised, he would convey to them the inquirers' personal greetings.[43] Another few months went by without a sign of life from Soviet Jewry. This understandably caused specific embarrassment to those Jewish personalities and circles in Europe and America who were known to be ardent Soviet supporters, or self-styled "progressive" Communists. They strove to repudiate what they called anti-Soviet calumny by the Jewish "knights of the cold war."[44] Yet they found it hard to produce plausible reasons for the sudden severance of their own relations with Soviet Jewish art and literary circles. And though they were still able to "discredit" the rumors of the arrest and disappearance of Soviet Jewish writers and artists, the sudden *silence* of Jewish literature and cultural institutions in the USSR remained an incontrovertible fact. Consternation at this disappearance and silence was forcibly expressed in an open letter addressed by an American Jewish writer and public figure to the Soviet ambassador to the United States, of which the following are excerpts:

I am told that the entertainment columns of the Moscow newspapers no longer mention the existence of a Yiddish theater. Yet only a few years ago the dramatic art in Yiddish had been highly praised. These are not military secrets which a government is justified in concealing.

And what happened to the Yiddish press in the Soviet Union? Has it committed suicide or has it been murdered? Is there no reading public for it? We know that the process of Russification has been intense among Soviet Jews, yet despite this process it is inconceivable that a whole people should forget its language in such a short time.

And what happened to the Yiddish writers? . . . We, in the United States, do not know whether these vanished Yiddish authors have been kidnapped, executed, exiled to forced labor, or whether they have committed suicide. . . . But what about other Yiddish authors, the ones not exiled or liquidated? . . . Have all the Yiddish authors in the Soviet Union been found guilty without exception? Has the Yiddish press proved to be counter-revolutionary in its entirety?

Assuming for the sake of argument that all Soviet Jews no longer

> need Yiddish and no author wants to write in that language, have they also lost interest in one another? . . . Is it possible that among 2,000,000 Jews in the Soviet Union there exists not the slightest need to read about Jewish matters in the Russian language?[45]

This open letter remained unanswered, just as no reply was given to a memorandum circulated by a group of American Jewish writers — from so-called progressive circles — to a number of Soviet personalities and institutions (among them diplomatic representatives, authors, artists, newspaper editorial offices, and others). The memorandum stated that no Yiddish books and newspapers had arrived from the Soviet Union for about two years; that the names of Jewish writers were no longer mentioned in the general Soviet press; and that Yiddish theater notices failed to appear. It pointed to the persistent rumor concerning the "exile, imprisonment, and even execution of well-known Jewish writers." The authors of the memorandum added, "We trust that all this is a misunderstanding, and if it has really happened, that the injustice will certainly be rectified." Receipt of the memorandum was not even acknowledged.[46]

In 1955 Soviet author Boris Polevoy, at a New York reception (largely attended by known Soviet sympathizers) was still forced to lie when asked what truth there was in the rumor that Kvitko, together with other Jewish writers, had been imprisoned and executed. Polevoy replied that such rumors were only "common anti-Soviet slander"; Kvitko, he said, was living in the same house where he (Polevoy) lived, was completing a translation, and was about to begin a new book; he had seen him just before he (Polevoy) left Moscow, "and Kvitko asked me to give his regards to his friends in America." This was after Kvitko and many other Jewish writers had been put to death.[47]

A deathly silence prevailed over Jewish culture in the Soviet Union. It is characteristic that in time, when the Soviet press widely condemned Russian writers of Jewish origin as "cosmopolitans" and the like, or deliberately stressed the Jewish-sounding names of swindlers and profiteers, or exposed, in pursuance of the anti-Jewish campaign, the murderous crimes of Jewish physicians — it reported nothing about the exposure of spies, saboteurs, and common deviationists among Jewish literary and cultural circles and institutions; in the course of the liquidation operations Soviet "public opinion" completely ignored them, as though they had never existed.

This attitude of ignoring the Jews or diminishing their image was also applied to scientific and historical publications. Suffice it to compare the first and second editions of the *Great Soviet Encyclopedia.* The first edition began to appear in 1926, and the entry "Jews" opens the twenty-fourth volume, published in 1932. This entry runs to 108 columns, or fifty-four pages, in addition to separate entries on such subjects as Jewish literature, the Jewish problem, the Yiddish language, the Jewish religion, Jewish music, the Jewish theater, Jewish art, the Jewish community, the Jewish Commissariat (attached to the Commissariat of Soviet Nationalities), and also on several Jewish parties, newspapers and periodicals, institutions, and important events in Jewish history (e.g., "Pogroms Against Russian Jews"). These additional entries run to another forty-five columns in the twenty-fourth volume. In the second edition of the encyclopedia (in volume fifteen, which appeared in 1952), the entry "Jews" covers no more than four columns, with an additional four-column entry "Jewish Autonomous Province" (of Birobidzhan); three of these columns are devoted to a geographical survey of the region.[48] This drastic curtailment can hardly be regarded as incidental.

The contents of the entry "Jews" in the encyclopedia's second edition are no less illuminating. The Jews are defined as "various ethnic groups, of common origin with the ancient Jews, a people that lived in Palestine from the middle of the second century B.C. to the first or second century A.D." Which implies that all that has survived of Jewish propinquity is a common origin dating back some two thousand years, or more explicitly, "the Jews do not constitute a nation." Basing itself on Stalin's essay *Marxism and the National Question* of 1913, wherein he outlined the essential distinguishing features of a nation, the encyclopedia stated in its second edition:

> The Jews do not constitute a nation, since they do not present a stable community of people that has become efformed in the course of history, and which has appeared on the strength of a common

language, territory, joint economic life, and also a common culture. Their economic, political, and cultural life is common to them and to the nations around them. Therefore, the Jews are ethnographically closer to the nations among which they are living (though not to an equal degree in every place). . . . As a result of historical circumstances the Jews have not formed a compact ethnic entity; they have become dispersed over continents and countries, forming a number of separate ethnic groups, different in language, culture, and way of life. Throughout their history the Jews have been prone to become assimilated with the nations in whose countries they were living. This process occurred in a different manner at different times and in different places.

The implications here are glaringly obvious — a denial of Jewish unity not only in the present, but also throughout the generations. The entry then sets out to diminish the importance of the Jews' historical contribution to civilization. And there is a distinctly political ring about the reference to the language spoken by the Jews: "The vast majority of Jews speak the language of the nations among whom they are living"; some speak Yiddish, and "Russian Jews spoke Yiddish in the past." This is intended to imply that Jews used to speak this language only in Tsarist Russia, but not under the Soviet regime. This historical assertion contradicted even an abundance of cogent facts from the most recent past, yet was in keeping with the current intentions and activities of the authorities.

It is relevant to point out that after the Twentieth Party Congress, even Communists (outside the Soviet Union) complained of the contemptuous attitude towards the Jews manifested in the encyclopedia's second edition, to say nothing of the distorted facts. One writer pointed to the fact that even the Nentsy — an ethnic group living in the Arctic region, which numbered no more than 17,000 in 1926, and which first showed some glimmerings of culture under Soviet rule — was shown greater respect in the encyclopedia, which appended a bibliography to this entry and to the separate entry on the Nentsy language, whereas this had not been accorded to the entry "Jews" (or the separate entry "Jewish Autonomous Province").[49]

This contemptuous attitude to the Jews and their culture and the deliberate tendency to diminish their image or completely ignore them is conspicuous in the number of entries that are *missing* in the second edition of the encyclopedia, as compared to the first edition. To begin with, not a single Soviet Yiddish writer is mentioned throughout all the fifty volumes.[50] The first edition had given information about David Bergelson when he had still been living outside the Soviet Union; whereas there was no mention of him and his work in the second edition, after he had lived and created for fifteen years on Soviet territory and had been proclaimed a new classicist of Yiddish literature. Other Yiddish and Hebrew writers omitted from the second edition included Sholem Asch, S. Ansky, Ahad Ha-am, Yosef Bovshover, Y. L. Gordon, Jacob Gordin, Micah Yosef Berdichevsky, Morris Rosenfeld, Shaul Tschernikhovsky, and Avraham-Ber Gottlober, as well as the celebrated Jewish historians Graetz and Dubnow. Also omitted were such Jewish Russian writers as Isaac Babel and Osip Mandelstamm. Nor were the omissions confined to the province of literature only, but extended to Jews famous in various fields: Aaron Liebermann, recognized as one of the fathers of Jewish socialism; Maxim Vinaver, one of the founders and leaders of the Russian Constitutional Democratic Party; Ber Borokhov, foremost theoretician of Socialist Zionism, founder of *Poalei-Zion;* Mikhail Veltman (known also by his pseudonym M. P. Pavlovich), a noted Soviet public figure, whom the first edition (in an entry of three columns) described as a revolutionary, publicist, economist, historian, and Orientalist. Among other Jewish scholars, writers, and artists omitted from the second edition, are: Yehudah Halevi, Zalman Shmeyur, Moris Vinchevsky, Max Brod, Ludwig Zanenhof, Nachum Aronson, and Ber Brutskus.

The Habimah Theater, which was founded and made its initial steps in Moscow at the time of the revolution, was entirely passed over; it was not even mentioned under "Yevgeni Vakhtangov," the producer under whose guidance this theater had staged his and its crowning success, *The Dibbuk,* though the other plays he directed were listed. Even Theodor Herzl, founder of political Zionism who envisaged the Jewish state, was omitted. Two classical Yiddish authors, Mendele Mocher Seforim and Sholem Aleichem, were considered worthy of inclusion in the second edition, but a third writer, Yitzhak Leib Peretz, was passed over in the entire fifty volumes; he was referred to only in the supplementary fifty-first volume that appeared in 1958.

Let us now turn to the entries retained in the second edition, for the obvious purpose of highlighting their negative aspects. Chaim Weizmann, for instance, had been given ten lines in the first edition, where he was said to be "one of the leaders of the nationalist-bourgeois movement called Zionism." The second edition allotted him twenty-three lines, which explained that with the help of Weizmann, who "in his youth joined the reactionary nationalist-bourgeois movement, namely Zionism . . . Britain made use of the Zionists as a mainstay of her colonial rule in Palestine. Following the weakening of Britain's position, Weizmann is effecting a reorientation of Zionism in the service of U.S. imperialism. . . . On the instructions of the imperialists, who have turned Israel into their colony, Weizmann pursues a policy of suppressing the Jewish toiling masses and the Arab national minority, a policy of stifling the forces of peace and democracy inside the country." (The second edition entirely omitted the brother of Chaim Weizmann, Samuel Weizmann, a leading figure in Soviet industry, to whom the first edition devoted an entry of seventeen lines).

Neither was Hebrew poet Chaim Nachman Bialik ignored in the second edition. We learn that not only had Bialik "cast in his lot with the bourgeois Zionist movement," but that his work "bears the stamp of reactionary nationalism and *cosmopolitanism,*" and that "to the end of his days he remained a bourgeois nationalist and *cosmopolite.*" (Italics added.)

Highly instructive are the differences between the two editions of the encyclopedia in regard to the Bund. The first edition (volume 8, published in 1927) devoted to this party seventeen columns. Despite the critical approach to various positions of the Bund, a recognition of the party's historic importance and its valuable political contribution to the workers' movement was clearly evident. There is also a separate entry (two and a half columns) on the Bund press, which mentions that its list contains five hundred titles (legal and illegal) — mostly in Yiddish, but also in Russian, Polish, German, and other languages — and thousands of proclamations. In the second edition (volume 6, published in 1951) no more than roughly two and a half columns were allotted to the Bund and no good word has been left for it. The whole entry is in line with the opening definition that this party is "an agency of the bourgeoisie within the working class."

Also characteristic is the change of tone adopted in regard to Victor Adler and Friedrich Adler (his son). With all the criticism leveled at Victor Adler's reformistic and utopian errors, the reference to him in the first edition (over two columns, written by Karl Radek) nevertheless stressed the idealism of the founder of the Austrian Social Democratic Party in a distinctly sympathetic light. The second edition, which allotted him barely half a column, had hardly a good word to say about him; nor did it mention his Jewish origin, as did the first edition. In the new image given to Austrian socialist leader Friedrich Adler (famous, among other things, for his assassination of Austrian prime minister Count Stürgkh, as an act of protest against the war), there are certain prominent features consistent with the times; thus he was referred to as "an agent of U.S. imperialism," and charged with injecting the Austrian labor movement with "the venom of cosmopolitanism."

Consistent with this tendency to obliterate, there had vanished from the second edition of the encyclopedia all Jewish traces in the entries giving information on various Soviet towns and cities. The entry "Vilna" (the Jewish center dubbed the Lithuanian Jerusalem) is a striking example. This entry had concluded the tenth volume of the first edition, which appeared in 1928. In describing Vilna, as a cultural center, the entry had stated that there appeared in this city four Polish, *three Jewish,* and one Russian dailies; four Polish, three Belorussian, *two Jewish,* and one Lithuanian weeklies. Reporting on the initial growth of the workers' movement in the city (about the year 1887), the encyclopedia had stated that "Vilna at that time was primarily a center of the Jewish labor movement," and had listed a series of Jewish activities. Particulars were given of "the famous May Day demonstration of Jewish and Polish workers" (in 1902), following which the governor of the province, Von Vahl, had thirty of the demonstrators flogged; fury at this barbarous punishment drove a Jewish cobbler named Hirsh Lekert to assassinate Von Vahl on May 5, 1902. Lekert was hanged on June 11, 1902. His execution, the encyclopedia stated, "naturally did not dismay the [revolutionary] movement; on the contrary, it reinforced it." However, in the entry "Vilna" in the second edition (volume 8, approved for printing in November 1951), there is no mention of the city's Jewry, or of Jewish participation in the 1902 May Day demonstration. This demonstration, the entry stated, was organized by the Vilna Social Democrats and attended by over one thousand demonstrators; on the governor's orders, eighty-nine workers were arrested and thirty of them flogged; this maltreatment aroused indignation in various towns. . . . The share of Jews in staging the demonstration and Lekert's assassination of the governor and his hanging were not mentioned at all. As against this, the encyclopedia did not fail to record that a northwestern regional committee of the Russian Social Democrat Party was formed in Vilna in 1903, and that this committee united the workers of all peoples and fought the Bund, unmasking its real nationalist-bourgeois nature.

The missing entries relating to Jewish matters would form too long a list to be included here. It is worth noting, nevertheless, that the encyclopedia's second edition as a rule mentioned the national origin, alongside the Soviet citizenship, of a great many celebrated Russians and other nationals in various fields, thus: "Soviet Russian mathematician," "Soviet Ukrainian inventor," or "Soviet Georgian composer" — but only rarely did so in the case of celebrated Jews, who were mostly referred to as "Soviet physicist," "Soviet meteorologist," and so on.

The "flexibility" of the entries and the selectivity applied to their inclusion or omission were generally in keeping with characteristic Stalinist-Zhdanovite requirements of an encyclopedia, as set forth in a Moscow periodical: "A Soviet Encyclopedia cannot be simply an assemblage of information, presented in an objective, detached, apolitical manner. It must illuminate all aspects of human endeavor and knowledge from the standpoint of a militant Marxist-Leninist world outlook."[51] However, such a standpoint, as is well known, may be subject to fluctuation and change. Thus, the second edition of the *Great Soviet Encyclopedia* — as stated in the editors' introduction — set out to correct the "crude political errors" of the first edition. These corrections, it transpired, were numerous, including a complete reappraisal of a great many Western statesmen and thinkers, and no doubt also applied to the space and appraisals formerly allotted to Jewish affairs.

Corrections similar to those inserted in the encyclopedia's second edition were also made in other Soviet scientific publications. Thus, no more than twenty-five lines were allotted to the entry "Jews" in volume I of the *Encyclopedic Dictionary* (published by the *Great Soviet Encyclopedia*); though this volume went to press after Stalin's death, on September 9, 1953, it nevertheless adhered to the Stalinist spirit. In this entry, Jews are defined as one of the "ethnic groups," united by no more than their common descent from the ancient Jewish people. Most Jews, the entry states, speak the language of the nation among which they are living, while Yiddish is spoken only by "part of the Jews (in central Europe)." Again, what this implies is that all Soviet Jews have been excluded in toto from the Yiddish speakers. It must be stated that this arbitrary scientific pronouncement was later contradicted by authoritative Soviet sources, chiefly as a result of the census taken in January 1959: of the 2,268,000 Soviet citizens who declared their nationality to be Jewish, 471,744, or 20.8 percent, stated that Yiddish was their mother tongue.

There were further manifestations pointing to a deliberate and systematic Soviet drive to diminish the Jewish image and even eradicate its traces. From a so-called complete bibliography of the writings of Howard Fast — a member of the Communist Party in the United States, he was extremely popular and admired in the Soviet world of literature — there were omitted his books on Jewish subjects, namely: *Romance of a People,* which is a short history of the Jews, and *My Glorious Brothers,* which deals with the Hasmonean rising. In time, Fast himself came to regard this as an attempt on the part of Moscow to rob the Jews of their past.[52]

A similar trend was clearly apparent in the new Soviet thirty-volume edition of Maxim Gorky's writings (Moscow, 1948–56). Gorky, who was officially pronounced the founder of socialist literature, was known to have been attached to Jewish culture and to have admired the spirit of Judaism. He had on various occasions voiced his admiration for the Bible, for the poems of Bialik, for the Habimah Hebrew Theater during its early years in Moscow after the October

Revolution, and had frequently condemned anti-Semitic prejudice, which he regarded as a disgrace to the Russian people. Yet all this was not found worthy of inclusion in the abovementioned edition, which even omitted Lenin's remarks, in a conversation he had with Gorky, about the intelligence of the Jews — remarks that had been quoted by the author in the 1924 edition of his works.[53]

Characteristic of this trend was also the steady diminution of the importance attached to remote Jewish tribes in Soviet publications that appeared between the years 1949 and 1953, as compared to the references to them in former publications. In 1941, a Soviet Jewish source had remarked proudly on the development of a literature in the Jewish-Tadzhik language (a Persian dialect spoken by Jews who for generations had been living in some parts of central Asia) — a literature that had not existed prior to the October Revolution.[54] According to a postwar Soviet Jewish source, there was even a Jewish-Tadzhik theater in Uzbekistan.[55] Apart from the Jewish-Tadzhik language, there was also current among Oriental Jews in the Soviet Union a Tati-Jewish language, or "Mountain-Yiddish," as it is popularly referred to in Soviet terminology. (This, too, is an ancient Persian dialect, Persian Tat, spoken chiefly by Jews who have lived for centuries in the mountainous regions of North Caucasus.) It contains a great many Hebrew words and expressions, chiefly for objects and concepts of religious significance. The Tat Jews used Hebrew script until the Latin alphabet was instituted for the Turkmen peoples.[56] We learn from Soviet sources that the Tat Jews had popular ballad singers and storytellers, and that throughout the generations they had composed, orally, a great many ballads, tales, and legends — the collection, translation, and publication of which had been encouraged by the Soviet authorities. We know, in fact, of Tati-Jewish works that have been published.[57] The new Soviet policy towards the Jews, however, was also applied to these Mountain Jews. The second edition of the encyclopedia does, admittedly, contain an entry "Mountain Jews," but the less than twenty lines allotted to this entry speaks only of the great changes that occurred in the cultural and economic life of these Jews under Soviet rule, without a word about any specific literary or artistic creation produced by this Jewish tribe. On the other hand, the author of the entry took pains to point out that Judaism had been "the former current religion" of the Mountain Jews.[58]

This practice of diminishing the historical significance of peoples or of simply ignoring them, in the light of current political trends, was adopted by the Stalinist regime not only with regard to the Jews. Thus there disappeared from Soviet encyclopedic publications all mention of those minorities that were punished for collaborating with the Germans during the war. After they had been deported in large masses and their republics dissolved, all trace of them was frequently expunged from scientific and historical works. Yet one cannot disregard the difference between their cases and the practice adopted with regard to the Jews. The obliteration of the Kalmyks, Balkars, Chechens, and Ingushis was part of the collective punishment imposed on these peoples *after* many of their members had acted traitorously, whereas the Soviet authorities could not pin any such crime on the Jews. The demoting of the Jews from their historical position was perpetrated in pursuance of a prophylactic punitive campaign aimed at preventing "foreseeable" crimes, in keeping with the Stalinist logic of "looking ahead." As the Jews were actually a Soviet national group without a territory of their own, the reprisal and preventive measures taken against them could not take the form of dissolving their republic, as was done in the case of other minorities. These measures were therefore aimed at cultural liquidation, at eradicating every vestige of Jewish spiritual autonomy and independent expression. Nor did this liquidation spare the Jewish past.

This campaign in Stalin's latter years was nevertheless accompanied by an apparently surprising phenomenon: the attitude to Jewish organized ritual was less harsh than that adopted towards Jewish secular culture. While the latter was totally extirpated — and most of its exponents flung into prison and a great many put to death — the essentially atheistic regime allowed some synagogues to continue some form of existence, albeit wretched, and permitted some of the clergy to officiate to a limited extent.

This relative "favorable discrimination" may be put down to several possible causes. Moscow might have believed — with all its disregard of world public opinion — that to have dealt a death blow to the religious institutions after the liquidation of Jewish culture and other anti-Jewish measures would have been going too far at the time.

We have qualified this by saying "at the time," since it was not unlikely that in preparing further, more stringent measures, which became apparent with the Doctors' Plot, this final blow was planned as well. Meanwhile, at all events, several synagogues and rabbis were still retained as window dressing for the outside world — as some sort of alibi to refute the indignation, inquiries and protests expected abroad. In the early Fifties, a few foreign Jewish visitors were still taken to see the Moscow synagogue so that they should deny "malicious reports" of religious persecution. The rabbis the visitors met certainly did not venture to complain; in view of the fate that had befallen Jewish secular institutions and the general inimical atmosphere towards the Jews, they had become reserved and were instinctively more wary than before.

The synagogues provided for no communal or educational activities. The number of worshipers dwindled to a frightened handful. The public status of the rabbis dropped to the lowest social level: they no longer appeared at official receptions alongside the Christian and Moslem clergy. Nevertheless, despite the wretched existence accorded to the Jewish religion, the authorities could still wring some propaganda value out of it. We refer not merely to the fact that the rabbis were allowed to talk to a few Western visitors and repudiate "allegations" that the authorities were suppressing Jewish religious activities, but chiefly to the exploitation of the rabbis for international political ends. Thus, for example, at a peace rally for religious leaders held in Zagorsk in May 1952, the speakers included Rabbi Shlomo Shleifer from Moscow and Rabbi Yitzhak Shechtman from Kiev. The latter explained that for devout Jews the word "peace" has both a religious-symbolical and a general connotation; and when the enemies of peace threaten mankind with another world war, religious people cannot remain indifferent. Rabbi Shleifer spoke of great Stalin's foreign policy, which was based on peace and friendship, and of the duty of the Jews to join in the struggle against the war- and atom-mongers, who sin against God.[59]

A further possible reason for the concessions granted to the Jewish religion, as compared to the fate that befell secular Jewish culture, might have been the reluctance to rudely upset the formal balance between the various churches in the atheistic state. In the prevailing concrete social circumstances, the total rescission of Jewish religious rights might have appeared as an indication that a State Church was coming into being — which would have been too much, even at a time when the Communist regime was making an all-out effort to bolster Russian nationalism.

It would appear, however, that the principal reason for these "concessions" resided in the fact that the authorities regarded these last vestiges of Jewish ritual and religious institutions as a dwindling substance that had lost all vitality — a stunted branch that presented no danger and which would in any case shrivel of itself very soon. In the calculations of the Soviet ideologists and those who laid down internal policy, the synagogue had lost all significance and appeal, especially for the younger generation. By placing it under strict constraint and surveillance, it could still be allowed to exist as a kind of fossilized museum exhibit. The alert ears of the authorities were no doubt attuned to the national Jewish overtones in various parts of the liturgy, but they did not regard this religious feeling as having any significant influence. Moreover, the Jewish synagogue on Soviet soil appeared utterly isolated from the modern trends of world Jewry. To sum up: the "opium" had stopped having any effect, so there was no need to eradicate it by drastic measures.

It is in this light, too, that one may find a partial explanation for the more liberal attitude shown all along by the Soviet authorities to the religious life of the non-Ashkenazic Jewish communities, such as the Bokharan, Mountain, Georgian, and Krimchak (indigenous Crimean) Jews. Their religious observances were shown greater tolerance due to the fact that these communities were far away from Jewish centers and unlikely to be influenced by modern trends.

Conversely, it was just the secular Jewish Soviet culture that began to offer a danger to the regime. The Yiddish language, for all its de-Hebraization, and Yiddish literature, despite its adoption of an antireligious note and its repudiation of Jewish national values, nevertheless drank at the historical fountainhead of Judaism and gravitated towards its modern trends of thought and aspirations. Paradoxical as this might sound, it was just the "proletarian" Jewish literature — which had so carefully observed the general dictate of being "national [only] in form and socialistic in content" — that showed itself in the

Forties to be a focus of a Jewish renaissance, a force that might foster an awareness of the Jewish national identity and a sense of world Jewish unity. In other words, the authorities began to fear that the secular Soviet Jewish culture had taken over from the religious institutions their harmful nationalistic functions. The extinction to which this culture was doomed indicates that the authorities took account of the "dangers" inherent in its appeal and influence.[60]

It must be pointed out that in Stalin's latter years the Soviet regime did not rely entirely on the withering away of Jewish religion. The religious community was denied the possibility of training rabbis and other religious officials, as the present clergy became aged, had no access to religious literature, and met insurmountable difficulties in obtaining devotional articles. More than that, however, distinctly repressive measures were instituted against certain religious activities, and especially against uncompromising and overly active rabbis. Victims of threats and persecution were chiefly rabbis and cantors who were "revealed" to have laid particular emphasis on those prayers that mention Zion and Jerusalem — in which the prayer book abounds.[61] It appears that even Rabbi Shleifer of Moscow was imprisoned for some time,[62] though he strove with all his might not to give the authorities cause to level accusations against him and against the Moscow synagogue of which he was the spiritual leader. In 1950, the Kharkov rabbi, Shmuel Lev, was sentenced to ten years' confinement in a "rigid discipline" camp. Later, in the early Fifties, there began to arrive in the labor camps, under heavy sentences, groups of non-Ashkenazi worshipers and rabbis, among them the Sephardic rabbi of Tashkent.[63]

Nonetheless, the Jewish religion was less harshly treated than the secular Soviet Jewish culture. The latter was doomed to total extinction, which even embraced Jewish art and folklore and Jewish typescript.

After Stalin's death Soviet spokesmen occasionally set out to prove that what had befallen Jewish culture and its exponents was not specifically a Jewish tragedy. They claimed that the intellectuals of other nationalities, especially of the national minorities, had also suffered at the hands of "Beria's gang" and its infringements of the "socialist legality" as well as from the deviations from the "Leninist norms" induced by Stalin's personality cult. Such a comparison does not stand up to a quantitative test, to begin with. Even discounting the tortures and executions to which the Jewish writers were subjected, as compared to the sufferings of the other nationalities, one cannot disregard the essential difference inherent in the fact that in the case of the Jews an entire culture, and not merely some of its exponents, fell victim. The distinctive essence of the Stalinist anti-Jewish campaign was attested to by a Jewish Communist paper in Poland, thus:

> The fact that other nationalities suffered, especially in the years 1949 to 1953, does not refute the inescapable fact that not only were the leading Jewish writers and cultural leaders imprisoned and murdered, but the entire Jewish social and cultural life in the Soviet Union was liquidated. And this, to our deep regret, is not a fantasy, but the horrifying truth.[64]

It may well be asked whether the Jewish writers and communal leaders had any foreboding of the dangers that threatened them. Reading between the lines of some of the later works of several of the writers who were executed or tortured, one may discern a resigned note, occasionally hidden behind a kind of calm philosophical auto-dialogue.

Itsik Feffer, in a poem that appeared in his collection *Ofsnei* [Anew], published in 1948, speaks of the deaths that lurk at his door; but the poet overcomes them all and they retreat. He boasts of his overwhelming victory over his greatest foe, depression, and hints that he must similarly defeat fear. What echoes as a tragic irony, in view of Feffer's execution, is the line: "Death is trivial; terrible is fear, which turns a man into vermin."

In one of his last poems Leib Kvitko exchanges reflections, during a sleepless night, with his creaking, groaning bed. The atmosphere of the poem is reflected in its title, "Restlessness." The room is charged with harrowing dread. The bed, restless like the poet, speaks to him of evil forebodings.[65]

Shmuel Halkin, in his poem "My Word," published in 1945, asks his word, which he figuratively refers to as the house in which he is totally immersed: " . . . in desolate vineyards, how may I be your guardian . . . if with every light rustle of a leaf and tremor of a twig I adjure you with fear — If only it might end well! The heavy wing of my fate was your cradle, but between being and surcease you have flowered. With what may I now secure you, my word, shield you, when some other wing of fate may efface you from the earth?"[66]

In his poem "Pour Out," dated January 1949, Perets Markish writes: "How much longer will we be able to enjoy our lives — until the sad abyss? Pour out generously, then, and raise the glass to the stars [and drink] to our last wishes." The poet speaks of the summer that is ending and the fall that is setting in, and again raises his glass to "those who will come in our place," and to "those who will remember us kindly."[67]

It must be pointed out that these were not the dominant notes that pervaded Soviet Jewish literature in its last years. On the contrary, it was largely charged with what might be termed official optimism and echoed also with genuine hopes: not a few writers, in fact, believed in the rejuvenation and development of cultural Jewish life in the country.

In the light of the extinction of Soviet Jewish cultural life, these hopes no doubt assumed a most tragic flavor — optimism in the shadow of the gallows, as it were. One month before *Einikeit* appeared for the last time, its acting editor took pains to explain that anti-Semitism had been totally eradicated in the Soviet Union: in a country where the Stalinist brotherhood of nations flourished in a manner unparalleled elsewhere in the world, the Jewish people enjoyed full equality.[68] By the end of the summer of 1948, a Jewish writer in New York received from Itsik Feffer a gift of his last collection of poems, *Ofsnei,* "with a warm dedication." In October 1948, the same writer received from Perets Markish his book *War,* in which the author had inscribed an apology for his tardy correspondence, and had added, "let us start anew beginning with this book."[69] These were the last greetings received from these Soviet Jewish poets, who were among those executed in August 1952.

Yitzhak Nusinov — also executed in August 1952 — had written proudly in October 1947 of the large readership of Yiddish books in the Soviet Union. He saw fit to stress that "the Soviet Jewish book has a circulation undreamed of by any Jewish writer in the United States, which has a Jewish population of many millions."[70] At the beginning of 1948, *Einikeit* reported the publishing program of *Der Emes* publishing house, which proposed to bring out the first complete edition of the works of Sholem Aleichem, in twenty volumes, between 1948 and 1951. This, it was pointed out, would not yet be an "academic edition," which was unfeasible as long as there was no access to the Sholem Aleichem archives (which were not in Soviet hands and could not therefore be referred to), but the object was "to assemble and publish all that we can" of his writings.[71] Of this "complete edition" only three volumes were published, in 1948, and the completion of the project was scrapped. Two and a half weeks before *Einikeit* was closed down, the paper reported that several new Yiddish textbooks were in printing.[72] The paper's penultimate issue listed the contents of the seventh number of *Heimland,* which never reached the readers.[73] The final issue of *Einikeit* (dated November 20, 1948) published a report on a meeting of Moscow Jewish writers, convened to discuss the future of *Heimland.* The paper also wrote of the need to meet the growing need for a repertoire suited to the considerable expansion of Yiddish theater troupes, both professional and amateur, and of other problems and projects of Jewish cultural activity in the Soviet Union. In fine, all proceeded as usual with death looming up on the horizon.

A further case, both tragic and curious, may be cited. In 1949 there appeared in New York an anthology entitled *On New Roads,* containing works by sixty-seven Soviet Yiddish writers (the names of twenty of the writers, who had died or been killed in the war, were enclosed in black frames).[74] The material for the anthology had been sent to New York from Moscow, in keeping with the practice instituted during the war, when the Moscow Jewish Anti-Fascist Committee was in contact with Jewish centers in the West, especially with so-called progressive organizations. The material had been compiled by a writers' subcommittee of the JAC. The anthology was intended to sum up thirty years of Jewish literary work in the Soviet Union and also mark the thirtieth anniversary of the October Revolution (in 1947), but its preparation had been unduly prolonged and it appeared only at the beginning of 1949. In the preface to the anthology the New York publishers stated:

> Among the writers [whose work is presented in the anthology] there are some who have been active in the field of Jewish literature for tens of years, and others who are beginners, attesting to the growth of the abundant Jewish literary harvest in the Soviet Union. In no other branch of Jewish literature is there such a great number of young writers, who have burgeoned in recent years. This is proof of the vast creative force of Soviet Jewry.

This preface, which is dated January 15, 1949, is followed by an introduction entitled "Our Literature" by the Soviet Jewish authoress and critic, Rebecca Rubin. She lauds the Soviet Jewish literature even more fervently and stresses its variegation, bringing examples from the work of scores of writers in support. According to her, conditions in the Soviet Union led to the realization of "the dream of our classicists of a truly popular literature in the widest sense." She concludes her introduction on a confident note:

> No obstacles will prevent its growth [of Soviet Jewish literature]. It will flourish also in the future, just as our people — that has known so much tribulation and fight — will surely flourish and grow.

These words of assurance were written in Moscow in 1948. By the time they were published, early in 1949, all Jewish literary activity and practically all other cultural activity had been suppressed in the Soviet Union, and leading Jewish writers and artists were undergoing ruthless torture and interrogation in prison. Many of the prominent contributors to *On New Roads* were executed several years later.

Alexander Fadeyev, who visited New York in the spring of 1949, was given the anthology *On New Roads* by the American Jewish writers who had worked on its publication, in order "to present it to his Soviet Jewish colleagues."[75] Fadeyev was obviously putting up a pretense, for he surely knew of his Jewish colleagues' fate.

In comparing the course of Soviet Jewish culture in its final days with its cruel end, one gains the impression that the Soviet authorities were playing some cruel game with their victim while tightening the noose around its neck. There is no doubt, however, that the authorities tended to ignore the small "contradictions" between their acts and what even their own sources had said only recently about Jewish culture in the Soviet Union. At all events, the liquidation was perpetrated ruthlessly and strictly according to plan.

SIX

The Crimean Affair

One of the charges leveled against the twenty-five accused in the trial held in Moscow between July 11 and July 18, 1952 was that they had plotted to sever the Crimea from the Soviet Union and establish there a Zionist-bourgeois republic, to serve as an American imperialist base for aggressive anti-Soviet designs.[1]

The Crimean Affair presents one of the most intricate mysteries in the annals of Soviet Jewry in Stalin's last decade. In attempting to unravel it, we must needs have recourse to various scraps of evidence, and these, even when correlated, render more assumptions inevitable.

As mentioned, the Crimean allegation fits into a broadly shaped American conspiracy. The United States was alleged to have begun to plan a war against the Soviet Union while still her wartime ally, chiefly after Stalingrad, and to have sought to organize a fifth column inside the Soviet Union for the prosecution of this war. To this end, U.S. Jews were assigned the task of recruiting Jews in the Soviet Union. The operational arm which would execute the plan was to be the American Joint Distribution Committee (JDC), whose agents had manipulated the 1943 visit to the United States of Solomon Mikhoels and Itsik Feffer. The two had indeed met JDC leaders in New York, and thus the Moscow Jewish Anti-Fascist Committee was alleged to have become a hireling of American imperialism. American strategy was keen on establishing a secret base in the Crimean peninsula, which would be taken on the outbreak of the American-Soviet war. Hence, the JAC, it was alleged, was to request the authorities to turn the Crimea into a Jewish Autonomous Province instead of Birobidzhan. By dint of JAC supervision over the Crimean local authorities and leaders, the peninsula would become an American military base. Liaison between the JDC and the JAC in Moscow was allegedly maintained by the president of the American Committee of Jewish Writers, Artists and Scientists (B. Z. Goldberg) and by the editor of a New York Jewish Communist paper; the two had visited the Soviet Union shortly after the war. The same Jewish-American mechanism was later allegedly activated for the Doctors' Plot.[2]

As far as is known, the Crimean Affair has been mentioned no more than once by a Soviet official source up to the date of this writing; it was referred to by Soviet Premier Nikita Khrushchev in August 1956, when he received a visiting delegation of the Canadian (Communist) Progressive Labour Party (LPP) in Moscow. Khrushchev, who was at that time blazoning forth to the world Stalin's crimes and perversions, stated then that he was "in agreement with Stalin that the Crimea, depopulated at the time in consequence of the war against Germany, shall not become a Jewish settlement center, since in the event of war it would be turned into an American war base against the Soviet Union." He exonerated Solomon Lozovsky, one of the victims of the 1952 trial, in the following terms: "Our veteran and loyal Comrade Lozovsky perished through no guilt of his, since he had been dragged into the Crimean swindle."[3]

With all the malicious fabrications that made up the Crimean Affair, certain actual threads were nonetheless interwoven into this false legal libel. These were a conglomeration of rumors, exaggerated hints, "logical" conclusions and fanciful interpretations placed on certain indications; all in all, these were vague elements that had no real foundation, yet they were forceful enough to coincide with Jewish wishful thinking in the wake of the wartime tragedy.

For an understanding of the Crimean Affair, it may be useful to make a retrospective background survey of the place assumed by the Crimea in the life of Soviet Jewry.

It should first be noted that the regime established in Russia after the October Revolution "inherited not only a Jewish population of millions in the cities and towns . . . but also quite a large number of Jewish settlements in the south and west, which had become well established in previous years."[4] There was a significant number of these settlements in the Crimea. Some of the inhabitants claimed that their ancestors had settled in the Crimea many centuries ago.

Immediately after the new regime was established, the Soviet authorities and Jewish organizations and circles put forward various proposals for settling Jews on the land, under the current productivization and agrarization plans. These proposals aroused a great deal of controversy among the Jewish leadership. This controversy raised both practical problems (of the expected Jewish response to the settlement projects, financing, climate, etc.) and questions of the principle involved in the national and ideological aspects of the settlement projects (chiefly concerned with the establishment of *autonomous* Jewish settlements or regions). Initially the plans were largely nurtured by quite sincere ideas — on the part of both the authorities and the Jewish public leaders — concerning the objectively difficult conditions in which the revolution had placed a considerable part of Russian Jewry. On the one hand, the Jewish population at the time of the October Revolution contained negligible big business elements; on the other hand, the Jews constituted but a small part of the actual industrial proletariat. The Jews were predominantly small tradesmen, artisans, pedlars, middlemen, or members of specifically Jewish professions, such as clergymen and religious instructors. The revolution deprived these Jews of their livelihoods, though it was primarily aimed against the members of those classes in which Jews figured negligibly, namely estate owners, financiers, and business barons, and high officials in the Tsarist administration. The recurrent pogroms during the Civil War also served to undermine the economic foundations of the Jewish townships in the Ukraine and Belorussia. As industrialization projects had not yet been widely implemented at the beginning of the Soviet regime, solutions for the problem of ameliorating the position of these Jews were necessarily sought in the field of agricultural settlement. These ideas were accompanied by ideological and political considerations, evolved chiefly by Jewish Communist leaders. Some of these considerations were heavily motivated by the aim of creating an objective that would counterbalance the "Palestine psychosis." There were also utilitarian considerations involved, based on the prospects of recruiting the capital of world Jewish philanthropy in aid of the settlement projects — for the Soviet authorities and Jewish leadership were not averse to receiving bourgeois Jewish funds. And indeed, the settlement projects had a considerable impact on Jewish communities the world over. Following the establishment in 1924 of the KOMZET, the committee for the Rural Placement of Jewish Toilers attached to the Presidium of the Soviet of Nationalities, the Jewish settlement projects in the Soviet Union were systematically supported by overseas Jewish bodies. A special agency, Agro-Joint, was set up for this purpose by the JDC and operated in collaboration with other Jewish bodies. The settlement project prompted Jewish writers, communal leaders, and philanthropists to visit the Soviet Union. Soviet propaganda, which did not refrain from exaggerating the achievements of Jewish settlement, enlarged the scope of Jewish aid.

Prominent among the Jewish settlement schemes in the Twenties was the Crimea project. This was featured in a favorable light, as against the negative aspects of Jewish settlement in Palestine. It was stressed, for example, that the local non-Jewish population of the areas assigned for Jewish settlement would welcome their new neighbors. Yuri Larin, a prominent Jewish Communist, pointed out that there was enough land for everybody. Another Communist leader, M. Litvakov, stated with romantic zeal: "The Crimea is our Palestine . . . for surely you can't compare the Jordan to the Dnieper." He also claimed that "our" Moslems (the Crimean Tartars) were unlike the Palestine Moslems (who violently opposed Jewish settlement).

Mikhail Kalinin, chairman of the Central Executive Committee of the Soviet Union (VTSIK), showed himself in favor of the agricultural settlement projects. On several occasions he stressed the importance of turning the Jewish masses into farmers and concentrating them in specific areas in order to assure the continued national existence of the Jewish people. Kalinin's support of the specific Crimea project is of greatest relevance to our discussion. He attached particular importance to the mild Crimean climate as a factor that would attract Jews there and make for an easier transition from town to village life. The government, Kalinin said, "wishes to settle them in the mild southern climate to which they are accustomed, and in familiar surroundings. If we want the Jewish settlement project to succeed, we must take the climatic-geographical factor into account."[5]

The settlement activities in the Crimea continued also after the Birobidzhan project was launched in 1928. This, at first, was not regarded as an alternative plan, but as a complementary one, though the authorities appeared to give preference to the Birobidzhan plan. An official resolution stated, in fact, that if there should be favorable results from the scheme to settle Jewish workers in the region assigned to them in the Far East, "account must be taken of the possibility of establishing [there] a Jewish national administrative-territorial entity."[6] Nonetheless, Birobidzhan did not entirely overshadow the Crimea project in the late Twenties and early Thirties.

In the numerous debates on the subject of "Crimea or Birobidzhan?" and in the activities of the settlement agencies a certain balance was maintained between the two projects. Some Jewish leaders remained stoutly in favor of the Crimea. They included Yuri Larin (previously mentioned) and Abraham Bragin. Larin had at one time envisaged a Jewish republic in northern Crimea, with the town of Kerch as its capital. Bragin had conceived an even bolder plan: Jewish settlement in a large area along the shores of the Black Sea "from Odessa to Abkhazsk." The initial failures and difficulties in Birobidzhan reinforced the arguments put forward by the Crimea supporters.

In January 1928, KOMZET ratified a five-year plan whereby fifteen thousand families were to be transferred to the Crimea and twelve thousand families to Birobidzhan. At the Second Conference of OZET (Society for Colonizing Jewish Toilers on the Land, formed in 1925 to assist the KOMZET), held in Moscow in December 1930, the prolonged discussion over the question of the Crimea or Birobidzhan was settled by a compromise resolution, whereby both regions would serve equally for Jewish settlement. In 1932, however, resolutions adopted by both KOMZET and OZET stressed the prime importance and urgency of prosecuting the Birobidzhan project, though "this must not lead to neglecting settlement in the Crimea." Birobidzhan was thus accorded priority, though settlement activities still continued in the Crimea. The vision of Soviet Jewish "sovereignty" in the Crimea was thus dispelled. Nevertheless, a fourth Jewish national province in the USSR — Freidorf — was established in the Crimean Jewish settlement region in 1931; and in 1935, about a year after Birobidzhan was declared a Jewish Autonomous Province, on May 7, 1934, a further Jewish national province — Larindorf — was set up. In July 1937, the Soviet government ratified a plan to settle five hundred Jewish families in Crimean *kolhozes,* collective farms.[7]

According to various sources, the number of Jewish farming families in the Crimea during the Thirties was estimated at roughly five thousand.[8] The departure of some families was offset by new arrivals, who were colonized with the help of the settlement agencies. But though the number of families remained more or less static, the number of persons dropped significantly. In 1933, the five thousand Jewish farming families had numbered twenty-five thousand souls; in 1939 they numbered only eighteen thousand. This is attributable chiefly to the fact that large numbers of young people left their parents' farms for the towns, or did not come there in the first place. This dropping off is attested to by the reports of visitors to the Soviet Union. Author David Pinsky, who visited the region in 1937 and toured several Jewish collective farms was struck by the fine husbandry he saw. However, when he and other visitors remarked on the noticeable absence of young people, the farmers told him: "The boys and girls have left for the towns, to study or work in factories. There are no prospects for them here."[9]

Even after the Communist propaganda organs — and Soviet Yiddish writing along with them — had begun to lavish their praises chiefly on the Birobidzhan project, they occasionally still spoke favorably of the Jewish settlements in the Crimea — which had formerly been their main source of pride.[10] Yet it transpires from the few figures we have quoted that the scope of the Crimea settlement project remained extremely limited despite the high-flown talk, and despite the occasional governmental encouragement and quite extensive overseas aid it was given. Even without taking account for the moment of the pallid Jewish national image of the Jewish settlements in the region and their lack of Jewish cultural substance, their contribution towards the economic recuperation of the Jewish population in the Soviet Union and a change in its structure was practically negligible.

We do not propose to enlarge on the reasons for the failure of the Crimea project. We might say, however, that they had very much in common with the reasons for the failure of the Jewish Birobidzhan scheme, since both projects were not inspired by any deep inner Jewish national awakening. The flimsy national content of Soviet Jewish autonomy was hardly enough to rouse and attract the urban Jewish masses. There were, moreover, specific reasons that proved detrimental to the Crimea settlement project. One of them lay in the very fact that governmental interest veered away from the Crimea to Birobidzhan. A further reason — which is relevant to our discussion of the new Crimean Affair — inhered in the hostility and jealousy evinced by the local residents towards the new Jewish settlers. Contrary to the glowing propaganda accounts, the Crimean Tartars and other indigenous groups did not receive their new Jewish neighbors with open arms. It should be noted that at first the initiators of the Crimea settlement project spoke of the favorable attitude of the Tartars as a kind of stock formula; whereas later, some of them used the "natural resistance" of the Tartars as one of their arguments for favoring Birobidzhan over the Crimea. Their enthusiasm for the Birobidzhan project derived, admittedly, chiefly from their acquiescence to the line the authorities appeared to be adopting, and from the presumption that a really vast settlement project could be executed only in the Far East, whose "sovereign" nature might well overshadow the attractions of Palestine. However, they were not entirely unmotivated by the hostility towards Jewish settlement in the Crimean peninsula. Kalinin himself recounted that many were voicing their resentment to the authorities over the fact that the Jews who were being settled under the Crimea project were given preference over soil-starved farmers of other nationalities.[11] And indeed, the "handing over" of the Crimea for Jewish settlement caused anti-Semitic manifestations in various places, or was used as a rationalization for a resurgence of anti-Jewish feeling. "So you want a separate Jewish republic? Want to take the Crimea?" an irate Kharkov factory worker baited a Jewish workmate.[12] Yuri Larin, who supported the Crimea project, gave an account of a "seminar on anti-Semitism" that he conducted in August 1928 in one of Moscow's boroughs; one of the questions revealing anti-Semitic bias was: "Why were the Jews in the Crimea given good land, while the land the Russians get is not so good?"[13] In 1936, when Birobidzhan had almost entirely supplanted the Crimea as a state-sponsored project, Simon Dimanstein, one-time head of the Jewish Commissariat (attached to the Commissariat of Nationalities) and chairman of OZET, published an article in the first issue of the Birobidzhan quarterly, *Forpost,* in the spirit current at the time: he reproached the KOMZET leaders for seeking to set up an autonomous Jewish entity in the Crimea: "These leaders did not take into account the specific national nature of the Crimea as a republic of the Tartars, and the natural resistance that must naturally be aroused by the idea of dividing up the Crimean Republic between the peoples that have been living there for centuries, and newcomers who have no affinity with the peninsula." Dimanstein published a further article in issue no. 3(5) of 1937 of the same quarterly, where he pointed to "nationalistic elements" among the sponsors of the settlement agencies, who sought to establish an autonomous Jewish center in the Crimea at the expense of the Tartars. He attributed the importance of choosing Birobidzhan for Jewish settlement to the fact that "here is a place where we shall not be confronted with any national antagonism with regard to the allotment of land to Jews, as had been the case in the Crimea and the Ukraine."

Having concluded our background survey at this point, let us now return to the Crimean Affair of the Forties. As the war was drawing to its close, the Soviet Jewish leadership — through its organized bodies such as the Jewish Anti-Fascist Committee and Jewish literary circles — began to entertain thoughts of a renewed settlement project in the Crimea, strange as this "recidivism" must appear in view of the course the former Crimea project had taken. The series of events that had taken place in the Twenties and Thirties should have been enough to warn the Jewish leaders against harboring illusions and running risks: suffice it to mention the resurgence of anti-Jewish feeling engendered by the Crimea project, the fact that it was deprived of state sponsorship, and the purge of its supporters, who were easily classifiable as "nationalistic elements." It would appear that these Jewish leaders disregarded these unfortunate memories of the past. They even ignored the practical circumstances which might well hinder the development of the notion of renewed settlement in the Crimea. The anti-Jewish feeling, which was running high, was met by an opportunistic attitude on the part of the authorities, and it was inconceivable that at just such a time the government should decide to hand over the Crimea, the "Russian Riviera," to the Jews! The inflammatory effect that such a step on the part of the authorities might have had on anti-Semitic feeling is not lessened by the fact that not the whole of the Crimea is a flourishing region and vacation resort. Large parts of the peninsula have an inhospitable climate and are unsuited for cultivation. However, for generations the Crimea had been popularly romanticized as "the pearl of Russia" and was associated with the happy life. For years a great many Ukrainians, who might even be termed "nationalists," had been indignant over the severance of the Crimea from the Ukraine and its annexation to the federated Soviet Russian Republic.[14] It was hardly to be imagined that just at the end of the war, when Ukrainian nationalism and Judeophobia were at their height, Stalin should outrage the Ukrainians by turning the Crimea into a kind of Jewish republic. Yet as much as the Jewish leaders were able to bring themselves to ignore this aspect of reality, they derived from current events some "logical reasoning" for the prospect that the Soviet government would reallot the Crimea for mass Jewish settlement. This selectivity of their thoughts and feelings in regard to the indications of reality may be a subject of study for a social psychologist rather than for a historian, yet we must follow their course for a better understanding of the Crimean Affair.

The "Crimean Legend" was broached about one year before the end of the war. This legend was nurtured from a confrontation of two material facts: on the one hand, there were a great many difficulties in the way of the resettlement of the Jewish survivors who returned to their homes in former German-occupied territories — difficulties arising from the wartime devastation, and also from the mounting anti-Semitism widely manifested by the inhabitants of the liberated areas. On the other hand, there were extensive unoccupied areas in the Crimea, after a large part of the local population had been deported for collaborating with the Germans. We shall add a few remarks on the latter fact in order to clarify the psychological background of the "Crimean Legend."

The region was liberated by the Red Army in April 1944. The

authorities immediately instituted punitive measures against the Tartar population, many of whom had joined German-organized units to fight against the Red Army, or carry out sabotage behind the Soviet lines. In a book of memoirs about partisan fighting in the Crimea, a Russian author remarks: "Not only did the natural conditions [in this region] impede partisan operations. Many Tartar villages were situated near the forests, and many Tartars had turned traitors at the beginning of the war. As a result, the Crimean partisans did not have the support of the local population."[15] It was also officially stated that most of the Crimean Tartars "did not offer resistance to the traitors." In consequence, collective responsibility was imposed on the whole region. The Crimean Autonomous Soviet Socialist Republic was reduced to the status of an ordinary administrative province.[16] Shortly after the liberation of the peninsula, masses of its Tartar inhabitants were deported to remote northern and eastern regions of the Soviet Union. The "Crimean Legend" could thus be nurtured by two practical factors: the fact that the Jews were in need of rehabilitation, and the fact that large areas had been vacated in the Crimea. Added weight was lent by the contrast involved: the mass treachery of the Crimean Tartars, on the one hand, and the loyal fighting and the tribulations suffered by the Jews, on the other. In the imagination of the Jews, the punishment of the collaborators was somehow associated with the need to compensate the chief victims of German brutality. It should be noted that the German extermination machinery had operated at full blast in the Crimea, where the occupation authorities sought to curry favor with the Tartar inhabitants. Most of the Crimean Jews were unable to escape. The Jewish farms became the scenes of butchery and pillage immediately after the Germans occupied the region.[17] Alongside this, there is impressive evidence of daring Crimean Jewish operations in the fighting underground.[18]

The new wartime line adopted by the Soviet authorities towards Jewish nationalist manifestations must certainly have lent plausibility to the assumption that the authorities would be favorably disposed to the scheme of resettling Jews in the Crimea. By a combination of logic and fancy, the Jews might also possibly have entertained the idea that the Soviet government might make some grateful gesture to world Jewry, which had responded generously to Russia's wartime needs. And there was also the consideration — induced by this same combination of logic and fantasy — that this was an opportune moment (surely Moscow realized this . . .) to secure worldwide Jewish support for a Soviet resettlement scheme for its Jews. Soviet Jewish spokesmen presumably broached the idea of the Crimea project to Soviet leaders on various occasions and were encouraged by the apparent reactions, though they received no specific promises. Or possibly at these meetings they discussed something on a far more modest scale, such as the reconstruction of the devastated Jewish settlements in the peninsula.

So fantastic was the allegation that the Jews had plotted to sever the peninsula from the Soviet Union that this might naturally give rise to the assumption that the Crimean Affair, from the outset, was an infamous provocation planned by the authorities — a trap laid for the Jewish communal leaders and writers for the deliberate purpose of preparing a legal basis for their liquidation. However, the evidence we have heard and assembled does not support this assumption. It is more reasonable to assume that in regard to the Jewish question — as it appeared with the resurgence of anti-Semitism during the war and the return of Jews to their former homes in liberated areas — the Soviet leaders adopted a far from uniform approach. Some were completely indifferent, if not worse, to the fate of the Jews, while others contemplated the need to take steps to alleviate their spiritual and physical plight.

The Crimean Affair was among the subjects which this author discussed with several Jewish writers and actors of Polish origin who were living in the Soviet Union during the war. One of them recounted, on the strength of his personal contacts with Soviet Jewish writers and public figures, that "at 10 Kropotkin St. [the premises of the Jewish Anti-Fascist Committee] there at times prevailed an atmosphere of deliverance during 1944." According to him, a whole fabric of speculation had been woven around the Crimea, Palestine, and Birobidzhan, in respect of one of which the Soviet government was expected to institute some innovation. These rumors and hopes were full of contradictions, but of the three alternatives, the Crimea began to take precedence. The Crimea was presumably accorded prominence (in these speculations) on the strength of the following rationalization: the authorities were not yet prepared to withdraw their basic opposition to Palestine as a Jewish national home, whereas they knew that the Birobidzhan project was unpopular, but still they felt obliged and wished to "do something" for the Jews. The Crimea presented this opportunity.

The Jewish State Theater in Moscow was also agog with tense expectation. There — according to one of the persons the author talked to — Mikhoels, director of the theater and chairman of the JAC, was regarded as a man "who carried a great secret with him." Some could not keep from asking him what lay behind the Crimean rumors. His replies were noncommittal. Once, however, he hinted that at a meeting he had had with a Soviet leader the question of the Crimea had come up. But he advised the theater people not to talk about this too much in the meantime.

These verbal memoirs largely coincide with a mass of written evidence, chiefly also of Polish Jewish writers who were living in the Soviet Union during the war. According to Isaac Yonasovich, "expectation of some great event" prevailed among the Jewish writers in Moscow when the war had reached its final stages. This expectation induced a certain tension, which was also a source of elation. At the Jewish Anti-Fascist Committee, at the *Emes* publishing house, and at the writers' apartments, all spoke of the event that was about to take place "with hints and allusions, and lowered voices." It was a kind of secret which "birds twittered from the rooftops." "Quivering excitement" was caused by the rumor that "the Soviet government plans to allot the Crimean peninsula to the Jews of Russia, where they will be able to settle and establish, if not a Jewish Republic of their own, at least an Autonomous Jewish Province." According to a current rumor, Politburo member Lazar Kaganovich had told someone that "there was a hope that the Jews would get the Crimea." The Jewish writers, who were accustomed to speaking with exaggerated zeal of what was happening in the Soviet Union, "congratulated one another with the traditional *Mazel Tov* greeting and walked about intoxicated with joy." Some of them even fancied themselves as the future rulers of the Jewish state that was about to be established in the Crimea.[19]

Joseph Rubinstein recounts similar experiences of his stay in Moscow in 1944. An unusual air of enthusiasm prevailed among those present at a plenary meeting of the JAC. People whispered and exchanged secrets excitedly. The secret was the Crimea, the magnificent country that "the Kremlin proposes to give us in compensation for our bereavement." People speak of the traitorous Tartars, of vacant land that is waiting for working hands. Instead of the ruins and ashes that await them in their devastated Ukrainian townships, the Jews will rebuild their lives anew in the Crimea. Intoxicated with joy, writers exclaim proudly, "Such is our government! Such is our Soviet homeland!" . . . Bergelson is enthusiastic, Markish is aquiver, Kvitko is smiling, Kushnirov is excited . . . all are enthralled by the sweet rumors . . . a dream is coming true . . . Kaganovich promised . . . Of course! After such a calamity! . . . Imaginations are fired . . . but meanwhile it is better to keep quiet. . . .

In the course of the JAC plenary meeting, Rubinstein goes on to recount, Ilya Ehrenburg took the floor. He too, he said, had heard the rumors circulated there to the effect that Comrade Stalin proposed to give the Crimea to the Jews, but all that was "empty prattle"; the Jews would not return to the Crimea, but to Minsk and Zhitomir, to their former homes. To this, Shakhno Epstein, the JAC secretary, retorted that it was inconceivable that "after such a terrible calamity" the situation should revert to what it was before, without "some sort of compensation." This exchange caused consternation and alarm among the gathering.[20]

Poet Abraham Sutzkever recorded in his diary, in July 1944, an account of the representations made by a Soviet Jewish delegation that had recently been received by Litvinov, then deputy foreign minister. At this meeting, Jewish claims for a postwar settlement were discussed. Shakhno Epstein broached the idea of establishing a Jewish center in the Crimea. Litvinov, however, was of the opinion that if the Jews needed a territory of their own, this should preferably be in Palestine, which was supported by world Jewry. Ehrenburg, with whom Sutzkever discussed the matter, was inclined to agree with Litvinov.[21]

Sutzkever also mentions the Crimean idea in his reminiscences concerning Mikhoels. Though "Mikhoels was skeptical of the idea of a Jewish republic in the Crimea, he nevertheless came out with the following remark when he was directing a rehearsal of Bergelson's play *Prince Reuveni:* 'Comrades, it may well be that we shall celebrate the premiere of *Prince Reuveni* in Symferopol [capital of the former Crimean Autonomous Republic].' " Actor Zuskin then remarked that he had heard that Mikhoels would be the first president of the Crimean Jewish Republic.[22]

The Crimean rumors even reached author Moshe Grossman while he was in a prison camp in Uzbekistan: "They are going to establish a Jewish republic in the Crimea," he was told by an actor acquaintance, who had arrived in the camp, not as a prisoner, but to do some job there.[23]

Hershel Vaynrauch, a Soviet Jewish writer who managed to escape from the USSR, recalls that when he came back from the front to Moscow for a few days in 1944, he attended a meeting of Jewish writers at the premises of the Soviet Writers' Association. Markish spoke enthusiastically of the great achievements of Soviet Jewish literature, but author Professor Nusinov retorted that there was no point speaking of Jewish literature when there was no Jewish people. Pointing out that "the victory of the Red Army is already clearly apparent," Nusinov raised the question of where the Jewish survivors and evacuees would return to — were they to go back to their destroyed towns and villages in the Ukraine and Belorussia? He proposed that "we, the Jewish writers and the Jewish Anti-Fascist Committee, should request the government to repatriate the Jews evacuated to Siberia and Central Asia, not in the devastated cities and townships, but in some other place, some other territory, say the Crimea." Young poet Motl Grubian seconded Nusinov's proposal, but Bergelson maintained that "the Party and the government themselves know what to do with the Jewish evacuees. . . . Our business is only to write, to write well." Vaynrauch points out that Bergelson's remarks caused despondency and alarm among the gathering.[24]

It would appear that Vaynrauch's account of Bergelson's reaction to the Crimean project contradicts that of Rubinstein (and others), but in reality there is no contradiction, for the entire Crimean Affair turned out to be a short-lived episode. It flared up in 1944, and petered out that same year. According to several accounts, the Jewish writers and leaders were very soon told, or given broad hints, to stop "talking drivel." Within a few months the elation made way for disappointment and despondency. Bergelson himself — he was one of the most adaptable of the Jewish writers — ably voiced the change in climate in his usual smooth manner. Yonasovich, from whose memoirs we have quoted, recounts that when the "Crimea Legend" was at its peak Bergelson would say: "But of course! Our Soviet government alone will solve the Jewish question; only our Communist Party will reward the Jews for their loyalty and compensate them for what they suffered during the war." But only a short time later Bergelson had to claim that he had known from the outset that the Crimea rumors were a provocation instigated by "the enemies of our dear Soviet homeland," for "why do we, Russian Jews, need a territory? . . . We Russian Jews feel good wherever we are."[25]

Ehrenburg's skeptical attitude to the Crimea notion — as reflected in the accounts of Rubinstein and Sutzkever cited above — was apparently quite consistent. According to author Israel Emyot, too, Ehrenburg was against all that sort of talk; his opposition extended to both the Crimea and Birobidzhan projects. Before a group of Yiddish writers Ehrenburg expostulated: "You want to create a new Jewish ghetto!"[26] About twenty years later, Ehrenburg referred to the abortive Crimea project, in a talk with a Paris journalist, as "a rash plan to break into a home whose legal owner might still come back." In the course of that talk Ehrenburg revealed several important and illuminating details. First: the proposal to allot the Crimea for Jewish settlement, after the Tartar collaborationists had been deported from the region, had been mooted in a memorandum addressed to Stalin by the Jewish Anti-Fascist Committee. Secondly: "Molotov was sympathetically disposed to the Crimea project and was consulted before the memorandum to Stalin was drawn up."[27] B. Z. Goldberg, too, records that the JAC addressed its memorandum on the Crimea project to the Kremlin "on Molotov's advice."[28] It should be borne in mind that for many years Molotov was considered to be second to Stalin in the Soviet hierarchy. It cannot be ascertained whether the memorandum to Stalin spoke merely of mass Jewish resettlement in the Crimea, or specifically broached the idea of establishing an autonomous Jewish territory in the peninsula. What is beyond all doubt, however, is that in this project — as in the entire course of the birth and growth of the "Crimea Legend" — there was not the minutest trace of a Jewish conspiracy. At most it was a tragic illusion. Nor did the authorities have to go to particular pains to eradicate this illusion from Jewish minds.

It is relevant to point out that Jewish wartime and postwar publications, including *Einikeit,* made no allusion to the neo-Crimean notion. On the other hand, it was just in 1944, when the illusion of the Crimea began to be widespread, that these publications featured increasing propaganda about and for the Birobidzhan project. After no settlement activities had been carried out there for several years, the publications obviously set out to promote the resumption of Jewish migration to the region. While the Crimean rumors were still circulating among Jewish literary and public circles, there occurred the tenth anniversary of the Jewish Autonomous Province in Birobidzhan, an event to which *Einikeit* devoted several enthusiastic columns.[29] Birobidzhan representatives, who had come to Moscow to attend a JAC meeting, were received by Kalinin, who assured them that he firmly maintained that Birobidzhan was the most suitable place for mass Jewish settlement.[30]

At the beginning of 1946, the propaganda in favor of the Birobidzhan project was accompanied by organized measures to promote migration there. A resolution adopted on January 26, 1946, by the government of the Russian Federated Republic (in whose territory the Jewish Autonomous Province is situated), referred to "measures to reinforce and further develop the economy of the Jewish Autonomous Region." This resolution also directed the competent authorities to send there twenty doctors, chiefly Jews, in the third quarter of 1946, and fifty Jewish teachers during 1946. An order promulgated by the Central Soviet Government the next day, on January 27, 1946, called for the establishment and completion of several nationally important enterprises in Birobidzhan.[31] The Jewish propaganda stressed, in particular, the patriotic aspect of renewed migration to Birobidzhan and of the intensified socialist construction work there, but also strove to touch upon national Jewish sentiments. On the one hand, this propaganda pointed to Birobidzhan's integration into the first postwar Five Year Plan, for 1946–50, and strove, on the other hand, to bolster pride in the "Jewishness" of the region. We may be permitted to assume that the enthusiasm that was stirred up for Birobidzhan in those years was also designed to afford an escape from the Crimea notion — a notion that had fired the Jewish leadership when it was still no more than innocent wishful thinking. This escape no doubt wrought an effect on the rousing welcome that Moscow Jewish institutions gave the "Vinitza Contingent" that passed through the Moscow railway station on their way to Birobidzhan. It was met by representatives of the Jewish Anti-Fascist Committee, *Einikeit,* the Jewish State Theater and others, including Mikhoels, Feffer, Markish, and Kvitko.[32]

In addition to the call to share in building up "Soviet Jewish sovereignty" and in executing the Stalinist postwar Five Year Plan, Jewish migration to Birobidzhan was also motivated by the reintegration difficulties encountered by Jews in the newly liberated areas. It is an illuminating fact that contingents for migration to Birobidzhan were organized even in the Ukraine and Belorussia, where large reconstruction works were already in progress and no doubt needed a great deal of labor. The emigrants included a large number of men in essential professions and trades, such as engineers, technicians, tractor and truck drivers, electricians, agronomists, metal workers, and the like, who were certainly not redundant in Russia's western areas. This inevitably leads to the conclusion that their migration was induced by the prevailing anti-Semitic mood.

It should be noted in connection with the rise and collapse of the "Crimea Legend," that even Jews of Crimean origin figured prominently among the Birobidzhan contingents. The floodlights of publicity were turned in particular onto the travelers "from the shores of the Black Sea to the shores of the River Amur." The "Crimean Contingent," like the Vinitza Contingent before it, became a byword. At the beginning of 1948 *Einikeit* reported that it had consisted of 802 emigrants, "who now live with the single thought of settling quickly and becoming the honorable builders of the Jewish Autonomous Province."[33]

It may be assumed that also the veteran Jewish Crimean settlers, including the farmers, encountered resettlement difficulties there after the war. Thus, even the small former measure of Jewish identity in the Crimea was diminished after the war.

The Crimean illusion was indeed short-lived. Yet several years later, in the course of the liquidation of Jewish culture and the last vestiges of Jewish communal life, the authorities seized on this illusion, among other things, to fabricate the criminal charges which they leveled against a group of Jewish writers, artists, and other public figures.

SEVEN

Numerus Clausus, Numerus Nullus

The liquidation of Jewish culture and its institutions in the Soviet Union, together with the persecution or execution of many Jewish writers, artists, and public figures, constitute a massive series of deliberate measures that assumed the proportions of cultural genocide. But also in the light of other processes and events, the years 1948 to 1953 were "black years" in the history of Soviet Jewry.[1] One of these processes consisted in the ousting of Jews from various positions and fields of activity. The significance of this process will be more readily understood in the light of the position formerly occupied by Jews in Soviet officialdom; this survey will refer chiefly to the professional staffs of various services.

The beginning of the Soviet regime was marked by an acute shortage of loyal cadres. Many intellectuals left the country after the October Revolution and a large number of those who stayed on were not trusted by the new regime. This afforded the Jewish intelligentsia wide openings for entering the government and public service. The fact that they had been barred from state service during Tsarist days now increased their chances, since the Soviet regime was eager to employ qualified personnel that had no Tsarist affiliations. Moreover, a considerable section of the Jewish intelligentsia had been active in the revolutionary movement, or was known to have leftist inclinations. At all events, the anti-Soviet element among the Jews was estimated to be smaller than that among other national groups in the country, including the Russian people. Also, the fact remained that in Russia, with its essentially rural population, the Jews were largely an urban element and their educational level was higher than that of any other national group among the population. The predominant social background of the Jews — a decisive criterion in determining fitness for Soviet state service — was in their favor: most of the Jewish intellectuals came from the lower or middle classes, as did the majority of Russian Jews.

The entry of Jews into the various branches of state service was smoothed both by their professional qualifications, and also because of their political trustworthiness. This summation accords with Khrushchev's admission nearly forty years after the revolution, when speaking of the changes that had taken place in the "cadres" since then. At the beginning of the new regime, he stated, "we had a great many Jews at the head of the Party and at the head of the state, because they were more educated and possibly even more revolutionary than the average Russian."[2]

Jewish potential continued to be an undiminished source of cadres for Soviet state service. Though the desire for education had become general throughout the country, with all the material benefits this afforded, this in no way diminished the Jews' thirst for knowledge. On the contrary, the desire of Jewish parents to give their children an education, which is a universal Jewish national characteristic and tradition, was bolstered by governmental encouragement. If Jews had been able to maintain this tradition under repressive and discriminatory conditions and in dire economic circumstances, they were all the more prompted to do so when all the state schools were open to them and they could benefit from government education incentives. In the latter half of the Twenties and the first half of the Thirties, Jews accounted for roughly 14 percent of the total student body at all Soviet universities, while constituting some 2 percent of the total population — 1.78 percent according to the Soviet census taken in January 1939. We may again refer to Khrushchev, who, in remarking on specific Jewish traits (though not over-fondly), asserted that Jews are basically intellectuals and "never feel they have studied enough. Just give them a chance, and they go to a university without considering the sacrifice involved."[3] Hence it transpires that while Jews figured prominently on government staffs, they also flocked to the universities; and this led further to responsible posts in the various state services, where there was a growing demand for qualified personnel, with a correspondingly increasing general supply.

The years 1948–53 were marked by a clear reversal of Soviet policy in this regard. Jews were deliberately kept from ascending the hierarchic scale and were barred from employment in a number of services and branches that were considered "sensitive." It must be pointed out, however, that in the Soviet structure — where the state monopolizes all economic and cultural activity, and where political surveillance and ideological direction are an inseparable part of all fields of human endeavor — there is practically no limitation on classifying various fields as "sensitive."

At the beginning of the Soviet regime, Jews possessing the necessary qualifications were particularly in demand in the foreign service, where a theoretical and practical knowledge of world affairs and of foreign languages was required. It was not mere chance that combined anti-Soviet and anti-Semitic propaganda, eager to prove Jewish domination of the Soviet Union, pointed to the Soviet foreign office (derisively termed "the synagogue") as an example. Several Jews — Maxim Litvinov, Adolf Yoffe, Karl Radek — were prominent in the delegation that accompanied the Soviet people's commissar for foreign affairs, Georgi Chicherin, to the Genoa Conference in 1922, where the young Soviet diplomacy made its first impressive appearance on the international scene, and signed the Treaty of Rapallo with Germany. In the Twenties and early Thirties, there were a great many Jewish Soviet ambasadors and envoys, and many more held consular and other posts in overseas missions. A Jew, Jakob Suritz, was the Soviet minister to Germany even at the beginning of the Nazi regime. True, the number of Jews in the Soviet foreign service was reduced — presumably on orders from above — already while Maxim Litvinov, a Jew himself, was foreign commissar, but this was still a long way from rendering the Soviet foreign office *Judenrein.* Konstantin Umansky, a Jew, was appointed Soviet ambassador to the United States in 1939, and was later ambassador to Mexico. After the German invasion of the Soviet Union, Maxim Litvinov held this post from November 1941 to August 1943. Ivan Maisky, a half-Jew, was Soviet ambassador to Great Britain during the war. Between 1943 and 1946, Litvinov held the post of deputy foreign minister, a post also occupied for certain periods by Maisky and Solomon Lozovsky — though the powers of all three were extremely limited.[4] Professor Boris Stein was a member of the Soviet delegation to the United Nations for some time (when the Palestine question was under discussion). At all events, though the number of Jews in representative posts of the foreign service had been reduced during the ten years preceding 1948, Jews were still prominent in the "harmless" departments of the foreign office, where they engaged in research, review of events, or press relations. There was also a high proportion of Jews among professors and lecturers at diplomatic training colleges, where there was also a high Jewish student enrollment.

Against this background there stands out the stark fact that in the early Fifties Jews were barred, by dint of a total *numerus nullus,* from employment in the field of Soviet foreign relations, whether at the Moscow administrative level or in representative posts abroad; whether in the field of diplomatic training, or in specialist advisory and research posts. This applied even to the lower grades — Jews were suspended from posts as attachés or on technical and administrative staffs in foreign missions. Similarly, the staff of the ministry of foreign trade, where Jews had formerly figured prominently, was purged of Jews. Regular lists were published of officials authorized to negotiate transactions on behalf of the ministry and its ancillary organizations; of the eighty-seven names listed in January to April 1950, only two or three were Jewish.[5] Yet in the light of the anti-Jewish atmosphere that later prevailed, this situation could be looked back on as being ideal. Also characteristic of this atmosphere was the fact that Jews were expelled from foreign trade institutes and colleges, both as lecturers and as students.

Similar developments occurred in the Soviet Army, though the overall picture here was somewhat different for various reasons. First, military ranks are not automatically revoked on the cessation of active duty. Secondly, since Jews continued to be mobilized for military service, they could not very well be debarred from the lower commissioned ranks, at least. Thirdly, for many years Jews had largely held high ranks in such technical units as the Medical, Engineering, Signals, and Armored Corps, and they could hardly be demobilized, or dismissed, without this having an immediate detrimental effect on the defense system. Several Jews even continued to hold high-ranking command posts. Yet there remains the inescapable fact that the supreme military command was almost entirely purged of Jews during the black years.

A number of military leaders of Jewish origin were before the war affected by the liquidation of Marshal Tukhachevsky: Generals Yakir, Feldman, and Eidman were executed in 1937. General Gamarnik, dismissed from his post of chief political commissar of the Red Army, committed suicide. Later, when high-ranking officers who had been connected with Soviet aid to the Spanish republican forces were imprisoned or disappeared, they included such Jewish names as Generals Shmushkovich ("Duglas") and Stern ("Kelber").[6]

During the war, however, there again appeared to be a high proportion of Jews in the supreme command, but nothing was heard of them in the late Forties. Between 1948 and 1953, 63 Jewish generals, 111 colonels, and 159 lieutenant-colonels were retired. By 1953, there was not a single Jew among the hundred top-ranking officers — marshals, chiefs of staff, commanders of the twenty-three military regions, and generals on the active list.[7] Characteristic of this trend is the fact that in 1948–49 the Soviet authorities commenced to purge its administration and military forces in Germany of Jewish personnel; this was effected by transferring Jews to other units or discharging, if not imprisoning some of them. In the latter half of the Forties the military academies became barred to Jews, who were also weeded out from schools for subalterns. Milovan Djilas, who visited the Soviet Union with a Yugoslav delegation in 1948, was informed (with obvious gratification) by a Central Party official, that when the deputy chief of staff, General Antonov, was discovered to be a Jew, that meant the end of his career.[8] It is inconceivable that a man who had held the post of deputy chief of staff should have been able to conceal such a cogent biographical detail as his Jewish origin from those whose constant business it was to scrutinize the curricula vitae and dossiers of leading persons. It is more reasonable to assume that it was only in 1948 that the authorities saw fit to "uncover" Antonov's genealogy and draw the conclusions they found necessary.

From the Red Army let us turn to the leadership of the Communist Party. From the beginning of the Thirties (as opposed to the Twenties) up to Stalin's death, there was only one Jewish member, Lazar Kaganovich, in the Politburo, the most powerful unit of the Party.[9] Nevertheless, in the Thirties there was still a relatively large number of Jews in the Party's Central Committee. But in the Central Committee elected by the Eighteenth Party Congress in March 1939 there were only nine Jews among its seventy-one members, namely: Yemelian, Yaroslavsky, Lazar Kaganovich, Maxim Litvinov, Lev Mekhlis, Solomon Lozovsky, Mikhail Kaganovich — Lazar's brother — Rosalia Ziemlatska, Mark Mitin, and General Stern. Of these, only Lazar Kaganovich was reelected at the Nineteenth Party Congress in October 1952. All the rest were dismissed, apart from Yaroslavsky and Ziemlatska who had died meanwhile; Litvinov died several years after he was expelled from the Central Committee, and Lozovsky, as has been previously stated, was executed in August 1952. There was one Jew, G. D. Veinberg, among the sixty-eight candidates for membership in the Central Committee that was elected in 1939, but he too was expelled between the two Congresses. In the early Fifties, moreover, there was not a single Jew in the secretariat of the Central Committee and its organizational bureau (Orgburo), or among the first Party secretaries of the republics, and hardly among the provincial Party secretaries (Obkom or Kraikom). It has been more difficult to ascertain the number of Jews among the secretaries of the smaller Party units, the Raykom committees, which numbered some two thousand, but as far as is known the position here was no different. The same applied to the Komsomol and its various bodies.[10]

The purge of Party institutions and staffs of Jewish personnel was actually completed in the early Fifties, having been instituted several years previously. The man who smugly told Djilas of the discharge of General Antonov when his Jewish origin was "discovered," also told him of the purge of the Central Committee staff of Jews carried out by Andrei Zhdanov.[11] It transpires, however, that this purge was not limited to the Party staffs only. From a report of the Mandates

Committee of the Nineteenth Party Congress in 1952 we learn that 1,192 delegates and 167 candidate delegates represented nearly seven million members of thirty-seven nationalities. The report specified these nationalities, some of them tiny groups like the Yakuts, Ossetians, Mordovinians, Udmurts, Komis, Chuvashes, and Buriats, but did not list the Jews. If there were any Jews at all among the delegates or candidates, they were presumably listed among the "miscellaneous" nationalities stated in the report.

Jewish membership in the Supreme Soviet with its two chambers, the Soviet of the Union and the Soviet of Nationalities, steadily dwindled from one election to the next. After the war, however, the decline in Jewish membership was particularly steep, in line with the tendency to keep Jews almost entirely out of the leading representative bodies of the state. In the 1937 elections, 47 Jewish members out of a total of 1,143, namely 4.1 percent, had been returned to the two chambers of the Supreme Soviet. In the first postwar elections, in January 1946, only 5 Jewish members out of a total of 801, or 0.8 percent, were returned to the Soviet of the Union. (There is no authoritative data on the number of Jews elected to the Soviet of Nationalities; but it has been estimated that whereas in 1937 they had ranked there eleventh in the listing of nationalities, they ranked twenty-sixth in 1946.)[12] In the March 1950 elections the proportion of Jews in both chambers dropped to less than 0.4 percent: there were 5 Jews among the 1,316 members of both chambers (they included Lazar Kaganovich, Ilya Ehrenburg, and Rosalia Goldenberg, head physician at the Birobidzhan municipal hospital, who was the only Jewish representative of the Autonomous Jewish Province in the Soviet of Nationalities). A similar trend was also apparent in the Supreme Soviets of the Republics, and even in the elections to the municipal councils.

It should be borne in mind that the lists of candidates are drawn up by Party bodies, and they reflect political processes rather than demographic changes. The censuses taken in 1939, the last before the war, and in 1959, the first after the war, admittedly show that the proportion of Jews among the general population of the USSR dropped from roughly 1.8 percent to 1.1 percent; between the two censuses, on the one hand, the Soviet Union enlarged its Jewish population by the annexation of Belorussia, Western Ukraine, the Baltic countries, Bessarabia, and Northern Bukovina — and on the other hand, the Nazis had exterminated masses of Jews. However, the decline in Jewish representation was far from warranted by the tragic demographic changes.

The picture was no different in the Soviet government, which is not an authoritative political body, but rather a kind of central technical administration. A large number of Jews were expelled from leading positions in planning, economic, and industrial agencies. That the names of a few Jews still appeared among the holders of ministerial posts in the early Fifties hardly changes the general picture. These indications were also in evidence in the governments and administrations of the republics. There, the Jews were replaced, not necessarily by members of the local nationalities, but in many cases by non-Jews of other nationalities.

This deliberate tendency to oust Jews from all leading positions — governmental and Party, diplomatic and administrative, parliamentary and military — was in no way slurred over even by the impressive state funeral given to Lev Mekhlis, who died on February 13, 1953. Mekhlis had been politically dead since 1950. Nothing had been heard of him since the Presidium of the Supreme Soviet had in October 1950 released him ("for health reasons") from his post as minister of state control (he was presumably dismissed from the Central Committee at about the same time). Mekhlis had for many years held important posts: he had been on the staff of Stalin's personal bureau; for some time, after Gamarnik's suicide, he had been in charge of political supervision of the army; after the war, he had been entrusted with the sensitive task of state control, no doubt because of his unswerving loyalty, as well as his ability. One of the reasons for removing Mekhlis from his last post as state comptroller might possibly have been connected with the *political* preparations (regardless of the actual facts) that were being made to expose fraudulent conspiracy, largely attributable to Jews, in various economic and administrative bodies; this activity, which we shall deal with separately, was pursued with particular intensity in the early Fifties. At all events, the man who among those of Jewish origin had stood second only to Kaganovich in the political hierarchy, was summarily removed from the scene.

Isaac Deutscher advances the assumption that the state funeral accorded Mekhlis, was an indication of the growing strength of the liberal, anti-Stalinist element just before the ruler's death.[13] What is no less feasible is the assumption that the posthumous honor accorded to Mekhlis, one month after the sensational disclosure of the Doctors' Plot, was intended to refute the foreign reports of a total anti-Semitic campaign in the Soviet Union — a Stalinist ruse to "confuse the enemy."

As has already been remarked, in the Soviet scheme of things every service and every field of activity could readily be defined as "sensitive." In keeping with the line adopted towards the Jews, they could no longer have any place on the staffs of the internal security agencies. According to this pattern, where politics were inseparably interrelated with production, or propaganda with security, the trade unions, for example, were treated in no different way from the other branches of the state and Party, and the anti-Jewish purges swept their leadership, too. The times when a Jew — Solomon Lozovsky — could stand at the head of Profintern, which was under direct Kremlin supervision, seemed very far off indeed. The Jews began to be edged out of propaganda and information jobs, and not only from the key positions; it was not convenient at such a time to employ Jews as Party propagandists — lecturers, instructors, or directors of seminars. Jews also disappeared from among the representatives of the Soviet press and news agencies in foreign countries. For some three decades Jews had figured prominently in the Soviet press, from the leading newspapers, through the regional and local organs, right down to the thousands of brochures and wall newspapers published at various industrial plants and other economic enterprises. During the black years, they were weeded out from journalistic occupations, and especially from editorial jobs on the central newspapers. The few that remained belonged to the old guard, but they too were in for "surprises." Even David Zaslavsky (1879–1964), one of the few former members of the Jewish Anti-Fascist Committee who had survived, fell into disrepute. Zaslavsky bore the reputation of a man who toed the line — he had clearly shown his conformism in his blistering attacks on Israel. When the Doctors' Plot was exposed, he was removed from a key position on *Pravda,* after one of his colleagues reportedly claimed that he could not work together with a man who belonged to a race of traitors and poisoners.[14] Artificial difficulties were placed in the way of the advancement of young Jews, who were not admitted to schools of journalism. For some time it looked as though Jews working in the broadcasting services were not affected, but the systematic purge could not, in the long run, pass over this essential branch: radio announcers and commentators were charged not only with harboring Western sympathies, but even with having an insufficient knowledge of the Russian language. . . .

The purge also encompassed the universities, affecting teaching and research staffs and students alike. Many professors were dismissed. The Moscow University, for example, considered a stronghold of Russian culture, was extensively purged of Jewish lecturers.[15] According to one report, Jews had accounted for some 40 percent of the student body of the Moscow University's department of philology before the war; in 1951, only three Jewish applicants, out of a total of 250, were admitted to the department's first year studies.[16] A similar situation obtained in a large number of other institutions of higher education. The dismissal of the faculty members and the nonacceptance of students was not openly attributed to the fact that they were Jews, but these appearances became so widespread that their real reason needed no explanation.

The anti-Jewish purge extended its compass. Specific industrial branches and institutes of science were facilely classified as "sensitive areas." While the judiciary system was being primed to deal drastically with political and economic crimes, in which Jews were to figure largely, Jewish jurists — judges, prosecutors, and defense counsels — suddenly became redundant. In accordance with the hallowed Soviet principle that theory must not be divorced from practice, the condemnations and dismissals extended also to Jewish legal experts who had served the Supreme Soviet in professional capacities, and to scientists working at legal research institutes, such as that attached to the Soviet Academy of Sciences. What is illuminating is the combination of charges made against a number of Jewish jurists and legal experts: they were accused of ideological deviations (e.g., formalism, or dogmatism), as well as of contravening social and ethical norms of conduct, nepotism and the like. Among those condemned for both crimes in one *Izvestia* article, for instance, there figured such Jewish names as Trainin, Mankovsky, Gertsenson, Gringaus, Genkin, Karp, Eisenstadt, Rabinovich, and others. There were also non-Jews among those condemned, as at the time of the intensive anticosmopolitan campaign, but the proportion in which the deviationists of the different nationalities was represented left no room for any wrong conclusions.[17]

Some of the dismissals were performed in a brutal, open manner, and others in a roundabout way. In some places, Jewish employees were instructed to apply for their discharge on grounds of health, or agree to be demoted to relieve their pressure of work. When Jews in responsible posts committed the most trivial errors, these were blown up to grievous proportions and used against them in order to punish them, force them to resign, or curtail their powers. This engendered an atmosphere in which Jews were not encouraged to excel and attain leading positions. Rather than try to climb up the scale, they chose to be unobtrusive.

As we have observed, specific fields were almost entirely purged of Jews, and the few Jews who remained in them hardly change the general picture. We have also remarked that a regime such as that current in the Soviet Union reserves the right to decide who is a Jew and when he is a Jew. It is relevant to add that when the authorities accord their tutelage — as a rule temporarily — to a few Jews who are the exceptions, this is sometimes in effect a cruel act, since the protégés feel a psychological need to prove their loyalty: afraid for their skins, they might strive to join those condemning Jews and Judaism. Leading Soviet personages of Jewish origin never helped their people when anti-Jewish measures were instituted.

However, there were still several fields in which Jews continued to maintain a high proportionate representation. One of these was the field of Soviet — or more specifically, Russian — literature. By the early Fifties, not a trace of Jewish culture or Yiddish literature had survived. Yet when the Second Conference of Soviet Writers was held in December 1954, 72 authors of Jewish origin attended it, compared to 250 Russian delegates (who ranked first according to a national breakdown) and 71 Ukrainian delegates (ranking third).[18] This conference was held about a year and nine months after Stalin's death, but it more or less reflects the Jewish share in Soviet writing also during Stalin's latter years. Despite the anti-Jewish spearhead of the campaign against cosmopolitanism, and despite the inimical atmosphere engendered towards writers of Jewish origin — there was even a proposal to expel practically all of them from the Writers' Union[19] — Soviet literature was not subjected to an anti-Jewish purge, and more or less similar immunity was accorded to Jews engaged in other fields such as painting, sculpture, music, and ballet, and drama — despite the sharp attacks leveled against Jewish theater critics. It may be interesting to note that world chess champion Mikhail Botvinik, a Soviet Jew, retained his title throughout the black years and after, but the second edition of the *Great Soviet Encyclopedia* (Volume 5, published in 1950) did not mention his Jewish origin.

At the same time as the Jews clung to their literary and artistic pursuits despite the unfavorable climate — persons engaged in these pursuits presumably find it hard to abandon them — Jews relinquished such humanistic subjects as philosophy, historiography, pedagogy, and the like, which had always attracted Jews. Against this, Jews continued to be prominently represented throughout the black years in the exact sciences. This was not mere chance, but a direct result of the reality with which they were faced and the sociopolitical processes. There is doubtless some correlation between the disappearance of Jews from key administrative positions and their proliferation in the scientific and technological fields. Finding certain avenues barred to them, the Jews sought some other outlets of expression for their intellect, drive, and ability, particularly in view of the increased demand for scientific and technical skills. Against the background of the black years atmosphere, it is not surprising that Jews instinctively shied away from controversial fields of endeavor, which were subject to fluctuations of policy, and sought refuge in more "stable" branches. There, despite the doctrine that claimed that there was no such thing as an apolitical field of research or activity, they nevertheless felt less hampered by ideological and political programs, and were less in danger of slipping up and being suspected of diversionist tendencies. Jewish circles might have entertained the optimistic thought that in the physics or biology laboratory, engaged in mechanical tests or electronic development, their national origin might be less closely scrutinized and they would be less likely to be accused of cosmopolitanism or nationalism. Such occupations — as opposed to government, administrative, or Party posts — were also less "representative" and hence, it was hoped, less conspicuous.

This balancing out between the *numerus clausus* imposed on the Jews in specific fields and the prominent position they continued to occupy, despite the difficulties, in literature, the arts, and the exact sciences, might explain the fact that in 1952 Jews still constituted 8 to 9 percent of the recipients of Stalin Awards — a percentage far higher than their proportion among the total population, yet less than half of the percentage of Jewish prizewinners five years previously. Yet the crux of the problem does not lie in percentages, but in the fact that processes and measures were instituted in an overt manner to deprive Jews of their equality of rights and status as Soviet citizens. In principle — and, as we have observed, largely in practice, too — the entire Jewish community found itself reduced to the status of "fifth-rate invalids," as the Jews often referred to themselves. This "invalidity" relates to the fifth entry in the internal passport which all Soviet citizens must carry, indicating the bearer's nationality.[20] It also almost entirely diminished the value of such attributes as expert knowledge, capacity for work, excellent qualifications, and loyalty. The fifth entry requirement was applied indiscriminately, often claiming as its victims persons entirely divorced from Judaism from the religious, linguistic, cultural, social, or emotional aspects. In some respects the situation of the Jews had become worse than it had been under the Tsarist regime, which, despite its persecution and anti-Semitic repression of Jews on fanatical religious grounds, had nevertheless given Jews who embraced Christianity the possibility, theoretically at least, of attaining leading positions in the hierarchy. During Stalin's last five years the Jews were often confronted with a biological barrier, which even their repudiation of Judaism and assimilation did not enable them to break through.

EIGHT

Kafka in Prague, 1952

The history of the Jewish communities in the People's Democracies lies outside the scope of this study, but sometimes it must be touched upon because of its connection with events in the Soviet Union. Although what happened with respect to the Jews in these countries was to some degree dependent on local developments and on the nature of the leadership in each of them, the events were — with all their variations[1] — to a considerable extent a function of Moscow's "Jewish policy."

The degree of Stalinization, or satellitism, of the People's Democracies was also reflected in like fashion in its effects on the Jews. The diminution of democratic freedoms, the processes of political and cultural regimentation, and increasing adaptation to Soviet methods of government — these and similar phenomena directly influenced Jewish communal life which had been shrinking rapidly from the end of the 1940's. Communist supervision of Jewish cultural and welfare institutions became stricter; the activities of a number of them were reduced to almost nothing while others were completely liquidated. Most seriously affected were institutions receiving guidance and financial assistance from Jewish organizations abroad, primarily from the Joint Distribution Committee, which had been very active in helping Jewish survivors of the Nazi holocaust in eastern and central Europe. Jewish hospitals and orphans' homes, rehabilitation centers and charitable organizations devoted especially to Jews, and above all, separate Jewish schools became the targets of frequent charges of promoting bourgeois tradition, nationalism, clericalism, and the like. Of course, with the swift advance towards the model of a one-party state, any basis for the existence of Jewish political associations vanished. This was particularly true of organizations which by their very nature — ideologically if not by their organizational structure — were linked to worldwide movements.

It is not difficult to imagine the fear which gripped the leaders of the People's Democracies in the wake of the evident Soviet retreat from its initial, generally favorable, policy toward Israel (which was chiefly manifested in Moscow's strong support of the establishment of the Jewish state in 1947–48), in view of these countries' support of Israel's War of Independence. This support was expressed not only in the diplomatic sphere but also in a series of practical measures. The fact that Moscow itself had previously permitted these steps could not prevent the leaders of other Soviet bloc states from feeling the need to dissociate themselves from the shadow of the past, especially if they happened to be of Jewish extraction.

This need must have been more keenly felt when Soviet publications began accusing Israeli and Zionist organizations of stirring up Jews of eastern Europe and even of employing coercion among them to emigrate to the Jewish state. Local Communist officials experienced in Soviet propaganda and communication techniques may already have discovered the question directed to them between the lines — where had their "vigilance" been? Immigration to Israel from the Peoples' Democracies was drastically reduced at the end of the 1940's and was subsequently completely discontinued. Both in external policy towards Israel as well as in the attitude towards Jewish nationalist sentiments, it was possible in these countries to discern the change a short time after the publicaton of Ilya Ehrenburg's "About a Certain Letter" in the Moscow *Pravda* of September 21, 1948.[2] Here and there, leading Jewish Communists active in local Jewish public life helped in persecuting Zionists and furthering the prohibition of Jewish emigration to Israel. They adopted this line of action either out of excessive fear for their own skins or in the ambition to strengthen their power, regarding with concern a possibility of their position being undermined as the Jewish communities continued to diminish in size with the progress of their "Exodus." Following the example of the Soviet press, the newspapers in the People's Democracies often presented Zionism and Israel as tools of reaction and imperialism.

Zhdanovist processes in the countries of the Soviet bloc imitated the prototype, and in time, anti-Jewish notes were added to the local campaigns against cosmopolitanism and other foreign hostile influences. Attempts were made to link Titoism to Jewish elements. In the trial of Laszlo Rajek and his comrades which took place in Hungary in September 1949, "Zionist espionage detachments" were bracketed with the American intelligence services in charging the accused with treason.

Operations for purging the government and Party workers of Jews were energetically carried out, especially in 1951–52. The same held true for top ranks of the armed forces. One of the purposes of the purges was to endow the new regimes with a more nationalist, original image to make them more popular with the population. Sadly paradoxical is the fact that in a number of countries, this purge was for a time conducted with the active participation of Jewish topflight leaders, who were probably most anxious in this way to demonstrate their readiness to serve the local regimes and their masters abroad. A case in point is the statement made by Moshe Pijade of Yugoslavia concerning Matyas Rakosi and other Hungarian Communist leaders, who, as Jews "must conduct a particularly anti-Jewish policy in order to prove constantly their anticosmopolitan attitude."[3]

More and more the Jews were becoming objects of suspicion for disloyalty because of their bourgeois origins, their family ties with the West, their feelings for Israel, and similar pretexts. Arrests of Jews who had been active in public life increased; and these were not always persons playing central roles in politics. In a number of countries, Jews were "transferred" from "sensitive" cities or regions to "safer" areas.[4] The economic condition of many Jews was in any case undermined as nationalization was expedited and the spheres in which it was applicable expanded when even the existence of small private enterprises became very precarious. Simultaneously, an anti-Jewish note appeared in the propaganda and activities against various antisocial and "parasitic" elements.

It is important to discuss the "restitution" activities and clarify their background. In a number of countries of eastern and central Europe, laws for the "restoration of property" were enacted after the war. The reference was to property plundered from the citizens of these countries by the Nazis and their collaborators. As may well be imagined, Jews who had survived the holocaust were conspicuous among the individuals demanding the restoration of their property by law. These lawsuits were not only concerned with large enterprises and other assets subject to the nationalization laws but also with apartments or various personal and domestic items. Obviously, such suits not only involved compensation from state funds but also clashed with the interests of new private "owners." This aspect of vested interests here and there added fuel to hostile feelings towards Jews. For its part, the government bureaucracy also piled up obstacles in the way of the application and execution of the restitution laws, sometimes out of a mute response to popular feelings, and occasionally out of excessive Communist zeal to protect the interests of the state against those of individuals.[5]

The attitude of the Jewish population to the new regimes in eastern and central Europe is worth noting. There should be no talk whatsoever of a homogeneous attitude, just as the Jewish population was not possessed of a uniform political and social image. Generally, if the "Jewish policy" in all its forms of these regimes is ignored (and it was not a necessary outgrowth of their own logic), the Jews had no special reason for looking back in longing. The anti-Semitic nature of the previous regimes in a part of these countries was still well remembered. Similarly, the previous regimes had no special nostalgic attraction for the Jews economically since most of the Jewish population consisted of the lower middle class and a professional intelligentsia. Nevertheless, during the period of Stalinization, the authorities picked out this meager population as a symbol of actual and potential opposition to the new regimes.

The anti-Jewish developments in the People's Democracies referred to here in general terms were intensified during and subsequent to the arrest and trial of Rudolf Slansky.[6] The Prague trial, which beyond a doubt was inspired by Moscow, deserves to be discussed at length.

Czechoslovakia traveled quite a distance from the time it served as an important source of materiel in Israel's War of Independence to the Prague trial of November 1952. The days when the Czech foreign minister, Jan Masaryk, could say about the Palestine question, "I don't know very much about oil pipelines, but I know of another pipe through which Jewish blood has been flowing for many long generations,"[7] seemed to be archaeological discoveries against the background of the anti-Israel and anti-Semitic notes of the Slansky trial, although they were only separated by a span of six years. Four and one half years before the trial, in March 1948, about a month after the February coup, Antonin Zapotocky (who was prime minister during the Slansky trial) published the following statement on the occasion of a visit by a delegation of the Histadrut — the Jewish Federation of Labor in Palestine: "In my name and in the name of the workers of Czechoslovakia please convey cordial regards to the workers of Palestine. Czechoslovakia's new government will not only continue the traditional friendship for the cause of Palestine, but believes that this friendship between Czechoslovakia and Palestine will grow still more. The government will remain faithful to its policy towards Palestine and will not prevent any Czech Jew from participating in the rebuilding of the country."[8]

However, on December 18, 1951 — three weeks after the news of Slansky's arrest was made public in Prague — Zapotocky's speech rang with an entirely different note. He attacked the "foreign elements in the Party" and the "treacherous agents who abandoned their people," spoke of the "reactionaries" who wanted to "restore nationalized enterprises to Jewish capitalists," and pointed to the important part Israel had been playing in the international intrigues against Czechoslovakia. "We shall not stand for interference in our internal matters," he said, among other things, "and the exertion of any influence whatsoever from the outside, whether it be from Washington, London, Rome, or Jerusalem."[9]

The transformation which had occurred in the Jewish sphere and in relation to Israel reflected Czechoslovakia's general development in the process of Stalinization. Just as precisely a country with a

"Western" reputation was directed by Moscow to demonstrate the rejection of the remains of the "corrupt" liberal tradition, so it also had to dramatically repudiate the "episode" of its sympathy and help for Israel.

With the Prague trial of November 20–27, 1952, the country of John Huss and Thomas Masaryk achieved complete adaptation to the Stalinist model. In the city of Kafka, a Kafkaesque horror spectacle was conducted. Even leftist circles in the world regarded the Prague trial as "the most savage stab in the back that the Communists have inflicted on themselves since the Nazi-Soviet pact of 1939."[10] It bore many indications which brought to mind the large show trials which were conducted in Moscow in the 1930's: the Czech prosecutor Dr. Jozef Urvalek looked like a reincarnation of Andrei Vyshinsky; the accused monotonously repeated confessions of the most fantastic crimes; the appointed attorneys for the defense actually supported the charges with their speeches; the president of the "senate of the state court," Dr. Jaroslav Novak, acted like a prosecutor. The resemblance to the Moscow trials was also apparent in the reactions of the spectators, who doubtless constituted a highly selective audience, reminiscent of the atmosphere nurtured among the general population. "Comrades" and "toilers" were called upon to turn on their radios and listen in on the broadcast of the proceedings at the trial. Reports of the trial in the press and on the radio left no doubt as to its outcome. The opening session was described as follows: "Before the court there appeared the traitors, the Trotskyites-Titoists-Zionists, the bourgeois nationalists and enemies of the Czechoslovak people, the People's Democratic regime, and Socialism."[11] To complete the resemblance to the Moscow trials, letters to the president of the court from members of the families of the accused were not lacking. There was a letter from a son demanding the death sentence for his father, a creature "not to be called a human being"; a wife wrote to express her happiness at the detection and destruction of a "gang of traitors" to which her husband belonged.[12]

The Prague trial had a series of motives and objectives. Not all the trends which will be clarified below are of equal value, but the anti-Semitic and anti-Israel character of the proceedings was designed to serve nearly all of them.

Of the fourteen defendants, eleven were of Jewish extraction. They were Rudolf Slansky, formerly the secretary general of the Czech Communist Party; Bedrich Geminder, former director of the Party's department for international affairs; Ludvik Frejka, former chairman of the economic division of the president's office; Bedrich Rejcin, former deputy defense minister; Artur London, former deputy foreign minister; Vavro Hajdu, former deputy foreign minister; Evzen Loebl, former deputy minister for foreign trade; Rudolf Margulies, former deputy minister for foreign trade; Oto Fisl, former deputy finance minister; Oto Sling, former district secretary of the Communist Party in Brno; and Andrej Simon, former editor of *Rude Pravo* (the Party's central organ in Czechoslovakia). The three non-Jewish defendants were Vladimir Klementis, a Slovak, former foreign minister; Jozef Frank, a Czech, former deputy secretary general of the Communist Party; and Karel Svab, former deputy minister for national security.

The national origin of the accused men did not have to be deduced from their names or from the listing of their additional "original" names in parentheses for, as a new technique not resorted to in the Moscow trials, it was stated explicitly in the charge sheet together with the date of birth, place of residence, previous duties, and social background of the defendants. Citation of the social background conspicuously displayed the fact, no doubt deliberately, that only two of the accused men — both of them Czechs — came from "workers' families"; all the others, meaning all the Jewish defendants and the only Slovak, Klementis, came from bourgeois families. Description of the social origin of the Jewish defendants was more explicit than just a "bourgeois family" and was couched in such terms as "from a family of merchants," "son of a merchant and innkeeper," "son of a large merchant," "son of a factory owner," "son of the owner of a public bath," etc. Only one of the defendants was an exception to the mercantile-industrial pedigree and was presented as "the son of a physician"; this was Frejka. All this descriptive detail does not seem fortuitous or the result of routine record keeping.

Throughout the trial, an obvious trend was apparent to present the Jewish origin as a character trait creating a predisposition to deception and treachery, as if there were a natural link between the defendants' Judaism and their crimes. The prosecutor cited "testimony" to prove that traitors and enemy agents pinned great hopes on Rudele (Slansky), since he came from an "old Jewish family" and was highly intelligent, talented, and patient. When Slansky was asked by the prosecutor how he happened to have gone over to serving imperialism despite his long-standing membership in the Communist Party, the defendant pointed to his bourgeois origins and said, "The surroundings in which I grew up affected my personal traits and my character." Another accused, Geminder, explained to the court why Slansky had trusted him to carry out acts of sabotage against the state; not only had Slansky been aware of Geminder's cosmopolitan and Zionist inclinations but he had also known that "I am a scion of a family of Jewish bourgeois merchants and during my youth I had had no cares, and everyday troubles had actually never bothered me." The defendant Hajdu declared, "My past led me to the camp of the enemies of Socialism. I grew up in a Jewish bourgeois family and was educated in the spirit of bourgeois ideology and Jewish nationalism. I had no contact with the toilers — I did not know them and despised them." The accused Loebl had joined the Communist Party in 1934, but, "as a matter of fact, I never struck roots in it." Fisl had adopted a hostile attitude towards the Czech People's Republic because, he said, "I come from a petit bourgeois family, am the son of a merchant, and am a Jewish bourgeois nationalist." The defendant Sling had been led to hostile acts by his past and his Jewish-bourgeois-nationalist education; he had, it is true, joined the Czech Communist Party, but "I had never become part of the Party and was always an alien in it." Rejcin had indeed become a member of the Komsomol in 1926, but his education "in the spirit of Jewish bourgeois nationalism" continued to influence him; this spirit had been reinforced by his personal traits of frivolity, careerism, and the pursuit of honor. Frejka said about himself, "Although I had joined the Communist Party, deep within me I remained an undisciplined intellectual, a petit bourgeois, and a man without a nationality." Andrej Simon declared, "The working class was always strange to me. Therefore I was always surrounded by people close to my heart from the ranks of betrayers of the interests of the toilers, Trotskyites, right-wing Socialists, and bourgeois Jewish nationalists." In reply to a question he had to confirm that in his eyes a worker was an "inferior human being."

The conclusion to be reached from all these statements was that there is a sort of natural contrast between Jewish intellectuals, even if they adorn themselves in revolutionary feathers, and the true proletariat. A common denominator was even found for all kinds of corrupt manifestations in the Communist world and Judaism. Cosmopolitanism? Connections with the whole world? For these defendants it is a matter of business, a matter of society and family. Their partners, friends, and relatives are scattered over the face of the globe from Mexico to London, from Venezuela to Tel Aviv, from Chile to Prague. Trotskyism, like Zionism, is in their blood. When the prosecutor asks the defendant Simon, "How did Slansky react to your announcement concerning collaboration with Trotskyites and Zionists in the West?" he replies, "He accepted what I said as something taken for granted. He may already have known about it, or he may not have expected anything else at all." Moreover, betrayal is part of their nature. The same Simon enumerated for the court a long list of espionage services with which he was connected. The prosecutor asked him, "Actually, for whom did you not work?" and "How are we to understand that you so easily obligated yourself to serve all the capitalist countries?" To which the accused answered, "It stems from my character, from my origin."

The point should be stressed that these defendants were absolutely estranged from Judaism in its spiritual and emotional significance. As an observer put it, "Its victims were men with no trace of Jewishness except what the Nazis used to call 'racial origin.' "[13] They were certainly not Zionists. Generally, they were known for their struggle against Zionism and every other manifestation of Jewish nationalism. Among them were men who persecuted Zionists with a zeal which could be interpreted as morbid self-hatred. But this aspect in the past of the accused was not mentioned during the trial. On the contrary, the court rudely swept aside their attempts to point to their assimilation. In reply to a query by the president, Geminder said that he was a member of the Czech nation. The president continued to press him: "Do you speak Czech well? . . . Would you like an interpreter? . . . Do you understand questions in the Czech language and can you answer in it?" ("The defendant spoke broken Czech," a press report describing the proceedings at the trial wrote of Geminder's cross-examination.) In his summing-up speech, the prosecutor argued, "Slansky tried in vain to hide his nationalist, bourgeois Jewish character!" Despite the fact that the national origin of the defendants was noted in the charge sheet, as mentioned above, it was also pointed out that the "real name" of the accused Andrej Simon, for example, was Oto Katz. This was the formula for referring to other traitors, such as "Hanus Lomsky whose real name is Gabriel Leiben" (former Party secretary in Plzeň), "Koloman Mosko whose real name is Moskovic" (formerly one of the Party's secretaries in Slovakia).

The last two names belonged to men made to stand trial on other occasions. At this point, mention should be made of the fact that the Slansky trial was merely the most spectacular or most representative of a series of trials and arrests in Czechoslovakia in which the Jews were the most conspicuous victims. In this way, those "purged" included among others Viteslav Fuks, Party secretary in Ostrava; Ruzena Dubova, Party secretary in Brno; Ervin Polak, deputy minister of the interior; Zigmund Stein, who had served as legal adviser to the Soviet embassy in Prague; Richard Slansky (Rudolf Slansky's brother), who had served as chargé d'affaires in Iran and later, as deputy ambassador in Poland; Jarmila Tausigova, member of the central control board of the Party; Gustav Bares (Breitenfeld), deputy secretary general and director of the Party's propaganda department; Jozef Goldman, deputy director of the planning bureau; Mikulas Landa (Landau), Party secretary in Usti nad Labem; Rudolf Bistricky (Weichharz), ambassador to Britain; F. S. Weisskopf, ambassador to China; Eduard Goldsticker, minister to Israel; Alexander Kunosy, minister to Argentina; Arnost Tauber, minister to Switzerland; Jan Vinar, first secretary at the embassy in the United States; Evzen Klinger, director of the foreign ministry's press department.[14]

Some remarks should be made about the three defendants at the Slansky trial who were not of Jewish origin. The most outstanding of them was Vladimir (Vlado) Klementis. A study of his biographical background and the charges made against him leads to a number of interesting discoveries which can explain his inclusion among the distinguished Prague victims. He was presented at the trial as the personification of Slovak nationalist separatism. This was accordingly a warning by the central authorities in view of manifestations of unrest in Slovakia, which, among other things, stemmed from a feeling of discrimination in the Slovak section of the binational state. In addition, Klementis had spent the war years in the West, mostly in London, and the very fact that he was not a "Moscow man" like other Czechoslovak leaders served to make him suspect as not being too dependent on the Soviet Union. One of his sins, to which he confessed at the trial, is illuminating. He told the court, "In 1939, I openly adopted an anti-Democratic and anti-Soviet position towards the Russo-German pact and the military operations against Finland, and I misjudged the first period of the war."

Probably Klementis, who had been dismissed from his post as foreign minister in March 1950, and placed under arrest several months later, had to serve as scapegoat to atone for the heavy sin with which Czechoslovakia had been saddled since 1947 when it accepted Marshall Plan aid. However, it should be pointed out that the foreign ministry headed by Klementis was pictured at the trial as a ramified network of plotters actually controlled by Slansky by means of his cadres — the overwhelming majority of whom were Jews.

The remaining two non-Jewish defendants, Jozef Frank and Karel Svab, were presented at the Prague trial as involved to a considerable extent in the Jewish-Zionist conspiracy — and for greater clarity — as Slansky's tools. Frank confessed that he had committed war crimes about which Slansky had known. Slansky had used this as a means of blackmailing Frank in order to make him dependent on his favors. Svab had a similar wartime past. While a prisoner at the Sachsenhausen concentration camp, he had collaborated with the Nazi overseers and had tortured other prisoners, by his own confession in which he went on to say, "Slansky had taken advantage of my treachery in order to secure my cooperation and had given me a part in the activity of the central organization operating against the state"; he "had not made me stand trial but had ordered me to describe my crimes in writing in order to tie me to him with an additional bond." Frank indirectly indicated that in his corrupt traits which had led him to provoke the "people, the republic, and Socialism," he had been influenced by Jews. "Although I come from a workers' family, I myself had never been a workingman. From my youth on, I worked in offices of ready-to-wear clothing factories in the Prostejov district and I associated with petit bourgeois circles."

All the crimes of the defendants at the Prague trial were supplied with a Jewish background. The sources of inspiration of the "Central Organization for Plotting Against the State" headed by Slansky as well as the persons who had established contact with the accused for the purpose of subversion and espionage, included numerous names of prominent Jews: David Ben-Gurion, Henry Morganthau, Georges Mandel (who had been murdered by the Nazis in 1940), Ana Pauker, Moshe Pijade, Moshe Sharett, Bernard Baruch, and the Rothschilds. They were links in a chain which included Harry Truman, Dean Acheson, Herbert Morrison, Konni Zilliacus, and others. All these were not merely names but the symbols of Western imperialism, Israel in thrall to the United States, Zionism, worldwide espionage institutions, Titoism, the Jewish plutocracy, treacherous social democracy, rootless cosmopolitanism, the class enemy in disguise who had infiltrated the front ranks of Communist leadership in the People's Democracies, subversive Trotskyism, the exploiting bourgeoisie, etc.

Zionism was presented at the trial not just as a reactionary movement; it is "the loyal agency of American imperialism" which actually carried out espionage and sabotage functions. According to the charge sheet, Geminder testified, "By means of the Zionist agencies and their representatives in the Czechoslovak Socialist Republic, the American imperialists tried to undermine the political and economic foundations of the Czechoslovak People's Democracy. The Zionist organizations served as an advance position of American imperialism in its war against the People's Democracies and the Soviet Union." And in the same spirit, the prosecutor pointed out, "the danger of international Zionism increased with the establishment of the American *pashalik* called the state of Israel." He explained further that "the Zionist movement is not only a wrong current of thinking and false ideology" and pointed to the close ties — among other things, by means of *gesheften* ("business deals" in Yiddish; the prosecutor used the word in the original) — made by the gang ruling Israel with Zionist capitalists throughout the world and the American imperialists.

Slansky clearly stated in the course of his interrogation by the prosecutor during the trial that he had relied upon the Zionists because they "had been engaging in hostile activity the purpose of which had been the destruction of the People's Democracy in Czechoslovakia." To facilitate the achievement of this aim, "I placed various Zionist elements in important posts in the Party and economic establishments and covered up for them." Collaboration between Slansky's "Central Organization for Plotting Against the State" and local Zionist organizations was important because the latter maintained ramified ties with various similar groups in capitalist countries, chiefly the United States. "The entire world Zionist movement is in effect the work of imperialists, mainly of Americans." Thus, the Zionist organizations served as "a suitable link" between the Central Plotters' Organization and Western imperialists — chiefly Americans. Slansky went on to explain that the Zionist organizations served as an effective tool "for carrying out espionage and sabotage activity" for the imperialists.

Often in the course of the trial attention was drawn to American espionage activities, but it was always done by citing concrete examples in which the part played by Jews, Israelis, and Zionists was stressed, for example, "The American spies hiding behind Israeli diplomatic passports" (referring to the Israeli minister and legation officials); the fact that the witness Langer had returned to Czechoslovakia in 1946 from the United States where he had been staying with his family since 1938, "since I had been sent here by American Zionists." The American journalists Maurice Hindus and David Schoenbrun had also engaged in espionage activities in Czechoslovakia. According to the testimony, they "had hidden behind their press cards." Schoenbrun, the "son of a Jewish capitalist," allegedly said to the defendant Simon: "Among American espionage agents there are many with Zionist tendencies"; this was to have made it easier for Simon to carry out the subversive activities designed to overthrow the regime and restore capitalism. One of the foreign spies with whom Simon had come in contact was the British Labourite member of Parliament, "the Jewish nationalist" Richard Crossman (not a Jew at all).

The large part played by Jewish Zionists in acts of subversion and espionage against Czechoslovakia and other socialist states was not to have appeared fortuitous. Israel and Zionism were assigned a central function in the planning and implementation of these acts. The trial publicly exposed two great conspiracies closely related to each other, the Morgenthau Plot and the Avriel (Ueberall) Plot. They were planned as early as the middle of 1947, about a year before the official establishment of the state of Israel, at a secret meeting in Washington attended by President Truman, American Secretary of State Acheson, former American Secretary of the Treasury Morgenthau, the future Israeli Prime Minister David Ben-Gurion, and the future Israeli Foreign Minister Sharett. The plot determined the conditions for the support of the United States and its satellites for the program to establish a Jewish state and for subsequent aid to the new country. The terms included the handing over of all Israeli military bases to the United States, subordination of the Israeli army's general staff to American command, active participation by Israel in a Mediterranean bloc after its formation, and the cession of all Israeli ports, including a military port to be built in Haifa, to the Americans in the event of an armed conflict between the United States and the USSR. In addition, according to the charge sheet (based on the testimony of the "American spy Orenstein"), part of the plot provided that "Zionist organizations should be extensively used for the purpose of carrying out espionage activities and sowing destruction in the People's Democracies, in support of the efforts of American imperialists to seize power in the world." The charge sheet bracketed the Morgenthau and Avriel plots: "Implementation of the evil plots in Czechoslovakia was assigned to the important agent of the American espionage service and former Israeli minister to the CSR, Ehud Avriel-Ueberall."

From a series of testimonies and confessions, the Avriel Plot appeared to have had two aspects. First of all, it afforded cover for the sabotage and espionage activities against Czechoslovakia. Secondly, it was a central instrument for impoverishing Czechoslovakia.

In fact, one of the trial's important tendencies which the Avriel Plot was supposed to have served was to provide the public with an explanation for the economic failures and material distress in the country known for its high industrial standards. In other words, this was an attempt in the "classic" spirit to place the blame on a scapegoat. Both Prague and Moscow were equally interested in finding a scapegoat, since one of the reasons for Czechoslovakia's economic decline stemmed from Soviet exploitation. And so it was made "clear" that there was nothing wrong with the regime and that well-defined circles were guilty — enemies and swindlers who had infiltrated the government leadership. These miscreants were Slansky and his assistants (presented at this and at other trials) who — by their own admission — sabotaged industrial production, deliberately established low production quotas, directed the Czechoslovak economy towards dependence on imports from capitalist countries, made unnecessary, aimless investments, discontinued important enterprises, interfered with the reconstruction of agriculture in the spirit of socialism, and caused deliberate breakdowns in electrical plants. There is no need to enumerate further, since the catalogue of deliberate acts of sabotage included nearly all aspects of the economy, and the Jewish motif dominated the entire list. And not only were nearly all the defendants and almost all those mentioned as their partners in deceit and robbery Jews, but they plundered Czechoslovakia inspired and guided by Jewish organizations for the sake of Jewish interests and for Israel. The people of the "Central Plotters' Organization" helped Czechoslovak Jews emigrate to Israel. A "Report by Experts in Financial Matters" presented to the court had the following to say: "This emigration involved the illegal export of large sums of money which came from exploiting the toilers, from the illegal restoration of property, from funds, etc. In addition, the emigrants took out of Czechoslovakia an unjustified quantity of personal effects, a large amount of important machinery, workshop equipment, lathes, grinding wheels, electric drills, equipment for dental clinics, etc., which could have served the purposes of the five year plans in our enterprises."

Several of the accused even concealed the emigration of persons sought by the police. The defendant Loebl confessed that he had signed "agreements advantageous to capitalist merchants, particularly Jews, and harmful to Czechoslovakia." Loebl spoke of the pernicious transactions which he had carried out in the government's name with foreign business men, and with emphasis mentioned the American Zionist Kuhorn, the Jewish financier from Argentina Yizreel, the Jewish coal tycoon in Italy (an emigrant from Czechoslovakia) Gutmann, the Israeli Zionists Benjamin Gesundheit and Shimon Orenstein, the British Zionist (also an emigrant from Czechoslovakia), Leo Brenner. The latter "maintained close ties with the great Jewish financiers of the Rothschild family and with other Jewish capitalist circles." The defendant Margulies was asked by the prosecutor to cite "concrete facts" of the subversive activity against the economy of Czechoslovakia with the help of emigrants, and he listed the Zionist financier in England Schmitzer, the American Jewish capitalists of the Lindt family, the Jewish financier Becher in Argentina, Singer in Brazil, and others. All these men raked in profits at the expense of the sweat of the toilers of Czechoslovakia, or in the language of the prosecutor during Slansky's cross-examination, the Zionists accumulated "non-Christian profits."

A picture of Jewish nepotism was painted at the Prague trial. In the words of the prosecutor, "One hand washed the other." But this portrayal of nepotism did not just reflect family favoritism for the sake of material benefits and not even the mutual protection by the members of a community of their own interests. What had occurred here had been the deliberate "planting" of Zionist Jews in key positions as part of a worldwide political conspiracy. "The most important agent of the Israeli espionage service," Oto Fisl, "had been sent" to the ministry of finance to assume the position of deputy minister. To serve as Klementis's assistants, Slansky had sent the British intelligence agent, the millionaire's son and Zionist, Hajdu together with the prominent American espionage agent, the Trotskyite Artur London. The various confessions gave one to understand that "they" had put "their" men in all the sensitive spots, including the army and internal security establishments. Moreover, the conspirators had methodically acted to eliminate persons not associated with their circle from important posts so that they would be free to carry out their plotting without being detected by honest men.

A large part of the trial proceedings was devoted to "restitution" matters which were included in the "shady deals" carried out by Zionist Jews. This was a crude attempt to play on the anti-Semitic feelings of certain sections of the population. The prosecution "exposed" the personal greed of the defendants and their friends (the charge sheet listed the names of Slansky, Geminder, Margulies, Lomsky, and Landa) who "under the mask of restoring property acquired fortunes amounting to many millions of crowns." But this was not only the private acquisition of wealth; the restitution law (it should be pointed out that various "amendments" had already anyway cancelled its effective significance in Czechoslovakia, in addition to the pressure exerted on persons suing for the restoration of their property to waive their claims) was wholly "a Zionist tool for the plundering of the Czechoslovak state for the benefit of the capitalists, the imperialists, and Israel."

After this varied choice of acts of exploitation and robbery, the prosecutor was able to summarize: "It was clearly demonstrated to us that numerous difficulties which were often considered the side effects of our rapid reconstruction were the deliberate handiwork of these criminals. Like a thousand-armed octopus, they clove to the body of the state and sucked its blood and vitality."

Mention should also be made of the trial's tendency to supply proof of the direct ties between the activities of this "octopus" and the daily hardships of the masses of people. A low standard of living? A shortage of staples? No wonder, for the plotters "sent out meat and wheat from Czechoslovakia to the capitalist countries to the detriment of our toiling nation," the charge sheet said. Frejka explained that by means of agreements concerning compensation for nationalized enterprises "they stole hundreds of millions of crowns from the Czechoslovak working nation." He said that in the sphere of supply, the plotters created a situation which forced the authorities to maintain a system of rationing and that they made the policy of price reduction fail. The accused Margulies confessed to various activities which interfered with the supply of foodstuffs to the population. Among other things, he had "issued instructions to export meat to the capitalist world" and had helped "create a situation forcing the government to introduce the rationing of bread and flour." The defendant Fisl confessed that the plotters had checked the rise in the standard of living: "If not for our subversive activities, the standard of living of the toiling population would today be immeasurably higher."

To sum up, the people's resentment was directed into the channel of racial hatred. The Prague government generously bestowed "compensation" on its citizens. It is noteworthy that some people grasped at this spurious compensation to the extent of translating it immediately into violence. The day after the opening of the Slansky trial, houses of Jews were smeared with expressions like "Down with capitalist Jews!" or "Jews leave here." The police refused to take any action against deeds of this sort. Pointing to the premises of the Israeli legation in Prague, a guide explained to visitors, "This is the building serving as a center for espionage." It was difficult for Jews to be mistaken in understanding the significance of the events. The eighteen thousand Jews of Prague sensed a threat to their existence. Many of them were afraid to go to work or open their stores. The secretary of the Prague Jewish community, the Communist Erich Kohn, and his wife took their own lives. There were reports of other suicides.[15]

There is special significance in the confessions of a number of defendants concerning activities against the state under the pretext of combating anti-Semitism. The Czech Jozef Frank testified: "Under the mask of fighting anti-Semitism we granted immunity to Zionist organizations and supported Zionists. Under the mask of fighting anti-Semitism, to tell the truth, the class war against the Zionists, that is to say, the Jewish capitalists, was put to sleep. Honest people who pointed out the hostile acts of the Zionists and bourgeois Jewish nationalists were called anti-Semites and thus intimidated."

This testimony echoed Slansky's confession: "I also defended the Zionist organizations by taking advantage of the war against anti-Semitism. In supporting the campaign against anti-Semitism, I exaggerated its danger and suggested adopting various measures against it such as articles, pamphlets, lectures, etc. On the other hand, I did nothing against Zionism."

Certain elements must have concluded from these statements by Slansky and Frank — as well as by others — that there was nothing wrong in hating Jews. On the contrary, steps against anti-Semitism were described as being antipatriotic.

Merging the acts of robbery in Czechoslovakia with Israel's interests was calculated to impress the Arabs. One of the aims of the Prague trial was to indicate to the Arab world the readiness of the Soviet bloc to join it in an anti-Israel campaign. From the accusations against Slansky and his friends the Arabs were to reach the conclusion that they and Czechoslovakia had the same enemy, for these traitors had weakened the defensive power of Czechoslovakia in handing over to the Jews of Palestine important military equipment for waging war against the Arabs. By affording assistance to the emigration of Jews, by aiding Jewish displaced persons reach Palestine, by helping out in the transfer of capital, and by similar acts, they had simultaneously sabotaged Czechoslovakia and increased the power of the Israeli aggressors. Part of the plan of the traitors standing trial was to harm the relations between the Democratic People's Republic and the Arab states. They alone are responsible for the support given to Israel several years before, backing which was actually one of their destructive plots. Did not others know anything at all about the aid given to Israel? Indeed, Slansky had to admit that he had at the time succeeded in misleading Comrade Klement Gottwald with the argument that Israel was conducting an anti-imperialist war. In other words, Prague made a concentrated and spectacular effort in November 1952, to clear herself once and for all of the "stigma" of her position and behavior with respect to Palestine in 1947–48. It is quite certain that parallel to these overt verbal gestures in the court intensive action was taken at approximately the same time to win sympathy by generous offers (by Moscow and Prague) of military equipment and weapons to the Arab countries from the famous armaments industries of Czechoslovakia.

It may also be assumed that the stagers of the Prague trial felt no revulsion at an incidental tendency to exploit attitudes towards Germany. Moscow had long before begun to flatter "her" Germans, just as the West had been acting with respect to "its" Germans. The Slansky trial utilized a few tricks for the psychological bribing of the Germans. The numerous attacks on Benes were able to cause them some satisfaction since the deceased president of Czechoslovakia was occasionally mentioned in Germany as the murderer of innocent Sudeten Germans. The denunciation of Jewish greed revealed in the shrewd tactics for securing the restoration of Jews' property must have sounded pleasing to some German ears. And were there not Germans who enjoyed the degradation and end of Slansky, who was really a man called Salzman, the Jew from the Sudeten region?

Two Israeli citizens, Mordecai Oren and Shimon Orenstein, also appeared as witnesses at the Slansky trial. Both of them were brought to the witness stand from prison cells in which they had been languishing for a year (later, they had to stand trial themselves; in August 1953, Orenstein, "Prague convict no. 2392," was sentenced to life imprisonment, and in October 1953, Oren, "convict no. 2446," was sentenced to a fifteen-year term in prison). In the planning and direction of the trial, they were assigned the role of supplying the Israeli stamp of approval to the confessions of the defendants and other evidence in the possession of the prosecutor.[16]

Orenstein, who had been to Czechoslovakia on a mission for the Hagana before the establishment of the state of Israel and had later worked in the commercial department of the Israeli legation in Prague, appeared to the stage directors as the proper person to describe the operations of the Avriel Plot which impoverished Czechoslovakia. The activities carried out in Israel's name and for her benefit were part of the operations of the worldwide subversion plan of American imperialism. "All our hostile operations were conducted in accordance with American demands and based on policies laid down by them for the purpose of destroying the People's Democracies and particularly the Soviet Union," the court was told.

Oren, a leader of the Israel United Workers' Party, MAPAM, was known for his extreme left-wing attitudes in the party which defined itself as being both "Zionist-pioneering" and "Socialist-revolutionary" and was considered the nearest "neighbor" of the Communist Party in the Israeli political spectrum. He was arrested in Czechoslovakia, on December 31, 1951, on his way from East Berlin where he had participated in a conference of the World Federation of Trade Unions despite the fact that the Israel Federation of Labor, the Histadrut, had left the Federation in view of its having come under Communist domination. The events which befell Orenstein and Oren while they were under arrest in Czechoslovakia, the cross-examinations they were forced to undergo, their testimony at the Slansky trial, and their own trials shed much light on the "functions" which the rulers of Prague and Moscow (chiefly under the orders of the latter) assigned to the Jews, the Zionist movement, and Israel in a series of acts in both foreign and domestic policy.

The memoirs of Shimon Orenstein and Mordecai Oren are replete with hair-raising details of the physical and psychological means, both of abuse as well as honeyed words, which the investigators used against them. We should call attention to a number of "Jewish points" which colored their interrogation.

Orenstein recounted the following epithets hurled at him by one of the high-ranking officers of the secret police who "took care" of him: "Stinking Jewish spy . . . contemptible Zionist . . . blood-sucking Jew . . . Fascist Jew . . ." The rest of the expressions are not printable; he went on to say, "In any case, every sentence he uttered ended with the words 'foul stinking Jew.' "[17] Oren tells that he often heard "vivid anti-Semitic curses." When he pointed out to the investigator that the Polish secondary school which he had attended had been ridden with an atmosphere of anti-Semitism, the official retorted, "You are hated everywhere, and rightly so."[18] On another occasion, after the Slansky trial, the investigator asserted to Oren, "We have lately learned in Socialistic countries as well that the Jewish race of various prominent persons explains divers serious phenomena in lands building Socialism. It is not chance that most of the traitors sentenced to the gallows at the Slansky trial were Jews. Do you want to deny that Ana Pauker was Jewish?"[19]

At the Slansky trial, Oren first talked about himself; he revealed that he had been a professional spy and an agent of British Intelligence since 1934; from 1945 until his arrest he had carried out a number of Zionist assignments and operated as a spy in the People's Democracies "hiding behind the mask of a progressive public worker, a peace-lover, and a friend of the Soviet Union." But the most instructive aspect of Oren's testimony is the lumping together of the Avriel Plot and the evil designs of Tito and his gang. Oren himself served as the liaison between the Yugoslav traitors and those in Czechoslovakia just as he had been the link between these two groups and the British imperialist agents, the Labour Party leaders Morrison and Zilliacus.

In one part of his testimony, Oren disclosed, "Pijade told me that he had been keeping in touch with Rudolf Slansky through the Israeli legation in Czechoslovakia and particularly through Avriel-Ueberall. This was confirmed to me by Avriel himself when I came to Czechoslovakia from Yugoslavia in 1948."

Just like other parts of the Prague trial the Titoist aspect, too, was shot through with crass "Jewish" and "Zionist" references. This was a transparent attempt to discredit Titoism by identifying it with Jewish elements and Zionist and Israel plots. For this reason, Moshe Pijade had to be mentioned at the trial with special emphasis and among other terms Oren used to describe him were such designations as "the ideologist and theorist of the Fascist Tito gang." This was the significance of the Slansky-Oren-Pijade trio, despite the fact that Oren had never even met Slansky and had seen Pijade just once in 1947. When Oren made an effort to express amazement to the investigator with the words, "How can I . . . be conversant with details of meetings between these two anti-Zionist, Communist leaders [Slansky and Pijade]?" the official explained, "Slansky was revealed as a secret Zionist. Pijade is also a Zionist. That is why you went to see him. You are a Zionist. You were in general accustomed to visiting Communist leaders who are clandestine Zionists."[20]

In the end, Oren was compelled to help the investigators fabricate the meetings and conversations in Yugoslavia and Czechoslovakia in which they were interested. Once again, the investigator provided Oren with a "reasonable explanation" for the fact he had been the one to whom the Yugoslav traitors had divulged the secret of their preparations to carry out a Titoist coup in Czechoslovakia, too, by means of the Slansky gang. He said to him, "You are a Jew. Pijade is a Jew, too. Pijade told you that secret on the basis of your closeness as Jews."[21]

To every manifestation of "national Communism" either actual or potential, attempts were made in Prague to attach Jewish features. Thus, for instance, Klementis said in his testimony that the "cosmopolitan" Koloman Mosko had "served as a liaison officer between our nationalist, bourgeois Jews and similar groups operating in the Hungarian Communist Party," especially Zionists who were exposed during the Rajek trial. Morrison and Zilliacus, who were the object of particular denunciations at Prague, were not Jews, but these Labourite Tito sympathizers were known for their friendship to Zionism. Thus, superhuman efforts were expended in Prague to Judaize Titoism. An attempt was even made, during Orenstein's investigation, to interpret the fact that Jewish parachutists from Palestine had been dropped in Yugoslavia during the war as an old Zionist-Titoist-British-American conspiracy.[22] And the most cogent proof of the Titoism-

Judaism equation was in the defendants' box. Who were the men who wanted to cut off the Czechoslovak republic from the Soviet Union and the peace camp following the Titoist example, who were anxious to transform the Czechoslovak Party into a Tito-like instrument for restoring capitalism? Eleven of the fourteen traitors were Jews, and the others were their stooges.

No more examples of the "Jewish aspect" of the Prague trial will be cited, but the summing-up evaluation of Mordecai Oren will be given below. Although he declared after his release and return to Israel (in May 1956): "My years of suffering in Czechoslovak prisons did not impair my loyalty to my beliefs and my sympathy for the nations building Socialism," he explicitly wrote:

> Anti-Semitism undoubtedly played a large part in staging this trial. It was the purpose of the trial to purge the Party and the state of Jews. In this way, the political leadership responded to the anti-Semitic sentiments among the backward parts of the masses of people, who pointed to the new regime as the handiwork of Jews. The trial and what came with it — purging the government establishment and central Party setup of Jews — were designed to demonstrate to reactionary and anti-Semitic circles that the regime being built in the CSR is one of Czechs and Slovaks. Czechoslovak Communism had decided to win over and conciliate anti-Semitic reaction. It tried to do this by denouncing the leading Jewish Communists as enemies of the Czechoslovak people, foes of socialism, traitors, saboteurs, spies, murderers, and Nazi collaborators — and had them beheaded.[24]

And he reached yet another conclusion: "Anti-Semitism is then possible in regimes aspiring to socialism. And not only anti-Semitism among certain classes of the population which the new regime has not yet succeeded in uprooting but *anti-Semitism as a weapon in the hands of the upper echelons of the country's leadership itself*" (the emphasis is in the original).[25]

In the thaw which came to Czechoslovakia in 1968, it was proved beyond a doubt that not only had the general framework of the Prague trial been determined in the Soviet Union but that Soviet bodies and individuals had shaped nearly the entire proceedings. The prosecutor, Dr. Jozef Urvalek, himself admitted in an interview which appeared in *Rude Pravo* on April 14, 1968, that the prosecution had based its charges on prepared material which the Politburo had processed under the guidance of "Soviet advisers."[26]

During the same "springtime thaw," various confessions were also made in Czechoslovakia concerning the anti-Semitic trends and nature of the Prague trial. Rudolf Sansky's widow, Mrs. Jozefa Slanska, herself stated that the trial of her husband and his codefendants had an "unmistakable anti-Semitic character." "Slansky's enemies very skillfully made their tactical account that there is nothing easier than conducting anti-Semitic agitation and gaining the sympathy of the masses at the simple cost of spreading hatred of the Jews."[27]

It was Moscow's guidance, of course, which directed the trial into turbid anti-Semitic channels. The Slansky trial was a sort of dress rehearsal of the spectacle soon to be presented on the central stage of Moscow with doctors committing acts of sabotage playing the principal roles in one great worldwide plot against the Soviet Union and the other Socialist countries. The main sources of inspiration of this plot included Jewish organizations, Zionism, and Israel.

Separate chapters will discuss the Moscow doctors' affair. But at this point, attention will be called to two additional details of the Prague trial which even show a certain technical similarity to charges published a month and a half after its termination against the "murderers in white gowns." The first detail is concerned with the part played by the American Joint Distribution Committee ("Joint" for short) in the acts of espionage and sabotage in Czechoslovakia. The activities of this Jewish welfare organization in Czechoslovakia were completely suspended at the beginning of 1950. However, the men responsible for the Slansky trial brought up the horrors of the Joint in the court many times. The Joint was presented as a "secret branch of the American espionage service." The accused permitted its activity "with the pretext that it was engaging in welfare work" and actually this Jewish-American organization "engaged in espionage, sabotage, shady currency transfers, black marketing, and smuggling."

Another detail is the inclusion of an attempt to kill President Klement Gottwald by means of a physician. In the course of the Prague trial, mention was made a number of times of Dr. Haskovic, Gottwald's personal doctor, who treated him from 1945 to 1951 and who was shown to be a henchman of Slansky, from whom he took orders. Slansky admitted that he had hidden from President Gottwald the reprehensible political past of Dr. Haskovic who "had not given the President proper care and treatment, thus helping to shorten his life, meaning, hasten his death." Slansky asked for Dr. Haskovic's assistance in the knowledge that if "I wanted to seize power, it would be necessary to get Klement Gottwald out of the way."[28]

The close connection between the Prague trial and the bloody spectacle then being prepared in Moscow also emerges from the cross-examination of Mordecai Oren. Pressure was exerted on Oren to confess that he had also been involved in antistate, Zionist activity in the Soviet Union (where he had never been). A number of matters about which he was ordered to give details are actually part of the charges against the "murderers in white gowns." He was asked about his meetings with Jewish physicians in the USSR, conversations with the treacherous Zionist Mikhoels, and delegates from the Soviet Union who clandestinely attended Zionist congresses.

The investigator wanted to know who of the Soviet diplomats whom Oren had met was "a Jew or of Jewish extraction." During the grilling Oren was told that the "nationalist-Zionist underground" in the organization of which the Joint had had a large part had just been discovered in the Soviet Union and that "its leaders will soon be brought to trial in a Soviet court."[29] Oren was also informed of his own part in that underground and what was now being demanded of him. The investigator said: "We are in possession of all the facts that you, as an important emissary of international Zionism in charge of organizing Zionist activity in socialist countries, are among the leading organizers of the criminal nationalist-Zionist underground in the Soviet Union. Central Soviet personalities became victims of the intrigues of this underground and its clandestine terrorist activities. Your vital interests demand that you disclose the entire truth about this matter to us; otherwise we shall be compelled to take you somewhere very far from here and you will be investigated by someone else. There, they will undoubtedly get the truth out of you."[30]

Actually it is not impossible that the threats of a cross-examination elsewhere were not only made for the purpose of exerting pressure; in Moscow they may have been considering the possibility of presenting Oren as a defendant to testify at the doctors' trial being planned. His appearance at a "more advanced phase" of the show would be accepted as a natural and logical continuation of his "frank" testimony at the Slansky trial which, according to the definition of Zdenek Nejedly, the Czechoslovak minister of culture, was conducted in a "Communist atmosphere of truth."

At the end of the Prague trial, eleven of the defendants were sentenced to death (they were executed on December 3, 1952) and three (Artur London, Vavro Hajdu, and Evzen Loebl) were given life imprisonment. The trial was widely acclaimed in the Soviet press. Statements appearing in a literary periodical can serve as example of the style they adopted. *Literaturnaya Gazeta* compared the Prague defendants to "frogs near a clear spring" who dreamed of transforming Czechoslovakia into a "cosmopolitan possession of Wall Street ruled by American monopolies, bourgeois nationalists, and Zionists together with various kinds of rabble immersed in crime."[31]

However, the Moscow repercussion of the Prague trial far exceeded the scope of providing information and commentary. At this time, Soviet anti-Jewish campaigns were inaugurated or intensified which described criminals and crimes in a style and in metaphors resembling those resorted to in the Czech capital and even outdoing them.

NINE

Swindlers and Embezzlers

The Prague trial ended on November 27, 1952. Two days later the "Kiev Affair" was publicized in the Soviet Union. A short item in the *Pravda Ukrainy* of November 29, 1952, under the headline "Chronicle" reported that a group of people had been tried before a military court in Kiev for embezzling state property and profiteering. Three of them, H. Khain, Y. Yaroshetsky, and D. Gerson, were sentenced to death and the execution carried out. The others were sentenced to long prison terms. The defendants were the heads of a commercial textile "base" in Kiev attached to the ministry of light industries.

There was something new about the accused being judged in a military court. In this way, an economic offense was symbolically identified with high treason. The verdict even expressed this identification: the men sentenced to death were found guilty of "counterrevolutionary sabotage in the fields of commerce and supply." The death penalty was also an innovation and strengthened the identification of economic crimes with the most serious offenses against the state. When capital punishment was restored in the Soviet Union about two years previously, it applied to offenses such as espionage, subversion, and high treason. And although the Nineteenth Congress of the Communist Party of the Soviet Union (October 1952) gave the signal for an intensified propaganda and legal campaign against negligence and fraud in the economic life, it was difficult to ignore the demonstrative significance of the death penalty against three Jewish defendants. It soon became clear that the "Kiev Affair" served to inaugurate a flood of reports in the Soviet press concerning various kinds of "parasitic" libels, the leading figures of which were persons with Jewish names. Such reports or "accounts" became especially numerous from the publication of revelations regarding the "group of saboteur-doctors" (January 13, 1953) until Stalin's death (March 5, 1953).

A series of reports concerning economic crimes will be briefly cited below. They were selected from various Soviet newspapers which appeared during the four months between December 1952 and March 1953.[1]

Mendelson, the head of the department for cadres in a factory, installed his relatives in responsible positions. Raigorodsky, the former manager of a shoe factory, appointed a relative of his by the name of Rosen as head of the plant guards and played a large part in "production thefts." Shonin, the former deputy manager of a commercial administration, was placed under arrest. Greenberg swindled the warehouses of which he was in charge. Yakob Davidovich Meilman, the manager of the Thermos glass factory in Kiev, had all the jobs filled by his relatives and friends as if it were a family business. His niece, S. Meilman, his uncle Vintman, and persons called Halperin, Kaganskaya, Feivisovich, Obukhovsky, Singer, Shor, Shvartser, Shenker, as well as others all wasted the funds and materials of the plant for their personal use. Yakob Meilman allotted apartments belonging to the factory to relatives of his and to other individuals who were not entitled to them. Khalemsky was a partner of Meilman's in a transaction involving bribery. Lumer and Levitas swindled institutions engaged in retail trade. In the case of forged documents in a shoe factory, the principal offenders were mentioned as being the chief engineer Kershner and his assistants Levin and Khanin. Lev Rotenbergsky, a senior foreman in a construction administration at Maikop in the northern Caucasus, was involved in sabotage, counter-revolutionary activities, and large-scale systematic embezzlement. Lerner served as the man in charge of supply of four organizations at Pskov, despite the fact that he had never left Leningrad. Bachilo, Pelfuks, Taube, Kagan, and Lifshitz, all of whom worked in clothing enterprises at Brailov were involved in fraud and speculation; the courts were denounced for having permitted Lifshitz, Taube, and Pelfuks to get out of the matter unpunished (it was mentioned Pelfuks "was let off with only one year's corrective labor") after a lawyer by the name of Shain had played a decisive role in securing their release in exchange for a bribe of 50,000 rubles; Shain was later arrested and the attorneys Khazin, Nisenson, and Krimsky who had helped Lifshitz, Taube, and the others escape punishment (they were brought for a renewed trial) were dismissed from their posts. Berkovich, the manager of a slaughterhouse, and Lifshitz and Khaimsky trafficked on the black market in meat products. Katsman caused enormous losses in the Latvian Republic.

Abraham Natanovich Khaitin secured the position of director of a theatrical studio in Riga and as his assistants appointed Gerstein, Podriachik, Chekhanovitz, Greenberg, Silin, Morein, Kovadlo, and others; they abused their posts, embezzled property, and took bribes. Yevgenia Israilevna Chernina received her job in the office of the prosecutor in Kiev through fraud and blackmail, being a protégée of the deputy prosecutor; she took advantage of her position to conceal criminals who caused the state losses of thousands of rubles — Nodelman and Goryansky from the bureau of coal supply in Voroshilovgrad and Federman from Moscow. Israel Moiseevich Yoffe secured a position in the ministry of light metallurgy through Shapironsky. Leonid Moiseevich Roitblat, David Shabalevich Abramovich, Fainberg, and Furman received jobs through relatives and friends. In Armenia Garush Samuelian was responsible for embezzling one million rubles. Abraham Yankelevich conducted himself immorally with a number of women. Shaya (Isaiah) Khaimovich Rabirov, the former manager of a textile plant, was charged together with several others with stealing cloth.

Feldman, a senior investigator in the prosecutor's office, was guilty of criminal conduct during a trial. Bourgeois nationalists and Zionists penetrated numerous organizations in Lithuania especially a certain Edinovich who allowed American and British spies to work in the banking system. Shafranik transformed a government enterprise into a private possession of his. Rosen, who was employed by the division for constructing machinery of the ministry of railways, organized a whole group of criminals who embezzled state property to the tune of one million rubles. Peklis and Yushkevich built themselves houses with materials from the plant in which they worked as senior officials. Ludmirsky, the head of a number of departments and bureaus in the Rostov district executive committee, was accused of mismanagement and wasting government funds. Dvorkin, an official in a cooperative at Penza, obtained a large quantity of watches which his accomplice, Savatev, passed on to Moscow. Suppliers of the parts for assembling the watches bore the names of Ofman, Tashlitsky, Milyavsky, and Kogan; watch parts worth 600,000 rubles were found in the latter's house. Dvorkin's sister, Mrs. Koblents, was involved in these deals. With no justification, houses were built for the managers Davidov and Koval. In connection with an action against espionage, subversion, and other crimes, enemies of the people Yemets, the manager of a meat company in Kiev, the engineer Rofman, and the cashier Orel — whose real name was Kadchinsky — were arrested. Rofman was charged with evading military service at the beginning of the war. Mrs. Orel-Kadchinsky embezzled more than 240,000 rubles in government funds. Liberman, a high railroad official, took advantage of his position to build unusual vehicles for himself and for his assistants Milman and Gutermacher. Gorelik built himself a summer home with materials which belonged to a record factory in which he worked. Max Rimlind, an administrator in an enterprise for decorations, caused the state losses amounting to 280,000 rubles, and was also charged with drawing up fraudulent contracts and with blackmail.

Boris Yefremovich Bichkov had headed the Zionist organization in Chernigov before the revolution (with the knowledge of the Tsarist secret police); in 1932 he was sentenced for black marketing in foreign currency. When he later became the deputy manager of a company for marketing fish, he discharged "foreign" workers and in their place hired friends of his, Lazar Botvinik, Khaim Oksman (who had been expelled from the Communist Party), Lev Goldberg (who had a criminal past), Aaron Poperny (a former fish wholesaler), and Moishe Karpilovsky (who had been expelled from the Communist Party for antigovernment activity). Within three years these people embezzled more than 273,000 rubles. Sheleg, Zagursky, and Davidovich were mentioned as having had contact with them.

A number of cases of embezzlement were discovered in educational and scientific institutions. The persons mentioned were Segal, the principal of a Moscow school, and Levin of a district department of education. Rabinovich of the Ukrainian Academy for Nuclear Energy received payment for work which he had never done; Shvets and Yampolsky of the same institution were mentioned in connection with fraud. Keilin had been in charge of instruction in the bureau for higher education at Dnepropetrovsk despite the fact that he had never been graduated from a teachers' seminary; it was pointed out that this educator's father had speculated in wheat and horses. In the same city, a woman by the name of Volynskaya had been appointed to head a department in a pharmaceutical institute even though she had not completed high school. Professor Lembergsky's "scientific" work was allegedly based on plundering state property. Bushtet had been appointed senior lecturer in chemical technology on the basis of a forged diploma. Betty Spector had secured a teaching position through fraud. The teacher Yuda Maharshak was a swindler. Fraudulent dealings in connection with enrolling students were discovered in a Moscow institute for librarians; the accused included Khlebsevich, Domnits, Levin, Fried, Eikhenvolts, and Abramov. Various kinds of deceit were discovered in a Kiev publishing firm; the persons involved included Pismenik, Mikhailik, and Adelheim.

The list of Moscow lawyers denounced for their efforts to help criminals evade punishment included the name Berlin. Among those who undermined justice in the prosecutor's office of the Uzbek Republic at Tashkent were Gurvich, Alperovich, Kotliar, and Shvartsman.

Alexander Lazarovich Cohen was portrayed as a modern Fagin. This blind man claimed to have lost his sight while serving in the army during World War II, and was accordingly granted disability compensation from the state amounting to 21,000 rubles. Under false pretenses he managed to have boys from a Moscow orphans' home placed in his charge. Instead of concerning himself with their education as he should have done, he turned the youngsters into his servants and the tools of his shady deals. The last victim of this Fagin was the boy Yuri Pankov, the son of patriots who had given their lives for their country.

These accounts and stories appeared in a wide range of publications and included national, district, and local newspapers, papers for young people, labor unions, the army, and the navy, philosophical, literary, professional, and humoristic periodicals, and others. It may be added that these descriptions sometimes appeared under the heading of a humoristic column (so-called "feuilleton"). Such columns served as attractive reading material since they employed an easy popular style instead of the hackneyed, official, ideological, almost uniform pattern of many other parts of the Soviet press. Despite the fact that the column also presented a moral and did not lack a note of preaching, it nervertheless appeared at first sight as a smiling island in the sea of heavy phraseology, slogans, and quotations. For the same reason, the columns describing criminals with Jewish names in a colorful, humorous fashion wielded greater influence.

The collection cited above demonstrates the nature of the Soviet press and legal campaign. The "map" of economic crimes is striking, extending from the western republics to central Russia, from the Baltic republics to the central regions of the USSR and the Caucasus. In certain instances the practical and business connections among criminals from different areas were cited. The wide range of enterprises, in which fraud, embezzlement, and theft were carried out, is clearly delineated. Nevertheless, the broad range has a unifying factor; the enterprises were all chiefly engaged in producing consumer goods. "Public opinion" was directed to heinous deeds in connection with clothing and shoes, housing and building materials, food products in short supply, summer homes and private vehicles, watches and records, and the like. It was possible from the accounts of economic crimes and criminals to compile a list of merchandise in which the Soviet market was deficient and perhaps of "dream items" for the masses. The criminals who had been apprehended by the authorities were thus not enemies of the state in the abstract sense but also foes of "the Soviet common man."

The campaign described above graphically translated into personal terms the statements made at the Nineteenth Party Congress by Alexander Poskrebyshev, head of Stalin's private secretariat and the man who was considered the gray eminence in the Soviet hierarchy. Poskrebyshev said, "Every Party and government worker, every honest

Soviet citizen must regard the stealers of Soviet property not only as enemies of the state but also as their own personal enemies." This personal implication was bracketed by Poskrebyshev with the statement made many years before by his teacher Stalin who had declared that a person stealing socialist property was tantamount to a "spy and traitor, if not worse." This statement was cited in numerous publications.

Due to economic distress, and especially because of a shortage of vital products, the climate in the Soviet Union was now and then favorable to the spread of the "poor man's socialism," as August Bell defined anti-Semitism. This was all the more true after the war when against the background of the victims of the preceding years on the one hand and awareness of the great victory on the other, strong emotional food was supplied to the desire of the masses for an easier life. At the end of the 1940's and the early 1950's there were already hardly any Jewish commissars who could be blamed for economic failures; however, in organizations engaged in supply and in domestic retail trade and behind the counters of stores there were still many Jews. As a matter of fact, the Kremlin is always remote and unattainable. In his daily needs and chagrins, the man in the street does not come face to face with the regime, the economic system, and the massive power but with the living image of the salesman in the nearby government store or the person in charge of the neighborhood warehouse. If the latter happen to be Jews, a collective address for grievances and complaints is easily found.

This being so, anti-Semitism of the *ochered* (i.e., "line") — the institution which has become an integral part of Soviet life — reared its head. Anti-Semitism of the *ochered* was not a new phenomenon; "Abramoviches" handing out and distributing (common expressions in the Soviet popular jargon for the function of selling) commodities to "their own" people were from time to time the object of widespread resentment. The innovation since Stalin's last days was the fact that this time the authorities demonstrated their approval of these channels of indignation precisely when the proportion of Jews in the commercial services had already declined considerably. The government seemed to have adopted the "anti-Semitism of the line" in a series of measures and newspaper write-ups.

The Soviet reader was able to get an idea of the collective origin and nature of the criminals who just about stole from the pockets and homes of the citizens not only from the large number of Jewish names among them. Additional character traits and behavior patterns in the spirit of old primitive myths about Jews were provided: how *they* "manage," how *they* push themselves to the top posts of institutions, how *they* pull each other up to the "fat, cosy" jobs, how *they* cover up for each other. The accounts formed a picture of nepotism operating both on a family level and on a broader basis, that of the "congregation." Educated persons, intellectuals? Insinuations were made about their methods for securing diplomas; or explanations were provided to show how they abused their liberal and academic professions. Deserving of special attention is the singling out of individuals in the legal profession, both defense attorneys and investigators for the prosecution, as persons whose loyalty to their own kind took precedence over their duties towards justice and the good of the state. Of interest is the linking of certain criminals to banking transactions, which evokes associations of "classic" anti-Semitic tales, or at least placing them in jobs connected with handling money — a sort of graphic illustration to the thumbworn stereotype that their god is Mammon. Incidentally the evasion of military service was mentioned. The reader was given to understand by insinuation that the account of "Fagin" Cohen having been blinded during the war is doubtful. The greed of such characters does not recoil from harming the security of the state; on the contrary, here and there, acts of economic fraud are directly connected with serving foreign enemies, especially at the inspiration of Zionist agents. Where the surname of a certain criminal aroused doubts concerning his origin, it was clarified by adding his first name and his father's name. In cases where Russian names, such as Bichkov, left room for doubt, the account (the person's Zionist past) dispelled all uncertainty.

Sometimes a description of the physical features of the criminals was designed both to banish doubts regarding their origin and to stir up animosity (for instance, the "underground millionaire" with the long, fleshy nose who trembles in court). If anyone still believes that descriptions like these and the large number of Jewish names were fortuitous, the use of names in the plural is sufficient to dispel any further doubts. About a month and a half after the appearance of the "accounts" in *Pravda Ukrainy* concerning the sentences and executions carried out in Kiev, an editorial in the newspaper pointed out that "all those khains and yaroshetskys, greensteins . . . perses . . . and kaplans, and polyakovs" (all the names were spelled with initial small letters) "arouse the profound loathing of the people."

The role played by non-Jewish names in these publications deserves mention. First of all, the names of non-Jews in a Jewish criminal gang were calculated to give an air of "authenticity" to the various stories or to assure an alibi in case of anticipated charges of an anti-Semitic campaign. This was no longer a new tactic. Secondly, several of these non-Jews were mainly mentioned as accomplices — and usually as minor partners — and sometimes the accounts tried to create an impression that they had been seduced into participating in shady deals and had not been their initiators. This right — the initiative — was from the outset reserved for the crafty, diabolical Jewish mind. On the other hand, non-Jews served as a target of severe criticism for their sin of complacency with respect to the abominable swindlers — for having employed such corrupt characters without a sufficient check, for having detected their crimes much too late, for having been aware of their acts without denouncing them either because they did not care or for lack of courage. Furthermore, in the process of drawing a demonological picture of the Jews — even without explicitly using the word "Jew" — it sometimes happened that non-Jewish names became woven into the tales of criminals and crimes in an antipodal fashion — as their victims. Once in a while this contrast was presented in a gushingly sentimental form as in the case of the Moscow "Fagin" — of the poor orphan Yuri Pankov who was ruthlessly exploited by Alexander Lazarovich Cohen.

It should be pointed out that the descriptions of economic crimes repeated here are, per se, not necessarily the result of a fertile imagination. Black market deals, graft, personal contacts for the purpose of securing mutual favors in matters of supply, the misappropriation of materials from enterprises, bookkeeping manipulations in order to conceal deficits and similar phenomena and acts were a notorious part of the Soviet economic scene. The practice of employing *tolkachi* in various enterprises, especially in light industries which did not have top priority, was extremely widespread. The *tolkachi* are a sort of supply agents whose job it is to secure the materials necessary for the operation of an enterprise by all possible means; and they also do this by unofficially exchanging goods with other enterprises, by granting favors to certain people and circles, paying black market prices, and handing out bribes. There was a popular saying among the people: "*blat* is higher than Stalin." *Blat* is a slang expression meaning personal connections and influence by means of which everything can be obtained or arranged. *Blat* became a vital element both in institutional economic activity and the daily existence of individuals. In enterprises *blat* (the ability to make use of it was a leading trait of the *tolkachi*) was an important factor in determining production quotas ("plan") and calculating their fulfillment in addition to securing the official release of raw materials and other commodities; and in the life of the individual it was regarded as a magic means of getting around market shortages and rationing regulations.[2]

It is no wonder that this state of affairs gave rise to favoritism and discrimination, various forms of payoffs and bribes, under-the-counter sales, and all kinds of fraud. Soviet literature from the period of the post-Stalinist "thaw" — especially works dealing with the ruler's final years — is full of the descriptions of corruption, theft, and shady deals. The great innovation in the descriptions repeated above is not the facts which they expose but in their placing Jews in the center of the dirty deals or in presenting them as their exclusive main characters. Moreover, the Stalinist line in the press (comparable to "socialist realism" in literature) generally required the writers to stress positive aspects of Soviet life and conceal what was negative, to devote a great deal of space to tales of courage and devotion and as little as possible to stories of corruption. And the above facts have demonstrated that when the Soviet press did deviate from its accepted practice and opened its columns wide to descriptions of corruption and reports of swindles and crimes, it did so chiefly by means of Jewish names, which in many instances appeared in groups.

This special notoriety given to persons of Jewish extraction in publications discussing economic crimes could leave no doubt in their concentrated systematic manipulation.

TEN

Murderers in White Gowns

The second half of 1952 — as we have learned from previous chapters — confronted the Jews of the Soviet Union (and other countries in the Soviet bloc) with a series of highly significant events. On July 11–18, twenty-five Jewish writers, artists, and leaders were tried in a Moscow court and on August 12, twenty-four of them were executed; on November 20–27, the Prague trial took place; and on November 29, the Kiev Affair was made public.

Soon, a new depressing date was added to this time schedule.

On January 13, 1953, an account was published on the last page of the Moscow *Pravda* by the Soviet news agency Tass. This, too, was modestly headlined under "Chronicle," and reported the "Arrest of a Group of Saboteur-Doctors." It said that some time previously, the state security institutions had uncovered a terroristic group of physicians whose aim was to cut short the lives of Soviet leaders by means of medical treatment. Participants in the group included such names as Professors M. S. Vofsi, V. N. Vinogradov, M. B. Kogan, B. B. Kogan, P. I. Yegorov, A. I. Feldman, Y. G. Etinger, A. M. Greenstein, and Dr. G. I. Mayorov. The item stated that evidence from documents, investigations, and medical experts as well as the confessions of the accused proved that these criminals — secret enemies of the people — had deliberately sabotaged the health of their patients. Taking advantage of their positions as doctors, they had abused the trust of their patients by ignoring the data provided by tests, consequently establishing wrong diagnoses and unsuitable treatment which had brought on the death of the persons entrusted in their care. The criminals admitted that they had incorrectly diagnosed the illness of A. A. Zhdanov, concealing an infarct of his myocardium, and prescribed a regime counterindicated by this serious ailment, thus murdering him. They similarly treated A. S. Shcherbakov prescribing a regime and strong drugs which caused his death. First of all, the criminal physicians attempted to undermine the health of leading Soviet military personnel, put them out of action, and weaken the country's defenses. They tried to disable Marshal A. M. Vasilevsky, Marshal L. A. Govorov, Marshal I. S. Konev, General of the Army S. M. Shtemenko, Admiral G. I. Levchenko, and others. Their arrests disrupted the evil plans of the accused. It was proved — so the announcement went on to say — that all those doctor-murderers who had become monsters in human form, trampling the sacred banner of science and desecrating its honor, had been enrolled by foreign intelligence services as hired agents. Most of the participants in the terrorist group (Vofsi, B. B. Kogan, Feldman, Greenstein, Etinger, and others) were connected with the international Jewish bourgeois-nationalist organization, Joint, which had been established by American intelligence for the alleged purpose of providing material aid to Jews in other countries. Actually, this organization, under the direction of American intelligence, conducts extensive espionage, terrorist, and other subversive activities in numerous countries, including the Soviet Union. Vofsi told investigators after his arrest that he had received orders to "destroy the leading cadres of the Soviet Union"; he had received them from the United States through the Joint by way of a Moscow physician Shimeliovich and the well-known Jewish bourgeois nationalist Mikhoels. Other participants in the terrorist group (Vinogradov, M. B. Kogan, Yegorov) turned out to be old agents of British intelligence. The announcement ended with the statement that the investigation would soon be concluded.[1]

There are grounds for assuming that these "saboteur-doctors" — some of the greatest physicians in the Soviet Union, the heads of medical services in the Kremlin, and the personal doctors of leading political figures in the country, a sort of "court physicians" — had been arrested as early as the first half of November 1952. At about the same time, their names and articles stopped appearing in medical and scientific periodicals.[2] According to revelations made by Nikita Khrushchev about his former master, Stalin himself had given the order for their arrest, and he "personally issued advice on the conduct of the investigation and the method of interrogation of the arrested person." Khrushchev had added that Stalin had told the interrogators to have the academician Vinogradov chained and another prisoner beaten. Stalin had said to Semyon Ignatiev, a former minister of state security, "If you do not obtain confessions from the doctors, we will shorten you by a head." He had called in the investigating judge and personally instructed him in the methods for conducting the interrogation. "These methods were simple — beat, beat, and, once again, beat."[3]

There can be no doubt about the fact that when the announcement of the physicians' arrest was made, their fate had already been decided (although their so-called investigation was not yet finished). In the same issue of *Pravda* (January 13, 1953), an editorial on the front page was devoted to the discovery of the gang. Entitled "Foul Spies and Murderers in the Mask of Doctors and Professors," it for the most part repeated the crimes of the defendants calling the persons by name in a style almost identical with that of the announcement in the "chronicle" but adding a full measure of commentary to the event.

The editorial asked:

> Whom did these monsters serve? Who directed the criminal terrorist and wrecking activity of these vile traitors to the motherland? . . . It has been established that all the participants in the terrorist group of doctors were enrolled in foreign intelligence services, sold them their bodies and souls, were their hired, paid agents. . . . The dirty face of this Zionist espionage organization [Joint], concealing its foul work under a mask of charity, has been completely exposed. . . . Exposure of the band of poisoner-doctors is a blow at the international Jewish Zionist organization. Now all can see what charitable friends of peace hide under the "Joint" letterhead. . . . The bosses of the U.S.A. and their British junior partners know that it is impossible to secure mastery over other nations by peaceful means. Feverishly preparing for a new world war, they are sending more and more of their spies into the USSR and the people's democracies, trying to

succeed where the Hitlerites failed — trying to create a subversive fifth column in the USSR.

The editorial goes on to discuss mostly the need for "increasing . . . vigilance, carefully watching for all machinations of the warmongers and their agents" and the necessity to strengthen the armed forces of the Soviet Union and the defense against espionage and subversive activities. Referring to instructions and warnings issued by Stalin, the editorial denounces complacency, recalling the assumptions of Lenin and Stalin concerning the sharpening of the class struggle and not its subsidence as Soviet successes mount. The article then cites additional concrete conclusions and accusations not mentioned in the announcement in "chronicle."

The editorial continues:

The fact that a group of despised degenerates from among men of science were able to engage in their machinations with impunity for some time shows that some of our Soviet agencies and their officials lost their vigilance and were infected with gullibility. The agencies of state security did not discover the doctors' wrecking, terrorist organization in time. Yet these agencies should have been particularly vigilant, since history already records instances of foul murderers and traitors to the motherland conducting their machinations in the guise of doctors, such as the doctors Levin and Pletnev, who killed the great Russian writer A. M. Gorky and the outstanding Soviet statesmen V. V. Kuibyshev and V. R. Menzhinsky by deliberate wrong treatment, on orders from enemies of the Soviet Union. The heads of the USSR Ministry of Public Health also did not prove equal to their responsibilities. They failed to perceive the wrecking, terrorist work of the rotten degenerates who had sold themselves to the enemies of the Soviet Union. . . . The Soviet people wrathfully and indignantly condemn the criminal band of murderers and their foreign masters. They will crush like loathsome vermin the despised hirelings who sold themselves for dollars and pounds sterling. As for the inspirers of these hired murderers, they may rest assured that vengeance will not pass them by but will find a path to them. . . . All this is true of course. But it is also true that besides these enemies we still have one more enemy — the gullibility of our people. One cannot doubt that as long as we have gullibility there will continue to be sabotage. Consequently, to end sabotage it is necessary to put an end to gullibility in our ranks.[4]

The Tass announcement was published that day in a number of Soviet newspapers and many of them featured articles devoted to the discovery of the gang of physicians which did not differ much in spirit and style from the *Pravda* editorial.

If the announcement and the *Pravda* editorial are broken down into their components, many of the keys to the significance of the event will be found.

First of all, it should be pointed out that the charges against the defendants and the atmosphere which the authorities began to foster around them aroused associations of the trials of the 1930's. This leads to the conclusion that in this instance, too, Moscow was preparing a large legal spectacle, and now, just as then, the big public trial had been planned from the outset to serve as a sort of symbolical altar for the waves of terror and purges which would sweep the country. Indeed, it is characteristic that the *Pravda* article, like many others, called attention to the treacherous and murderous functions which famous doctors had fulfilled in previous times. In this connection, mention was made of physicians "such as the doctors Levin and Pletnev" and their deeds. This analogy drawn by the men who pulled the strings in the Kremlin deserves more information and additional clarification. The argument has been advanced that Dr. Pletnev, one of the greatest physicians at the Kremlin in the Thirties, had been sentenced to "disappear" in 1937 since he had by chance witnessed the murder of Sergo Ordzhenikidze. This incident suggests that the arrest of the doctors, which had been designed for "grandiose" aims, was also calculated to achieve a by-product — the elimination of a number of individuals who through their profession came in very close personal contact with the country's bigwigs and knew, or were suspected of knowing, some of the "court" secrets and intrigues. The Dr. Levin who was mentioned in the *Pravda* article was one of the physicians (together with Bukharin, Rykov, Rakovsky, Yagoda, and others) who was a defendant in the "Trial of the Twenty-One" or, as it was termed officially, the trial of the "bloc of rightists and Trotskyites" which was conducted in Moscow on March 2–13, 1938. At that legal spectacle, the accused doctors admitted to the prosecutor, Andrei Vyshinsky, and the judges that they had deliberately shortened the lives of prominent patients by means of wrong treatment. Levin and the others confessed what they had to, but it is worthwhile mentioning an instructive detail of Levin's testimony. When he was asked — ironically by the "defense attorney" — "Perhaps you belonged to some national party, Jewish, for example?" Levin replied, "Not to any party, only to the physicians' party."[5]

It would thus appear that the "theoretical" possibility of publicly bracketing medical murder conspiracies with Jewish nationalism had already been alluded to fifteen years before the plots of Professor Vofsi and his colleagues were exposed. Another detail which is more than piquant is the fact that one of the two expert witnesses (in medical matters) at the "Trial of the Twenty-One" who had confirmed that professionally "everything is quite clear" (that is, the charge had been proven) was Dr. Vinogradov, who was in 1952–53 recommended for chaining by Stalin. This was not the first time that the wheel of terror had come full circle and struck at the very persons who had helped it either through coercion or willingly. It is interesting that in the early 1950's, as in the later 1930's, information about the murder of leaders by medical means was made public several years after their death. Viacheslav Menzhinsky — a former head of the GPU — died in 1934; Valerian Kuibyshev, in 1935; Maxim Gorky, in 1936; but news of their malicious murder by doctors at the inspiration of Fascist and Trotskyite enemies at the order of Yagoda did not reach the public until the trial held in March 1938. Shcherbakov died in 1945 and Zhdanov in 1948, but they had to wait in the next world until January 1953 for the "truth" of their premeditated death at the hands of abominable physicians to come to the knowledge of the public.

However, with all the analogous features, recourse of the Soviet judicial apparatus to doctors towards the end of Stalin's life was distinguished by a number of original qualities. One of them undoubtedly was the emphasis on Jewish aspects. This became apparent at first sight from the "ethnic" proportion of the composition of the defendants whose names were listed — six Jews and three non-Jews. It may be assumed that even had the proportion been reversed, public opinion would have tended to pick out more easily the minority of "aliens" in the list. They were all the more conspicuous for being the majority. But it was immediately made clear that the ethnic composition was not fortuitous since the principal acts of the imperialist plots against the Soviet Union were now being carried out by Jewish organizations headed by the Joint; they had, as it were, inherited the place reserved for Trotskyite groups from abroad in the anti-Soviet conspiracies of the Thirties. Implicating the Joint graphically pointed both to the principal source of inspiration of the current anti-Soviet plots — the United States — and to the identity and nature of elements within the USSR on which the foreign espionage services based their calculations and prospects.

A number of the names mentioned — both of persons arrested and those associated with them — are of interest: Mikhoels was the chairman of the Jewish Anti-Fascist Committee and one of the two "representatives" of Soviet Jewry who personally came in touch with the Jews of the United States and other countries in 1943; as mentioned previously, he was killed under mysterious circumstances in January 1947. Professor Miron Vofsi, a former leader in the Soviet army's medical corps with the rank of major-general, was a relative of Mikhoels (whose surname had originally been Vofsi) and had also been one of the personalities connected with the Jewish Anti-Fascist Committee (in the main, only formally, in order to lend it prestige). Dr. Boris Shimeliovich, a quondam director of the Botkin Hospital in Moscow, one of the largest and best in the Soviet Union, was also a member of the Committee, serving on it as a sort of spokesman to Jewish physicians abroad and handling the campaign to raise medical help for the Soviet army among Jewish communities in other countries. Dr. Shimeliovich was arrested together with other members of the committee when it was disbanded, and he presumably died — or was killed — in prison.

As for the two leaders who were allegedly the victims of the doctors' lust for murder — Zhdanov died on August 31, 1948. His death certificate, which was made public on September 1, 1948, bore the signatures of five doctors, all of them non-Jews: Vinogradov, Yegorov, Mayorov (these three were included in the list of doctors who had been arrested, according to the announcement of January 13, 1953), Fiodorov, and Vasilenko. Zhdanov was considered the rising star of the Soviet hierarchy and was regarded by many persons to be the first in line to inherit the leadership from Stalin. This is an important detail because the announcement and the editorial in *Pravda* suggested internal struggles among the Soviet leaders which were traditionally accompanied by intrigues and plans for purging and liquidating actual or potential rivals. A clear indicator of this is the emphasis on the negligence displayed by the institutions of internal security (and less stressed — of the ministry of health). It seems noteworthy that in his final years, Zhdanov exemplified Soviet anti-Westernism and he was considered the spiritual father of the campaign against cosmopolitanism which in time began to reveal its anti-Semitic sting. The second victim, Shcherbakov, died on May 10, 1945. During the war, he served as a sort of censor and chief political supervisor of the information agencies. There is evidence to support the allegation that he was responsible for concealing or obliterating the Jewish aspect of the Nazi atrocities for the purpose of preventing the emergence of an impression that Russia was conducting a "Jewish war." He also showed dissatisfaction when Jews were featured in stories of heroism.[6] Rumor had it that he was the source of the implied, if not explicit, plot to check the advance of Jews in the army. By means of these names, Zhdanov and Shcherbakov, the doctors' libel may have attempted incidentally to allude to the possibility of an act of reprisal by a vengeful people.

The prominence given to the doctors' intentions to impair the health of the military leaders is important. Of all the foci of Soviet power, and perhaps, in contrast to the rest, the military leaders were the most loved and admired by the population both because of their positive achievements during the war and (negatively) because they are not directly involved in the citizens' daily difficulties in getting along and in the authorities' repressive actions. Accordingly, putting a spotlight on the military personalities as the doctors' target could only add to the blazing agitation against these criminals and their like.

The announcement of January 13, 1953, served as the point of departure for a large-scale propaganda campaign for "revolutionary vigilance," as has been indicated above. In this campaign, the gang of saboteur-doctors served as widespread illustrative material for proving the evil intrigues of the imperialists and their agents and the existence of a danger stemming from lack of alertness to them. A number of examples (in addition to the *Pravda* article from the date of the announcement) showing the viciousness in the choice of illustrations in the doctors' affair follow:

The crimes of the terrorist group of saboteur-doctors . . . show that there is no crime to which the imperialists and their despised hirelings will not descend. . . . It has been established that all the participants in the terrorist group of saboteur-doctors were in the hire of foreign intelligence services. Most of the participants in this group were enlisted by a branch of the American intelligence service — the international Jewish bourgeois nationalist organization "Joint." Other participants in the terrorist group are old agents of British intelligence.[7]

The U.S. monopolists make extensive use for their odious purposes of Jewish Zionist organizations, including the international Jewish bourgeois nationalist organization "Joint," which acts at the orders and direction of American intelligence. Zionism has become the tool of the American-British warmongers. Relying upon a group of Jewish bourgeois nationalists, the wreckers and murderers from "Joint" have developed their criminal activity in our country. . . . The monstrous crimes of these base agents of American and British intelligence — Vofsi, Kogan, Feldman, Greenstein, Etinger, Vinogradov, and others — evoked the indignation of the entire Soviet people. Executing the will of its masters — the imperialists of the U.S.A. and Britain — this despicable band of wreckers which posed as learned doctors sought to cut short the lives of public figures in the Soviet Union. Comrades A. A. Zhdanov and A. S. Shcherbakov fell by their hands. The subversives in white gowns attempted to undermine the health of leading Soviet military cadres, to put them out of action, and to weaken the country's defense.[8]

That is how the horror story of the plots of the Joint and other Jewish nationalist elements was repeated in a number of publications giving the impression of a contest to see who could use the most venomous style. It is interesting to note that it was the humoristic magazine *Krokodil* which attained new heights in the use of this style; apparently its smiling countenance, as it were, brought the inciting statements on its pages closer to the hearts of the readers.

The following are examples of *Krokodil*'s "humor":

Vofsi, B. Kogan and M. Kogan, Feldman, Greenstein, Etinger, Vinogradov, and Yegorov knew how to change the expression in their eyes to give their wolves' souls a human aspect. . . . For this purpose, they attended a well-known school directed by the hypocrite Mikhoels, to whom nothing was sacred and who, for thirty pieces of silver, sold his soul to the "land of the yellow devil" which he chose to be his homeland. The poisoners also took lessons in camouflage from their medical comrade, the criminal, Shimeliovich. Vofsi, B. Kogan, Feldman, Greenstein, and Etinger were the hirelings of the espionage and terrorist organization Joint operating in the United States. This society advertised itself as a philanthropic organization, very dear to Israel, and designed to help its brothers and sisters of the same blood. That was an arrogant lie. . . . In the people's memory they [the arrested doctors] are the personification of baseness and abomination, the same kind as that Judas Iscariot. The gang of Judas Iscariot has been dealt a crushing blow. . . . The black hatred of our great country has united in one camp American and British bankers, colonialists, kings of arms, Hitler's defeated generals dreaming of vengeance, representatives of the Vatican, loyal adherents of the Zionist *kahal.*[9]

To supplement this description, a cartoon was printed on the entire back page of the same issue of *Krokodil.* It showed a bloodthirsty, dollar-lusting physician with the hand of justice gripping his white gown from behind. Both the mask pulled from his face and the predatory countenance exposed underneath had stereotyped "Jewish" features.[10]

Three weeks later, a Soviet writer described and interpreted in *Krokodil* foreign reactions to the doctors' affair as follows: "Weeping was heard by the rivers of Babylon, the most important of which is the Hudson. The Joint — the carrion vulture wrapping itself in the feathers of a dove of loving-kindness and philanthropy — was plucked. . . . The bourgeois newspapers shed tears of ink. . . . The embarrassed grieving of the leaders of Zionist organizations extends from Jerusalem to London."[11]

At the same time the Soviet organs were fulminating against all kinds of traitors and complaining against the "complacent ones," a campaign was being conducted to build up the woman doctor Lydia Timashuk as an exemplary figure. A week after the announcement of January 13, 1953, she was awarded the decoration of the Order of Lenin "for her help to the government" in discovering the saboteur-doctors.[12] Three years later, the nature of this aid was made clear by remarks of Khrushchev's on the doctors' affair and Stalin. He said: "Actually there was no 'affair' outside of the declaration of the woman doctor Timashuk, who was probably influenced or ordered by someone (after all, she was an unofficial collaborator of the organs of state security) to write Stalin a letter in which she declared that doctors were applying supposedly improper methods of medical treatment. Such a letter was sufficient for Stalin to reach an immediate conclusion that there are doctor-plotters in the Soviet Union."[13]

The service rendered by Lydia Timashuk did not remain the secret of the institutions for state security or Stalin and his assistants but was brought to the knowledge of the masses. The details of her "help to the government" in connection with the doctors' affair sometimes reverberated like a frightening children's legend. She worked in a hospital as an expert in electrocardiography. Her suspicions were aroused when she noticed that a distinguished professor did not interpret her electrocardiograms properly and determined a wrong diagnosis for the patient. She remarked to the professor about what had at first seemed to her an inadvertent error, but he reprimanded her sharply. She then embarked on a campaign "in very difficult and complex conditions." The professor was supported by many important physicians who expressed doubt in the "political maturity and honesty" of Mrs. Timashuk; but in the end, she won.[14] The stories of Lydia Timashuk's war were designed to depict a "Russian soul" — a woman who had honesty and loyalty in her blood, a devoted loving mother (her only son, a pilot — it was pointed out — had been severely wounded in World War II), and a responsible worker without special pretensions. But it was this "small" Russian woman doctor who stood firm against important and powerful "professors."

The Soviet Union rang with the praises of Lydia Timashuk. And these praises were drenched in waves of venom and agitation directed against the "antipode," as it were, of this pure soul. An article published one month after she was awarded the Order of Lenin which also featured letters to her is a good example of the atmosphere in which the authorities built up the image of the heroine:

A man in a white gown stands beside the patient's bed. Whatever the man does, whether he picks up a hypodermic needle, checks the result of a blood test, or writes a prescription, the eyes of the sick person follow him tensely and hopefully. "Doctor!" There is boundless human faith in this word. . . . A white gown is the symbol of purity . . . the symbol of the probity and altruism which is the mark of this profession. With the exception of high treason, there is no more monstrous crime than betrayal of the patient's faith; there is no criminal more abominable than the murderer dressed in the white gown of a doctor. And here two persons in white gowns meet beside a patient's bed. One, the man, is a celebrated scholar with high scientific degrees; the other, a woman, has no academic repute but possesses much experience and a wealth of knowledge acquired in more than twenty years of working in medicine. And she is filled with a strong sense of duty towards the health and lives of the Soviet people. Both the man and the woman hold the same analyses in their hands; both observe the same symptoms of the illness. But the woman sees that the man with the academic degrees makes a wrong diagnosis. A wrong diagnosis — a wrong treatment, and death is the result. . . . Yes, before her stands an enemy; and not one enemy but a gang of foes of the Soviet Union, evil, crafty, and well disguised. A struggle began, a very hard one. For these men with academic degrees and in high grades occupied important positions and surrounded themselves with their own people. But the woman fought on as one combats enemies of the homeland — heedless of the danger to her life. Perhaps in those days she had a vision of a flaming airplane in her mind, and in the aircraft, a Soviet flier, her only son. . . . For her help in exposing the disgrace of the accursed doctor-murderers, L. F. Timashuk was awarded the highest decoration of honor — the Order of Lenin. News of this has spread to all parts of our country. Lydia Fedosyevna Timashuk has become near and dear to the hearts of millions of Soviet people.

The article goes on to cite excerpts of letters to the "saving doctor," the "doctor-patriot," and "a daughter dear to our motherland." Letters were sent in by pupils, soldiers, retired people, mine workers, factory workers, doctors "who serve their country honorably and faithfully," members of collective farms, housewives wishing to shake hands with her and requesting her picture to put into the family album. The communications contained verses in her honor and denounced the enemies she had exposed, thanked her for restoring honor and purity to the white gown, and promised or called on others to follow in her footsteps against diverse enemies and their plots with patriotic, revolutionary vigilance.[15]

While letters of this kind were streaming to Lydia Timashuk or to government and party institutions and to the offices of newspapers, some Jews drew a comparison in their memories and minds between the current heroine and a certain Vera Cheberiak, one of the central figures in the Kiev blood libel of 1911 which led to the Beilis trial (1913); the Cheberiak woman had testified that the Christian boy, Yushchinsky, had been murdered by the defendant in order to make use of his blood for baking *matsot* (unleavened bread for Passover). However, one could not help contemplating the differences: those had been other times with an entirely different regime, and the witness had been a vulgar woman of the marketplace and a professional swindler. The present "witness" represented the best of the new Soviet intelligentsia.

The descriptions of the murderer-doctors were enough to arouse a certain amount of panic in the population. The man in the street was easily able to imagine the wall of protection and surveillance maintained around the Kremlin's top men or the generals and marshals and with what rigid security measures the physicians treating them were selected; nevertheless, the latter had "succeeded" in disguising themselves and had already managed to carry out a part of their plot. And if this is how the Vofsis, Greensteins, Kogans, and Shimeliovich's were, who could guarantee the honesty of other doctors of the same background? Actually, the fears of the "little man" of the "monsters in white gowns" were deliberately stimulated as evidenced by a series of accounts and stories in the Soviet press about doctors or other workers in institutes and institutions connecting medicine with Jewish names. The following excerpts are from the period between January 13 and the end of February, 1953.[16]

A group of physicians in Belorussia were denounced for negligence and abuse of their positions, including handing out fraudulent sickness slips. Among the names mentioned were those of Asia Epstein, Zila Markovich Nisnevitz, Regina Bloch, Kantorovitz, Slobodskaya, Kokesh, and Dora Moiseyevna Paperno. Mira Izrailyevna Chernyakova (née Bloch) used to throw specimens into the wastebasket instead of carrying out tests and did not report malignant growths, thus endangering the lives of cancer patients. M. Z. Izraelit worked as a specialist in venereal diseases without a medical diploma. Valentin Kazhdan worked with a fake diploma from a medical school; although he was exposed now and then, he managed to secure good jobs in various places with the help of his father, Boris Yankelevich Kazhdan, and his father's friends Prupes, Zeltsovsky, and Zalman Abramovich Pozyumin. Professor Batkis preferred medical workers or students who did not know anything and were unreliable and cheaters, such as Rabinovich, Meler, and Reich; and, on the other hand, he discriminated against honest workers and students. Dr. Zalmanson gave a young Jewish doctor, a friend of hers, a certificate to prevent him from being sent to work in the country. Professor Feinberg, the former director of the clinic for forensic psychiatry of the Institute for General and Experimental Pathology (which was attacked for various scandals and ideological deviations) brought "many friends and relatives of hers from Odessa" to work at the clinic; some of their names were Kholetsky, Kalashnik, Turnbiner, Freyer, Luntz, Shtiller, and Korsunsky. Physicians from various places were mentioned as having taken bribes from patients. (In this connection, there were rumors that the lists of retired persons were being revised because many of them — mainly Jews — had appeared on them on the basis of forged medical certificates). A large number of physicians in Kiev and Nikolaev were charged with being unfit for their duties and with swindling and embezzling large sums of money; the names mentioned were Roitelman, Geller, Makarovskaya, Vasserman, Ravich, Lirtsman, Zaslavsky, Gendelman, Professor Luria, Zlatman, Rapaport, Kogan, Magaziner, Professor Olshanetsky, Erlichman, Geshelin, Kogan-Yasni, Levin, Sheftel, Trachtenberg, and Patsyuk. A group of about twenty physicians were arrested in Zhitomir; Ukrainian newspapers called them "child murderers."

In this way, a "medical element" was introduced into the fabric of Jewish criminality connected with the daily existence of the Soviet citizen. Here lies one of the differences between the Thirties and the beginning of 1953: in the former period, there was talk of a number of physicians who had been treating top leaders; in the latter, the canvas was broadened and with the unmasking of the famous doctors and professors, encouragement and a sign were given to popular indignation against many other physicians — persons of the same extraction as most of the members of the Moscow gang. In deliberately worded publications and by means of various "atmosphere" pieces all these were presented as plotting against the lives of ordinary men, women, and children.

The stories and accounts about the corruption, negligence, nepotism, and fraud of doctors contain features analogous to those found in the descriptions of economic crimes; partial blame for the suffering of the little man was placed on Jewish physicians. For the purpose of understanding the significance of this, it is important to know that in Soviet society the doctor sometimes serves as a key figure making available various means of easing the citizen's daily life. He is authorized to distribute work releases and slips for rest, enabling the citizen to take care of personal matters. A well-known feature of Soviet life is the strong pressure brought to bear on doctors working in clinics attached to various places of employment by people who are really sick and malingerers for work releases. In view of the strict laws against absenteeism and lateness, the medical certificate sometimes saves the worker from fines and imprisonment. It is characteristic that while persons coming to clinics employed all kinds of tricks to influence the physicians, the latter were exposed to the counterpressure of managers and the authorities because of their excessive liberality in handing out work releases which harms and sabotages production. There was a practice in force of quotas in handing out releases for medical reasons which were generally smaller than the number of candidates. Another kind of pressure exerted on doctors (certainly not as common as the one for work releases) was for a medical permit for the termination of a pregnancy.[17] Under such circumstances, a doctor in the Soviet Union could sometimes appear in a light similar to that of a salesperson in a store or a person in charge of supplying commodities; great hopes were pinned on him and he also served as a focal point of grievances.

The number of doctors in the Soviet Union rose from 20,000 in 1913 (in Russia) to approximately 215,000 in 1951.[18] This growth testifies to great progress in medicine and an improvement in the field of social insurance as well as to wider educational opportunities. The number of Jews among Soviet medical workers is unknown, but it is reasonable to believe that there were proportionately more of them than the percentage of Jews in the Soviet population. The medical profession with a rich Jewish tradition certainly did not lose its attraction for Jews in the Soviet way of life, too. Evidently, just because Jews were conspicuously represented in the medical profession, and this profession came into sensitive contact with the "little man" were accusations and libels expressly directed against doctors with Jewish names. The same threads bind them to the various economic criminals and the terrorist group of doctors discovered in Moscow.

One of the illuminating and tragic phenomena of the reality of the early months of 1953 in the Soviet Union was the relative ease with which the doctors' libel was given credence by the population. Many people — including some not particularly infected with hatred of Jews — tended to believe it. Yevgeny Yevtushenko in his *Precocious Autobiography* tells of the poet K., who had been a schoolmate of his. K. glowed with joy at the publication of the account of the gang of doctors which he regarded as the confirmation of his opinions on the Jews; "See?" he called out, waving the newspaper. "What did I tell you? Jews, the whole lot of them!" And even though his friend's outburst of joy displeased Yevtushenko, and the account of the doctors did not make an anti-Semite out of him, he pointed out, "I must admit that I believed the report."[19] In telling the story of his life and discussing the acquittal of the doctors after Stalin's death, Yevtushenko says that the news "stunned the general public, who, by and large, had believed in their [the doctors'] guilt."[20] This belief rested a great deal on Stalin's authority. It was also nourished, paradoxically, by the grandiose dimensions of the crimes described; it was difficult to imagine that crimes like *these* could be a fabrication of the imagination. Thus the effectiveness of the rule laid down by Hitler and Goebbels that the bigger the lie, the better its chances of being accepted by the masses if it is repeated often enough with conviction, was proved.

And just as many people "responded" to the great fiction of the notorious doctor-spies, the murderers of Zhdanov and Shcherbakov, so panic was aroused in the population in connection with Jewish doctors in general. After having been set in operation by various publications, the rumor mill began working under its own motive power. The number of patients waiting outside the rooms of Jewish doctors in clinics was sharply reduced. Persons coming to the clinics were heard saying, "They killed Zhdanov, they are also liable to kill us." People told one another of friends or relatives who died because of deliberate wrong diagnoses, incorrect prescriptions, sabotaging operations, and the like. Rumors spread of sabotage in medical industries and of poison introduced into stores of medicines. There were rumors that an order had been issued to investigate a series of deaths in recent years, especially of army officers. People whispered to each other that the cleaning women in hospitals had known that something was wrong but had been helpless against the Jewish doctors. Rumors followed one another in rapid succession. Someone had seen a Jewish doctor pouring poison into medicines; tens of women victims were attributed to a Jewish gynecologist who was said to have induced intrauterine poisoning in them by a syringe; a Jewish doctor infected a student with tuberculosis.[21] In his memoirs Ehrenburg attests to the atmosphere in Moscow after the announcement of January 13, 1953, and he writes:

> People repeated the story that it is hell in the hospitals. Many patients regard the doctors as brutal villains and refuse medicine. An agronomist went to Yalta on his vacation. He left early. He told me that his wife had frightened him: "We are leaving the rest home this very day — they will poison us here." A woman doctor said, "Yesterday I had to take pills, powders, ten medicines for ten ailments — the patients were afraid I was a plotter." In the Tishin market [in Moscow] a drunk shouted, "The Jews wanted to poison Stalin."

Ehrenburg also gave expression to the lack of confidence in Jewish doctors which spread through the population immediately after the announcement of January 13 in his story "The Thaw," which he began to write, he said, right after the announcement of the acquittal of the doctors and from which he drew inspiration for the title[23] (which in the West came to refer to the new period which began after Stalin's death). One of the characters in the story is Dr. Vera Sherer who works in the hospital of an industrial plant. Her husband and the members of her family died during the war, but she apparently also has another source of grief "since the announcement" (the announcement of January 13). When she was summoned to examine the daughter of the plant's manager, the latter began remarking to his wife, "She's supposed to be very good. I've got nothing at all against her. Still, you have to be careful whom you trust, no doubt about it."[24] At the same time a number of patients in the hospital shouted that doctors like Vera should not be trusted.

It is not hard to describe the physical and mental condition of Jewish physicians. They were gripped by nervousness and fear. The death of a patient whom a Jewish doctor had been treating constituted an actual threat against his life. Insults and suffering were also the lot of non-Jewish woman doctors married to Jews.

From her personal experiences in Moscow at the time, a woman subsequently relates in her memoirs that efforts to explain to people that the rumors about doctors were groundless were mostly doomed to failure.[25]

ELEVEN

The Darkest Days

It may be recalled that the period in the life of Soviet Jewry from the end of 1948 until Stalin's death was defined by some people as the "black years." In the anti-Semitic campaigns of those years the distinction between Jews as a national group and as individuals was progressively obliterated. Not only personalities who were directly or otherwise associated with Jewish public life and cultural activities sensed the dangers to their existence but masses of ordinary Jews as well. The British author Max Hayward who lived in Moscow two years, in the gloomiest period of Stalinist rule — as he put it — pointed out that the Jews of the Soviet Union were gripped by the fear lest their fate resemble that which had several years previously befallen the Jews in the lands under German occupation. He went on to say that they were dominated by a horrible feeling of helplessness.[1]

This feeling took possession of the Jews as the consequence of events which could be interpreted as a sort of coordination of official policy and the instincts of the mob. It seemed that official Russia was aiding and giving her blessing to popular anti-Semitism. An illuminating detail is the fact that a second edition of a standard history textbook omitted material in the first edition which had denounced the anti-Semitic policy of Tsar Alexander III.[2]

For Jews, the horrors of the 1930's paled by comparison with those of the "black years." In the 1930's "you had to be important to be arrested or shot. In the '40's it made no difference. Anyone could be arrested. Literally anyone." (Hayward, who was just quoted, related that once he, too, had been the victim of an anti-Semitic attack when he had been mistaken for a Jew.) Ordinary Jewish citizens lost their jobs, were exiled, or disapppeared, and the question "why" was everywhere to be heard. The police, too, may not have known the answer, as, for example, in the case of a certain watchmaker. His name just happened to be on a list, or it may have been confused with someone else's. In any event, he was arrested and shot a few days later.[3] Some were arrested for having had Jewish books in their possession, and others, for having concealed their Judaism. Sometimes Jews actually tried to get rid of their passports because of the nationality registered in them, but their exchange involved considerable risks. Many Jews realized that there was no sense in complaining to the authorities and the preservers of the law of anti-Semitic outbreaks; and sometimes such complaints involved danger — the person registering them was exposed to arrest and the charge of spreading defamatory anti-Soviet propaganda.[4]

In the atmosphere of the "black years," the Soviet press devoted much space to attacks on Israel and Zionism. This externally directed propaganda campaign was accompanied by domestic repressive measures. Under such circumstances, a Jewish family could be sent to Siberia because its ten-year-old daughter had in school asked where Israel was.[5] There were reports that in a number of places in the western districts the authorities had provocatively announced the registration of Jews wishing to emigrate to Israel, and those who had yielded to the impulse to sign up were arrested or exiled. For a long time after Mrs. Golda Meir, Israel's first minister to Moscow, had left the Soviet Union, the number of "Golda's prisoners" (the term applied to persons accused of showing excessive enthusiasm at the arrival of the Israeli legation to Moscow) continued to mount.

Relations between the USSR and Israel, which were deteriorating steadily from the end of the 1940's, reached their tensest point during the Slansky trial and the doctors' libel. Israeli public opinion was aroused by the spate of imaginary accusations and calumnies from

connection between the juridical spectacle in Prague and the doctors' affair in Moscow. The Israeli government also pointed up the connection between them and denounced the doctors' libel in the sharpest terms.

Speaking for the government, Foreign Minister Moshe Sharett said:

> In the consciousness of the Jewish people, the Moscow libel is equated with the charges leveled at the Jews in the Middle Ages of poisoning wells and murdering Christian children for religious purposes. It reminds all of us of the Beilis trial which was staged by the Tsarist regime, with this difference — that that regime did not coerce Beilis into confessing his crime and also afforded him the possibility of defending himself with the best lawyers in Russia. Large numbers of citizens in the state of Israel and masses of Jews throughout the world are convinced that the accused are innocent, even if they have been forced to admit to deeds which they never committed. Also, anyone familiar with the activity of the Joint is certain of the complete purity of its actions and contemptuously rejects the libel flung at it.[6]

From the sentencing of Slansky and his comrades until Stalin's death, attacks against Israel and Zionism became more frequent in the Soviet press. The definition of Zionism as "a reactionary trend of the Jewish bourgeoisie" or presenting Israel as being sold to American imperialism were no longer new, but with the Slansky trial and subsequent to it a novel note was added to this explanation; great emphasis was attached to espionage and concrete acts of subversion carried out in the Soviet Union and other Soviet bloc countries by Israel and Zionism for the benefit of the United States.[7] Even if now and then the distinction between anti-Semitism and anti-Zionism was pointed out, it was difficult not to discern, at least an anti-Semitic "tone" made by the anti-Israel music — understood, for example, from the statements about Israeli retail peddlers doing business by supplying spies wholesale to Washington out of a congenital penchant for trading.

Soviet publications repeated the story spread at the Prague trial concerning the secret meeting which David Ben-Gurion had held in Washington in 1947 with American leaders at which the "Morgen-

story under the headline "Zionist Agents of the American Intelligence Service" declared Zionism was chiefly supported by American capitalist families — Strauss, Lehman, Rockefeller, and Morgenthau; that the American diplomat Benjamin Cohen was the liaison between the State Department and Zionist organizations; that the Zionists supported the revival of Nazism and the establishment of Fascist regimes in a spirit of bestial racism; and that the Zionist movement was helping the American intelligence services to set up a fifth column in the Soviet Union and the People's Democracies.[8]

A series of Soviet publications featured the history, activity, and nature of the Joint. The readers were told that almost from the beginning of its existence, this organization had been involved in subversive activities against the Soviet Union as evidenced, for example, by its participation in Herbert Hoover's delegation to Russia in the early 1920's; when hunger was throttling the young Soviet republic, the ARA (Agricultural Research Administration) came to it together with the Joint for the apparent purpose of aiding the hungry but actually to work for the toppling of the Soviet regime. This was the permanent face of the Joint, about which the following was said: "Irrefutable facts testify that 'Joint' is one of the most important branches of the American Intelligence Service. Murderers, spies, and saboteurs who are members of this organization carry out the vilest assignments of Wall Street, not disdaining any, even the most inhuman, means. U.S. imperialist circles generously finance their Zionist Agency."[9]

The Soviet citizen learned that just as the richest American families support the Joint so they (the Rockefellers, Warburgs, Lehmans, Fords, and others) dominate the Joint which was directed against the Soviet regime immediately after its establishment. Thus, in the 1920's, for example, the Joint spent 16,000,000 Czech crowns in Ukrainian Carpathia (the region annexed by the Soviet Union in 1945) for supporting subversive Jewish societies and institutions, including the Jewish gymnasium in Mukachevo serving as a "recruitment center for agents and saboteurs." The writer who disclosed these facts also knew of criminal Zionist activity in Ukrianian Carpathia supported by dollars through the efforts of a Bratislava lawyer, Barukh Tomashoff, a relative of "the well-known American atom monger [Bernard]

Baruch." The aim of this activity was "to transform Transcarpathia into a military springboard against the Soviet Union."[10] Variations on the themes Zionist-Israel-Joint appeared in other publications.

On February 9, 1953, a bomb was placed in the Soviet legation in Tel Aviv wounding a number of workers and causing considerable damage to the building. Despite the fact that the Israeli government, the president, and the Knesset denounced the attack and the government expressed its sympathy to the Soviet government and announced its readiness to pay compensation for the damage, Moscow severed relations with Israel on February 12, claiming that the attack proved that minimal conditions for the activity of a Soviet diplomatic representation did not exist in Israel. A note in this connection which was handed to the Israeli minister to Moscow, Shemuel Elyashiv, spoke of provocative articles published in the press of Israel's ruling parties and of defamatory anti-Soviet speeches delivered in Parliament. The speech made in the Knesset on January 19 by the foreign minister (the government's announcement concerning the arrest of the doctors in Moscow) was described as open incitement to act against the Soviet Union.

Moscow continued to argue that Israel's leaders had launched a campaign of hate against the USSR which grew in intensity especially after the Joint's dirty deeds in the Soviet Union and in a number of People's Democracies were exposed.[11] These "dirty deeds" were chiefly exposed by the Prague trial and the doctors' investigation and threads were discovered which linked Slansky and the doctors and other saboteurs to the plotters Rajek (Hungary), Kostov (Bulgaria), and Gomulka and Spichalsky (Poland).[12] It was also pointed out that the vicious crimes of the doctor-murderers, the actions of Zionists who were members of the "Central Organization for Plotting Against the State" in Czechoslovakia, and the terrorist act against the Soviet legation in Tel Aviv were links in the same chain.[13] It was thus clear that Moscow wanted to utilize the anti-Semitic, anti-Zionist, anti-Israel campaign for the purpose of unifying the Soviet bloc held in the power-grip of Stalinization.

In the fight against all kinds of "hostile views" arguments well known from the period of the attacks against "cosmopolitanism" were heard again and their anti-Semitic overtones were repeated. In connection with ideological deviations, anti-Marxist opinions, and the like, the names Landsman, Rubin, Zilberfarb, and Professor Bernshtam were mentioned in February and March, 1953, for example. At a performance of the puppet theater in Moscow, which among other things also cast jibes at corrupt Western art, people from Hollywood with so-called typical ugly Jewish features were shown.[14] Calls for "revolutionary vigilance" and ideological preparedness for battle were also accompanied in the period of the doctors' libel by model accounts of persons who had infiltrated various institutions and constituted a danger to the security of the state — and once more, Jewish names predominated. A certain Korshun had served as an adviser in the ministry of nonferrous metallurgy, although he had been expelled from the Party, and he was linked to the disappearance of a secret document.[15] G. L. Zaslavsky, a high-ranking worker in the ministry for geology, took secret documents home and showed them to strangers. I. G. Khanovich, head of a department in the Krylov Academy of Leningrad, a man who admired objects from abroad, wrote a number of books in which he revealed secret data concerning Soviet inventions that he obtained from a research institute.[16] It was thus possible to discern in the Khanovich story points of contact between "cosmopolitanism" and concrete security offenses.

The center of a more complicated and dramatic espionage libel was occupied by a certain S. Gurevitz, an old-time Trotskyite who had grown up in a Menshevik home and had been a member of the Jewish socialist Bund. In the period 1914–17, he lived in the United States and on his return to Russia, he became an active participant in an anti-Soviet Trotskyite group; in 1927 he gave the Party a declaration of renouncing Trotskyism, but this was only pretense. In 1939 he established ties with a foreign intelligence agency and for years, he supplied it with espionage information which he secured by means of other collaborators.[17] A man by the name of Gurevitz actually was known in the circles of Western representatives in Moscow, who chiefly regarded him as a person authorized to keep in touch with foreign correspondents. This gave rise to the impression that Gurevitz was liable to serve in an imminent show trial (perhaps the doctors' trial) as one of the "living exhibits" to prove the existence of connections between traitors from the Soviet Union and American diplomats and correspondents in Moscow.[18] It should be pointed out that about three weeks before the publication of the Gurevitz libel, the Bund was mentioned in an article by Frol Kozlov, the Party district secretary in Leningrad, among the foreign elements connected with "bourgeois, nationalist, counterrevolutionary elements" which had infiltrated the Party.[19]

Security dangers and violations were pointed to by reports of the discovery of Jewish, bourgeois, nationalist or explicit "Zionist nests" in various places. A Zionist nest was discovered at the University of Odessa.[20] A man by the name of Eisen, a member of an anti-Soviet Zionist organization was active in the ministry of education of the Moldavian Republic. Another bourgeois nationalist in Moldavia was a man by the name of Buchumensky, a senior engineer in the department for construction planning.[21] Zionists infiltrated enterprises and institutions in Ashkhabad, the capital of the Turkestan Republic.[22] Zionist-imperialist spies were active in Latvia. Sometimes a Zionist coloring was given to reports of economic crimes; the accounts stated that the guilty persons had carried out thefts and fraudulent activities for Israel's benefit or at the inspiration of nationalist "nests." Thus, Zionism was raised to the degree of a daily, concrete enemy of the Soviet people. Now and then Zionist traitors were mentioned together with other nationalist enemies. According to reports, bourgeois nationalists, cosmopolitans, and stateless persons, both Jews and Lithuanians, were discovered in Lithuania engaged in espionage and sabotage in the service of American imperialism. Jewish and Ukrainian bourgeois nationalism and Zionism were mentioned at a Komsomol meeting in Kiev as the abominable agents of American imperialism.[23] The manifestations of Ukrainian and Lithuanian nationalism troubled the Soviet authorities and their bracketing with Jewish nationalism and Zionism was designed to add still another black mark to their names. This combination was also calculated to serve as a severe warning to various nationalist elements since it was obvious what sharp measures were taken against Jewish nationalists.

There is interesting testimony of the reflection of the "Jewish policy" in prison camps from the time of the doctors' affair. Behind barbed-wire fences Jewish prisoners sensed the climate in the country. In many places they were excluded from easier kinds of work and from responsible duties. German prisoners and persons sentenced to prison for collaborating with the Nazis began to assume a lofty bearing towards them. Various kinds of Jew-haters took courage as if they once more sniffed the approach of propitious times. In some cases, they made threatening remarks to their fellow prisoners of Jewish origin in the style of "Your end is coming nearer." In the camps there was much talk of many doctors, even professors, due to arrive soon from Moscow. It was being said that for a long time, Jews were not seen in the camps because Kaganovich used to protect them, but they had finally all been caught and incarcerated.[24] Members of the security and administrative staffs at the camps made frequent anti-Semitic remarks. It seems that the close ties between Israel and American imperialism were well known in the isolated country of persons deprived of their freedom, and served as a pretext for picking on Jews. At the beginning of 1953 a rumor spread throughout the northern camps that on a flight from New York to Canada Israel's prime minister David Ben-Gurion, the widow of Israel's first president, Vera Weizmann, and a number of Israeli ministers and top-ranking army officers, as well as American Zionist leaders, all of whom had been active in the United States on behalf of a big campaign for Israel, had been killed in an airplane accident. A former prisoner who told the writer about this rumor assumed that its dissemination had been a deliberately planned act of the MGB (ministry for state security) for the purpose of finding out on the basis of reactions to the tragedy which prisoners were interested in Israel and were grieving at the death of her leaders. On the strength of such reactions, the authorities could lay their hands on Zionists and also learn who the Jewish leaders in the camps were. It may also be that the subterfuge was necessary in order to make preparations for a "Zionist trial."[25]

Everything "impossible" became reasonable during Stalin's last days. Vyacheslav Molotov's wife, the Jewess Pauline Zhemchuzhina Molotov, was exiled from Moscow.[26] Among her sins there probably figured the following: in addition to having a brother living in the United States, she had been cordial to Mrs. Golda Meir on the Israeli minister's arrival in Moscow and could not conceal her excitement at the establishment of the state of Israel; during a reception which Molotov, as commissar for foreign affairs, gave on November 7, 1948, in honor of the anniversary of the revolution, Mrs. Molotov said to the Israeli minister in Yiddish, *"Ich bin a Yiddishe tochter"* ("I am a Jewish daughter"), a phrase with warmer overtones than a merely factual "I am Jewish." She also said, "May things go well with you [meaning Israel]. If all will be well with you, things will go well for Jews in the whole world."[27]

If, according to various signs, "anti-Semitism had become the secret policy of the Stalin regime"[28] in its final years, the implementation of this "secret policy" became obvious and open during the last months of the dictator's life, particularly since publication of the "chronicle," as it was termed (the announcement of January 13, 1953), about which the *New York Times* correspondent in Moscow reported, "It chilled my blood."[29] In fact, the atmosphere which subsequently settled over the country went beyond the "everyday fear" to which people had become accustomed; there was a feeling that an unusual terror was beginning, "Terror with a capital T."[30] The horror years of Yezhov and Yagoda came to mind, but it could certainly be said that "the bloodshed of the Thirties would have seemed but a few drops compared with the slaughter which was being prepared in the weeks before the old dictator met his death."[31]

Fear of what was to come was not felt by Jews alone but encompassed various circles. At this point the influence of the anticipated "Terror with a capital T" on Stalin's comrades-in-arms (as other Soviet top-flight leaders were called) should be discussed in greater detail.

These men well knew that in addition to political considerations, the aging dictator was also guided by clear pathological motives by which he was trapped. His suspicion assumed unusual dimensions, even by comparison with the morbid suspicion with which his associates had long been familiar. His nose — always exaggerated — for all kinds of "oppositions" and attempted "plots" against him sharpened to the extent of constituting an immediate danger to their safety. Khrushchev related in his "secret" speech at the Twentieth Congress that "Stalin toyed [also] with the absurd and ridiculous suspicion that Voroshilov was an English agent. . . . A special tapping device was installed in his home to listen to what was said there. . . . Stalin forbade him [Voroshilov] to attend the Political Bureau sessions and to receive documents. . . . It is not excluded that had Stalin remained at the helm for another few months, Comrades Molotov and Mikoyan would probably not have delivered any speeches at this Congress." Quoting Bulganin, Khrushchev went on to say, "It has happened sometimes that a man goes to Stalin on his invitation as a friend. And when he sits with Stalin, he does not know where he will be sent next, home or to jail." And, in general, "Stalin evidently had plans to finish off the old members of the Political Bureau."[32]

And so it happened that while Stalin was often imagining himself surrounded by "enemies of the people" or his personal foes, his associates were troubled by the question where would the Terror stop. They outdid each other in panegyrics to the *vozhd* (leader) and competed with each other in calling for vigilance, fully aware at the same time that they themselves had to be unusually alert in face of the potential threat to their existence by the "Great Father." The unprecedented expansion of the Politburo (the name of which was changed to "presidium") on October 16, 1952, after the Nineteenth Party Congress (October 5–14, 1952) from twelve members to twenty-five as well as increasing the number of alternate members to eleven and doubling the members of the Party secretariat to ten — all brought home to the members of the Old Guard the dangers facing them. Being well acquainted with Stalin's character and experienced with his techniques, they detected in these moves his intention to prepare a new, obedient group of leaders who would supplant them. It is certainly not by chance that as early as March 6, 1953, before Stalin's body had grown cold, his successors hastened once more to reduce the presidium to ten members and the number of alternate members to four, removing nearly all the new faces from it.

Stalin was a crafty, ruthless ruler. But his entire court was never a school for moral rectitude. During Stalin's last years it must certainly have been ridden with corruption and crawled with ambitions and intrigues. Stalin's "comrades-in-arms," as much as each and everyone of them seemed to be a fearful ruler, knew that their position and privileges had been granted to them only on his sufferance. In this connection, an apparently paradoxical situation developed. In their search for ways to save themselves, Stalin's servants, who were the foreordained victims of his persecution complex, fed this complex.

They trembled at his manic behavior, but at the same time, they inflated and encouraged his suspicions. As his loyal followers and protectors, as it were, for the purpose of winning his affection, they allowed accounts or whisperings to get through to him of various enemies secretly bent on harming the country and him. It may be assumed that by this cunning bit of work they wanted not only to make themselves safe from him in the present but also to assure themselves a part in the legacy, for the struggle of the gods over it on the Red Olympus began while Zeus himself was still alive.

It should be mentioned that "enemies" became the daily bread of Soviet totalitarian rule. They were necessary as emotional cement holding society together, for justifying supervision and speeding up the tempo of work, for reasons of "morale," and for concealing all kinds of defects and mistakes. While preserving the Communist-papal principle of infallibility, the real or imaginary enemies had almost a permanent function in clarifying various situations — it is their fault that the state has not yet "withered away," that the Communist messianic age is late in coming, that tanks come before butter, and so on. In addition, the regime almost always needed internal "enemies" parallel with foreign ones. And in the late 1940's where was there a "convenient" source of supply for these? It was only with bitter irony that one could recall at the time that at the beginning of 1934, in his speech to the Seventeenth Party Congress ("The Congress of Victors"), Stalin said in citing the defeat of certain anti-Leninist groups, that "It seems there is nobody to beat." However, about fifteen years later, after the mighty triumph over Germany when the Soviet Union was at the peak of her international status and when there was not the trace of a threat to Stalin's absolute rule (Trotsky had long before that been killed), what internal "enemy" could still easily be "digested" by the imagination of the masses? Accordingly, the new witch-hunt was directed against the Jews collectively, especially since reports and rumors of Jewish sins, including their evil plots, were easily taken in by Stalin's imagination.

But once more, as time passed, particularly during the final months of Stalin's life, the "enemy" hysteria and its turbid anti-Jewish wave also began threatening Stalin's entourage, or part of it, which had been participating in its nurturing. In the doctors' libel and the bracketing of Soviet Jews together with the conspiracies of foreign intelligence services, chiefly the American, it manufactured a perfect specimen, as it were, of a "desirable" enemy. And the danger of that hysteria to the lackeys of the ruler themselves assumed a concrete form.

Against this background, certain questions concerning the place and function of Lavrenti Beria during the "black years" in general and the doctors' affair in particular may become clarified. These questions deserve to be studied since they shed light on the state of affairs during Stalin's final years — a state of affairs the principles of which a Polish poet defined as "Fascization, demoralization, and careerism."[33]

After having served as head of the police and later, as Party secretary in Georgia, Beria became director of the NKVD in 1938. In 1946 the powers in matters concerning internal security were divided between two ministries, the ministry of the interior (MVD) and the ministry for state security (MGB) with separate ministers. However, there were various indications to show that the supervision of both of them remained in the hands of Beria, who had been appointed deputy prime minister. And, indeed, just as after his transfer to Moscow his loyal followers and protégés remained in key positions in Georgia (sometimes this republic was considered to be a sort of personal bailiwick of his), so both arms of the security service (after its division) with their headquarters in Moscow continued to be manned by his men. Of special interest is Viktor Abakumov, one of Beria's cronies, who served as minister of state security during the late 1940's and in 1951.

The power concentrated by Beria continued to grow. He also controlled the forces of internal security. By means of the "prisoners' kingdom," he exerted a great deal of influence on manpower, development programs, and the national economy. According to certain sources, the supervision of the development of atomic energy was entrusted to him after the war. There is no doubt that his swift rise was due to his personal loyalty to Stalin. He not only did the practical dirty work for his master, particularly in the purges, but was also one of the leading architects of his personality cult (which included writing a prerevolution history of the Bolshevik organization in Transcaucasia, so distorted that it became "simply Stalinist hagiography").[34] It may be assumed that, knowing his master's mind, he fed him with apprehensions of all kinds of enemies and even succeeded in implanting in him suspicion of all those who surrounded him. By this method of inflating external and domestic dangers and plots, he struck directly at Stalin's psychological traits while convincing him of the need to strengthen the power of the police under his supervision.

However, because of Stalin's personal nature and the character of the Stalinist regime, this method of Beria's had a sort of "dialectic" of its own. Who better than Stalin realized that a secret police has an internal developmental logic of its own, that in its expansion and growth it tends to free itself of external obedience and becomes a state within a state? It is quite certain that in the personal organization at his disposal he established arms parallel to the various departments of the government and the Party to serve as his eyes and ears — just like in the security institutions under Beria;[35] and even when Beria himself was at the peak of his power, Stalin never fully trusted him, even while honoring him. Moreover, eventually Stalin must have come to the conclusion that the "Moor" had already done his work and the time had come for him to go, just as previously, the time for getting rid of Beria's precursors, Yagoda and Yezhov, had come. Their loyal service to Stalin and their collaboration in his crimes had not conferred immunity on them; on the contrary, when the time came, they seemed to be the most fit for serving as scapegoats. At any rate, it was difficult to gamble on privileges which fate, for some reason or other, had bestowed on Beria.

There can be no doubt that Beria had had an active guiding hand in the postwar terror operations, without excluding the acts against Jews. But, as the scope of the witch-hunt grew, Beria's position became more shaky. Despite the fact that in November 1951 he was still the most important speaker on the thirty-fourth anniversary of the revolution, he himself must have already then begun to sense that he was no longer on firm ground — experienced cynic and sadist that he was. He should have been afraid of the accelerated intensification of the measures against national minorities which was conducted as a struggle against bourgeois nationalism, especially since Georgia was one of its prominent theaters. The fact that Stalin was also a native of Georgia could not calm his fears; Stalin had long before ceased to have the label of a minority attached to him and could decide to what minority a person belonged according to whatever current considerations he found convenient. Beria's fears were also grounded in actual events. During this period (November 1951), a group of leaders of the Mingrelian minority (close to the Georgians) — the racial stock of Beria and some of his followers — were arrested. They were charged with a Mingrelian nationalist plot. In 1952, there was a series of purges in Georgia, Beria's home territory, which brought a number of persons hostile to him to power — one of them was A. Mgeladze, who became the first secretary of the Party in the republic — to supplant his supporters. The fact that the new key men in Georgia paid lip service to Beria and that he himself bestowed his blessing on these purges can testify to the political morality which prevailed in the Stalinist-Soviet jungle of intrigues but by no means to Beria's real position and feeling. The action in Georgia was a planned blow against him. Actually, it was not the first sign of the decline of his prestige. His position at the Party center became more precarious. In effect, his "kingdom" was slipping out of his hands. At the end of 1951 or the beginning of 1952, Abakumov, who had been a loyal follower of Beria since the Caucasus period, as pointed out above, was replaced as minister for state security by Semyon Ignatiev, a known enemy of Beria.[36] Mikhail Ryumin, who had evidently before that been in charge of matters concerning state security in Stalin's personal secretariat, began serving as Ignatiev's deputy, or one of his deputies. Ryumin was also appointed head of the investigation department in the ministry for state security and was the man responsible for investigating the "murderers in white gowns" which was conducted under Stalin's supervision. There are grounds for supposing that Ignatiev and Ryumin were also assigned the duty of compiling a dossier against Beria by means of the doctors' affair.

It should be mentioned that the *Pravda* article of January 13, 1953, concerning the discovery of the Doctors' Plot denounced "the agencies of state security [which] did not discover the doctors' wrecking, terrorist organization *in time*" (italics added). "In time" refers to the period when Beria's men controlled the security services since, after all, the Doctors' Plot was discovered when the ministry for state security was already in the hands of Ignatiev and Ryumin. The numerous accusations in the Soviet press concerning the criminal "sleepiness" (that is, lack of vigilance) of the institutions of state security in connection with the Doctors' Plot expressly referred to Beria and his loyal followers, since they had been in charge of these institutions when the physicians succeeded in murdering Shcherbakov (1945) and in hastening Zhdanov's death (1948).

It is not impossible that the stock of future accusations against Beria also held in reserve aid to Zionism. It should be recalled that he had been active — after the German invasion of the Soviet Union — in making the initial contacts for the establishment of a Jewish anti-Fascist committee, and the committee discussed then was supposed to have been worldwide. If the assumption is correct that he had an important part in the initiative to send a Jewish delegation from the USSR (Mikhoels, Feffer) to Jewish communities in other countries, it is possible to implicate him in the Joint's network and its plots.

In any case, here and there rumors were heard to the effect that Beria was of Jewish extraction — some people even said that he had changed his real name, Berman or Berenson, to a Georgian-sounding one — or was partly Jewish, on his mother's side. The rumors were evidently figments of somebody's imagination, but it is a fact that in Georgia, Beria was spoken of as a friend of the Jews, and people told of his sympathetic attitude to the Jewish communities in the republic. As special proof of his favorable attitude towards Jews it was possible to point to the Jewish Ethnological Museum at Tiflis (Tbilisi) which was founded at his initiative; its wealth of exhibits had no antireligious flavor and was actually designed to encourage awareness of the Jewish historical heritage and stimulate admiration for it. The fact that it remained open for at least part of the "black years" could be taken as another indication of Beria's love of the Jews. Beria may also be credited with the fact that there was still a relatively large number of Jews in the institutions of internal security even after a clear anti-Jewish policy had been introduced into various other sensitive organizations.[37] In a word, it was possible, if not to discover Jewish blood in Beria's veins, then at least to dig up, when necessary, material for accusing him of encouraging Jewish nationalism.

The assumption that Beria and his men had been designed as victims of punitive action by means of the doctors' affair is strengthened by a series of happenings which occurred immediately after Stalin's death, although for the most part, they are connected with the struggle over succession. The first was the reunification of the two arms of internal security into a single ministry of the interior (MVD) under Beria's command; this was done with striking haste, within twenty-four hours after the announcement of Stalin's death. Apparently, Beria returned to rehabilitate himself in his old base of power from which he counterattacked those who had forced him out of that base and had planned additional acts for his downfall.

Within a short time, a "purge of the purgers" began, inspired by Beria at the return of his loyal followers, the victims of his enemies, to key positions, especially in Georgia, his former fortress, but also in other places. In the middle of April 1953, it was reported that the Party secretary in Georgia, A. Mgeladze, the republic's minister of the interior, N. Rukhadze, and others had been charged with violating the rights of citizens, extracting confessions by illegal means, and of juridical libel which also consisted of false accusations of nationalism — a clear allusion to the "Mingrelian Affair." It should also be noted that when the Party presidium was again reduced to ten members and four candidates right after Stalin's death, there was only one among them, M. Bagirov, who had not been a member of the expanded presidium selected after the Nineteenth Congress; he, too, was well known for his loyalty to Beria and had been an old collaborator of his since the Caucasus period. On the other hand, Semyon Ignatiev, who had been a member of the expanded presidium, was not taken into the new presidium, not even as a candidate for membership.[38]

But above all, it is significant that it was the ministry of the interior under Beria which announced the quashing of the Doctors' Plot and cited the nationalist incitement involved.

It can be established that Beria's decline and the fate which awaited him according to the signs appearing at the publication of the doctors' affair caused no concern to Stalin's other "comrades-in-arms." On the contrary, they, too, were disturbed at his growing power, which was certainly nourished by his proximity to Stalin. It may be conjectured that not only did they regard the deterioration in confidential relations between the two with satisfaction, but they also contributed to it with intrigues as best they could. For the purpose of cutting Beria down to size or catching him in a trap they would not even recoil from a crude use of anti-Semitic methods.

But Stalin's entourage quickly learned that Beria and his men were only one object of the dictator's goals. The doctors' affair, the anti-Jewish nature of which was clear from the beginning, seemed to be branching out in a number of directions. Charges against various persons responsible for economic and administrative matters began to accompany denunciations of the security organizations. In this way, every VIP was able to see himself next in line for dismissal, exile, arrest, show trial, and execution. For this reason, the doctors' libel also aroused the opposition of persons who had previously contributed to Stalin's anti-Semitic hysteria and had participated in the anti-Semitic operations of the "black years." Under these circumstances, a sort of ad hoc front of men of the Old Guard apparently began to take shape against Stalin and the new leaders whom he had just elevated to power. Even Georgi Malenkov, who had been portrayed as a figure midway between the two generations of leaders, was not able to feel secure; it was to him that Stalin had handed his mantle, as it were, by letting him deliver the principal speech — the report of the Central Committee — at the Nineteenth Congress. If his peace of mind was not disturbed by the escalation of anti-Semitic activities and propaganda, waves of criticism and measures taken against persons from administrative and technocratic circles to which he could be regarded close gave him the danger signal.[39] This unique state of affairs during Stalin's final months provides the logic for various speculations which suggest the possibility that Stalin's "comrades-in-arms" had a hand either in his death or in hastening his end. This point is likely to remain hypothetical forever, but, as the *New York Times* correspondent in Moscow wrote: "While murder cannot be proved there is no question that motive to murder existed. For . . . if Stalin was dying a natural death it was the luckiest thing that had ever happened to the men who stood closest to him."[40]

But as long as the new waves of terror were likely to wash over not only Jews, but over additional circles and individuals, there were clear indications that "Stalin was resorting to anti-Semitism as a basis for a new purge."[41] It was possible to detect signs of the *Protocols of the Elders of Zion* of the beginning of the century. There was nothing missing: the *kahal* with its secret plots, the talent for disguise and pretense (the "humanitarian" Joint), Jewish world domination (from the "banks of the Hudson" and the shores of the Thames to Moscow, from Tel Aviv to Prague), greed, and blood lust.

There is interesting literary evidence of the Doctors' Plot and its times in the phantasmagoric story written by Andrei Sinyavsky, who called himself Abram Tertz, entitled *The Trial Begins.* The two leading characters in the story are the public prosecutor Globov and the citizen Rabinovich. The latter is a gynecologist charged with having unlawfully procured an abortion. For the prosecutor, Rabinovich is neither just a name or a personal "file." His heart and mind are in advance inclined to the "collectivization" of the case which he is handling. Globov is proud that he was the one who exposed not merely Rabinovich but Rabinovich as a symbol. For him this name is almost automatically associated with Trotsky, Radek, Zinoviev, and Kamenev, with "homeless cosmopolitans . . . people with an inborn love of treachery."

Actually, he "had already had occasion to prosecute at least one Rabinovich," he recalls, "if not two or three. Indeed, they were too many to remember." The times of the trial and the case against the last Rabinovich are reflected not only in his occupation and the nature of the charges against him. In Globov's words, "Every schoolboy knew today that these people with their petty-bourgeois instincts were born enemies of socialism." In one part of the story, a certain interrogator explains his Rabinovich case to the prosecutor: "Needless to say, he's not the only one. . . . It's on a country-wide scale, my dear fellow. . . . Medicine! See what I mean? And all . . . you know — these chaps with long noses . . . cosmopolitans! every one . . . ." This explanation corresponds very well to the words which Globov says in the courtroom before the judge's vacant seat at night while rehearsing his speech: "No Rabinoviches shall undermine the basis of our society, we shall not allow our enemies to destroy us. It is we who shall destroy them!"[42]

And in fact, the Jewish population felt that the mighty power of the government was directed against it. Jews were exposed to a ceaseless barrage of suspicions, libels, and accusations. Anti-Semitic elements felt the backing given to their sentiments by the authorities. The air was saturated with venom which was felt more sharply in places where people rubbed elbows — in stores, clinics, public transportation, and in the common areas of dwellings. Now and then at meetings of tenants demands were made to forbid Jewish tenants to use the common kitchen and toilets, as a precautionary measure against their poisoning plots. Mixed couples suffered special distress and agony. There were cases of non-Jews loyally sharing the tragic fate of their Jewish spouses. But there were also incidents of divorces — some of them fictitious, until the storm would blow over, and some of them real, under the influence of the atmosphere or the pressure of the environment. This was a period when Jews began to be dismissed from their jobs without the need of special pretexts. In various places of employment, Jews were abused and there were not a few incidents of physical violence. In the lines which formed it was possible to hear the Jews addressed in the following language: "Hey, Joint, move!" or "Go to America!" and "Go to Israel!" There were cases of Jews being thrown off public transport. Jew hatred was transmitted from adults to children and it found unbridled expression in schools, youth clubs, streets, and neighborhood yards.[43]

A sort of borderline situation prevailed in an atmosphere suggesting the beginning of actual pogroms. This term *pogrom,* which during the period of the Tsars was donated to the world's dictionary by the Russian language, seemed during the last months of Stalin's rule to return to its native land.

A Russian woman from the Rostov district wrote to a Russian friend of hers: "You know that I have always been hostile to the Jews; but you also know that I do not overdo things. But I must admit that never in my dreams had I foreseen for the Jews what is befalling them now. They are being persecuted and driven out of every place; they are being persecuted horribly. They do not dare show themselves in the streets. In my youth, I saw rioting, but now, not only feathers from Jews' pillows are flying in the air but their lives are also in danger. And now certainly no one can come to their aid."[44]

The contempt and hatred of the Jews dished out daily by the Soviet press rang with the tone of the old Russian slogan, "Beat the Jews, save Russia!" In view of the signs of mutual understanding between the mobs and the authorities, the Jews found themselves isolated. Unlike the gloomy times of the Tsarist period, they no longer had any hopes of protests by writers such as Tolstoy, Saltykov-Shchedrin, Korolenko, or Gorky. The Russian conscience was paralyzed and in the course of degeneration of the Stalinist regime, the Soviet intellectuals reconciled themselves with helpless obsequiousness — where they did not actually collaborate — to its atrocities. There were certainly numerous Russians who were touched by the Jews' conditions, and some regarded the official policy as a disgrace to Russia, like the person who in strict privacy said, "After all this I am ashamed of being a Russian."[45] But generally, even this kind of person had to stifle his pain inside him.

Jews as such, without excepting persons who had long lost their mental and cultural ties with their origins, Jews of various classes and with diverse occupations regarded the doctors' affair as an immediate, concrete threat against them. Many of them were dominated by a feeling of resignation. They were ready for the worst. Some anticipated coming events by committing suicide. Preparing a bundle to take along on a journey to the unknown became a common feature of Jewish life.

Various details support the assumption that in the period between publication of the announcement about the Doctors' Plot — January 13, 1953 — and the first official communiqué of Stalin's illness, the dictator crystallized a plan which had been in his mind previously — of the mass evacuation of Jews from many regions of the Soviet Union, particularly from the western areas, to remote eastern and northern parts of the country. This plan was to have been carried out in an inflamed atmosphere of mass anger against people of the same origins as the "murderers in white gowns." At the publication of the doctors' sentence (expected in the near future) the organized exile of Jews would have either looked like a response to the demands of the "people" for punishing the open and secret partners of the traitors or as a preventive measure for the "defense" of Jews against attempts by the masses to take the law into their hands.

Activities at the two ends of the great operation — areas from which Jews were to be expelled and places designed to take them —

served as evidence of the decision of mass expulsion. In the first, it was possible to detect unusual steps to prepare the means of transportation for mass movements of people; and in the latter, obvious preparations were being made to set up an inordinate number of dwelling huts with the addition of an increased supply of materials such as rolls of barbed wire. On the basis of anticipated transports of Jews, various enterprises in outlying areas were promised additional "manpower" to enable them to maintain and expand their production quotas.[46] Birobidzhan may also have been included in the list of places designed to take in the expelled; probably because of its desolate areas and distance rather than its "autonomous" status. Other objectives were Siberia, the steppes of Kazakhstan, and the Arctic region.

Although many people could not logically digest the thought of such a mass expulsion, if only because of the economic and technical complications involved (among other things they were troubled by the question of filling the positions which would become vacant almost simultaneously in various enterprises and services), the feeling grew that a Jew's turn for being taken from one town or another depended only on a timetable now being prepared or already drawn up. Among the non-Jewish population there were people who openly spoke of the apartments which would be vacated and some already had their eyes on property which the expelled would leave behind.

The planning and practical preparations for the expulsion operation were apparently executed by the MGB institutions and men from Stalin's personal office. But Stalin — according to certain sources — also presented the plan (evidently after its crystallization) to the presidium of the Central Committee. It cannot be assumed that the members of this institution had no previous knowledge at all of the plan but it is possible to conjecture that they did not dare ask Stalin about it — or express an opinion about it — on their own initiative. However, when the dictator himself presented it to them at a meeting held at the end of February 1953, it evoked reactions among some of the old members. They may really have been surprised at the overall dimensions of the plan and they could not easily accept its far-reaching brutality. Perhaps they feared a political and economic decline in the country or foreign reactions, within the world Communist movement, too, in the wake of such an uncurbed adventure in violence. And among these last survivors of the "October Generation," there might have glimmered sparks of conscience which deterred them from a new terror. And above all, there is no doubt that their sixth sense, which had become sharpened during the years of terror, signaled the dangers to themselves.

For one reason or another, or because of all of them combined, there were some who dared express reservations of Stalin's plan; this very boldness was enough to surprise the dictator. The impression is that at the outset, the manifestations of opposition to the expulsion plan did not go beyond attempts to clarify its scope and soften its impact somewhat. Thus, the story is told that Kaganovich — the only Jew on the presidium — wanted to know whether or not the plan was designed for *all* the Jews of the Soviet Union without exception, and Stalin replied that a "certain selection" would be made. Molotov — the man who for many years had been in charge of the USSR's foreign relations — called attention to the bad impression that the expulsion would have on world public opinion. Mikoyan spoke in a similar vein. More firm and militant was Marshal Voroshilov who argued that the plan was terrible and that acts like these had aroused the world against Hitler. The story has it that Voroshilov even threw his Party membership card down on the table, saying that the projected measures violated the honor of the Party and if they were carried out, he would be ashamed of being a member; at this, Stalin became enraged and the fury brought on a stroke from which he never recovered. As much as it is impossible to guarantee the accuracy of the details cited above, it is reasonable that there were certain reservations concerning the expulsion plan among the Soviet Union's top leaders. In any case, existence of the expulsion plan itself has been confirmed by important testimony.[47]

It was not until Stalin's death that the nightmares which had begun to envelop the Jews of the Soviet Union during his last months began to fade. Officially the doctors' libel was not quashed until a month later, but unofficially, it almost disappeared right after March 5, 1953. Its absence from the important newspapers was particularly striking since in January and February, their readers had become accustomed to finding it there nearly every day. Some space was still devoted to the doctor-murderers in a number of regional and local newspapers, but this was apparently the result of inertia or faulty coordination and contacts between the center of power and the periphery in the first weeks after Stalin's death. The coincidence of the disappearance of the doctors' libel and the end of the dictator speaks for itself, although the day before his death, Moscow's Chief Rabbi, like other religious dignitaries, prayed for him and called upon the members of his congregation to fast and pray for his life.[48]

The official annulment of the doctors' libel came with the publication of an announcement by the ministry of the interior on April 4, 1953, which put an end — according to one definition — to "eighty-two days of anxiety" (from January 13 until that date) of the Jews of the Soviet Union.[49]

The following is the announcement in full:

The USSR Ministry of Internal Affairs has carried out a thorough verification of all the preliminary investigation data and other material in the case of the group of doctors accused of sabotage, espionage and terrorist acts against active leaders of the Soviet state.

The verification has established that the accused in this case, Professors M. S. Vofsi, V. N. Vinogradov, M. B. Kogan, B. B. Kogan, P. I. Yegorov, A. I. Feldman, Y. G. Etinger, V. K. Vasilenko, A. M. Grinshtein, V. F. Zelenin, B. S. Preobrazhensky, N. A. Popova, V. V. Zakusov and N. A. Sheresevsky and Dr. G. I. Mayorov, were arrested by the former USSR Ministry of State Security incorrectly without any lawful basis.

Verification has shown that the accusations against the above-named persons are false and the documentary sources on which the investigating officials based themselves are without foundation.

It was established that the testimony of the arrested, allegedly confirming the accusations against them, was obtained by the officials of the investigatory department of the former Ministry of State Security through the use of impermissible means of investigation which are strictly forbidden under Soviet law.

On the basis of the conclusion of an investigatory commission especially appointed by the USSR Ministry of Internal Affairs to check this case, the arrested M. S. Vofsi, V. N. Vinogradov, B. B. Kogan, P. I. Yegorov, A. I. Feldman, V. K. Vasilenko, A. M. Grinshtein, V. F. Zelenin, B. S. Preobrazhensky, N. A. Popova, V. V. Zakusov, N. A. Shereshevsky and G. A. Mayorov and others accused in this case have been completely exonerated of the accusations against them of sabotage, terrorist and espionage activities, and, in accord with Article 4, Paragraph 5, of the Criminal Procedure Code of the Russian Republic, have been freed from imprisonment.

The persons accused of incorrect conduct of the investigation have been arrested and brought to criminal responsibility.[50]

A study of this announcement and its comparison with the one issued on January 13 shows that the list of names of the arrested persons in both do not overlap. First of all, two names are conspicuously absent from the list of the persons exonerated, Professors M. B. Kogan and Y. G. Etinger. They quite probably died in prison and it is not farfetched to conjecture that the tortures inflicted on them hastened their end. On the other hand, the exoneration announcement contains six new names of accused persons: Professors Vasilenko, Zelenin, Preobrazhensky, Popova, Zakusov, and Shereshevsky. Of all these names, only the last may attest to the Jewish origin of the person bearing it. The new "ethnic" picture of the victims of the doctors' libel shows a majority of one non-Jew to Jews — eight to seven. The names can of course be misleading as far as the person's origins are concerned — the list of the persons exonerated ends with the phrase "and others" — but apparently the new proportion was presented to the public deliberately and perhaps the January 13 announcement did not mention the names of all the doctors who had been arrested; there may have been more arrests during the period between that announcement and Stalin's death. It should be noted also that despite the fact that the savage agitation against Jews in the Soviet press dwindled immediately after Stalin's death and at the beginning of April nearly ceased, the exoneration announcement does not contain a word about the Joint, Zionism, or Jewish bourgeois nationalists. Thus, it omitted all details which gave the structure of lies of the doctors' libel its unmistakable anti-Semitic coloring.

But the very public admission of the lack of any foundation to the accusations which the officials of the "former Ministry of State Security" had made against the doctors and their release was enough to make it possible for Soviet citizens, Jews particularly, to breathe more easily. In addition, on the same day on which the announcement of the exoneration of the doctors was published, on April 4, 1953, the presidium of the Supreme Soviet announced that Dr. Lydia Timashuk had been deprived of the Order of Lenin. It had been this "model woman" and "hero of the people," the winner of the highest decoration for her contribution to the discovery of the gang of doctors, who had two and one half months previously symbolized the authorities' blessing on the upsurge of anti-Semitic feeling.[51] Additional relief came to the Jews two days later, on April 6, 1953, with the publication of an editorial in *Pravda* entitled "Soviet Socialist Law is Inviolable" which was devoted to a retraction of the doctors' libel and to conclusions arising from the affair. The article laid the principal responsibility for the false accusations on the deputy minister for state security and on the ministry's director of the department of investigation, Ryumin (the article stated that he had been arrested), and it denounced Ignatiev, the minister for state security, for having "displayed political blindness and heedlessness" and for having been led around "by such criminal adventurers as Ryumin." The Jews paid special attention to that part of the editorial which said that by their false investigation "despicable adventurers of the Ryumin type tried . . . to inflame in Soviet society . . . feelings of national antagonism, which are profoundly alien to socialist ideology. For these provocational ends they did not stop at mad slander of Soviet people. Careful investigation has established, for example, that an honest public figure, USSR People's Artist [Solomon] Mikhoels, was slandered in this way."[52]

Thus, indirectly, Mikhoels, who in the "chronicle" of January 13 had been presented as one of the chief contact men between the Joint in the United States and the terrorist gang of doctors, was exonerated. Once again, although nothing was said in the article about quashing the charges against the Joint itself or other Jewish organizations, this conclusion followed logically and by association. The mention of inflaming "feelings of national antagonism" suggests an indirect admission that the doctors' libel had been designed to harm the Jews — if only in view of the national composition of the gang of "murderers in white gowns" fabricated by the corrupt investigators. It is thus no wonder that the days of April 4–6, 1953, aroused hope among the Jews of the Soviet Union of a "new page" in the policy of the authorities (Stalin's successors) towards them. At any rate, so great was the fatalistic anticipation of serious events in the wake of the doctors' libel that the Jews spoke of its annulment as of the cessation of a plague.

TWELVE

Premeditated Anti-Semitism

On reaching the limits of this study — Stalin's death and the annulment of the doctors' libel — we shall summarize a number of questions on the motives of the "Jewish policy" in the "black years," although they have been discussed in various chapters.

To regard the Soviet regime as a "secular theocracy" encourages attempts to seek ideological sources likely to nourish its anti-Jewish acts. This search is aided by the fact that a number of assumptions made by Lenin and Stalin which looked upon a Jewish national existence negatively or disparagingly basically foresaw assimilation for the Jews as both inevitable and desirable.

These assumptions were formed even before the October Revolution. In part they stemmed from Lenin's basic conception, which was derived from other Marxist thinkers, that the merging of nations and cultures is a progressive process. Of the two opposing tendencies which Lenin found in the later development of capitalism, one leading to the crystallization of separate nations and the other to the obliteration of national differences and assimilation, he welcomed the latter. In this connection he wrote that whoever is not ridden with national prejudices cannot help seeing great historical progress in the process of capitalism leading to the assimilation of nations. As for socialism, according to Lenin, it aims at the formation of an international proletarian culture which will constitute a synthesis of everything positive in the various national cultures.

Lenin's approach to the Jewish question suited his general conception concerning "historical progress" in the national sphere. That is the reason he regarded the best in Jewish culture and tradition to be their internationalist and assimilationist trends whereas their isolationist tendencies appeared as signs of backwardness to him. From this point of view, for example, he set up the "civilized world" of Western Europe and the United States, where the prospects of rapid assimilation of the Jews are good, as an ideal to be emulated by backward Galicia and Russia and their Jewish populations. Lenin abominated anti-Semitism and fought it, considering also Jewish separatism an outgrowth of the laws of discrimination and restrictions — "the fault of the Purishkevichs." He was in full agreement with Karl Kautsky who said that the only possible solution to the Jewish problem is merging the Jews with the "general mass of the population." Lenin believed that the idea of a separate Jewish people is scientifically groundless and politically reactionary.

This position of Lenin's also stemmed from actual political considerations. The strategist of the revolution saw the prospects of its realization dependent on party centralism. Among his strong fears of the centrifugal, detrimental influence of autonomous and federative trends on the organized revolutionary proletariat, he regarded as particularly concrete the danger presented by the strivings for autonomy in the ideology of the Jewish Socialist Bund. His hatred of the Bund and his fierce war against it apparently strengthened Lenin's negative attitude to the manifestations and aspirations of Jewish separatism.[1]

Stalin's concepts on the national question in general and in relation to the Jews in particular were developed along the lines of Lenin's thinking, but expressed more decisively and sometimes quite vulgarly. He treated Jewish tradition and the "Jargon" — as he called Yiddish — with conspicuous disparagement and denied the existence of a common fate and national ties among Jews dispersed in various countries of the world. He spoke contemptuously of the "petrified religious customs and evanescent psychological remains" of the Jews, which are not enough to define them as a nation. Regarding the problem of national autonomy for the Russian Jews, as the Bund demanded, he argued that this question was assuming the nature of a curiosity: autonomy was being offered to a nation being denied a future whose existence had yet to be proved.[2]

It is not important for the subject of our discussion to what extent the prerevolutionary conceptions are able to stand the test of facts and theory. On the other hand, it is important to mention that from the point of view of practical Soviet policy they became frozen almost from the beginning of the regime; and within the limits of this study, their political relevancy certainly has not grown. Even if Soviet Communism has not entirely abandoned the idea of the amalgamation of nations and cultures, this has been preserved for some future date — a fact which in no way affects policy in the foreseeable time to come.

Lenin may have continued to believe to the end of his life that a separate nation has no intrinsic value and is a transitory phenomenon in history. But Lenin also raised the practical needs of the revolution and the regime to the degree of a guiding principle. Consequently Bolshevism compromised at least from the beginning of its rule with the existence of deep-rooted national sentiments. This compromise was designed to help the regime gain support among the peoples which had been suppressed in the Tsarist "prison for peoples" (not to mention the necessity of conducting propaganda activity among the masses in their own language) and to constitute an attraction for subjugated nations outside Russia. Adaptation to national facts brought Lenin right after the revolution to back the country's federative structure in which Soviet republics would be included on a national basis, despite the fact that he had strongly opposed ideas of federation previously. Without divorcing the vision of a merger of nations, ideological legitimacy was accorded to the uniqueness of nations and their cultures. In any case, Lenin believed that humanity would reach the inevitable fusion of nations by way of a transition period in which all peoples would be liberated, while it was the view of Stalin, whose personality embodied a rare combination of Communist scholasticism and a utilitarian calculating machine based on what was good for the regime, that there is no contradiction between the aspiration for a future merger of cultures and the promotion of national cultures in the present, in the period of the proletarian dictatorship. In his opinion, "National cultures should be allowed to develop and expand while revealing their potential qualities for the purpose of creating conditions necessary for their fusion into a single common culture with a single common language at the triumph of socialism throughout the world. The flourishing of cultures national in form and socialist in content under conditions of the dictatorship of the proletariat in a single country for the sake of their fusion into a single common socialist (both in form and content) culture with a single common language when the proletariat will triumph in the entire world and socialism will become a way of life — that is the expression of the true dialectic of the question of national culture as it was presented by Lenin."[3]

Thus, within the sanctioned framework of "national in form and socialist in content" there remained living space for national cultures, despite the rigorous supervision to see that they did not threaten governmental centralism and political uniformity. And in spite of the fact that Stalin previously mocked (in a polemic with Karl Renner and Otto Bauer, the Austrian Social Democrats) those who regarded it as the function of the proletariat to "organize" or "found" nations,[4] during his dictatorship, government aid was extended for the basic development of the cultures of tiny peoples, some of which were at the tribal stage and even required the creation of a written language and an alphabet which they lacked.

With respect to the Jews, the Soviet regime from the beginning deviated considerably from the prerevolutionary conceptions of Lenin and Stalin cited above. The latter, first as commissar for nationalities and later as all-powerful ruler, seemed to ignore his theories and allowed a nation, the existence of which he denied, quite a large field for autonomous cultural activity. Numerous separate Jewish institutions existed in the Soviet Union — schools, publishing houses, newspapers, theaters, research institutes, a number of local councils and courts conducted in Yiddish, and colonization activities — including the "Jewish Autonomous Province" in Birobidzhan. All these institutions, even taking into account their gradual decline and attenuation of national feeling and tradition from the point of view of spirit and content, were not reconcilable with Stalin's negation of the future of the Jewish people and the statement he made in 1913 that the very existence of the Jewish people still had to be proved.

Generally speaking, the Soviet ideocracy is noted for the flexibility it displays regarding its own "precepts." It knows how to enable them to coexist with current needs. The importance of doctrines in the Soviet world of thought should not be disparaged, but Communist Moscow never displayed haste in sacrificing current interests and considerations on their altar. Both Lenin and Stalin argued that theory must not become dogma but a guide for action. In practice, the Soviet regime accumulated a rich tradition of ideological rationalism for the sake of tactical interests and measures. For this reason, Soviet ideologists are sometimes compared to a sharpshooter who marks his target on a spot he has just hit. In view of the numerous changes in the official evaluation of certain ideas and movements, countries, persons, and even past events, it is not easy to establish what is stable and what is transitory in Soviet theory. The widespread use of the adjective "present" in Soviet, Communist terminology (for example, the present phase, the present conditions, the present time and place), like the entire common formula concerning "creative development of Marxist-Leninist theory," constitute a ready-made source of ideological justification for worthwhile turning points in policy. In this way, theory becomes excessively functional. It may be that their "ecclesiastical" education does not make it easy for Soviet leaders to admit that their attitude to problems is thoroughly pragmatic and stems from self-interest. Perhaps they are subject to a certain autosuggestion and tend "naturally" to identify their current positions either with "historic law" or a basic philosophy. However, experience has proved that no less than ideology influences Soviet policy are the ideological formulas subordinate to policy with all its changes and metamorphoses.

From what has been said thus far it should stand to reason that it was not hallowed doctrines which guided Soviet practice with regard to the Jews until 1948 — and there are no grounds for attributing the severe anti-Jewish policy (including the liquidation of Jewish culture) during the "black years" to ideological motives. It is difficult to interpret this policy as a regression to assimilationist assumptions with respect to the Jews (with the new addition of forced assimilation by brutal means) if only in view of what is known that it harmed people who had long been cut off from their Jewish origins. Moreover, this policy made assimilation more difficult and led to the strengthening of Jewish national consciousness in the Soviet Union by arousing bitter reactions to it. Certainly it cannot be assumed that after the Jews had established an independent state of their own — with the political support of the USSR — Stalin still clung to the definition which he had formulated five years before the October Revolution that the Jews do not constitute a nation.

A negative rule implies the affirmative. The anti-Jewish policy of the "black years" did not stem from ideological sources but was entirely based on opportunistic, "mercantilist" considerations. It was brutally calculated to correspond to Soviet needs, either real or imaginary, and profit weighings, right or wrong, both in connection with the country's internal developments and its foreign relations.

We shall continue stressing in our summing-up what we have attempted to do in various chapters — that with all the reasons and special qualities of the anti-Jewish policy in the "black years," we do not treat it isolated from the general developments in the Soviet Union. It is first of all closely connected with the tightening of totalitarian rule in the postwar years.

The natural expectations of the masses of Soviet people after the war for a relaxation of tension and an easing of living conditions were countered by Stalin with demands for new sacrifices. When the war ended, the people hoped that Stalin himself, wearing the laurel wreath, would initiate "de-Stalinization" — in the apt words of an authority on Soviet problems.[5] The desire to return to normalcy — a common human desire at the end of wars — had a special flavor in the Soviet Union; here the longing was not just for the "normal" prewar condition with its distress and terror but for a state of affairs which Soviet citizens had almost not experienced. The popular feeling was expressed in a remark made by a Russian officer in Moscow on VE Day, "Now it is time to live," and he certainly must have meant not only relief from the hardships of war but the end of "normal" suffering, want, and fear. However, confronted with the natural desire of a drained people and "exhausted heroes" for a little relaxation, Stalin actually announced the resumption of a long period of intensified effort, tightening the belt, and daily sacrifice on the altar of the future. This — for the masses of people — was one of the points of great significance brought out in the speech made by the dictator on

February 9, 1946, when he appeared as an election candidate and presented the general outlines of three new five-year plans, "if not more," particularly built around the development of heavy industry in order to make the country secure against any surprise.[6]

Stalin took early precautions against a potential "Thermidor." On the contrary, his old thesis that "the growth of the power of the Soviet State will intensify the resistance of the last remnants of the dying classes"[7] continued to serve as the guiding principle of the relations between the government and the citizen. In effect, that thesis could be interpreted as an intensification of the class war precisely together with the glorious victory; and a rational justification of greater "vigilance" and supervision was found.

In the government's deployment of its forces against popular "demobilizationary" tendencies, the Jews could easily become a scapegoat. It is true that liberal sentiments could cling to the Jews (or be preserved by them) relatively with greater ease than to other groups in the population, but, essentially, it was convenient and "worthwhile" for the authorities to label the Jews with them. Since the expectations for a "new period" (in addition to the victory) also nurtured friendship and collaboration with the Western democracies, the attraction of identifying the holders of such hopes with the Jews grew. Historical experience teaches that the Soviet terror campaigns almost invariably pointed or alluded to a deviant or criminal group — whether it be ethnic, social, class, religious, professional, literary — and its victims were designed to represent a collective enemy. Thus, also after the war — through reliance on prejudices — a desirable and suitable group embodiment of the processes of "relaxation" was found: Who loves an easy life more than the Jews? Who are individualists and egotists like them? Who like them regards the large outside world with yearning? The growth of Russian chauvinism and xenophobia, the intensification of the cold war, the inflation of anti-Westernism, and the encouragement of hatred of the United States certainly helped direct the blame for all kinds of mishaps and dangerous trends against the Jews. In citing as a goal of exposing the doctors' plot the creation of an atmosphere of war fever and nationalist hysteria and the cutting off of all contact between the Communist bloc and the West, Isaac Deutscher rightly contended:

"In such a mood the 'alien,' the citizen suspected of 'divided loyalties,' is naturally regarded as the worst 'security risk.'. . . And who could be a worse 'security risk' than the Jew with Zionist sympathies or the 'rootless cosmopolitan' whose brothers or cousins lived in the West?"[8]

Now let us examine the importance of Stalin's personal feelings concerning the anti-Jewish policy. To be more specific, was Stalin himself an anti-Semite, and if so, to what extent did his personal hatred of Jews determine what happened during the "black years"?

A series of testimonies and probabilities combine to prove that Stalin did not like Jews; and in any case, he did not have the biographical and psychological background to be sympathetic towards them. From the beginning of his emergence as a political figure, he was apparently consumed by envy and hate for the "intellectual" revolutionary leaders — the theoretical magicians, the famous orators and writers, the masters of polemic, the men of the world, the persons fluent in many languages. These people represented the qualities which Stalin lacked or in which he was inferior — and the fact that they were mostly and conspicuously Jews must have left traces on his mind. A similar dose of anti-Semitism is detectable in Stalin's political animosity to the Mensheviks and Social Revolutionaries, since there were numerous Jews among the leaders of these two factions. Quite characteristic is one paragraph in Stalin's "Report on the London Congress" in which the writer called attention to the "interesting" national composition of the congress of the Russian Social Democratic Party held in 1907. Stalin wrote that "statistics showed that most of the Menshevik faction consisted of Jews. . . . On the other hand, the overwhelming majority of the Bolshevik faction consisted of Russians. . . . For this reason, one of the Bolsheviks (it seems, Comrade Aleksinski) remarked in jest that the Mensheviks were a Jewish faction and the Bolsheviks, a true Russian one; consequently, it would not be a bad idea for us, the Bolsheviks, to organize a pogrom in the Party."[9] The pleased repetition of this joke in the land of pogroms does not indicate that Stalin was too sophisticated, but — what is more important — it does reveal some of the mental sediment in his personality. This is to some extent also attested to by the high percentage of Jews among Stalin's prominent victims. Unconscious hate and vindictiveness could not be influenced by the fact that men like Zinoviev, Kamenev, Sokolnikov, Radek, and others had no ties with Judaism except for their origin and that they and their complete Russification were precisely the facts symbolizing the extinction of the Jewish people which Stalin had foreseen. Operating here was his instinctive identification of Jews with intellectual, revolutionary "bright children" or Jews with "cosmopolitans." Stalin's deep hatred of Trotsky must have to no small degree been influenced by the latter's being a living symbol of the former's inferiority; and the fact of the national extraction of Trotsky, the archfiend, should not be belittled in considering Stalin's attitudes to the Jews.

On the instinctive and primitive level, Stalin's mind transformed Jewish intellectualism into cunning and egoism. It is interesting to note how much he clung to stereotypes of an anti-Semitic nature despite the obvious facts which refuted them right under his nose in his own country. He was well aware of the fate of the Jews under Nazi rule and could not help knowing of the relatively important part played by the Jews of his country in the war against Hitler. Nevertheless, in a conversation which he conducted on December 3, 1941, with General Wladislaw Sikorsky, prime minister of the Polish government in exile, who had come from London on a visit to the Soviet Union, and with General Wladislaw Anders, commander of the Polish forces which had been organized in Soviet territory, he repeatedly said, "The Jews are rotten soldiers," or "poor soldiers."[10] Ironically, in this evaluation, the Soviet ruler found a common language with a person who just several months before had been his prisoner, General Anders, a man with a reputation for both being anti-Semitic and anti-Soviet.

Milovan Djilas mentioned that even in old age, Stalin, at the height of his glory, was not free of his preoccupation with the Jews. During a banquet which he held in his villa at the beginning of 1948 in honor of the Yugoslav delegation, he suddenly and provocatively asked Djilas, "Why aren't there many Jews in the Yugoslav Party and why don't the few who are in it fulfill any important function?" After that he added, "In our Central Committee there are no Jews," accompanying his boast with a laugh and a teasing jest, "You are an anti-Semite; you, too, Djilas, are an anti-Semite."[11]

A window to Stalin's private and family life, which was hidden from the public by a curtain within a curtain, was opened by his daughter Svetlana (by his second wife, Nadezhda Alliluyeva) after her flight from the Soviet Union in 1967. She also related revealing details which shed light on Stalin's personal attitude to the Jews. He apparently bore a grudge against Molotov's Jewish wife Pauline Zhemchuzhina since Nadezhda Alliluyeva's suicide in 1932, attributing to the bad influence of this close friend of his wife's a certain importance in making her fatal decision. He disapproved of the marriage (his second) of his eldest son Yakov to a Jewess, Yulia. Mentioning this incident, Svetlana Alliluyeva points out, "He [Stalin] never liked Jews, though in those days [the middle 1930's] he wasn't yet as blatant about expressing his hatred for them as he was after the war." His morbid anti-Semitism is attested to by his suspicion of Yulia that she had had a hand in delivering Yakov to the Germans — he had been taken prisoner by them at the beginning of the Soviet-German war; she was arrested and kept in prison for about two years. The man called the "Father of Peoples" could not tolerate the love affair of his own daughter in the winter of 1942–43 which she carried on with a Jew, Alexei Kapler, a motion picture scenario writer, when she was seventeen. In anger he flung at her that she "couldn't even find herself a Russian." "Writer!" he said contemptuously of her lover. "He can't write decent Russian!" He claimed that Kapler was a British spy. The man was sent to Vorkuta for five years and immediately on his return, in 1948, he was again arrested and sentenced to another five-year term which he spent working in the mines of the camps near Inta, in the far north; after Stalin's death, he was brought to the Lubianka Prison in Moscow and in July 1953 he was released. It seems that in order to dispel doubts concerning the reasons for Stalin's attitude towards Kapler, Svetlana found it proper to point out, "Apparently the fact that Kapler was a Jew was what bothered him most of all." In the spring of 1944, Stalin grudgingly agreed ("To hell with you. Do as you like") to his daughter's marriage to another Jew, a fellow student of hers, Grigory Morozov ("He was Jewish, and my father didn't like it"), but only on condition that his son-in-law never enter his home — and Stalin indeed "never once met my first husband [Morozov] and said quite firmly that he never would." A remark which Stalin made to his daughter regarding Morozov is quite characteristic: "He's too calculating, that young man of yours. Look at that. It's terrible at the front. People are getting shot. And look at him. He's sitting it out at home." This marriage ended in divorce three years later for entirely personal reasons, but Stalin continued to remember the fact that Morozov was a Jew. Grigory Morozov's father was among the persons arrested in the campaign against "cosmopolitanism." At that time, Stalin told his daughter, "That first husband of yours was thrown your way by the Zionists." When Svetlana replied that "the younger ones couldn't care less about all this Zionism," Stalin retorted: "No! You don't understand. The entire older generation is contaminated with Zionism, and now they're teaching the young people, too."[12]

To sum up, unmistakable anti-Semitic features can be discerned in Stalin's psychological and emotional makeup. However, at the same time he must be credited with propaganda and legal activities against anti-Semitism on various occasions. This conduct of his did not stem from emotional distress caused by anti-Semitism but from the fact that he realized what dangers it involved for the regime and that it might open dams to nationalistic currents and serve as a tool in the hands of existing or potential counterrevolution. The man who had been amused by a jest about a pogrom approved quite a great number of publications in the 1920's denouncing anti-Semitism and the imposition of relatively severe penalties for anti-Semitic outbreaks. It was certainly no excessive love of Jews that impelled him to say strong words against anti-Semitism on January 12, 1931, when he bracketed it with "national and racial chauvinism" constituting a survival of practices of the "cannibalistic period." In addition to propaganda considerations for foreign consumption — he made the statement to the Jewish Telegraphic Agency of the United States — Stalin realized that anti-Semitism is "profoundly hostile to the Soviet regime."[13] As much as Stalin's sincerity in making such a statement in January 1931 can be questioned on the basis of the fact that it was not made public in the Soviet Union until the end of November 1936, when it was quoted by Molotov, permission to publish it (even belatedly) is instructive. Without Stalin's approval, even the words Molotov added in his own name, denouncing "the cannibalism of our time from the camp of the Fascist anti-Semites," and accompanied by expressions of brotherhood to the Jewish people, would not have been said.[14]

In view of the contradictory revelations cited above, Stalin's attitude towards the Jews cannot be summed up by defining it as merely ambivalent. They express Stalin's unique talent for now and then separating his personal feelings from a sober political or administrative consideration. As much as Stalin knew how to hate with unusual intensity, he was a man who often did not allow his instincts to guide his political steps. In accordance with his own assessment of what was good for the regime and even out of egoistic, utilitarian considerations, he was capable of forcing a sort of depersonalization on himself. Other Soviet leaders who served him had also been tamed to act in this fashion. Is it possible, for example, to learn about the personal loathing or affection of Moscow's great men from the prohibition or sanctioning of jazz in the Soviet Union? As a matter of fact, there is a foundation to the "distinct impression" of a student of Soviet problems that stories which Andrei Zhdanov, the person who had been the arbiter of literary matters in the USSR during Stalin's lifetime, had approved and praised were no more according to his taste than the ones which he had rejected and denounced during the period of literary purges, for "Indeed the essence of the totalitarian approach to art is that taste, including the taste of the totalitarian leader, is *irrelevant* to its evaluation."[15]

This depersonalization was valid in various spheres and had numerous aspects. The fact that Molotov had a Jewish wife caused him no mental anguish while signing the friendship pact with Ribbentrop and later, while vehemently defending it. Mrs. Molotov's banishment at a time when her husband was and continued to be at the peak of an official status is but a marginal phenomenon of "depersonalization." A number of top-flight Soviet leaders had or have Jewish wives (or Jewish sons- and daughters-in-law) but it has no political relevancy. Perhaps this is the place to note the stubborn rumor about Stalin's living together with a Jewess, Rosa Kaganovich, Lazar Kaganovich's sister, either as his wife or mistress; it is difficult to ascertain the reliability of this rumor, but, in any case, any attempt to clarify this matter will only remain a piquant titbit, the results of which would have no importance for Stalin's "Jewish policy." The Kremlin is not the soil for producing modern Purim legends of the kind described in the biblical Book of Esther.

Stalin's rare power to ignore his personal sympathies and antipathies out of dry "arithmetic" and sometimes to take steps against anti-Semitism despite his own anti-Semitic instincts is particularly conspicuous considered against the background of his uninhibited, domineering personality. He loathed Jewish "intellectuals" and destroyed quite a number of them, but as long as he needed their talents or their contacts, he did not hesitate to keep these "intellectuals" around him and drain the last drop of service (or obsequiousness) out of them. At the very least, emotional antagonism was unavoidable between a man like Stalin and one like Litvinov, and nevertheless the latter was Soviet foreign minister for about ten years. Eventually he was discarded, but when Litvinov's "liberalism" and even his Jewish identity once more appeared to be "useful" qualities, Stalin must have suffered no mental pangs when he again restored the right man to the right post as Soviet ambassador to the United States during the Soviet-German war. In Stalin's view, as we have related, the Jews are "rotten soldiers" (perhaps he also wanted to win over his Polish guests by making such a statement), but at the same time, he played up Jewish courage in propaganda directed to the Jewish world. Until Stalin's death, Kaganovich was one of his protégés. He did not flinch from making use of the services of Lev Mekhlis. Ilya Ehrenburg was one of his most prominent court writers, despite the fact that politically and socially, he was no symbol of Bolshevik purity. (Parenthetically: one of the striking examples of Stalin's selectivity in remembering his servants' past stains is the career of Andrei Vyshinsky, a scion of the Polish nobility and a Menshevik, who was promoted to the rank of his "Grand Inquisitor.") In not a few instances, Stalin acted in accordance with the saying that if you need the thief, you take him down from the scaffold. Moreover, he was used to exploiting even persons slated for the firing squad some day for the sake of the interests of the state and of his rule.

Stalin did not have to wait until his old age, when there were no limits to his power in the country and when his hate of the Jews became more open and brutal, to make a calculated use of anti-

Semitism for his own interests. Even during the 1920's, when the Old Guard, as much as it had been trained to sanctify means for the sake of the end, could still find it seriously immoral or unaesthetic to utilize anti-Semitism for political purposes, Stalin was resorting to premeditated anti-Semitism. After having taken advantage of the collaboration of two Jews (Zinoviev and Kamenev who in 1922–23 had together with Stalin constituted a faction called the "triumvirate") in maneuvers to prevent a third Jew (Trotsky) from becoming Lenin's successor, he made use of anti-Semitic tricks in his struggle against his two former partners when the time came. He saw to it that during the appearances of the Party's official propagandists, the distinction between Trotskyites and followers of Zinoviev was obliterated and a hint given to the rank and file of the members that it was no accident that the leaders of the two opposition groups were Jews. At Stalin's inspiration, propagandists made an effort to plant the notion that a struggle was going on in the Party between native Russian socialism and aliens seeking to pervert it.[16]

The next thirty years of Stalin's rule certainly did not raise his morality and did not increase his fastidiousness regarding the choice of means which he was ready to make use of for the sake of special interests. During his final years, when he had already used a wide variety of scapegoats, he was certainly not likely to exercise more self-control, especially with regard to the Jews, and refrain from a deliberate exploitation of anti-Semitism in order to advance his ends.

Nevertheless, it seems that Stalin did not create for himself a clear purpose to which his inflammatory acts with respect to the Jews would lead. There is a story about Konstantin Pobedonostsov, the ruler of the Holy Synod (the supreme religious institution of the Russian Orthodox Church in Tsarist Russia) and a notorious anti-Semite, who was considered the architect of the Jewish policy of the last two Tsars — Alexander III and Nicholas II; in 1890 he told the Jewish writer Alexander Zederbaum how it would be possible to solve the problem of the Jews in Russia, who then amounted to about five million persons — one third would be allowed to perish, one third would be baptized, and the remaining third would emigrate.[17] It is difficult to imagine that Stalin would have been prepared to adopt a solution of this sort. Translated into the Soviet vernacular baptism means assimilation and adoption of the Communist "religion"; however, we have seen that assimilated and Communist Jews did not gain Stalin's sympathy either. He certainly did not consider the possibility of permitting one third of Soviet Jewry to emigrate. And what would he gain, he could ask himself, from decreeing the physical destruction of the remaining third? The thought is consequently inescapable that in his anti-Jewish policy — as much as it was implemented with cruelty — Stalin during the "black years" was not guided by a "final solution," to use a horrifying term borrowed from the Nazi dictionary. This policy was essentially reactive — his reply to situations and needs as he understood them within a foreseeable range. Since this was so, his resorting to anti-Semitism did not result from a single "arithmetical" consideration. Sometimes it appeared profitable for the purpose of diverting attention from internal economic difficulties, sometimes it was considered desirable for eliminating obstacles to his power, sometimes it was designed to win the support of the Arabs, sometimes it was considered helpful in increasing hatred of the West, especially the United States, sometimes it was convenient in the intrigues against the leaders (or for their struggles among themselves) — and there were still other current profit accounts in operation.

In effect, cynical and crude "arithmetic" determined the course of the "black years." Unlike Hitler, it is difficult to imagine Stalin yielding to anti-Jewish feelings to the extent of ignoring the needs of the regime.[18] To take another example from Russia's previous rulers, it is unbelievable that he would grasp at anti-Semitic fanaticism as did Yelizaveta, the daughter of Peter the Great; to the Senate's request to soften the harshness of her expulsion decree against the Jews who had been living in Russia temporarily (1742) or at least permit them to attend the fairs in accordance with the interests of the state treasury and Christian merchants, she replied with a "resolution" written in her own hand on the Senate's memorandum that she did not want to make any profit from the enemies of Jesus Christ.[19] On the other hand, Stalin could bring to mind the owner of a summer resort in prewar Poland about whom a joke was told that he had said, "I am an anti-Semite, but not during the season."

It may hypothetically be assumed that even had Stalin harbored personal affection for the Jews, he would not have refrained from brutal acts towards them if he had made his calculation and found that they would bring him political benefits. According to this hypothesis, the special severity of the policy of the "black years" probably stems from the fact that calculations of state expediency simultaneously overlapped the morbid personal inclinations of Stalin and of other top Soviet leaders with regard to the Jews. The meeting, as it were, of what seemed to be the *raison d'état* with anti-Semitic instincts made the adoption of the anti-Jewish policy easier and added the enthusiasm to carrying it out.

CHAPTER NOTES

1: The War Years

1. Quoted in Soviet Premier Khrushchev's letter to Swedish Prime Minister T. Erlander, published in *Mezhdunarodnaya Zhizn* [International Life], no. 12, Moscow, December 1961, p. 8; see B. Z. Urlanis, "Loss of Life in the Wars," *Voprosy Istorii* [Problems of History], no. 5, Moscow, May 1965, p. 47.
2. As stated by the Soviet State Commission in its report on *Material War Damage,* Moscow, 1945, pp. 1–3; *Bolshaya Sovetskaya Entsiklopedia* [Great Soviet Encyclopedia], 2nd ed. (Moscow), vol. 7 (1951), p. 191; and vol. 50 (1957), p. 239.
3. According to the census taken in the Soviet Union in January 1939, the Jewish population numbered some 3,020,000 (see L. Zinger, *Dos Banayte Folk* [The Rejuvenated People] (Moscow: *Der Emes* publishers, 1941), p. 35). To this figure must be added an estimated Jewish population of 2,180,000 in the territories annexed by the USSR in 1939–40 (i.e. Lithuania, Latvia, Estonia, Bessarabia, northern Bukovina, and part of Poland), and a natural increase set at 60,000 for the two years 1939–41 (Yaakov Lestchinsky, *The Dispersion of the Jews,* published by the World Zionist Organization's Department for Education and Culture in the Diaspora (Jerusalem, 1961), p. 249). Hence, Soviet Jewry may be assumed to have numbered some 5,260,000 at the time of the German invasion of the USSR.
4. Jewish loss of life in the USSR during the war has been variously estimated at one and a half to nearly three millions. The two million figure was quoted, inter alia, by Shakhno Epstein (one-time secretary of the Jewish Anti-Fascist Committee) in the Yiddish-language *Einikeit,* Moscow, June 23, 1945.
5. Hermann Fest, *Bolschewismus und Judentum: Das jüdische Element in der Führerschaft des Bolschewismus* (Berlin-Leipzig, 1934).
6. Walter Laqueur, *Russia and Germany, a Century of Conflict* (Boston and Toronto: Little, Brown & Co., 1965), pp. 193–195.
7. Alexander Dallin, *German Rule in Russia, 1941–1945* (London: Macmillan, 1957), p. 9.
8. Ibid., p. 65
9. Binyamin West, ed., *In the Throes of Extinction* (Hebrew) (published by the Labor Archive, Tel Aviv, 1963), p. 13 (quoted from the records of the Nuremberg Trial).
10. Perets Markish, *Trot fun Doires* [March of the Generations]. The novel was completed in 1948, but only in 1956 — about four years after Markish's execution — did the existence of the manuscript become known. Parts of the novel began to be published outside the Soviet Union, in

Folks-Shtimme and *Yiddishe Shriften* (Warsaw). In 1963 excerpts from the novel were also published in the Soviet Union, in *Sovetish Heimland* (Moscow). *Trot fun Doires* (in the original Yiddish) was printed in book form in Moscow at the end of 1966 or the beginning of 1967, but a number of episodes and themes expressing Jewish national character were excluded from that edition, evidently as a result of political-ideological censorship (see "Two Sections of Perets Markish's Book *March of the Generations,* Which Were Missing in the Soviet Edition," *Behinot,* no. 1, Tel Aviv, 1970, pp. 180–189).

11. Vasily Grossman, *The Aged Teacher,* first published in Russian in Moscow, 1942; the reference is taken from the Yiddish translation that appeared in *Heimland,* Moscow, 1943.

    That the Jews "took precedence" among Nazi victims is again stressed by Grossman in his documented reportage on Treblinka, written shortly after its liberation by the Red Army. He states that there were "two camps — Labor Camp No. 1, for prisoners of various nationalities, chiefly Poles, and Labor Camp 2 for Jews. . . . The internees in Camp 1 were fully aware that there existed something a hundred times more horrible than their own camp. There [in the Jewish camp] nothing accorded with life, for all was in readiness for death." This excerpt is quoted from *Treblinker Gehenom* [The Treblinka Hell] (Moscow: *Der Emes* publishers, 1945), pp. 4, 11.
12. From the testimony of Otto Ulendorf at the Nuremberg Trial, as quoted by Binyamin West: "History of the Holocaust and Jewish Partisan Activity in the Soviet Union," *Gesher,* nos. 2–3 (Jerusalem, September 1966), p. 241.
13. Quoted by Gideon Hausner in his case for the prosecution at the Eichmann trial, Jerusalem: *The Attorney-General v. Adolf Eichmann* (Jerusalem, 1961), p. 77.
14. B. West, in *Gesher,* op. cit., p. 240.
15. From the testimony of General Bach-Zelevsky at the Nuremberg Trial, cited in *The Judgment of the International Military Tribunal* (Hebrew) (Jerusalem: *Yad Vashem* Martyrs' and Heroes' Remembrance Authority, 1961), p. 212.
16. Estimates and opinions differ widely as to the number of Jews evacuated and the Soviet authorities' share in facilitating their evacuation. Some historians of the period claim that the authorities initiated large-scale operations, at great risk, to save the Jews from the certain doom that awaited them under German occupation, while others maintain that no special measures were undertaken to evacuate Jews as distinct from the rest of the population. The latter view is prominently upheld by Solomon M. Schwarz in *The Jews in the Soviet Union,* Appendix: "Evacuation and Re-Evacuation of the Jews in the War" (Syracuse, N.Y.: Syracuse University Press, 1951), pp. 219–238. See also, by the same author, "Der Churb'n fun die Yidden in Sovietenferband" [The Annihilation of the Jews in the Soviet Union], *General Yiddish Encyclopedia,* vol. 6 (New York, 1963), pp. 256–262. Aryeh Tartakover states (in *Shivtey Yisrael,* vol. 2: *European Jewry in Present Times,* (Tel Aviv, 1966), p. 76, fn. 24)

that the number of Jews evacuated from German-occupied territory "presumably did not exceed half a million."

17. See entries on Collaborators and Jew-Baiters, regarding Soviet-occupied territories, in Jacob Robinson and Philip Friedman, *Guide to Jewish History under Nazi Impact* (Jerusalem: Yad Vashem, and New York: YIVO, 1960); also in Philip Friedman, ed., *Bibliography of Books in Hebrew on the Jewish Catastrophe and Heroism in Europe* (Hebrew) (Jerusalem: Yad Vashem, and New York: YIVO, 1960); Emmanuel Brand, "Trials against Nazi-Criminals and Their Collaborators in U.S.S.R., 1961–1965," in *Yediot Yad Vashem,* Jerusalem, June 1966, pp. 15–22; Philip Friedman, "Ukrainian-Jewish Relations at the Time of the Nazi Occupation," *Shmuel Niger Book* (Yiddish) (New York: YIVO, 1958), pp. 230–263.
18. L. Dmiterko, "The State and Functions of Literary and Theater Reviewing in the Ukraine," *Literaturnaya Gazeta,* Moscow, March 9, 1949.
19. Yaakov Lestchinsky — in *The Jewish Postwar Dispersion* (Hebrew) (B'terem, 1948), p. 48 — points to the illuminating fact that "Jewish children constitute the smallest percentage of survivors in Poland and the USSR," for whereas the adults might have been able to survive without having recourse to (the local population's) aid, "the survival of Jewish children was dependent solely on the wishes of the Christian population."
20. Quoted from Molotov's memorandum of April 27, 1942 (circulated to the governments of all the countries with which Moscow had diplomatic relations) on, "The atrocities . . . perpetrated by the German-Fascist invaders during their occupation of Soviet territory, and the responsibility of the German government and Military Command for these crimes." (*Pravda,* April 28, 1942.)
21. *Einikeit,* November 25, and December 2, 1943. Publication of Grossman's unfinished series of articles was discontinued after the latter date.
22. This survey of the situation of the Jews among the partisans is based partly on Moshe Kahanovich, *The Fighting of the Jewish Partisans in Eastern Europe* (Hebrew) (Tel Aviv, 1954). The excerpts are taken from pp. 78, 199, and 201.
23. Salo W. Baron, *The Russian Jew Under Tsars and Soviets* (New York: Macmillan, 1964), pp. 302–303.
24. Josef Stalin, "The Great Soviet War in Defence of the Homeland," (Moscow: *Der Emes* publishers, 1945), p. 9 (Yiddish version, based on the 4th Russian-language edition).
25. Winston S. Churchill, *The Second World War,* vol. 1, *The Gathering Storm* (Boston: Houghton Mifflin Co., 1948), p. 393.
26. *Nazi-Soviet Relations, 1939–1941: Documents from the Archives of the German Foreign Office,* ed. Raymond J. Sontag and James S. Beddie (Washington: Government Printing Office, 1948), p. 75.
27. Y. Barzilai, *Zohar Behatzot* [Brilliance at Midnight], (Tel Aviv: Am Oved, 1962), p. 176.
28. Gleb Struve, *Soviet-Russian Literature, 1917–1950* (Norman: University of Oklahoma Press, 1951), pp. 298–299.
29. Ilya Ehrenburg, *Memoirs, 1921–1941,* tr. Tatania Shebunina and Yvonne

Kapp (Cleveland and New York: World Publishing Co., 1963), pp. 502–503.

30. Ibid., pp. 485–486. Here, incidentally, Ehrenburg discloses a curious fact concerning Ivanov, who was sentenced to five years' imprisonment in September 1941: Ivanov's dossier, opened at about the same time as the conclusion of the Soviet-German pact, was completed some three months after the Nazi invasion.
31. Knesset (Israeli Parliament) Member Rabbi Mordechai Nurock, in his Knesset speech on January 19, 1953: Jerusalem, *Knesset Record,* vol. 13, p. 488.
32. Ehrenburg, op. cit., p. 467.
33. Churchill, op. cit., pp. 366–367.
34. Ehrenburg, op. cit., p. 498.
35. German report on Soviet supplies, quoted in *Nazi-Soviet Relations,* pp. 339–341.
36. G. Z. Israeli, *MPS, PKP, MKI: A History of the Communist Party in Palestine and Israel* (Hebrew) (Tel Aviv: Ayanot, 1953), pp. 153–160, 170. Walter Laqueur, *Communism and Nationalism in the Middle East* (London: Routledge and Kegan Paul, 1961), pp. 104–108.
37. Edward J. Rozek, *Allied Wartime Diplomacy: A Pattern in Poland* (New York: John Wiley & Sons, and London: Chapman and Hall, 1958), p. 37.
38. From Molotov's address to the Supreme Soviet on October 31, 1939, quoted in *Pravda* the following day.
39. Ibid.
40. *Izvestia,* October 9, 1939.
41. *Pravda,* December 25, 1939.
42. F. Grim (Moshe Grossman), *In the Enchanted Land of the Legendary Dzhugashvili: My Seven Years in Soviet Russia, 1939–1946* (Yiddish), 2nd ed., (Paris: Emes un Freiheit, 1950), pp. 35–36.
43. Sheine-Miriam Broderzon, *On the Road of Suffering with Moshe Broderzon* (Yiddish) (Buenos Aires: Central Association of Polish Jews in Argentina, 1960), p. 31.
44. B. Z. Goldberg, *The Jews in the Soviet Union* (Yiddish) (Tel Aviv: Peretz Publishing House, 1965), p. 245.
45. Yitzhak Yanasovich, *With Jewish Writers in Russia* (Yiddish) (Buenos Aires: Kiyum, 1959), p. 159.
46. Joseph Rubinstein, *Megilas Russland* [Scroll of Woe of a Polish Jew in Russia] (New York: CYCO, 1960), p. 44.
47. Mordechai Bilurai, in *Sefer Hashomer Hatzair,* vol. 1 (Merhavya: Sifriat Hapoalim, 1959), p. 448.
48. Yanasovich, op. cit., p. 159.
49. See Yehoshua A. Gilboa, *On the Ruins of Jewish Culture in the Soviet Union* (Hebrew) (Tel Aviv: Peretz Library, 1959), p. 56.
50. Rafal Abramovich, in the *General Encyclopedia in Yiddish,* vol. "Yidn"-D (New York: Dubnov-Fund and Cyco, 1950), p. 188.
51. Yaakov Lestchinsky, *Soviet Jewry, Its Past and Its Future* (Yiddish) (New York: a *Yiddisher Kempfer* publication, 1941), p. 342. Tartakover

(*Shivtey Israel,* op. cit., p. 75) considers Lestchinsky's estimate exaggerated.

52. Aryeh Tartakover, "Destruction in the Course of Liberation" (Hebrew), in *Davar Yearbook for 5712,* ed. David Zakai and Zalman Shazar (Tel Aviv, 1951), p. 113.
53. An editorial entitled "Our Sorrow and Our Consolation" which appeared in the Warsaw *Folks-Shtimme* of April 4, 1956, dwells on "the sad consequences" of the terror of the Thirties, "borne [also] by the creative activity of the Jewish population of Soviet Russia, and by a large number of its communal and cultural leaders" who were "the prime victims of this plague." The article states, moreover, that "then, when their talents were at their highest peak, there were uprooted such creators of our culture as Izi Kharik, Max Erik, Moshe Kulbak, Yasha Bronstein, K. Dunetz, and other upright and talented men."
54. The Jewish Sections in the branches of the Communist Party of the Soviet Union. Founded (like some other non-Russian sections) in 1918 for the purpose of conducting political work among the Yiddish-speaking masses, and for securing the proletarian dictatorship on the "Jewish street." Dissolved in 1930.
55. K. Shmeruk, *Jewish Culture in the Soviet Union* (Hebrew), *Gesher,* nos. 2–3, September 1966, pp. 66–72.
56. L. Ostrovsky, in *Di Goldene Keit,* Tel Aviv, no. 32, 1958, p. 184.
57. Yanasovich, op. cit., p. 95.
58. K. Shmeruk, ed., *Jewish Publications in the Soviet Union, 1917–1960* (Hebrew) (Jerusalem: The Historical Society of Israel, 1961), pp. 57, 91.
59. Memoirs of Yaakov Ben-Shlomo, in B. West, ed., *Naftuley Dor* (Hebrew) (Tel Aviv: Overseas Mission of Tzeirey Tzion, 1955), vol. 2, pp. 56–57.
60. Zinger, op. cit., p. 121.
61. K. Shmeruk, "Jewish Publications in the Soviet Union (From the End of the 1930's till 1948)," in *Yad Vashem,* Jerusalem, 1960, pp. 110–112. The author points out, inter alia, that "the publication of children's books in Yiddish was virtually suspended in 1939; in 1940–1941, children's books were again printed in Yiddish, in editions of 2,000 to 3,000 copies."
62. Ibid., p. 91.
63. "One tree after another was felled . . ." from an interview with the poetess Rachel Korn, reported by R. K., *Maariv,* Tel Aviv, March 27, 1959.
64. Moshe Grossman in *Heimish,* Tel Aviv, February–March, 1960.
65. F. Grim (Moshe Grossman), op. cit., p. 34.
66. "Memoirs of 'A Lithuanian,' " in *Naftuley Dor,* op. cit., vol. 2, pp. 67–68.
67. The account of how Akselrod met his end is corroborated, with minor variations, in a great many sources, notably the following: F. Grim and Sheine-Miriam Broderzon, in the books cited above; Shmerl Kaczerginsky, *Between the Hammer and the Sickle* (Yiddish) (Paris, 1949); Hershel Vaynrauch, *Blood on the Sun* (Yiddish) (Brooklyn, N.Y.: *Mensh un Yid,* 1950); an article by the poet Isaac Platner, published on the occasion of Akselrod's sixtieth birthday in *Folks-Shtimme,* Warsaw, January 1, 1965; Rebecca Rubin, "Derhoibene Shtilkeit" [Sublime Si-

lence], *Sovetish Heimland,* Moscow, no. 1, 1963; a brief news item published in *Sovetish Heimland,* no. 6, 1964.

68. This poem was included in a collection of Akselrod's poems, *Lieder,* published by YKUF, New York, 1961 (with a comprehensive preface by Nachman Meisel).
69. The poem appeared in full in a selection of Markish's poems, *Yerusheh* [Heritage] (Buenos Aires: YKUF, 1959), pp. 15–38; part of it was published in *Yiddishe Shriften,* Warsaw, no. 7, July 1958. Lavreniev's observation is quoted from his preface to a book of Markish's poems which appeared in Russian translation in Moscow, 1957.
70. Avraham Ben-Yosef, "Bibliography of Yiddish Works Printed in the Soviet Union from 1941 to 1948," in *Yad Vashem,* Jerusalem, 1960, pp. 133–135.
71. *Einikeit,* June 7, 1942.
72. The review of Soviet Jewry's part in the war and resistance is based on copious material that appeared in a great many publications, among them: Kahanovich, op. cit.; B. West, ed., *In the Throes of Extinction,* op. cit.; Y. Kantor in *Folks-Shtimme,* Warsaw, April 18, 1963; Yosef Guri in *Yediot Yad Vashem,* Jerusalem, October 1964, April 1965, June 1966; Yosef Litvak, "Soviet Jews in the Second World War — In the Armed Forces and Partisan Movement," *Gesher,* nos. 2–3, September 1966, pp. 186–217.

    For Jews as leaders of the Soviet POW underground, see: *Novy Mir,* Moscow, no. 6, June 1964, "From the Gestapo Archives in Munich," by Professor A. Brutsky.

    For particulars of Jews decorated for bravery and awarded the order "Hero of the Soviet Union," see, inter alia: L. Zinger, op. cit.; Shlomo Rabinovich, *Jews in the Soviet Union* (Moscow, 1965); *Einikeit* of May 9, 1946, lists the Jewish recipients of the "Hero of the Soviet Union" decoration.

    A list of 104 Jewish wartime Red Army generals was drawn up by Yosef Guri. Itsik Feffer, on his visit to the United States in 1943 on behalf of the Jewish Anti-Fascist Committee, put their number at 100.
73. I. Nusinov, "Great Summings-up: Thirty Years of Jewish Soviet-Socialist Culture," *Heimland,* Moscow, no. 1, 1947.
74. *Sovetish Heimland* of May 1965, reproduced works by the twenty-one poets who had fallen in battle.
75. *Novy Mir,* Moscow, no. 2, February 1958.
76. Apart from the Germans of the Volga region, also the Kabard, Kalmuck, Chechen-Ingush, Balkar, and Crimean Tartar peoples were subjected to mass deportation, and their autonomous republics dissovled.
77. Alexander Dallin, op. cit. Soviet postwar fiction, too, deals widely with themes of treachery. The indictment of collaborators has continued to the time of this writing.
78. *Einikeit,* March 15, 1943.
79. *Pravda,* March 16–17, 1944.
80. A. Sutzkever, "Ilya Ehrenburg (*Memoirs, 1944–1946*)," *Di Goldene Keit,* no. 61, 1967, p. 30.

81. Zvi Portnoi's testimony recorded at *Yad Vashem* and published in *In the Throes of Extinction,* op. cit., p. 130.
82. Frederick C. Barghoorn, "Notes on Life and Travel in Russia," *The Yale Review,* vol. 37, no. 4, June 1948.
83. The various accounts of the tension in Kiev in mid-1944 differ in a great many details. The episode related here is based on the testimony referred to in note 81. According to another account, sixteen Jews were killed in an anti-Jewish outbreak in Kiev following the murder of a Russian officer by a non-Jewish woman, mistakenly thought to be a Jewess. This is quoted by S. Schwarz, op. cit., pp. 347, 350 (note 46), from *Bulletin of the Joint Rescue Committee of the Jewish Agency for Palestine,* March 1945.
84. Binyamin West, "Soviet Jewry in its Agonies," in *Naftuley Dor,* op. cit., vol. 2, p. 27 (footnote).
85. B. Z. Goldberg, *The Jewish Problem in the Soviet Union* (New York: Crown Publishers, 1961), p. 61.
86. Léon Leneman, *La Tragédie des Juifs en U.R.S.S.* (Paris: Desclée de Brouver, 1959), pp. 175–179.
87. West, *Naftuley Dor,* op. cit., vol. 2, pp. 25–26.
88. Kaczerginsky, op. cit., pp. 31–50.
89. Ibid., pp. 73–74.
90. Quoted from *Yiddishe Kultur,* New York, no. 2, February 1944.
91. *Einikeit,* December 27, 1942.
92. *Pravda,* April 11, 1945.
93. *Pravda,* April 18, 1945 (also reproduced in *Krasnaya Zvezda*).
94. Ilya Ehrenburg, "Persons, Years, Life," *Novy Mir,* no. 3, March 1963, pp. 130–131.
95. Ehrenburg, op. cit., p. 499.
96. Itsik Feffer, "Mazel Tov," *Einikeit,* May 10, 1945. He concludes his article thus: "And may it be granted that we call out, according to the ancient Jewish custom: Mazel Tov to you, brothers and sisters! May we live in good fortune!"; L. Kvitko, *Mazel Tov* (poem), *Einikeit,* May 12, 1945; S. Mikhoels, "Gut Yontev, Brieder," *Einikeit,* May 9, 1946 (on the anniversary of the victory).
97. S. Holevsky, "The Jews of Minsk," in *In the Throes of Extinction,* op. cit., p. 197, quoted from *Book of the Partisans* (Hebrew) (Merhavya: Sifriat Hapoalim, 1958).
98. G. L. Zhigalin, *Accursed heritage — On Anti-Semitism* (Moscow-Leningrad, 1927).
99. A fairly complete list of Soviet writings against anti-Semitism published in 1926–30 appears in Schwarz, op. cit., pp. 290–291 (note 30).

2: "Our Jewish Brethren the World Over!"

1. Announced at a press conference for foreign correspondents in Kuibyshev by Solomon Lozovsky, deputy chief of the Soviet Information Bureau, on April 23, 1942.

2. The first issue of *Einikeit* appeared on June 7, 1942. Up to July 27, 1943, the newspaper appeared every ten days in Kuibyshev, and thenceforth weekly in Moscow. On February 24, 1945, it began to be published thrice weekly. The last (known) issue, no. 140 (700), came out on November 20, 1948. (Source: K. Shmeruk, ed., *Jewish Publications in the Soviet Union* (Hebrew) [Jerusalem: The Historical Society of Israel, 1961], p. 334, reference 3510.)

   It is interesting to note that the American Committee of Jewish Writers, Artists and Scientists, which cooperated closely with the JAC, also called its organ *Einikeit.* This appeared irregularly in New York until January 15 , 1944, when it became a biweekly, and later a monthly.
3. *Pravda,* August 25, 1941.
4. The election of Solomon Mikhoels to the chairmanship of the JAC, in August 1941, is noted in a memorial anthology in Russian entitled *Mikhoels,* ed. K. L. Rudnitsky, (Moscow: 1965), p. 606. At the first plenary session of the JAC, held on May 28, 1942, the Committee's secretary, Shakhno Epstein, announced that the Committee was founded shortly after the "public gathering of representatives of the Jewish people" which assembled in Moscow, on August 24, 1941.
5. For a reconstruction of events concerning the fate of Erlich and Alter, see the memorial work *Henryk Erlich und Viktor Alter* (New York: *Unser Zeit,* 1951), especially an account by Lucien Blitt, pp. 96–115.

   Stanislaw Kot (Polish ambassador to the USSR, 1941–42), *Conversations with the Kremlin and Despatches from Russia* trans. H. C. Stevens (London: Oxford University Press, 1963), pp. 60–62, 102, 159–160, 162, 169, 200–201, 227, 245–246.

   Jan Ciechanowski, *Defeat in Victory* (Garden City, N.Y.: Doubleday, 1947), pp. 120–121.

   Edward J. Rozek, *Allied Wartime Diplomacy: A Pattern in Poland* (New York: John Wiley & Sons, and London: Chapman and Hall, 1958), pp. 98–103.

   The execution of Erlich and Alter was not officially acknowledged by the Soviet authorities until about a year later. Following a series of protests and insistent demands, the charges brought against the two men and the fact of their execution were contained in a letter addressed by Maxim Litvinov, the Soviet ambassador to the United States, to William Green, president of the American Federation of Labor.

   In December 1956, following the "Polish October," the Polish newspaper *Zycie Warszawy,* in an article written by its editor, Stefan Arsky, demanded that the names of Erlich and Alter be cleared, claiming that charges brought against them by the Soviet authorities had been unfounded (reported in a dispatch by Philip Ben, *Maariv,* Tel Aviv, December 13, 1956).
6. The excerpts quoted from the JAC's publications, or connected with its activities, were largely taken from Binyamin West, ed., *In the Throes of Extinction* (published in Hebrew by the Labor Archive, Tel Aviv, 1963). Most of this material was obtained from Soviet sources, chiefly from *Einikeit.* Excerpts relating to the activities of the Jewish Anti-Fascist

Committee appear in a special section of the book (pp. 225–253). See also, *The Second Soviet-Jewish Anti-Fascist Meeting, Moscow, May 24, 1942,* (Moscow: Foreign Languages Publishing House, 1942).

7. *Einikeit,* June 17, 1942.
8. Ibid., March 15, 1943.
9. A. Poliakova, in a review of *Mikhoels,* in *Novy Mir,* Moscow, November 1965, p. 272.
10. This was told to the author by B. Z. Goldberg, who asserted he had heard it from Mikhoels.
11. Moshe Katz, in *Yiddishe Kultur,* New York, October 1943.
12. This bibliography, by Menashe Unger, appeared in *Yiddishe Kultur,* New York, January 1944, pp. 52–56, and February 1944, pp. 53–56.
13. *Yiddishe Kultur,* January 1944, p. 51.
14. At a meeting with members of the All-World Jewish Cultural Association (YKUF), on July 15, 1943; reported in *Yiddishe Kultur,* August and September 1943, pp. 88–90.
15. From a conversation between Itsik Feffer and Nachman Meisel, recounted in *Dos Yiddishe Shaffen un der Yiddisher Shreiber in Sovietenverband* [Jewish Creative Activity and Jewish Writers in the Soviet Union] (New York: YKUF, 1959), p. 64.
16. *Calling All Jews to Action,* published for the Jewish Fund for Soviet Russia, London, 1943.
17. Winston S. Churchill, *The Second World War,* vol. 1, *The Gathering Storm* (Boston: Houghton Mifflin Co., 1948), pp. 331–333.
18. S. Levenberg, in *Jewish Labour,* London, September 1943. Reprinted in *Calling All Jews to Action,* op. cit., pp. 99–100.
19. From a letter addressed on November 20, 1942, by Yitzhak Rabinovitz, member of the Jewish Agency's Committee for Soviet Affairs, to Moshe Shertok (later Sharett, Israel's foreign minister), then head of the Jewish Agency's Political Department.

    For material relating to the *yishuv*'s contacts with the USSR, the author had recourse to Shimon Redlich's paper, "The Ties between Palestine and the Soviet Union during World War Two," submitted to the Hebrew University, Jerusalem. This paper was based on material culled from a number of Palestine archives (chiefly the Zionist Archives, Jerusalem).
20. Ben-Gurion's talks with Maisky in London and Palestine are confirmed in Ben-Gurion's letter to the author of January 31, 1967, in reply to the author's inquiries. Ben-Gurion recounts that six months after Maisky's visit to Palestine, he (Ben-Gurion) met Labourite theoretician Harold Laski in London, and that the latter spoke like an "ardent Zionist." When Ben-Gurion showed his surprise, Laski stated that he had become a Zionist after reading Maisky's report on his Palestine visit.

    Bartley Crum, in *Behind the Silken Curtain* (New York: Simon and Schuster, 1947), pp. 63–64, recounts his conversation with Soviet statesman Dmitri Manuilsky in London, in 1946, in the course of which Manuilsky told him that Maisky, after his Palestine visit, had submitted to the Kremlin an enthusiastic report on the progress which the Jews had achieved in Palestine. (Quoted by Aharon Cohen, *Israel and the Arab World* (Hebrew) (Merhavya: Workers' Library, 1964), p. 338.) See also Golda Meyerson's report on Maisky's visit in *Histadrut Workers' Almanac,* October 1943, p. 11 (quoted in Aharon Cohen, op. cit.).

21. Other addresses were broadcast by Moshe Smilansky and Yitzhak Greenbaum. Some of the addresses were in Hebrew, others in Yiddish and Russian. The author obtained this material from the private archives of Yitzhak Rabinovitz.
22. The statement was drawn up by B. West and edited by Berl Katznelenson; it was reproduced in B. West, ed., *Naftuley Dor* (Tel Aviv: Overseas Mission of Tzeirey Tzion, 1955), vol. 2, p. 405.

    On March 19, 1942, the Vaad Leumi sent a cable to Mikhail Kalinin, chairman of the presidium of the Supreme Council of the USSR, extending Palestine Jewry's heartiest greetings to the government and peoples of the Soviet Union and to their brave forces engaged in a heroic struggle against Fascist aggression.The cable expresses the hope that the "Soviet Government will understand and view with sympathy [the] aspiration [of the] Jewish people for [the] re-establishment [of] its national life in Palestine on [the] basis [of] equality with all free nations, and will speed up [the] release [of] exiles and prisoners previously detained [on] account [of] their Zionist views and activities and [their] work for Jewish culture and traditions."
23. Jeremiah Ben-Jacob, in *Congress Weekly,* no. 14, New York, April 20, 1953.
24. From a report (in Russian) in Rabinovitz's archives.
25. *Davar,* Tel Aviv, August 28, 1942.
26. Ibid.
27. The addresses and remarks exchanged at the Afikim reception are quoted from records in Rabinovitz's archives.
28. Facts concerning the Volkovich episode were personally conveyed to the author by Rabinovitz, and corroborated by documents from his archives (including a record of a conversation between Rabinovitz and Volkovich which took place in Jerusalem on February 1, 1943).
29. Aharon Cohen, *With the Ambulances to Teheran* (Hebrew) (Merhavya: Workers' Library, 1943), pp. 66–71.
30. Ibid., pp. 64–65.
31. From a record in Rabinovitz's archives.
32. *Mishmar,* Tel Aviv, December 15, 1944; quoted in Aharon Cohen, *Israel and the Arab World,* op. cit., p. 338.
33. Elisha Rodin, *Laben* [To My Son] (Tel Aviv: Am Oved, 1943). The book opens with a letter to Rodin by the commissar of the division, informing him that his son "gave his life with heroism and uprightness for the sake of our homeland and to the glory of his parents," and also Rodin's application to the military censorship.
34. The particulars and quotations presented in the last two paragraphs are largely based on documents in the Zionist Archive files (to which Redlich also had recourse for his abovementioned paper).
35. From the minutes of the V League Secretariat meeting held on September

26, 1945, and a report thereupon by S. Kaplansky (in Rabinovitz's archives).

36. According to an interview (recorded by Redlich) with Meriminsky-Marom, from the archives of the Institute of Contemporary Judaism of the Hebrew University, Jerusalem.
37. *Calling All Jews to Action,* op. cit., pp. 96–97.
38. *Birobidzhan un Eretz Yisroel,* in *ICOR Almanac,* New York, 1943, p. 38.
39. "Is America a One-Storeyed Structure?" — an article jointly penned by Mikhoels and Feffer, in *Voina i Rabochy Klass* [The War and the Working Class], no. 3, Moscow, 1944. This article also appeared in *Mikhoels,* (see note 4), 1965 edition, pp. 257–266, and 1960 edition, pp. 212–222.
40. "Five Days in Mexico," jointly written hy Mikhoels and Feffer, in *Voina i Rabochy Klass,* no. 4, 1944. The article also appeared in *Mikhoels,* 1965 edition, pp. 296–301.
41. At the JAC plenary session of April 2, 1944.
42. *Dos Yiddishe Folk in Kampf kegen Fashism* [The Jewish People in the Struggle against Fascism] (Moscow, 1945). Quoted by Solomon M. Schwarz, *The Jews in the Soviet Union* (Syracuse, N.Y.: Syracuse University Press, 1951), p. 217, note 31.
43. B. Mark, in *Gesher,* Jerusalem, April 1960, p. 89.
44. B. Z. Goldberg, *The Jewish Problem in the Soviet Union* (New York: Crown Publishers, 1961), pp. 65–66.
45. *Einikeit,* March 2, 1946.
46. Ilya Ehrenburg, "People, Years, Life," in *Novy Mir,* no. 2, February 1965, p. 23.
47. Ibid., pp. 54–55.
48. Ibid., p. 55.
49. *The Black Book: The Nazi Crime Against the Jewish People* (New York: The Jewish *Black Book* Committee, 1946).
50. Albert Einstein, "Unpublished Preface to a Black Book," in *Out of My Later Years* (New York: Philosophical Library, 1950), pp. 258–259.
51. *Einikeit,* March 2, 1946.
52. Y. D. Sosis, "Sketches from the History of the Jewish People in Russia" (Yiddish), in *Bletter for Geshichte* (organ of the Jewish Historical Institute in Poland), Warsaw, vol. 16, pp. 3–25. The fate of this work is dealt with in an editorial preface, p. 3.
53. At a reception for Professor Kapitza, on his fiftieth birthday, Mikhoels referred to him as a "fighting humanist" and addressed him in the following terms: "I shall never forget your excellent appearance at the anti-Fascist rally. I am greatly in your debt. And though I have gone to great pains to spread the fact of your being a Jew — an object which I have achieved — I have remained indebted to you." (From the memoirs of A. Pototzkaya-Mikhoels, widow of Solomon Mikhoels, in *Mikhoels,* 1965 edition, p. 528.
54. Shmerl Kaczerginsky, *Between the Hammer and Sickle* (Yiddish) (Paris, 1949), p. 53.
55. *Einikeit,* May 10, 1945.
56. Ehrenburg, "People, Years, Life," *Novy Mir,* no. 2, 1965, p. 51. See also

in this regard, Joseph Schein, *Arum Moskver Yiddishen Teater* [About Moscow's Jewish Theatre] (Paris, 1963), pp. 192–193; A. Sutzkever, "Mit Shlomo Mikhoels," in *Di Goldene Keit,* no. 43, Tel Aviv, 1962, pp. 156–157. The author has also heard firsthand reports by people who worked with Mikhoels at the Jewish State Theater in Moscow, among them Israel Beker, who later became a Habimah actor in Israel.

57. I. B. Saltsberg (member of the Canadian delegation), in *Morgn Freiheit,* New York, November 22, 1956.
58. Alexander Tishler, "I See Mikhoels," in *Mikhoels,* 1960 edition, p. 504. He states: "I accompanied the body to [the premises of] Professor Zbarsky, who applied makeup to Mikhoels's face, covering a deep gash on the left temple. Mikhoels lay uncovered. The body was intact, unhurt." The author was a painter regularly employed by the Jewish State Theater. See also Schein, op. cit. p. 203.
59. Ehrenburg, *"People, Years, Life," Novy Mir,* no. 2, 1965, p. 51.
60. Eliahu Falkovich, ed., *Mikhoels, 1890–1948* (Moscow: *Der Emes* publishers), 1948, p. 174.
61. Ehrenburg, "People, Years, Life," *Novy Mir,* no. 2, 1965, p. 51.
62. Ibid.
63. *Mikhoels,* 1965 edition, p. 360; 1960 edition, p. 259.
64. The author heard similar accounts, with slight changes, from various sources. See also Zev Ben-Shlomo, "A New Light on the Death of Mikhoels" (Hebrew), in *Haaretz* daily, Tel Aviv, January 17, 1958.
65. From an article by Der Nister in Falkovich, op. cit.; reprinted in *Di Goldene Keit* no. 43, Tel Aviv, 1962, pp. 222–225.

3: The National Awakening in Soviet Jewish Literature

1. The process of Russification was more intensive among Soviet Jewry than among other national groups in the USSR. National elements in some Soviet republics even pointed to the Russificatory function performed by the Jews resident in these territories.
2. Hyman Levy, *Jews and the National Question,* rev. American ed. (New York: Cameron Associates, 1958), p. 47. The author, a Jewish professor of mathematics, and at one time a British Communist Party leader, was expelled from the Party for his criticism of the Soviet policy towards the Jews.
3. According to a population census taken on January 17, 1939 — that is, before the Baltic States, Western Belorussia and Ukraine, Bessarabia, and Northern Bukovina were annexed to Soviet territory — some 50.8 percent of Soviet Russia's 3,020,171 Jews were living in the Ukrainian Republic, and 12.4 percent in the Belorussian Republic.
4. Solomon M. Schwarz, *The Jews in the Soviet Union,* (Syracuse, N.Y.: Syracuse University Press, 1951), p. 198.
5. Reported in an interview with Shlonsky by Roman Prister, *Al Hamishmar,* Tel Aviv, August 10, 1962.

6. From Ehrenburg's address at the "public gathering of representatives of the Jewish people" in Moscow, on August 24, 1941.
7. Ilya Ehrenburg, *People and Life, 1891–1921,* trans. Anna Bostock and Yvonne Kapp, (New York: Knopf, 1962), pp. 12–13.
8. *Znamya,* Moscow, September 1945), pp. 1–28; "The Jewish Chapter," pp. 16–18 (Hebrew), trans. Ezra Zussman in *Ittim,* Tel Aviv, October 9, 1946.
9. In time, Soviet literary critics tended to ignore *The Aged Teacher,* though they lavished praise on Grossman's other writings on wartime themes. This is presumably due to the Jewish aspect presented in *The Aged Teacher.*
10. During the campaign against "cosmopolitanism," these and other works of Pervomaisky were brought up against him when he was charged with nationalism and other deviationist tendencies. He was also reminded of his sins of the 1920's, when he had wrongly appraised the Zionist cause. See L. Dmiterko, in *Literaturnaya Gazeta,* Moscow, March 9, 1949.
11. Shmuel Elyashiv, *Modern Soviet Literature* (Hebrew) (Tel Aviv: Tversky Publishing House, 1953), p. 191. We have referred to this book in adducing several examples of the "emotional return" to Judaism. See also: Bernard J. Choseed, "Jews in Soviet Literature," in Ernest J. Simmons, ed., *Through the Glass of Soviet Literature* (New York: Columbia University Press, 1953), pp. 110–158.
12. See Yehoshua A. Gilboa, "Jews and the Themes of Destruction and Revolt in Polish Literature," in *Gesher,* Jerusalem, March 1964, pp. 112–127.
13. Shlomo Bickel, "National Motifs in Soviet Yiddish Literature," in *Di Goldene Keit,* Tel Aviv, no. 29, 1957, p. 51.
14. At a meeting with YKUF representatives in New York on July 15, 1943; reported in *Yiddishe Kultur,* New York, August–September 1943, pp. 88–90.
15. Yitzhak Yonasovich, *With Jewish Writers in Russia* (Yiddish) (Buenos Aires: Kiyum, 1959), pp. 42–43.
16. K. Shmeruk, "Yiddish Publications in the Soviet Union (From the End of the 1930's up to 1948)," in *Yad Vashem,* no. 4, Jerusalem, 1960, p. 120.
17. Ibid., p. 121. According to this source, the number of Yiddish publications dwindled considerably during the war, but their average circulation increased.
18. Ibid., p. 128.
19. N. Notovich and S. Roitman, "October and the Soviet Yiddish Literature," in *Heimland,* Moscow, no. 1, October 1947.
20. I. Nusinov, "Great Summings-Up," *Heimland,* Moscow, no. 1, October 1947.
21. A. Aizen, in *Zukunft,* New York, February 1951.
22. *Einikeit,* September 11, 1945.
23. *Einikeit,* September 26, 1946.

24. Bergelson used only part of the verse from Psalms as the title of his play; the complete verse is, "I shall not die, but live, and recount the works of the Lord." This play was never published or performed in the Soviet Union. It was performed by Habimah in Palestine in 1944, in Avraham Shlonsky's Hebrew translation.
25. *Prince Reuveni* was never published or performed in the Soviet Union, either. The play was published in New York in 1946 by YKUF.
26. *Einikeit,* August 30, 1945.
27. Jacob Glatstein, "Itsik Feffer," in *Zamlbicher,* New York, no. 8, 1952, p. 168.
28. This poem was not included in the collections of Markish's poems published in the USSR.
29. M. Kamenstein, in *Shtern,* Kharkov, 1932; quoted by N. Meisel, "Soviet Yiddish Literature," in *Yiddishe Kultur,* October 1957.
30. A. Holdes, in *Almanack of Soviet Jewish Writers,* Kharkov, 1934; quoted by N. Meisel, op. cit.
31. A. Sutzkever, "Perets Markish and His Environment," in *Di Goldene Keit,* no. 43, 1962, p. 36.
32. *War* appeared in Moscow at the end of 1948. In 1956, this work was published in two volumes in New York by YKUF.
33. B. Mark, in *Yiddishe Shriften,* Warsaw, no. 12 (222), December 1965, p. 3.
34. Yanasovich, op. cit., p. 316.
35. Ibid., pp. 133–135.
36. Ibid., pp. 172–174, 197–200.
37. See note 30.
38. Yanasovich, op. cit., pp. 45–46.
39. Ibid., p. 31.
40. An Anonymous Soviet Jew, *To My Brethren in the State of Israel: Uncensored Letters from the Soviet Union* (Hebrew) (Jerusalem: Kiryat Sefer, 1957), pp. 142–143. The author's identity was disclosed to this writer after his death (in 1964) as Baruch Mordechai Weissman.
41. M. Viner, in M. Viner and A. Gurstein, *Problems of* [*Literary*] *Criticism* (Moscow: Emes, 1933).
42. Published by YKUF together with the first volume, reprinted from the Moscow edition.
43. *Vidervuks* [Regrowth] was published in *Yiddishe Kultur,* New York, nos. 6 and 7, 1946, with the remark that the story had been "specially sent over."
44. *Yiddishe Kultur,* nos. 4, 5, 6, and 7, 1949; the date when the story was written was given as April–May 1946.
45. *Einikeit,* June 29, 1944. Shloimke Olitsky (his real name is Shlomo Perlmutter) indeed managed to reach Israel and fight in the War of Independence.
46. *Einikeit,* August 30, 1947; *Heimland,* Moscow, no. 1, October 1947, pp. 108–118.
47. The play was included in Halkin's *The Tree of Life* (Moscow: *Der Emes*

publishers, 1948). The Moscow Jewish State Theater decided to include it in its repertoire in 1945, but it is not known whether it was actually performed in public.

48. This article was included in the collected writings of Itsik Kipnis: *Untervegns* [On the Road] (New York: YKUF, 1960), pp. 347–352.
49. *Dos Naye Leben* [The New Life], Lodz, May 19, 1947.
50. *Einikeit,* July 3, 1947.
51. Chaim Loitsker, "For Jewish Purity in Our Literature," in *Der Shtern,* Kiev, no. 2, 1948, p. 112.
52. Quoted from Leib Kvitko in *Einikeit,* July 5, 1947.
53. Ibid.
54. See note 51.

4: The Rootless Cosmopolitans

1. Gleb Struve, *Soviet-Russian Literature, 1917–1950* (Norman: University of Oklahoma Press, 1951), p. 331, note 8.
2. Ibid., pp. 316–317.
3. P. Vyshinsky, "Soviet Patriotism and Its Great Force," in *Bolshevik,* Moscow, no. 18, November 30, 1947, pp. 32–33.
4. Stalin's personal interest and intervention in the literary and philosophical "ideological front" was remarked on by various sources. Even Zhdanov stressed this in one of his speeches. Ehrenburg relates in his memoirs that he heard from author Konstantin Simonov that "Stalin attaches great political importance to the campaign against self-abasement before the West" ("People, Years, Life," in *Novy Mir,* no. 2, February 1965, pp. 42–43). In his speech at the Nineteenth Conference of the Soviet Communist Party, V. Andreyanov noted that the Central Committee's resolution against the Leningrad periodicals *Zvezda* and *Leningrad* — the first of a series of resolutions of this nature — "was adopted at the instance of Comrade Stalin" (*Pravda,* October 8, 1952).
5. This itemization, which must needs be somewhat sketchy, was culled from many, chiefly Soviet, sources. The last episode, in regard to baseball, is according to Harrison E. Salisbury, *Moscow Journal* (Chicago: University of Chicago Press, 1961), p. 280.
6. Ilya Ehrenburg, "People, Years, Life," in *Novy Mir,* no. 2, February 1965, p. 43.
7. This trend — it was openly admitted — was the guiding line of a two-volume collection entitled *Russian Men of Science,* reviewing the lives and work of 127 former Russian scholars, which appeared in Moscow in 1948; Jean Daniel, *Nationalism and Nations in the Soviet Regime* (Hebrew) (Tel Aviv: Tversky, 1953), p. 136.
8. Quoted on the strength of a Hebrew translation of selected speeches of Zhdanov (A. A. Zhdanov, *On Culture and Society* (Merhavya: Sifriat Poalim, 1949), p. 153). For the English version of Zhdanov's speech at the inaugural conference of the Cominform, see Andrei Zhdanov, *The*

International Situation (Moscow: Foreign Languages Publishing House, 1947).

9. *Arbeiter Zeitung,* Vienna, March 24, 1949.
10. A. Leontev, in *Novoe Vremya,* April 6, 1949.
11. *Voprosy Filosofii,* Moscow, no. 2, 1948.
12. A. Deborin, in *Voprosy Filosofii,* no. 6, 1951 (quoted in Daniel, op. cit., p. 47).
13. Albert Einstein, "Open Letter to the General Assembly of the United Nations," in *Out of My Later Years* (New York: Philosophical Library, 1950), p. 157.
14. The open letter of the Soviet scientists was published in *Novoe Vremya* and reprinted in Einstein, op. cit., pp. 161–168. See also Einstein's "A Reply to the Soviet Scientists," Ibid, pp. 169–175.
15. M. Mitin, in *Literaturnaya Gazeta,* March 9, 1949.
16. Professor Boris Kedrov, in *Kultura i Zhizn,* Moscow, March 22, 1949.
17. Ehrenburg, "People, Years, Life," in *Novy Mir,* no. 3, March 1965, pp. 113–114.
18. Herbert McClosky and John E. Turner, *The Soviet Dictatorship* (New York: McGraw-Hill, 1960), p. 143 (note).
19. Salisbury, op. cit., pp. 28–29.
20. Jeremiah Ben-Jacob, in *Congress Weekly,* New York, April 20, 1953, p. 13.
21. These quotations from Zhdanov's speeches are based on the Hebrew translation in Zhdanov, op. cit.
22. *Einikeit,* March 4, 1948.
23. Reported, inter alia, in *Newsweek,* May 2, 1949.
24. *Krokodil,* Moscow, March 23, 1949; also recounted in Salisbury, op. cit., p. 15.
25. Also before 1949, official Soviet announcements were in the habit of stating both the pseudonyms and real names of some persons in cases of appointments or conferment of prizes or decorations, where formal indentification was necessary. There could be no formal reason, however, warranting the mention in newspaper articles of the Jewish names of persons charged with cosmopolitanism; particularly as some of these persons, at least used their new names not only as literary noms de plume, but as their current, legally adopted names.
26. Harry Schwartz, in *New York Times,* May 12, 1949.
27. *Commentary,* New York, December 1963, p. 435. Gide, the name of the French author, and "Gid," a derogatory epithet for a Jew in Russian, have a similar sound.
28. Daniel, op. cit., p. 177; Edward Weintal, in *Newsweek,* April 4, 1949.
29. Galina Nikolayeva, *Bitva v Puti* [Battle on the Way] (Moscow: Sovetski Pisatel, 1958).
30. Yuri Bondarev, *Tishina* [Stillness], in *Novy Mir,* February, March, and April 1962.
31. Anna Valtseva, *Kvartira N. 13* [Apartment No. 13], in *Moscow,* no. 1, January 1957.

32. Milovan Djilas, in *Borba,* Belgrade, December 14, 1952.
33. Quoted by Alexander Pomerantz, *The Soviet Martyrs* (Yiddish), (Buenos Aires: YIVO, 1962), p. 81.
34. Aryeh Harel (former Israeli ambassador to the Soviet Union, who heard this from Semyon Kirsanov in the winter of 1960): "Meetings with Yevtushenko and His Poetry," in *Mibifnim,* Ein-Harod, November 1963.
35. Quoted by Eliahu Tsherikover, *Jews in Times of Revolution* (Hebrew) (Tel Aviv: Am Oved, 1957), p. 374.
36. Lenin, *Writings,* 4th Russian ed., vol. 20, p. 10.
37. Stalin, *Selected Writings* (Russian) (Moscow, 1948), vol. 10, p. 51. Many Soviet statesmen and writers repeated Stalin's interpretation of internationalism.
38. Eugene Lyons, "Reflections on Stalinist Anti-Semitism — A Symposium," in *Midstream,* New York, Spring 1957.
39. *Bolshevik,* Moscow, May 10, 1945.
40. *Izvestia* (and other papers), May 25, 1945.
41. Khrushchev, in an interview with *Le Figaro* correspondent Serge Groussard, as reported in that paper on April 9, 1958. These remarks were omitted from the version that appeared in *Pravda* and *Izvestia* on March 27, 1958. Radio Moscow (in its foreign broadcasts) denied the remarks concerning the Jews attributed to Khrushchev, but Groussard's report is considered most reliable.
42. This phenomenon is noted by Dr. Haim Beinart, *Conversos on Trial by the Inquisition* (Hebrew) (Tel Aviv: Am Oved, 1965), p. 11.
43. P. Pnimy, *The Soviet Jews and their Fate* (Hebrew) (Tel Aviv: Am Oved, 1959), pp. 77–78.
44. See Jerzy G. Gliksman, "Social Prophylaxis as a Form of Soviet Terror," in Carl J. Friedrich, ed., *Totalitarianism,* The Universal Library (New York: Grosset and Dunlap, 1964), pp. 60–74.
45. Ignazio Silone, referring to the persecution of Jews in the Soviet Union, in a letter to Ivan Anissimov (editor of *Inostrannaya Literatura,* Moscow); see "A Troubled Dialogue," in *Encounter,* London, June 1957, pp. 60–67 (reproduced from *Tempo Presente,* Rome, February 1957, pp. 85–98).
46. Ehrenburg, "People, Years, Life," in *Novy Mir,* no. 2, February 1965, p. 55.
47. *Izvestia,* February 26, 1949.
48. *Pravda,* December 23, 1948.
49. "Love for the Homeland — Hatred for the Cosmopolitans," in *Literaturnaya Gazeta,* February 12, 1949.
50. Ehrenburg, op. cit., p. 56.
51. *Pravda,* January 28, 1949.
52. *Pravda,* February 11, 1949.
53. *Novy Mir,* no. 12, December 1956, pp. 249–251.
54. *Pravda,* February 26–27, 1949.
55. G. Gurko, in *Sovetskoye Iskustvo,* Moscow, February 19, 1949.
56. *Pravda,* February 16, 1949.

57. P. Vishynsky, in *Bolshevik,* no. 18, September 30, 1947, p. 33; Struve, op. cit., pp. 341–342.
58. P. Pankovsky, "The Formalism and Eclecticism of Professor Eichenbaum," in *Zvezda,* Leningrad, no. 9, September 1949, pp. 169–181.
59. Struve, op. cit., pp. 338–339.
60. *Zvezda,* Leningrad, no. 1, January 1949, pp. 66–108.
61. *Zvezda,* no. 3, March 1949, p. 207.
62. Ibid.
63. *Sovetskoye Iskustvo,* February 12, 1949, and March 5, 1949; *Pravda,* February 25, 1949, and March 4, 1949; *Literaturnaya Gazeta,* February 16, 1949; Daniel, op. cit., pp. 170–171.
64. For the cosmopolitans referred to in the various spheres, see: *Bolshevik,* no. 3, February 15, 1949, p. 45; *Izvestia,* February 19, 1949; *Komsomolskaya Pravda,* March 6, 1949.
65. Salisbury, op. cit., p. 13.
66. Peter Viereck, *Conservatism Revisited* (New York: Scribner's Sons, 1949), pp. 175–176.
67. The references to the cosmopolitans in the fields of historical research, political economy, jurisprudence, and philosophy are taken from: *Bolshevik,* no. 17, 1947, pp. 50–51; *Voprosy Ekonomiki,* Moscow, no. 3, 1949, pp. 116–117; *Bolshevik,* no. 24, December 30, 1947, p. 64; Daniel, op. cit., pp. 83–85, 174–176; Salisbury, op. cit., pp. 318–319.
68. *Pravda,* March 4, 1949.
69. *Literaturnaya Gazeta,* February 26, 1949.
70. *Literaturnaya Gazeta,* February 19, 1949; Daniel, op. cit., pp. 171–173.
71. L. Dmiterko, in *Literaturnaya Gazeta,* March 9, 1949.
72. Daniel, op. cit., p. 173.
73. See note 71.
74. See note 49.
75. *Pravda,* March 5, 1949.
76. *Literaturnaya Gazeta,* February 23, 1949, and March 10, 1949; *Kultura i Zhizn,* March 10, 1949.
77. *Znamya,* no. 1, 1947, pp. 130–142.
78. M. Lukonin, at a meeting of poets in Moscow; *Literaturnaya Gazeta,* March 19, 1949.
79. *Vechernaya Moskva,* March 14, 1949; Salisbury, op. cit., pp. 13–14. Isbakh's story, translated by Bernard Choseed, was published in *Commentary,* October 1953, pp. 328–333.
80. A. Yelistratova, in *Literaturnaya Gazeta,* March 2, 1949.
81. *Voprosy Istorii,* no. 3, 1949.
82. Y. Kovalchyk, in *Literaturnaya Gazeta,* February 12, 1949.
83. Yaacov Talmon, *Unity and Distinctiveness: Essays in Historical Thought* (Hebrew) (Tel Aviv: Schocken Publishing House, 1965), introduction.

5: A Culture Uprooted — A People Effaced

1. L. Dmiterko, in *Literaturnaya Gazeta,* March 9, 1949.
2. The bibliographical particulars of the newspapers and periodicals men-

tioned are according to K. Shmeruk, ed., *Jewish Publications in the Soviet Union, 1917–1960* (Hebrew) (Jerusalem: Historical Society of Israel, 1961). The particulars regarding *Birobidzhaner Shtern* are quoted from additional sources, chiefly: Jacob Lvavi (Babitzky), *The Jewish Colonization in Birobidzhan* (Hebrew) (Jerusalem: Historical Society of Israel, 1965), pp. 322–328.

3. *Siddur Hashalom: Prayers for All the Year,* compiled by Rabbi Shlomo Shleifer, head of the Moscow Religious Community, published by the Religious Community in 1956.
4. As observed by Abraham Brumberg, who visited the Odessa library thirteen years later. See Joseph and Abraham Brumberg, *Sovyetish Heimland: An Analysis* (New York: Anti-Defamation League of B'nai B'ith, 1966), p. 51.
5. News dispatch of the Jewish Telegraphic Agency, March 13, 1950.
6. *Einikeit,* June 29, 1946.
7. A. Holdes, in *Einikeit,* June 29, 1946.
8. According to various sources, among them: Alexander Pomeranz, *The Soviet Martyrs* (Yiddish) (Buenos Aires: YIVO, 1962), pp. 44–45; Esther Rosenthal (Schneiderman), "Eliahu Spivak," in *Di Goldene Keit,* no. 44, 1962, pp. 135–144.
9. Esther Rosenthal (Schneiderman), "Itsik Kipnis as I Knew Him," in *Di Goldene Keit,* no. 61, 1967, pp. 148–150.
10. In assembling particulars of the liquidation operations, including the names of the victims, the author had recourse to hundreds of items culled from various newspapers, chiefly Soviet and Communist; scraps of information taken from other Soviet publications (see the Appendix); reports of visitors to the Soviet Union, including delegations, after Stalin's death, especially after the Twentieth Party Congress; articles that appeared in various papers; personal conversations with members of the families of some of the victims, including the family of one who was executed. Talks with Jewish writers of Polish origin, who had been in the Soviet Union during the Forties, helped the author in depicting the atmosphere that preceded the liquidation.

    The author also referred to the following works: Yitzhak Yanasovich, *With Jewish Writers in Russia* (Yiddish) (Buenos Aires: Kiyum, 1959); Hershel Vaynrauch, *Blood on the Sun* (Yiddish) (Brooklyn, N.Y.: *Mensh un Yid,* 1950); Sheine-Miriam Broderzon, *On the Road of Suffering with Moshe Broderzon* (Yiddish) (Buenos Aires: Central Association of Polish Jews in Argentina, 1960). (With Mrs. Broderzon — the widow of Moshe Broderzon, who was sentenced to ten years' imprisonment in 1950 but was released in 1955 — the author had a long talk, in the course of which he heard a great many details concerning the liquidation. Moshe Broderzon arrived in the Soviet Union at the beginning of the war together with other Polish refugee writers. He returned to Poland after his release, in July 1956, and died in Warsaw three weeks later, on August 17, 1956); An Anonymous Soviet Jew, *To My Brethren in the State of Israel: Uncensored Letters from the Soviet Union* (Hebrew) (Jerusalem: Kiryat Sefer,

1957); N. Meisel, "Soviet Yiddish Literature," in *Yiddishe Kultur,* October 1957; Israel Emyot, *The Case of Birobidzhan* (Yiddish) (Rochester, N.Y.: published by Shlomo Bogorod, 1960); Lvavi (Babitzky), op. cit.

11. In reviewing the developments in Birobidzhan the author had recourse to sources some of which are quoted in note 10, especially: Emyot, op. cit., and Lvavi (Babitzky), op. cit. Further sources are quoted separately.
12. *Einikeit,* March 30, 1948.
13. *Einikeit,* July 22, 1948.
14. Ben Ami [Arieh Eliav], *Between Hammer and Sickle* (Hebrew) (Tel Aviv: Am Oved, 1965), pp. 191–193 (among other sources). It was published in English in 1967 by the Jewish Publication Society of America, Philadelphia.
15. Harrison E. Salisbury, *American in Russia* (New York: Harper, 1955), pp. 282–283.
16. Ibid., p. 282.
17. Harrison E. Salisbury, in *New York Times,* August 12, 1958, based on a conversation with Israel Emyot (among other sources).
18. Salisbury, *American in Russia,* p. 281.
19. Ben Ami, op. cit., p. 189.
20. Salisbury, *American in Russia,* p. 284.
21. Ibid., pp. 279–281.
22. Ben Ami, op. cit., pp. 193–194. Against a possible contention on the part of the Soviet authorities that the Jews did not make use of the opportunity offered to them by Birobidzhan, Ben Ami quotes an interview of *Figaro* correspondent Serge Groussard with Khrushchev, in which the Soviet leader spoke, among other things, of the individualism of the Jews, in general, and of the fact that they had abandoned Birobidzhan, in particular (reported in *Figaro,* Paris, April 9, 1958).
23. A. Sutzkever, in *Di Goldene Keit,* no. 41, 1961, pp. 198–199.
24. The list was compiled (and particulars regarding it given to the author) by Eliahu Shulman, who has consistently followed up developments in various fields of Jewish culture in the Soviet Union and has written a series of articles on the subject.
25. *Morgn Freiheit,* New York, July 28, 1956.
26. A prominent example of this is Emanuel Kazakevich (son of the erstwhile editor of the *Birobidzhaner Shtern,* Henekh Kazakevich). A well-known Yiddish writer, he took to writing in Russian in the mid-Forties and established a reputation in Soviet Russian literature.
27. Maurice Shapps, in *Jewish Currents,* New York (here quoted from a Hebrew translation that appeared in *Al Hamishmar,* Tel Aviv, February 21, 1964).
28. *Einikeit,* September 24, 1946.
29. *Einikeit,* December 14, 1946.
30. M. Notovich and S. Roitman, "October and the Jewish Soviet Literature," in *Heimland,* Moscow, no. 1, 1947.
31. Chaim Loitsker, "For the Ideological Purity of Our Literature," in *Der Shtern,* no. 2, 1948.

32. B. Z. Goldberg, *The Jewish Problem in the Soviet Union* (New York: Crown Publishers, 1961), pp. 140–145.
33. Ilya Ehrenburg, *Memoirs, 1921–1941,* tr. Takania Shebunina and Yvonne Kapp (Cleveland and New York: World Publishing Co., 1963), p. 499.
34. According to one report, Lina Shtern's life sentence was commuted to twenty-five years' imprisonment. She was released and exonerated in the course of the de-Stalinization of the mid-Fifties. She died in March 1968 at the age of ninety.
35. The author saw a copy of one of the "rehabilitation" certificates that were issued to the widows of executed writers. This is important for determining the date of the trial. It states that "the charge against ——— was reexamined by the military collegium of the Supreme Court of the Soviet Union on ——— 1955," and that the "verdict of the military committee of July 11–18, 1952, passed on ——— has been changed in the light of new facts that emerged. The charges against him are dropped for lack of evidence of the crime attributed to him."

    The American Jewish journalist Leon Cristal, who toured the Soviet Union at the beginning of 1956, was one of the first who publicly disclosed the fact that twenty to thirty Soviet Jewish writers had been executed on August 12, 1952, having received his information from "those in the know" (*Forverts,* New York, March 7, 1956). It would appear that at that time the Soviet authorities were not interested in suppressing the publication of this information. It was later confirmed that twenty-four men had been executed; they included, apart from writers, also several Jewish artists and public figures, and reportedly six Jewish engineers from the Stalin vehicle assembly plant in Moscow.
36. To mark the sixty-fifth birthday of Perets Markish, Shlomo Belis published an article entitled "His Volcanic Poetry Lives" in the Warsaw *Folks-Shtimme* of December 3, 1960. In it he wrote: "We [on this day] scatter a spray of dry words . . . on his *anonymous grave.*" (Italics added.)
37. A great many rumors became rife concerning the disgraceful cowardly behavior of Itsik Feffer, which served the prosecution's ends in the 1952 trial. It is only fair to point out, however, that other rumors spoke of the brave stand adopted by Feffer, who was among those executed. In this connection, it is relevant to quote Mrs. Tsipeh Bergelson (widow of David Bergelson, who was executed together with Feffer): "Is it possible and must one believe all these rumors? And have we — those who survived — the right to judge a man who went through Beria's inquisition cells and might have been driven mad?" (From an article by Haim Shoshkes, following a visit to the USSR, in *Letzte Nayes,* Tel Aviv, June 1, 1960.)
38. See note 27.
39. Ilya Ehrenburg, "People, Years, Life," in *Novy Mir,* no. 2, February 1965, p. 57. On several occasions, and also in his memoirs, Ehrenburg claimed that he owed his survival to chance as though in a lottery; his number simply had not come up.

40. Alexei Surkov (then chairman of the Soviet Writers' Association), in a talk with Israeli writers Avraham Shlonsky and S. Yizhar (Smilansky) during their visit to the Soviet Union; according to Roman Prister's interview with Shlonsky, published in *Al Hamishmar,* Tel Aviv, August 10, 1962.
41. Esther Rosenthal (Schneiderman) commends the behavior, for example, of Ukrainian authors Pavlo Tichina and Maxim Rilsky (in *Di Goldene Keit,* no. 61, 1967, p. 154).
42. B. Z. Goldberg: *Jews in the Soviet Union* (Yiddish) (Tel Aviv: Peretz Publishing House, 1965), pp. 34–36.
43. Nachman Meisel, *Jewish Creative Activity and Jewish Writers in the Soviet Union* (Yiddish) (New York: YKUF, 1959), p. 98.
44. Editorial entitled "The New Unbridled Vilification" in *Yiddishe Kultur,* New York, June 1949; Moshe Katz, "What Are They Really Shouting About?" in *Yiddishe Kultur,* August 1949.
45. Hayim Greenberg, "What Is Happening to Soviet Jewry? — An Open Letter to the Soviet Ambassador to the U.S." in *Jewish Frontier,* New York, February 1951, pp. 5–8.
46. Meisel, op. cit., pp. 99–100.
47. Howard Fast, *The Naked God: The Writer in the Communist Party* (New York: Praeger, 1957). The quotations are based on the Hebrew translation published by Am Oved, Tel Aviv, 1959, pp. 126 and 174. See also the author's interview with Howard Fast, in *Maariv,* Tel Aviv, April 25, 1958.
48. It is noteworthy that the second edition of the encyclopedia devoted a great deal of space to the national literatures of the many Soviet peoples, including the literatures of ethnic groups that had only recently adopted an alphabet, but did not allot an entry to Jewish literature.
49. M. Mirsky in *Folks-Shtimme,* Warsaw, January 24, 26, 1957.
50. It was only in supplementary volume 51, which appeared in 1958 (after the "rehabilitations"), that space was allotted to the four Soviet Yiddish authors: David Bergelson, Shmuel Halkin, Perets Markish, and Leib Kvitko.
51. *Kultura i Zhizn,* Moscow, August 20, 1947.
52. Howard Fast, op. cit. Hebrew translation, p. 135; the author's interview with Fast (see note 47); Salo W. Baron, *The Russian Jew Under Tsars and Soviets* (New York: Macmillan, 1964), p. 325.
53. Boris Souvarine, "Gorky, Censorship and the Jews," *Dissent,* New York, Winter 1965, pp. 83–85 (reprinted from *Preuves,* Paris).
54. L. Zinger, *Dos Banayte Folk* [The Rejuvenated People] (Moscow: *Der Emes* publishers, 1941), p. 109.
55. I. Elkin, "Meeting with Bukharan Jews," in *Einikeit,* December 28, 1946.
56. According to the entry "Jews" in the first edition of the *Great Soviet Encyclopedia,* vol. 24, 1932.
57. The *shirohos,* or verses, of the Tati-Mountain Jews have become known. One of them, originating in Caucasian Dagestan, was translated into Yiddish by Soviet Jewish author M. Helmond and was widely published.

It tells of a dynasty of heroes — Samson the First, Second, and Third — who lived centuries ago, and includes these lines: "We are brothers, of one family of people, one large beehive in an eagle's eyrie, one stronghold — a mountain-rock tribe, the sons of Judah." (See *Einikeit,* February 14, 1946; *Yiddishe Kultur,* New York, November 1946, pp. 19–21.) There are *shirohos* from the Stalin era, written in Mountain Yiddish, glorifying the leader as "the chosen of the chosen ones, the mountain eagle."

58. The entry "Mountain Jews" appears in the second edition of the *Encyclopedia,* vol. 12, which went to press on May 28, 1952. Vol. 13, which went to press on June 27, 1952, has an entry "Dagestan Autonomous Republic." The Mountain Jews are mentioned in the section "Population" but not in the section "Literature."
59. Harrison E. Salisbury, *Moscow Journal* (Chicago: University of Chicago Press, 1961), pp. 254–255; Esther Vilenska, in *Kol Ha'am,* Tel Aviv, September 27, 1954.
60. It should be pointed out that the Soviet authorities' expectation that the Jewish religion would of itself become voided of all attraction proved incorrect. In the years after Stalin's death — a period beyond the scope of this research — it became manifest that in the absence of any alternative expression of national identification, the synagogue again began to exercise a stronger attraction.
61. Namely: "Bring our scattered ones among the nations near unto thee, and gather our dispersed from the ends of the earth"; "And may our eyes behold thy return in mercy to Zion"; "Next year in Jerusalem"; "And a redeemer shall come to Zion"; "On account of our sins we were exiled from our land"; "O cause a new light to shine upon Zion, and may we all be worthy soon to enjoy its brightness"; "And make us go upright to our land."
62. Goldberg, *The Jewish Problem . . . ,* op. cit., p. 101.
63. Emyot, op. cit., pp. 103–104.
64. "An Open Letter to Comrade Leonid Ilichev," by the editors of *Folks-Shtimme,* Warsaw, November 3, 1956.
65. Published, inter alia, in *Yiddishe Shriften,* Warsaw, December 1956, and in *Folks-Shtimme,* Warsaw, November 5, 1960.
66. Published in *Yiddishe Shriften,* Warsaw, January 1958.
67. Published in *Pariser Zeitshrift,* nos. 15–16, 1956–57.
68. G. Zhits, "Unser Heimland" [Our Homeland], in *Einikeit,* October 19, 1948.
69. Nachman Meisel, in *Yiddishe Kultur,* New York, November 1958.
70. I. Nusinov, "Great Summings-Up," in *Heimland,* Moscow, no. 1, October 1947.
71. A. Frumkin, in *Einikeit,* October 2, 1948. (Frumkin was chief editor for classical Yiddish literature of *Der Emes* State Publishing House.)
72. *Einikeit,* November 2, 1948.
73. *Einikeit,* November 18, 1948.
74. *On New Roads: Thirty Years of Soviet Jewish* [*Literary*] *Creation* (New York: YKUF, 1948).
75. Meisel, op. cit., p. 98.

6: The Crimean Affair

1. According to various sources, including a conversation the author had with a relative of one of the executed victims. See also: Zev Ben-Shlomo, in *Haaretz*, Tel Aviv, January 24, 1958.
2. B. Z. Goldberg, *The Jewish Problem in the Soviet Union* (New York: Crown Publishers, 1961), pp. 142–145.
3. I. B. Saltsberg (member of the Canadian LPP delegation), in *Morgn Freiheit*, New York, December 12, 1956, and in *Vochenblatt*, Toronto, December 26, 1956. This conversation took place on August 29, 1956, during one of the four meetings which the delegation had with Soviet leaders in Moscow. (It was devoted entirely to the Jewish question and Khrushchev did most of the talking.)
4. Aryeh Tartakover, *Jewish Colonization in the Diaspora* (Hebrew) (Tel Aviv: Neumann, 1959), p. 79.
5. M. Kalinin, "The Jewish Question and the Resettlement of Jews in the Crimea," in *Izvestia*, July 11, 1926. The desire of the Soviet government to allot land to Jewish settlers in places where "climatic and other conditions were suited to the habits of the Jewish population" (such as the Crimea and the southern regions of the Ukraine) was stressed by Kalinin also in his address to the First All-Union Convention of OZET, held in Moscow, November 15–20, 1926. See the stenographic record of the Convention, published in Yiddish by the Central Directorate of OZET, Moscow, 1927, p. 41. It is relevant to point out that Kalinin's remark about "the mild southern climate" did not prevent him, in later years, from giving his preferred support to Jewish colonization in Birobidzhan in the Far East.
6. Paragraph 5 of the resolution of the presidium of the Central Executive Committee of the USSR, adopted on March 28, 1928.
7. Jacob Lvavi (Babitzky), *The Jewish Colonization in Birobidzhan* (Hebrew), Galuyot Series (Jerusalem: Historical Society of Israel, 1965), pp. 52–57.
8. The figures as of January 1, 1938, place the number of Jewish homesteads in the Crimea at 4,992; L. Zinger, *Dos Banayte Folk* [The Rejuvenated People] (Moscow: *Der Emes* publishers, 1941), p. 90.
9. David Pinsky, *Travelogue* (Yiddish), vol. 2 (Warsaw: David Pinsky Books, n.d.), p. 216.
10. The December 1940 issue of *Nei Leben — New Life*, published in New York in Yiddish and English by ICOR, contains an article entitled "Jewish Collective Farm Is Now Pride of Crimea," which describes the Mayfeld *kolhoz* and its grape-growing achievements. The Mayfeld farmers are depicted as former Pale of Settlement residents — former tailors, cobblers, and petty shopkeepers. Not so long ago, all they knew about grapes was that one bought a few for the High Holidays in the autumn, and that raisin wine was needed for the Passover ritual. Now they had become fine grape-growing experts. The author of the article adds that most of the Crimea's grapes were grown in the southern coastal area, where the climate is similar to that of Italy.

11. See note 5.
12. Mikhail Gurev, *Against the Anti-Semites* (Russian) (Moscow and Leningrad, 1928). Quoted in Solomon M. Schwarz, *The Jews in the Soviet Union* (Syracuse, N.Y.: Syracuse University Press, 1951), p. 244.
13. Yuri Larin, *Jews and Anti-Semitism in the USSR* (Russian) (Moscow and Leningrad, 1929). Quoted in Schwarz, op. cit., p. 251.
14. In February 1954, the Crimea was transferred from the federated Russian Republic to the Ukrainian Republic.
15. Ivan Kozlov, *In the Crimean Underground: Memoirs* (Russian) (Moscow: Sovetski Pisatel, 1947), p. 76.
16. *Izvestia,* June 26, 1946; *Great Soviet Encyclopedia,* 2nd. ed., vol. 23, 1953, p. 547. An edict (*ukaz*) issued by the presidium of the Supreme Soviet of the USSR on September 5, 1967, stated that "the facts relating to the active collaboration with the German invaders of a certain section of the Tartars who lived in the Crimea were attributed without foundation to the entire Tartar population of the Crimea," and that these generalized charges must be cancelled.

    The Crimean Republic was one of the five autonomous units that were dissolved after these territories were liberated from the German occupation. The other units were: the Chechen-Ingush Autonomous Soviet Socialist Republic; the Kalmyk ASSR; the Balkar section of the Kabardine-Balkar ASSR; the Karachai Autonomous Oblast. A sixth autonomous unit, the Volga German ASSR, was previously dissolved, in September 1941.
17. Binyamin West, ed., *In the Throes of Extinction* (Hebrew) (published by the Labor Archive, Tel Aviv, 1963), pp. 138–145 (culled chiefly from Soviet sources).
18. Kozlov, op. cit.
19. Yitzhak Yanasovich, *With Jewish Writers in Russia* (Yiddish) (Buenos Aires: Kiyum, 1959), pp. 255–257.
20. Joseph Rubinstein, *Megilas Russland* [Scroll of Woe of a Polish Jew in Russia] (New York: CYCO, 1960), pp. 215–217. Rubinstein dwells on the Crimean Affair also in his *Polish Jewry: A Lament* (Yiddish) (New York: CYCO, 1964), p. 36.
21. A. Sutzkever, in *Di Goldene Keit,* no 61, 1967, p. 32.
22. A. Sutzkever, in *Di Goldene Keit,* no. 43, 1962, p. 159.
23. F. Grim (Moshe Grossman), *In the Enchanted Land of the Legendary Dzhugashvili: My Seven Years in Soviet Russia, 1939–1946* (Yiddish), 2nd ed. (Paris: Emes un Freiheit, 1950), vol. 2, p. 251.
24. Hershel Vaynrauch, *Blood on the Sun* (Yiddish) (Brooklyn, N.Y.: *Mensh un Yid,* 1950), pp. 10–11.
25. Yanasovich, op. cit., pp. 257–258.
26. Israel Emyot, *The Case of Birobidzhan* (Yiddish) (Rochester, N.Y.: published by Shlomo Bogorod, 1960), p. 8.
27. Menahem Flakser, in *Letzte Nayes,* Tel Aviv, December 20, 1963.
28. B. Z. Goldberg, *The Jews in the Soviet Union* (Yiddish) (Tel Aviv: Peretz Publishing House, 1965), p. 96.
29. *Einikeit,* May 11, 1944.

30. Emyot, op. cit., p. 7.
31. Lvavi (Babitzky), op. cit., pp. 68–69.
32. *Einikeit,* June 20, 1947.
33. *Einikeit,* January 10, 1948. See also *Einikeit,* January 3, 1948.

7: Numerus Clausus, Numerus Nullus

1. The term "black years" — or such analogous variations as "black days," "nightmare period," "sad years," etc. — recurs in the reports and articles of a great many visitors (delegations, journalists, or ordinary tourists) to the Soviet Union after Stalin's death. A British Communist delegation published a report of its October 1956 visit to the Soviet Union in the Party's official organ, *World News* (London), of January 12, 1957. The report stated that it transpired from the talks which Hyman Levy (a delegation member) had with Jews in the USSR that the years 1948–52 were known as the "black years," during which Jews were dismissed from their jobs, and Jewish poets and writers arrested, accused of treason, and executed.

   See also Harrison E. Salisbury, *To Moscow and Beyond* (New York: Harper, 1959), p. 65. ("The black days were the days from late 1948 until Stalin's death in March 1953, when a secret but deadly anti-Semitic policy was pursued by the Kremlin.")
2. From Khrushchev's talk with a French socialist delegation, Moscow, May 12, 1956; *Réalités,* Paris, May 1957.
3. From Khrushchev's interview with *Le Figaro* correspondent Serge Groussard, *Le Figaro,* Paris, April 9, 1958.
4. Litvinov, isolated in his latter years, died in Moscow on December 31, 1951; Maisky is believed to have spent two years in a labor camp, and to have been released after Stalin's death. See Louis Fischer, *Russia Revisited* (Garden City, N.Y.: Doubleday, 1957), p. 25. Lozovsky was executed on August 12, 1952.
5. Solomon M. Schwarz, *The Jews in the Soviet Union* (Syracuse, N.Y.: Syracuse University Press, 1951), p. 363.
6. Fischer, op. cit.
7. Joseph Schechtman, *Star in Eclipse: Russian Jewry Revisited* (New York: Thomas Yoseloff, 1961), p. 53.
8. Milovan Djilas, in *Borba,* December 14, 1952; Milovan Djilas, *Conversations with Stalin,* trans. Michael B. Petrovich (New York: Harcourt, Brace and World, 1962), p. 170.
9. Kaganovich was elected to the Politburo in July 1930, after the Sixteenth Party Congress (having been a member-designate since July 1926). He remained a member of the presidium (as the Politburo came to be called after the Nineteenth Party Congress) until his expulsion in June 1957 together with other members of the "Anti-Party Group."
10. In reviewing the position of Jews in the Communist Party leadership the author has referred to an article on the subject by A. Hiram, quoted from *Haaretz,* Tel Aviv, in *The Situation in the Soviet Sphere,* mimeographed

publication of the Institute of Jewish Affairs, World Jewish Congress, New York, 1953 (introduction by Nehemiah Robinson), pp. 15–16.

11. Djilas, op. cit.
12. Schwarz, op. cit., pp. 354–355.
13. Isaac Deutscher, *Russia — What Next?* (New York: Oxford University Press, 1953), pp. 192–193.
14. Salo W. Baron, *The Russian Jew Under Tsars and Soviets* (New York: Macmillan, 1964), p. 324.
15. Salisbury, op. cit., p. 14. See also Edmund Stevens, in *Christian Science Monitor,* Boston, January 10, 1950 (quoted by Joseph Gordon, in *American Jewish Year Book,* vol. 52, 1951, p. 329).
16. David Burg (a Soviet university graduate), in *Sotsialistichesky Viestnik,* New York, December 1957.
17. *Izvestia,* January 23, 1953.
18. "At the Second Conference of Soviet Writers (Facts and Figures)," in *Novy Mir,* January 1955.
19. Salisbury, op. cit., p. 74. Here, the author recounts that at a meeting of the Soviet Writers' Union one member called for the expulsion of a long list of members — all Jewish. Whereupon Ehrenburg observed that there was one thing wrong with the list: his own name had been omitted.
20. The bearer's nationality is entered on his internal passport, in accordance with a regulation promulgated on December 27, 1932. This is fixed on the strength of the nationality of the parents. Where the parents have different nationalities, the nationality of either one may be chosen. The nationality may not be changed after it has been entered in the passport. This was the legal position at the time of the present writing.

8: Kafka in Prague, 1952

1. The conduct of Bulgaria and Poland should be pointed out as a certain exception to the general line of the "Jewish Policy" in the Soviet bloc. Of the approximately forty-nine thousand Jews remaining in Bulgaria after World War II, about forty thousand emigrated to Israel until 1951. Even in the early 1950's, the tone of anti-Zionist propaganda in Bulgaria was softer than in other People's Democracies. The Polish authorities also exercised greater restraint with respect to Jews, although they did not refrain from purging the civil service of Jews or from conducting a propaganda campaign against Zionism and Israel. This approach was apparently influenced by fear of an anti-Semitic flare-up in the country, three million of whose Jews were destroyed by the Nazis. Dissatisfaction with a policy of closely hewing to the line marked out by Moscow accompanied by certain attempts to shy away from extreme Stalinization (the operation of these factors could be detected in the careful behavior with respect to the Catholic Church or in the failure to make Wladyslaw Gomulka stand public trial despite his arrest) also acted somewhat to moderate the "Jewish Policy" in Poland.

2. Ehrenburg's article, which was copied in the Moscow *Einikeit* from *Pravda,* was also published in the Warsaw *Folks-Shtimme* of October 8, 1948. In the countries of the Soviet bloc, the propaganda agencies energetically began to "discover" the reactionary-imperialistic-bourgeois character of Israel, which they had previously praised a good deal. A number of resolutions by Party organizations or by groups dominated by Communist Parties (without excepting Jewish organizations and institutions) called for a more intensive struggle against Zionist influences. An example is the resolution adopted by the Political Bureau of the Romanian Workers' Party (Communist) in December 1948, which declared: "Zionism in all its aspects is a reactionary, national, political current of the Jewish bourgeoisie seeking to isolate the toiling Jewish population from the peoples in the midst of whom they dwell and to prevent them from joining the ranks of progressive forces in the struggle against capitalism and their bourgeoisie." The resolution called for a struggle against Jewish nationalism serving Jewish big business and Anglo-American imperialists. For this purpose, the "Jewish Democratic Committee" in Romania, which had anyway been under complete supervision by the authorities and the Party, was reorganized.
3. Alfred Joachim Fischer, "Yugoslavia's Moshe Pijade," *Congress Weekly,* New York, June 1, 1953, p. 10. The author, a journalist from Britain, wrote the article on the basis of a personal interview with Pijade.
4. Peter Meyer et al., *The Jews in the Soviet Satellites* (Syracuse, N.Y.: Syracuse University Press, 1953), pp. 471–480 ("Hungary" by Eugene Duschinsky), pp. 540, 550 ("Rumania" by Nicolas Sylvain), and passim; *European Jewry Ten Years after the War,* Institute of Jewish Affairs of the World Jewish Congress, 1956 (prepared and published under the direction of Nehemiah Robinson), pp. 53–54, 74–77, 104–106.
5. Meyer et al., op. cit., pp. 40–41 (Introduction by Peter Meyer), and passim.
6. A number of Communist leaders of Jewish extraction were the object of criticism for deviating from the Party line and became the victims of dismissals and purges. One of the most outstanding cases was that of Ana Pauker in Romania, who for years was considered the number two personality in the leadership of the state and the Party. She lost her status gradually as the charges against her continued to pile up, and her final expulsion came at the beginning of July 1952, when the announcement of her dismissal as minister for foreign affairs was made.
7. David Horowitz, *State in the Making,* trans. Julian Meltzer (New York: Knopf, 1953), p. 250.
8. *Davar,* March 28, 1948.
9. A. A. Ben-Asher, *Foreign Relations, 1948–1953* (Hebrew) (Tel Aviv: Ayanot, 1956), p. 206.
10. Critic, in *New Statesman and Nation,* London, December 20, 1952.
11. The details and quotations referring to the trial which are cited in this chapter are taken from the Hebrew work, *The Prague Trial: A Complete Report,* published in Tel-Aviv in 1952–53 by the Israel Labor Party and

based on the report of the proceedings which were published in *Rude Pravo* in Prague during the trial. Only references to other sources will be cited below. See also: Meyer et al., op. cit., pp. 153–191, 201–204 (notes) ("Czechoslovakia" by Peter Meyer).

12. Thomas Frejka about his father, Ludvik Frejka; Lisa London about her husband, Artur London.
13. Peter Meyer, "Stalin Follows in Hitler's Footsteps," in Elliot E. Cohen, ed., *The New Red Antisemitism: A Symposium* (Boston: Beacon Press, 1953), p. 16.
14. See Joseph Gordon in *American Jewish Year Book,* vol. 54, 1953, pp. 346–347.
15. Miriam Kubovy, *Wife of the Israeli Minister in Prague and Warsaw* (Hebrew), trans. from French by Miri and Michael Kubovy (Tel Aviv: Massadah, 1964), p. 155; Peter Meyer, as in note 13, p. 18.
16. Shimon Orenstein, *Adventure in Prague* (Hebrew) (Tel Aviv: *Am Hassefer,* 1968); Mordecai Oren, *Notes of a Prisoner in Prague* (Hebrew) (Merhavia: Sifriat Hapoalim, 1958).
17. Orenstein, op. cit., p. 47.
18. Oren, op. cit., p. 57.
19. Ibid., p. 309.
20. Ibid., p. 164.
21. Ibid., p. 237.
22. Shimon Orenstein, "The Story of Czech Arms in the War of Independence," *Maariv,* August 17, 1956.
23. Oren, op. cit., p. 7.
24. Ibid., pp. 345–346.
25. Ibid., p. 311.
26. Shortly after the Slansky trial, the assumption was made that the first copy of the charge sheet had been drawn up in Russian. See Peter Meyer, "Czechoslovakia" in Meyer et al., op. cit., p. 203 (note 1).
27. Interview given by Jozefa Slanska (in Prague) to David Giladi, *Maariv,* August 9, 1968.
28. Gottwald died on March 14, 1953, not long after his return from Moscow where he attended Stalin's funeral. The short interval between his trip to Moscow and his death gave rise to speculation that his demise had not been entirely due to natural causes.
29. Oren, op. cit., pp. 286–297.
30. Ibid., p. 287.
31. Quoted from *Literaturnaya Gazeta* by I. Ehrenburg, "People, Years, Life," *Novy Mir,* no. 4, April 1965, p. 55. Other examples from the Soviet press on the Prague trial: *Pravda* and *Izvestia,* November 22, 25, 26, 27, 1952.

9: Swindlers and Embezzlers

1. In addition to Soviet newspapers in the original, the author had recourse to *The Current Digest of the Soviet Press* (*CDSP*), especially vols. 2, 4,

and 5; *The Jewish Situation in the Soviet Sphere,* a mimeographed publication of the Institute of Jewish Affairs, World Jewish Congress, New York, 1953 (Introduction by Nehemiah Robinson); Isaac London, "Days of Anxiety: A Chapter in the History of Soviet Jewry," in *Jewish Social Studies,* New York, July–October, 1953, pp. 275–292, with highly valuable notes, pp. 287–292; Harrison E. Salisbury, *Moscow Journal* (Chicago: University of Chicago Press, 1961). In the three sources listed above the names of the Soviet newspapers and the dates of the accounts and stories cited in the text are given.

2. Joseph Berliner, "Blat Is Higher than Stalin," in *Problems of Communism,* January–February 1954; Merle Fainsod, *How Russia Is Ruled,* revised ed. (Cambridge, Mass.: Harvard University Press, 1963), pp. 507–509.

10: Murderers in White Gowns

1. *Pravda,* January 13, 1953. *Current Digest of the Soviet Press* (*CDSP*), vol. 4, no. 51, January 31, 1953, p. 3.
2. Robert Conquest, *Power and Policy in the U.S.S.R.* (London: Macmillan, 1962), pp. 163–166.
3. From the speech delivered by Khrushchev at a special secret session of the Twentieth Congress on February 24 and 25, 1956; according to a copy obtained by the American Department of State and released for publication on June 4, 1956 (*New York Times,* June 5, 1956) and published in numerous newspapers and periodicals outside the Soviet Union. (Henceforth referred to as Khrushchev's "secret" speech). According to this text, Khrushchev completely ignored the Jewish aspect of the doctors' affair.
4. *Pravda,* January 13, 1953. *CDSP,* as in note 1, pp. 3–4.
5. John A. Armstrong, *The Politics of Totalitarianism* (New York: Random House, 1961), pp. 70–71.
6. Ilya Ehrenburg relates that he was once asked by the Sovinformburo to write an appeal to the Jews of the United States in which he would tell of the German atrocities and discuss the necessity of destroying the Third Reich at an early date. One of Shcherbakov's assistants, Kondakov, rejected the text written by Ehrenburg with the contention that there was no need to mention the heroism of Jewish soldiers in the Red Army. According to Kondakov, "This is bragging." Ehrenburg complained to Shcherbakov of Kondakov who argued (although he praised the writer's articles), "The soldiers want to hear of Suvorov and you quote Heine . . ." (I. Ehrenburg, "Men, Years, Life," *Novy Mir,* no. 2, February 1963, p. 126). There is no doubt that Kondakov's argument concerning the bravery of Jews reflected Shcherbakov's attitude. It should be pointed out that despite the fact that the Sovinformburo was headed by Solomon Lozovsky, his "possibilities were limited: it was Shcherbakov who made

the decisions" (Ehrenburg, "Men, Years, Life," *Novy Mir,* no. 1, January 1963, p. 70.

It is nevertheless told that at the end of 1943, Shcherbakov gathered leading Party workers in Moscow and explained — apparently because of widespread overt hatred of Jews — that anti-Semitism is not government policy and its manifestations should be curbed. (See Harrison E. Salisbury, *To Moscow and Beyond* [New York: Harper, 1959], p. 68; Maurice Hindus; *House Without a Roof* [Garden City, N.Y.: Doubleday, 1961], p. 311). But this statement of Shcherbakov's is not enough to contradict the testimony of his personal anti-Semitic attitude. What he said suggests that anti-Semitism had spread so freely that it was able to appear to many people as an official line — and this state of affairs was not desired by the authorities with the war still going on full blast and the sympathy of world public opinion sought after.

7. Editorial, *Pravda,* January 18, 1953. *CDSP,* vol. 4, no. 52, February 7, 1953, p. 3.
8. Editorial, *Trud,* January 17, 1953, *CDSP,* ibid., pp. 7–8. In a similar vein, and sometimes in almost identical language, many other articles were published, including editorials in *Komsomolskaya Pravda,* January 15, 20, 1953; and an editorial in *Izvestia,* January 15, 1953.
9. "The Poisoners," *Krokodil,* January 30, 1953.
10. Cartoon "The Trail of Crimes," ibid.
11. Nikolai Gribachev, "The Plucked 'Joint,' " *Krokodil,* February 20, 1953.
12. *Izvestia, Pravda,* January 21, 1953.
13. From Khrushchev's "secret" speech, op. cit.
14. Harrison E. Salisbury, *Moscow Journal* (Chicago: University of Chicago Press, 1961), p. 333. This is a piece written by the *New York Times* correspondent in Moscow on February 24, 1953, relying on an account in *Meditsinski Rabotnik.*
15. *Pravda,* February 20, 1953. (See also *CDSP,* vol. 5, no. 5, p. 13.)
16. The excerpts are drawn from *The Jewish Situation in the Soviet Sphere,* mimeographed publication of the Institute of Jewish Affairs, World Jewish Congress, New York, 1953 (introduction by Nehemiah Robinson).
17. Harold J. Berman, *The Russians in Focus* (Boston: Atlantic–Little, Brown, 1953), pp. 87–92.
18. Ibid., p. 82.
19. Yevgeny Yevtushenko, *A Precocious Autobiography,* trans. Andrew R. MacAndrew (New York: E. P. Dutton, 1963), p. 80.
20. Ibid., pp. 89–90.
21. Salisbury: *To Moscow and Beyond* p. 77. Salisbury, *American in Russia* (New York: Harper, 1955), p. 155. Esther Feldman, *A Prison Without Bars* (Hebrew) (Tel Aviv: *Am ha-Sefer,* 1964), pp. 150–151.
22. I. Ehrenburg, "Men, Years, Life," *Novy Mir,* no. 4, April 1965, p. 57.
23. Ibid., p. 71.
24. Ilya Ehrenburg, *The Thaw,* trans. Manya Harari, in *A Change of Season* (New York: Knopf, 1962), p. 23. In his characteristic fashion, Ehrenburg does not forget to add that at about the same time, Dr. Vera Sherer

received a pot of cyclamens with a note "from a group of workers."
25. Esther Feldman, op. cit., p. 151.

11: The Darkest Days

1. Said at a symposium devoted to the Jews of the Soviet Union conducted in London, October 22, 1961.
2. Frederick C. Barghoorn, *Soviet Russian Nationalism* (London and New York: Oxford University Press), 1956, pp. 301–302 (note 16 to chapter 5).
3. Harrison E. Salisbury, *To Moscow and Beyond* (New York: Harper, 1959), pp. 65–66, 69.
4. See note 1.
5. Salisbury, op. cit., pp. 78–79.
6. Announcement made by Foreign Minister Moshe Sharett at a session of the Knesset on January 19, 1953; *Divrei ha-Knesset* (Official Parliamentary Record), vol. 13, p. 493.
7. Harrison E. Salisbury, *Moscow Journal* (Chicago: University of Chicago Press, 1961), p. 308 (dispatch to *New York Times,* December 22, 1952, quoting *Bloknot Agitatora,* Moscow).
8. V. Minayev, *Novoe Vremya,* January 21, 1953.
9. N. Sergeyev, "Zionist Agency of the Dollar," *Trud,* February 13, 1953 (*CDSP,* vol. 5, no. 5, p. 10).
10. N. Klimpotyuk, "Zionists are Accursed Foes of Working People," *Sovetskoye Zakarpatye,* February 6, 1953; reprinted in *Pravda Ukrainy,* February 13, 1953 (*CDSP,* vol. 5, no. 5, pp. 10–11).
11. "What Is Joint?" *Literaturnaya Gazeta,* February 24, 1953 (*CDSP,* vol. 5, no. 9, pp. 6–7).
12. *Izvestia,* February 18, 1953.
13. M. Mitin, "The Zionist Agency of the American Imperialism," *Komsomolskaya Pravda,* February 24, 1953. See also: "Terroristic Act in Tel Aviv and Fraudulent Game of Rulers of Israel," *Pravda,* February 14, 1953 (*CDSP,* vol. 5, no. 5, pp. 9–10).
14. *The Jewish Situation in the Soviet Sphere,* mimeographed publication of the Institute of Jewish Affairs, World Jewish Congress, New York, 1953.
15. *Pravda,* January 18, 1953.
16. *Pravda,* January 31, 1953. (*CDSP,* vol. 5, no. 2, pp. 3–4.)
17. *Pravda,* February 6, 1953.
18. Thomas P. Whitney, *Russia in My Life* (New York: Reynal, 1962), pp. 264–265. (The author was A.P. correspondent in Moscow at the time.)
19. *Kommunist,* Moscow, January 14, 1953, pp. 46–58.
20. Salisbury, *Moscow Journal,* p. 326 (dispatch to *New York Times,* February 13, 1953, based on a report in *Pravda Ukrainy*).
21. *Sovietskaya Moldavia,* February 25, 1953 (*CDSP,* vol. 5, no. 9, pp. 13–14).
22. Salisbury, *Moscow Journal,* p. 317 (dispatch killed by censor on January 19, 1953).

23. *Pravda,* January 31, 1953; *New York Times,* January 30, 1953 (as quoted in *The Jewish Situation in the Soviet Sphere,* op. cit.).
24. Israel Emyot, *The Case of Birobidzhan* (Yiddish) (Rochester, N.Y.: published by Shlomo Bogorod, 1960), pp. 113–115.
25. From a conversation with Dr. L. Heselson.
26. John Gunther, *Inside Russia Today* (London: Hamish Hamilton, 1958), p. 139. Several weeks after Stalin's death, Mrs. Molotov returned to Moscow from her place of exile. (Harrison E. Salisbury, *American in Russia* (New York: Harper, 1955). See also Svetlana Alliluyeva, *Twenty Letters to a Friend,* trans. Priscilla Johnson (New York: Harper, 1967), pp. 119, 206.
27. Marie Syrkin, *Golda Meir, Woman with a Cause: An Authorized Biography* (New York: Putnam, 1963), pp. 230–231.
28. Salisbury, *To Moscow and Beyond,* op. cit., p. 69.
29. Salisbury, *Moscow Journal,* op. cit., p. 312.
30. Salisbury, *American in Russia,* op. cit., p. 140.
31. Ibid., p. 142.
32. Khrushchev's "secret" speech. See also: Merle Fainsod, *How Russia Is Ruled,* rev. ed. (Cambridge, Mass.: Harvard University Press, 1963), pp. 322–324.
33. W. Woroszylsky, in *Nowa Kultura,* Warsaw, November 13, 1956; quoted by Robert Conquest, *Russia After Khrushchev* (New York: Praeger, 1965), p. 130.
34. Robert Conquest, *The Great Terror: Stalin's Purge of the Thirties* (London: Macmillan, 1968), p. 88.
35. Fainsod, op. cit., p. 461.
36. No announcement was published concerning Ignatiev's appointment as minister of state security (and his serving in that capacity was learned only after the annulment of the doctors' libel at the beginning of April 1953); but in 1952, observers began noticing that Abakumov stopped appearing among the top dignitaries at official functions and receptions in Moscow.
37. Salisbury, *American in Russia,* op. cit., pp. 89–91; Salisbury, *To Moscow and Beyond,* op. cit., pp. 70–71.
38. The fate which in time befell the personalities mentioned here — Beria and his followers on the one hand and his rivals on the other — in the course of the vicissitudes accompanying the internal struggles among the top leaders during the early years after Stalin's death are outside the province of this study.
39. Boris I. Nicolaevsky, "The Strange Death of Mikhail Ryumin," *The New Leader,* October 4, 1954, pp. 15–18.
40. Salisbury, *American in Russia,* op. cit., p. 157.
41. Whitney, op. cit., p. 261.
42. *The Trial Begins,* Abram Tertz's work was first published in English (translated by Max Hayward) in *Encounter,* January 1960 (pp. 3–36), a short time after his original Russian manuscript managed to find its way outside the Soviet Union. After the author's identity was discovered, Andrei Sinyavsky — Abram Tertz — was brought to trial in Moscow in

February 1966 and sentenced to seven years in prison. (The second defendant at this trial was Yuly Daniel — "Nikolai Arzhak" — who was sentenced to a five-year term in prison.)

43. On the basis of the author's conversations with persons who had lived in the Soviet Union during this period.
44. Y. Ben-Mash (i.e. Yosef Barzillai), "Five Years After the Doctors' Libel," *Davar,* February 11, 1958.
45. Esther Feldman, *A Prison Without Bars* (Hebrew) (Tel-Aviv: *Am ha-Sefer,* 1964), p. 151.
46. See note 44.
47. The principal source for the account of the presidium's session in which the expulsion plan was discussed is an article by Michel Gordey which appeared in *France-Soir* on June 7, 1957 (and was quoted in the *New York Times* on June 8, 1957). It was believed that he secured his information from Panteleimon Ponomarenko, who had been an alternate member of the Party presidium during Stalin's last days and in the period of the "Thaw" had served as Soviet ambassador to Poland. (It is reasonable to assume that following the Twentieth Congress, Soviet personalities were interested in leaking information to the West stressing Stalin's exclusive responsibility for various criminal acts and implicitly suggesting their own dissociation from such deeds; it should be pointed out that in 1956–57, Poland served as an important source for divulging details connected with Stalin's last days.) More about the expulsion plan — the diplomatic correspondent of the London *Times* referred on April 16, 1956, to accounts concerning this matter cited by Khrushchev at a small meeting of the Party heads in Moscow after the Twentieth Congress (quoted in the daily *Haaretz,* April 17, 1956). It appears that after the "rejection" of Stalin, Khrushchev tried to bring to the attention of world public opinion accounts of his opposition to the dead dictator's expulsion plan. Dr. Jerome Davis, an American Christian sociologist, was told in 1957 (during a visit to the Soviet Union) by Khrushchev that he had "saved" the Jews "and by his opposition, together with that of other members of the Party's Politburo . . . forced Stalin to stay his hand" (*The Times,* London, September 8, 1959). It is noteworthy that there is no additional testimony to Khrushchev's personal share in this opposition. Finally, mention should be made of the fact that plans and operations for the mass expulsion of whole peoples do not appear extraordinary in view of Stalin's customary reactions. Referring to mass deportations of a number of minorities suspected of disloyalty during the war, Khrushchev declared, "The Ukrainians avoided meeting this fate only because there were too many of them and there was no place to which to deport them. Otherwise, he would have deported them also" (Khrushchev's "secret" speech).
48. Salisbury, *Moscow Journal,* op. cit., p. 336.
49. Isaac London: "Days of Anxiety: A Chapter in the History of Soviet Jewry," in *Jewish Social Studies,* New York, July–October, 1953, pp. 275–292.
50. *Pravda, Izvestia,* April 4, 1953.

51. An Anonymous Soviet Jew, *To My Brethren in the State of Israel: Uncensored Letters from the Soviet Union* (Hebrew) (Jerusalem: Kiryat Sefer, 1957), pp. 56–60.
52. *Pravda,* April 6, 1953.

12: Premeditated Anti-Semitism

1. For Lenin's prerevolutionary concepts on the national question in general and the Jewish question in particular, see mainly: Lenin, *Works* (Russian), 4th ed., vol. 20 (Moscow, 1948), pp. 1–34 ("Critical Remarks on the National Question") and passim. Purishkevich (Vladimir Mitrofanovich) (1870–1920), mentioned by Lenin ("the Purishkevichs"), a reactionary statesman and extreme anti-Semite in the Tsarist period, the founder of the organizations of the "Black Hundreds" which played a central role in pogroms against the Jews.
2. Stalin, *Works* (Russian) (Moscow, 1949), vol. 2, pp. 290–367 (the 1913 article "Marxism and the National Question").
3. Stalin, ibid., vol. 12, p. 369 (in the political report of the Central Committee at the Sixteenth Congress of the Communist Party of the USSR, June 27, 1930).
4. Stalin, ibid., vol. 2, p. 329.
5. Robert C. Tucker, *The Soviet Political Mind* (New York: Praeger, 1963), p. 50.
6. Ibid., pp. 20–24, 48–51.
7. Stalin, *Leninism, Selected Writings* (New York: International Publishers, 1942), p. 268.
8. Isaac Deutscher, *Russia — What Next?* (New York: Oxford University Press, 1953), p. 192.
9. Stalin, *Works,* op. cit., vol. 2, pp. 50–51. (The report was first published in *Bakinsky Proletary,* June 20, July 10, 1907, under Stalin's underground pseudonym Koba Ivanovich.)
10. Stanislaw Kot, *Conversations with the Kremlin and Despatches from Russia,* trans. H. C. Stevens (London: Oxford University Press, 1963), p. 153.
11. Milovan Djilas, *Conversations with Stalin,* trans. Michael B. Petrovich (New York: Harcourt, Brace and World, 1962), p. 154.
12. Svetlana Alliluyeva, *Twenty Letters to a Friend,* trans. Priscilla Johnson (New York: Harper, 1967), pp. 171–173, 185–194, 197–200, 204, 206.
13. This statement was widely published; among others, in the *New York Times,* January 15, 1931. It is cited in the entry "Anti-Semitism" in *Great Soviet Encyclopedia,* 2nd ed. (Moscow), vol. 2, p. 513. Also see Solomon M. Schwarz, *The Jews in the Soviet Union* (Syracuse, N.Y.: Syracuse University Press, 1951), pp. 292-293.
14. Molotov's speech on the new Soviet constitution, *Pravda,* November 30, 1936.
15. Alex Inkeles, in Carl J. Friedrich, ed., *Totalitarianism,* The University Library (New York: Grosset and Dunlap, 1964), p. 103.

16. Isaac Deutscher, *The Prophet Unarmed: Trotsky, 1921–1929* (London and New York: Oxford University Press, 1959), pp. 257–258.
17. Salo W. Baron, *The Russian Jew Under Tsars and Soviets* (New York: Macmillan, 1964), p. 59.
18. See Carl J. Friedrich, in Friedrich, op. cit., pp. 54–55.
19. Yitzhak Ma'or, *The Question of the Jews in the Liberal and Revolutionary Movements in Russia (1890–1914)* (Hebrew), (Jerusalem: *Mosad Bialik,* 1964), pp. 8–9.

APPENDIX

Excerpts from Communist and Soviet sources that mention or allude to Soviet Jewish writers who were imprisoned or executed during Stalin's latter years.

Z. VENDROF (David Vendrovsky)

To mark Vendrof's eightieth birthday in January 1957, the Warsaw *Folks-Shtimme* published his feuilleton, "A Charm against Old Age (An Interview with Myself)," where he hints at what he went through: "We asked Comrade Vendrof whether he was lying down because he didn't feel well. Comrade Vendrof answered that he didn't feel a single day older than stated in his passport. He was lying down, he said, because from his own experience he had learned that it was better to lie down than to 'sit' [i.e. in prison]."

NATHAN ZABARE

In the New York *Yiddishe Kultur* of December 1961, Yehoshua Lubomirsky (of Moscow) writes of him: "What happened to many Soviet writers did not spare author Zabare, too. . . . It was only in 1956 that Nathan Zabare returned from the Far North — from Kolyma — to his native town of Kiev, free, exonerated, encouraged, full of creative energy and new plans."

ISAAC PLATNER

After Platner's death, Hersh Smolar wrote of him in the Warsaw *Folks-Shtimme* of August 1, 1961: "Isaac Platner, who loved the new socialist life, did not escape the fate meted out to many by traitors of Beria's ilk. He returned home dangerously ill, but with his faith unshaken in the great ideals to which he had dedicated his life, all his poetic talent. . . ." The November 1964 issue of *Yiddishe Shriften,* Warsaw, published a poem by Platner, which the latter had sent to Smolar after his release from prison camp, with a request not to publish it during his lifetime. This poem, entitled *Mark of Suffering,* is a kind of answer to Smolar's questions concerning the charges leveled against the poet.

SHLOMO RABINOVICH

Folks-Shtimme of March 18, 1964, marking the sixtieth birthday of Rabinovich, stated: "For his part in the fighting, Rabinovich was awarded three combat decorations and a medal, for achievements on the battlefield. After the war he worked on the Yiddish paper *Einikeit.* The cruel personality cult period severely affected Rabinovich as well. But it did not break his spirit, his energy, his faith. We again see S. Rabinovich in the foremost ranks of Soviet journalism."

DAVID HOFSTEIN

On August 10, 1962, Ukrainian author Mikola Bodzhan wrote of Hofstein in a Ukrainian journal: "Ten years ago, the poet fell a victim to unfounded accusations. . . ."

MOSHE TAIF

Shlomo Rabinovich (mentioned above) wrote of him in *Kol Ha'am,* Tel Aviv, of July 31, 1964: "To our regret, the tyranny of the Stalinist cult also claimed Taif as a victim. For a long time his poetic voice was silenced. But after the Twentieth Congress . . . the notes of his poems were again heard."

ITZIK KIPNIS

On Kipnis's seventieth birthday, Shlomo Belis wrote of him in the Warsaw *Yiddishe Shriften* of December 1966: "White [-haired] as a dove is my seventy-year-old Itzik Kipnis. The evil did not spare him. And I know that under the most trying conditions he shared his bread with his innocent comrades."

LEIB KVITKO

A chapter is devoted to Kvitko in Kornei Chukovsky's book *My Contemporaries,* vol. 2 of *Collected Works* (Moscow 1965), pp. 459–472. Here, the author writes that Kvitko "was a victim to dark suspiciousness, libels, and violence, and perished at the time of the Stalinist lawlessness."

In an introduction to Kvitko's *Liam and Petrik* (translated from Yiddish into Russian and published in Moscow in 1958), Viera Smirnova states that Kivtko's life "was cut off in a tragic manner" in 1952.

PERETS MARKISH

Ilya Ehrenburg devoted a chapter to Markish in his memoirs, *People, Years, Life,* of which the following is an excerpt (based on the Hebrew translation by Eliahu Porat, vol. 2 [Merhavya: Sifriat Hapoalim publishing house, 1962], p. 87): "The last time I saw Markish was on January 23, 1949, at the Writers' Association, at the funeral of poet Mikhail Golodny [M. S. Epstein, born 1903]. Markish clasped my hand, a look of sadness in his eyes. We looked at one another, as though trying to guess on whom the die would fall next." Ehrenburg later quotes from Boris Lavreniev's introduction to a collection of Markish's poems, published in a Russian translation in Moscow 1957: "Markish was in the flowering prime of his mighty talent, and he would no doubt have produced many more magnificent creations, had not his life been cut short at the height of its burgeoning. He fell a victim to the enemies' false libels. The enemies of the homeland doomed the poet to physical extinction, but have been unable to kill his echoing poetry." And Ehrenburg adds: "Markish was arrested on January 27, 1949. He died on August 12, 1952."

A poem by Perets Markish's son, Russian-language poet David Markish (published in *Znamya,* Moscow, no. 11, November 1964), also alludes to his father's "death": "Mother does not write to me that the apples are falling from the trees in our garden. The sun has long shriveled the garden, and the charred tree trunks are mingled with the ashes. . . . Mother does not call me to father's house; the house is in ruins, and its great, cheerful owner was buried somewhere by human hands. . . ."

DER NISTER

M. Bielenky wrote in the Warsaw *Folks-Shtimme* of November 4, 1964, that Der Nister fell a victim to the ravages of the Stalin personality cult in 1950. But for this, "the writer would have led his characters [referring to *The Mashber Family* saga] up to present times."

The *Small Soviet Encyclopedia* (vol. 6, 1960, p. 643) gives the date of Der Nister's death as June 4, 1950. (He is known to have died in prison or a labor-camp hospital.)

NOAH LURIA

A eulogy on Luria's death signed B. M. (presumably Berl Mark) which appeared in the Warsaw *Yiddishe Shriften* of April 1960, stated: "He was not spared the heavy, tragic blows of the personality cult. Fortunately, he recovered from them and took up his pen anew."

SHMUEL PERSOV

A collection of Persov's stories and articles was published (in a Russian translation) in Moscow 1957. S. Golubov writes in the introduction: "The author of this book is no longer alive. His life was cut short in 1952."

CHAIM LOITSKER

On Loitsker's seventieth birthday, Muni Glaizer wrote of him in the March 1968 issue of *Yiddishe Shriften:* "At the height of the personality cult, early in 1949, Loitsker met the same fate that was meted out to other celebrated Jewish cultural exponents. . . . He was rehabilitated in the autumn of 1954."

Volume 51 of the 2nd edition of the *Great Soviet Encyclopedia* (1958) is a supplement to the regular 50 volumes. It is generally regarded as a "rehabilitatory" volume, containing entries on various persons who were excluded from their alphabetical place in the body of the encyclopedia, having previously been considered unworthy of mention. In the supplementary entries on David Bergelson, Leib Kvitko, and Perets Markish, they are stated to have "died" in 1952. Similar reference is made to the "death" of liquidated Jewish writers in the *Small Soviet Encyclopedia* and the *Short Encyclopedia of Literature.*

Various sources refer to the end of Solomon Lozovsky. Vol. 51 of the *Great*

Soviet Encyclopedia gives the years of his birth and death as 1878–1952. Ehrenburg states in his memoirs, *People, Years, Life,* that Lozovsky was arrested in 1948 together with the leaders of the Jewish Anti-Fascist Committee, sentenced to death and shot at the age of 74, and posthumously exonerated. In April 1963, *Izvestia* published an article on Lozovsky, entitled "The Life of a Revolutionary," by V. Ivanov and L. Terentev. The article stated that Lozovsky "perished in 1952, having been imprisoned on a false charge."

Hence, the year 1952 — and sometimes the exact date, August 12, 1952 — is given in several Communist and Soviet publications as the year in which a number of Yiddish writers, as well as Solomon Lozovsky, met their end. This refers, though not explicitly stated, to the execution of twenty-four of the twenty-five persons accused and sentenced in the trial held in July 1952.

INDEX

INDEX